THE MATCHLESS GENE RAYBURN

by
Adam Nedeff

BearManor Media

Albany, Georgia

The Matchless Gene Rayburn

Copyright © 2015 Adam Nedeff. All Rights Reserved.

No part of this book may be reproduced in any form or by any means, electronic, mechanical, digital, photocopying or recording, except for the inclusion in a review, without permission in writing from the publisher.

Published in the USA by
BearManor Media
P.O. Box 71426
Albany, GA 31708
www.BearManorMedia.com

ISBN-10: 1-59-393865-9 (Softcover edition)
ISBN-13: 978-1-59-393865-9

Title logo designed by W. Travis Echard.

Printed in the United States of America

Table of Contents

Acknowledgements ix
Prologue xi

Chapter 1 – Made in America   1
Chapter 2 – A Hell of a Town   9
Chapter 3 – Do You Remember Radio?   29
Chapter 4 – The Start of Something Big   59
Chapter 5 – The Sky's the Limit   81
Chapter 6 – Staged   99
Chapter 7 – The Monitor Beacon   131
Chapter 8 – Perfect Match   143
Chapter 9 – Due East   181
Chapter 10 – Re-Match   207
Chapter 11 – The Match Makers, On Stage and Off   231
Chapter 12 – Match Game After Dark   261
Chapter 13 – More Games   289
Chapter 14 – No Smiling   307
Chapter 15 – Coming Unbuttoned   323
Chapter 16 – Saturday Morning Fever   353
Chapter 17 – Hour Without Power   369
Chapter 18 – How Good He Had It   385
Chapter 19 – Left Out   395
Chapter 20 – Game Over   405
Chapter 21 – Don't Forget   415
Chapter 22 – The End, and The Continuation   427

Appendix A – Gene Rayburn's Resume   433
Appendix B – Gene Rayburn's Match Game *episode guide*   437
Bibliography   507
Endnotes   513
Index   515

Acknowledgments

Thank you once again to Fred Wostbrock for his typically magnificent contributions. Newspaper clippings and photos from Gene's own collection were generously supplied, as well as Fred's own photographic memories of conversations past.

Thank you to the wonderful people who knew and worked with Gene and were happy to share their insights: his lovely daughter Lynne; Orson Bean, Dick Gautier, *Match Game* writers Robert Sherman & Dick DeBartolo; *Bye Bye Birdie* cast mate Kay Cole; Goodson-Todman research staffer Chris Clementson; *Saturday Morning Live* regular Warren Eckstein; sometimes-dinner companion Randy West; personal friend (and Master of *The Hollywood Squares*) Peter Marshall; and *Dough Re Mi* production assistant Ron Greenberg; Josh Jacobs was instrumental in making contact with Warren Eckstein and Orson Bean. John Michael Sala helped make contact with Dick Gautier and Kay Cole.

Thank you to Mike Burger, Brendan McLaughlin, and Matt Ottinger for their diligent research for the most minute details. Their shared generosity, and consistent knack for going above and beyond when given a fact to find are admired and appreciated. Thank you also to Matt Ottinger for supplying videos from his vast collection. Chelsea Thrasher also provided valuable support in helping to complete this project.

(Fred Wostbrock Collection)

Prologue

Match Game taped what turned out to be its final episode in January 1982. The show was officially canceled in March 1982, and in most of the country, it aired for the last time in September 1982. I, the author, was born in November 1982.

I'm an unlikely biographer for Gene Rayburn, I admit that. I was born after he dominated radio in New York City, after he helped get *The Tonight Show* off the ground, after he had starred in *Bye Bye Birdie*, and after his long, successful run as host of *Match Game*.

But my entire life, I've been a fan of game shows. I've watched every one of them, sometimes with curiosity, sometimes with enthusiasm and rarely with disappointment. But I watch game shows. In the 1990s, a cable channel called Game Show Network came along and exposed a kid who thought he knew everything about game shows to a smorgasbord of games he had never heard of. When I first got the channel, I was looking forward to the reruns of *The Price is Right*, *Super Password*, *Family Feud*, *Jeopardy!*, *Tic Tac Dough*... shows that I knew. Shows that I remembered.

To my amazement, the shows that I knew almost immediately took a backseat to the fandom I developed for a show that aired before I was alive. I became captivated by a show called *Match Game*. The host had a seemingly rubber face that exaggerated every expression he conveyed tenfold. He was a tall man with a distinctive frame (I initially thought the host must be a retired football player because he had the widest shoulders I had ever seen). And like his face, his body seemed built to amplify anything he did with it, whether it was doing a quick softshoe, rolling down the stairs as his name was announced, running through the aisles of the audience for no reason, or climbing over the seats and shaking the camera in the back of the studio. Every funny thing a person could do just looked funnier because he was doing it.

And he didn't even have to do physical comedy. He was surrounded onstage by people to converse with. He swapped jokes, reacted with laughter at some, shock at others, and occasionally with disdain whenever he heard "a rotten answer."

That was Gene Rayburn, the man who helped make *Match Game* appointment TV for viewers in the 60s, 70s, and 80s, and for at least one teenager in West Virginia, the 90s, too. I had aspirations of doing something with television, and I think what drew me to Gene was that he seemed to embody everything that I hoped working in television could be: a chance to do something you did well, have fun with it, and do it surrounded by people that you liked.

Years later, that kid has written multiple books about TV game shows and decided it was time to write about Gene. The agent for Gene's estate, Fred Wostbrock, happily handed over several files that Gene had stuffed with personal letters, newspaper clippings about himself, interviews that he had given, and crammed in the back, several pages of handwritten notes.

Fred explained, "Gene wrote those. He was getting ready to write his autobiography at one point. And that didn't happen, unfortunately."

The hazards of old age—particularly dementia—had robbed Gene of the opportunity to share a tale that he had decided it was finally time to share, just as he was getting started. I sat down and began writing this

Prologue

book but wanted to give it the feeling of being that book that didn't get written in the late 1990s. **The quotes from Gene contained in this text came from a variety of sources; primarily, newspaper clippings and interviews conducted by Fred Wostbrock & David Hammett.** They are presented here in first-person, and in some cases, with the tense altered, to give Gene the opportunity that he had missed out on: the chance to tell you part of this story himself.

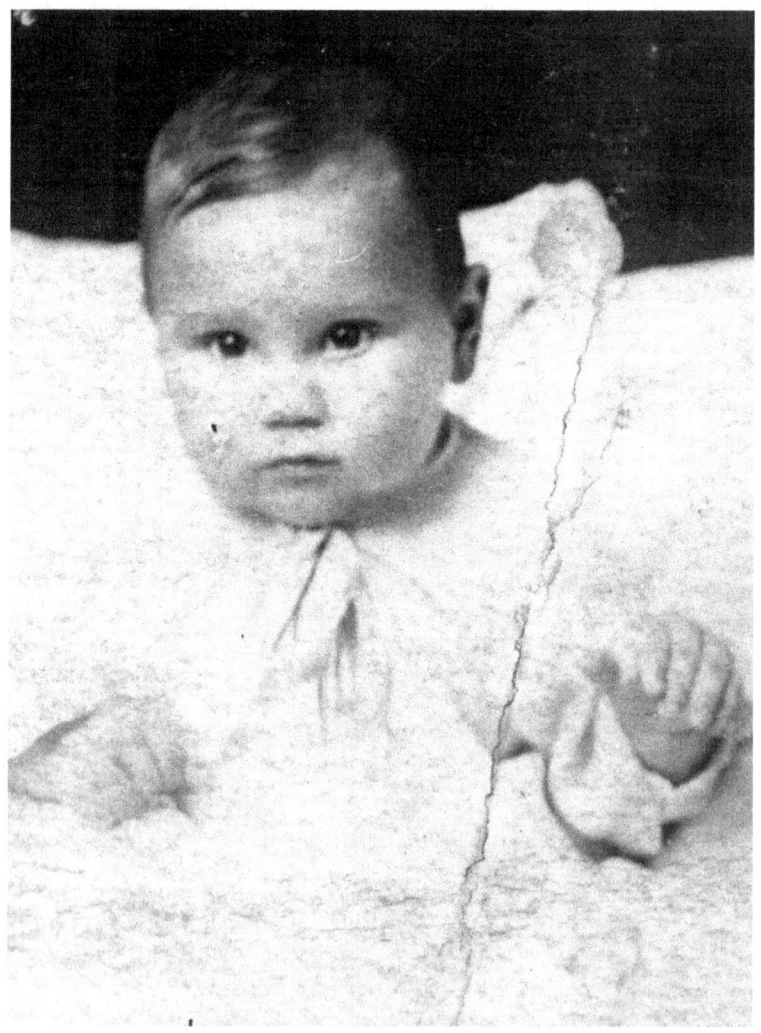

Baby Gene, six months old. (Fred Wostbrock Collection)

Chapter One
Made in America

Fans of the HBO series *Game of Thrones* would have an easy time recognizing the town of Dubrovnik, Croatia. Dubrovnik "plays" the role of King's Landing, the show's setting. St. Dominic Street, the Lokrum island olive groves, the Benedictine monastery, the Knezev dvor and Sponza palaces, the Fort of St. Lawrence, Fort Bokar, and the Minceta tower... if you've seen the show, you know all these sights.

Just outside of Dubrovnik is a small village called Selo Toplo; its name is a Slavic phrase literally meaning "hot village." Dubrovnik, which means "oak forest," was once exactly that. Venetians made use of the oak trees for building their war ships until there was no forest left, and with no mighty oaks to provide adequate shade, the nearby village became extremely hot—hence the name Selo Toplo.

In this village in 1893, Petr Jeljenić was born. (The J's were pronounced as Y's, and the accent mark over the C denotes a "ch" sound).

The "ić" ending carries the same meaning as the "O" at the start of an Irish name: "son of." "Jeljen" refers to deer, which means his ancestors were probably deer hunters.

When Petr reached adulthood, he made his way to America, and settled down in the small town of Christopher, Illinois. He met a Yugoslavian woman, Mary Hikec, who grew up near the Italian border. They were wed, and in 1915, they welcomed their first child, Alfred, into the world. Two years later, on December 22, 1917, they had a second child: another son, named Eugen Peter Jeljenić; the first name was pronounced "Oy-guhn," but he was called "Gene" for short.

Unfortunately, Petr didn't live to enjoy the experience of being a father for very long. In 1918, a flu pandemic circled the globe, killing an estimated 30-50 million victims, among them approximately 675,000 Americans. Gene's entire family became infected in the pandemic. For several weeks, Petr, Mary, Alfred, and Gene were lying side by side in the same bed, until one by one, they gradually recuperated. Mary recovered from the flu. Alfred did too. And then so did baby Gene. But Petr never got out of bed.

> *He was a coal miner. He had all that black gunk in his lungs.*

The flu and the gunk were a lethal combination. Petr didn't survive.

On November 10, 1919, Gene's mother married for a second time in a ceremony in Detroit. Her new husband was another Croatian immigrant, a man born Milan Rubesah (pronounced RUE-buh-shuh). Milan had been a metal worker in Croatia before leaving the country with his brother at the beginning of World War I. They only had enough money to buy one ticket for the ship that would take passengers across the Atlantic Ocean, so together, the Rubesah brothers built a crate from two-by-fours, making the crate just large enough to hold one human being comfortably. Together, they boarded the boat, one as a ticket-holding passenger and the other stored inside the crate as "cargo." The crate was stored in an area of the ship where it wasn't easily seen. Every four hours, the brothers would trade places, until they had reached America.

Once they arrived in the USA, the spelling of their last name was anglicized to Rubessa (rue-BESS-ah). When Milan & Mary were wed, Milan legally adopted her two sons, whose names became Alfred & Gene Rubessa. The Rubessas relocated to Chicago and would welcome two more children, Phyllis May (1920-1986) and Milan Jr. (who went by "Jim," 1923-1981). Together, the Rubessas lived in a cozy house at 6000 South Whipple in Chicago, before moving to a suburb, Cook, and a small house at 6119 South Kostner Avenue.

Gene's father instilled in him a sense of pride for both of his homelands. Milan was a sweet and simple man who had lost the hearing in one ear. When he arrived in America, he couldn't hear the new language very well, and what little English he heard, he couldn't bring himself to learn. As a result, Gene became fluent in the Croatian language at an early age, and for most of his life, he would eagerly greet somebody of similar heritage by saying a few words in the native tongue. He also fondly recalled that the happiest day of his father's life was the day that he became an American citizen. Gene recalled that the reason his father was so excited was that citizenship gave him the right to vote, and he loved living in a country that encouraged and expected it of him.

> *My stepfather was a very gifted man.*

Milan Rubessa worked for Dodge as a millwright, a machinist, and a tool & die worker. As a hobby, Milan built models. He lost an eye in an accident while working on one, but recovered and went right back to building. Milan built extremely realistic and functional models, including a five-foot-long replica of Delphine, Horace Dodge Jr.'s yacht. Milan's model even had a functioning motor, and all the working parts were dipped in fourteen-karat gold that never tarnished.

> *(My mother) was a mean broad, but a wonderful cook... She taught us how to eat nutritionally. As a Slav, she knew the value of things like animal livers and hearts. When my parents first came to the United States they were shocked to learn that livers and hearts were thrown to the dogs. Broiled, they're quite delicious.*

Gene rarely spoke of his childhood and his family. The few things he said in public were always positive. But when he reached adulthood and recounted his early life in private conversations, he painted a very different picture.

As an adult looking back, he always referred to his mother as "Crazy Mary," remembering her as a very demanding and very undereducated woman. Milan was a quiet and reserved man whose approach to life was to keep to himself and do whatever Mary asked of him because it was just easier that way.

Gene's earliest best friend in life was his older brother, Alfred. They were as close as brothers could be, and always looked out for each other, holding hands whenever they had to cross a street. One day, Gene let go of Alfred's hand for just a moment. Alfred was struck by a car and killed instantly. Mary blamed Gene, and told him so.

A few years later, Gene wanted a dog. Mary was obsessed with cleanliness and repeatedly refused. Gene insisted that he just wanted a small dog, one that wouldn't be much of a chore to care for. Mary obliged, but only on the condition that the dog was only allowed in one room of the house and in the backyard, nowhere else. Gene agreed to the terms. A few months later, Mary decided that even the one room of the house was more than she was willing to give, and gave the dog away to a neighbor. Every day, on the walk to school, Gene had to go past the house where his dog was living.

Gene did come to find some happiness in his childhood by stepping onto a stage whenever he could. Throughout his years attending Marquette Grammar School, he performed in every drama production, although merely going onstage and playing the role he had prepared for seemed to be too much to ask. Early on, he had to deal with a bout with stage fright.

> *I was bitten so hard that when I first went on stage, I couldn't say my lines.*

He shook off whatever fear was biting him and before long, Gene's teachers were probably wishing he had stayed bitten. In a school performance of *Robin Hood*, Gene used his bow and arrow to puncture a bass drum. For another school play, Gene, playing the role of George Washington, had a stirring speech to deliver. The young boy stepped forward in his knickers and powdered wig, took a deep breath, and recited a poem:

"Lizzie Borden took an axe, and gave her mother forty whacks. And when the job was nicely done, she gave her father forty-one..."

Gene was suspended from school for a week after that performance.

Gene in 1933, on the night of his graduation from grammar school. (Fred Wostbrock Collection)

For all of his goofing off in school, he actually did fairly well in his early school days, even winning a spelling bee while he was in third grade. Gene attended Lindblom High School in Chicago. He steered clear of athletics, save for fencing, but a glimpse of his yearbook indicates that he was an outgoing, active student, and if not a big man on campus, certainly a kid who cast a wide net and captured a lot of friends. Most of them called him "Gene," although among a handful of classmates, he was affectionately nicknamed "Rube." He was Senior Class President (although in one passage of his yearbook, he jokingly said he preferred to call himself "Dictator"). He played the title role in *Robert of Sicily*, a play about a wicked king who is visited by an angel, and also performed in *Mrs. Wiggs of the Cabbage Patch*, about an impoverished family. He was the chairman of the school's Party Committee; he helped arrange a series of programs to entertain students regularly on Fridays and organize the first outdoor prom in Lindblom history. He was also a member of the Senior Boys' Council, putting together charity drives for numerous causes.

Gene graduated in 1936, and served as class valedictorian. Like every kid with a yearbook, he gathered notes and signatures from the friends he was saying goodbye to. In later interviews, Gene rarely talked about his childhood or teenage years. The messages in the yearbook are some of the only insights about what kind of fellow he was in those formative years.

I could say a lot more than I can write. It has been an extreme pleasure to know one of the swellest fellows in Lindblom. I sincerely hope you are successful. To a great friend—luck, success, and best wishes. Charles.

Dear Gene, You've certainly made a swell name for yourself here at Lindblom and I know whatever you do you'll do it the same way. I knew when you were just a "little boy" at Harper that some day you would be "<u>The</u> Gene Rubessa." Now you see I was right, wasn't I? Good luck and Good-bye... Ethel.

Dear Gene: When I first met you, I never thought I would have the honor of going out with you. I really enjoyed every moment I spent with you. I wish you weren't leaving so soon—I think we were just getting acquainted. But of course, I know you really can't take anyone seriously. Loads of luck to the swellest fella I've ever met. Love, Loraine. P.S. Whenever you have a lot of time—Come out to the Indian Village.

Gene dons the cap and gown for his graduation in 1936.
(Fred Wostbrock Collection)

Well, Rube, we had a great time here in Lindblom, didn't we? I only wish that I had a closer relationship with you in my earlier years at Harper and at Lindblom. I don't have to tell you how much I enjoyed being with you at school and at all our social engagements. (Say, this is gettin' too darn formal. What I oughta say is "Listen you lousy jerk, why the heck didn't ya shove your ugly lookin' mug in front of me long before this?") Anywhoo... [No signature]

> *Gene—It's been fun working with you. Of all crazy people, you're the craziest! But somehow or other, you've got brains and personality. That's a combination that's really worth something. Regardless of how worried I ever was about anything, you made me forget about it because of your wit, humor, and perfect nuttiness. But honestly, it has been a pleasure knowing you, Gene, and I can only wish you the best of everything this world holds. There is no doubt that you'll succeed. You've got what it takes… Ginny.*

And so Gene Rubessa headed out into the real world. For what he sought to achieve in life, he seemed to be in the right place at the time. Chicago was a strong performing arts hub, with a thriving radio industry and television looming just around the corner. Despite a modest upbringing, Gene had the chance to attend college nearby. And yet, trouble was brewing overseas and the best opportunities Gene saw for himself would mean leaving Chicago. The next few years would take Gene far from home.

Chapter Two
A Hell of a Town

(Fred Wostbrock Collection)

Gene's graduation ceremony at Lindblom took place on a Friday evening. On Monday, he started attending classes at Knox College.

> *I went to college for about twenty minutes.*

It was only a slight exaggeration for Gene. His time at Knox College in Galesburg, Illinois lasted just long enough for him to conclude that he didn't need to be there. For an extracurricular activity, he tried archery, which turned out dismally. Picking up exactly where he left off in high school, Gene joined the school's drama club and performed in a single production, *Noah*, Andre Obey's retelling of the story of Noah's Ark in the form of a fairy tale.

Gene later cryptically said that the dean of students "wanted to keep an eye on" him and forced Gene to enroll in a class taught by the dean himself, Comparative Greek and Roman Literature I.

Gene, coming from a working class family, didn't have all the financial resources he needed for college. He couldn't afford to live in the dorms on campus, so he found a room for rent in a large home just off campus. The two owners, a pair of little old ladies, let Gene live there rent-free, as long as he did all the gardening and a few other chores around the home. Gene also made a little money working for the Knox athletic department, performing track maintenance.

But it wasn't financial strain that was bothering Gene at college; it was impatience. Gene felt he was meant for bigger things, and he was meant for them right now. He was going to college at a time in America when higher education was still viewed more as a luxury than a necessity, and Gene concluded that college was holding him back.

Regional theater would probably have been a viable option in Chicago, but, whether you call it confidence or hubris, Gene decided not to settle for anything less than the Great White Way. In 1937, Gene headed off to New York City.

Work didn't come. Even a seasoned performer can have trouble landing roles on Broadway, and it didn't take long for Gene to realize that a nineteen-year-old with little more than high school dramas under his belt had a lot more to do before he could even get an audition. After exploring Broadway for a while and realizing he couldn't find a job, Gene recognized that maybe he needed a little seasoning and sought training for opera.

Lessons were going to cost four dollars a week, and Gene just didn't have the money. He pounded the pavement, looking for any job that would have him. But finding a job just to pay the bills proved as difficult as finding an audition. It was 1936, after all; America was still deep into the Great Depression. Gene was on the verge of packing it in and returning to Chicago when a friend suggested a possible job working as a page for the National Broadcasting Company.

> *This chap... a wonderful man named Keane Crockett... I met him at the commencement exercises at Knox College, where I was finishing my freshman year. He had graduated the year before but came back to visit some friends. And I told him I had planned to come to New York. My money ran out and I couldn't continue college and my father had no money. And he said "If you need a job, come and look me up."*
>
> *And I eventually did look him up when I got to New York, and he had some connection with the personnel department [at NBC], and jobs in the late 1930s were tough to get because it was the Depression. These jobs paid fifteen dollars a week. But he got me in there and as soon as I finished my training course, I became a guide and took studio tours, and that paid twenty dollars a week, so all of us, as soon as we finished page training, took that extra training to be guides for that extra five bucks a week.*

In the depths of the Great Depression, Rockefeller Center set an extraordinary standard in design and presentation. Gene, for the rest of his life, would describe the lavish surroundings he was thrust into when he got hired; gold embedded in the walls, marble floors in the hallways, and offices lined with carpeting so plush that his feet sank into it every time he took a step.

NBC had just launched its page program in the 1930s. NBC pages had a wide variety of duties—opening, sorting and replying to mail, answering phone calls, leading tour groups through the facilities, relaying messages between departments, serving as go-fers for the various radio shows in the Rockefeller Plaza studios. Gene wasn't making a fortune, but at the time, fifteen to twenty dollars a week was just enough to get by.

At the time Gene was hired, NBC's training for pages came in the form of classes. His classmates in the NBC page program included Dave Garroway, who became the original host of *Today* in 1954, and Efrem Zimbalist, Jr., who would enjoy a long and successful career as a television actor, with *77 Sunset Strip* and *The FBI* among his most notable credits

> *We had quite a good bunch of pages and guides in that era. I think I was the only one without a college degree. It was really an elitist group. Except for me.*

The NBC page program was a valuable job because, as one page put it, it gave a foot in the door to people who didn't have relatives in high places. Gene got face time with plenty of the bigwigs at the network, he got experience, and he got to know a little bit about numerous areas of the network broadcasting business.

Gene developed camaraderie with his fellow pages. They were enthusiastic, they loved what they were doing, and they enjoyed being around each other.

Gene (sitting, far left) and the rest of the "white braid" pages at NBC. The braids on the shoulders indicated a page's rank. Red braids were for part-time pages, blue braids were for full time pages. The white braids seen here meant the pages were employed full time and that each had his own sets of keys for the entire Rockefeller Plaza complex. (Fred Wostbrock Collection)

> *We were all young and full of fun. And many times, when you worked the late shift, which ended at eleven o'clock, a bunch of us would go to 52nd Street. They had some great beer joints there. So we sat there and drank beer. That's what young people did.*
>
> *And I stayed up all night once drinking beer. I had to sober up because I was working the early shift, taking the studio tours through. I went down to the Prometheus Fountain down at Rockefeller Center, took off my outer garments, and jumped in that fountain there. It refreshed me, sobered me up a little bit… I swam around a bit before I got fished out by a guard.*
>
> *I went upstairs and I had ordered some breakfast to be delivered to the page and guide locker room. But I was called down for the first tour, so I had to go and I met the guy halfway, took the breakfast, and I started the tour. I said "Sir, would you take my coffee? Madame, would you take my English muffin?" And I ate and talked and did the tour.*
>
> *Lo and behold, I happened to run into my boss. I thought surely I was going to get fired on the spot. But he thought it was so funny that he just burst out laughing and disappeared. And I finished my breakfast and the tour. And there you are.*

The pages assisted with various odd jobs in the production of NBC radio broadcasts. Gene was frequently assigned to help with broadcasts involving Arturo Toscanini and the NBC Symphony Orchestra. Toscanini, an Italian conductor born in 1867, came to prominence very early in life. When he was nineteen years old, he was a member of a touring orchestra. While in South America, the maestro abruptly quit, and the nineteen-year-old Toscanini stepped up and led the orchestra through a two-and-a-half-hour concert, entirely from memory. He continued traveling the world as a maestro for decades to follow until settling in the United States for good in 1937. Very shortly after Gene arrived at NBC, the network created the NBC Symphony Orchestra and signed Toscanini to be its conductor. Studio 8H in Rockefeller Plaza was renovated to his specifications, to give the acoustics more reverberation.

They worked hard, they played hard. Gene (Second from left) and his fellow pages play with some of the scripts and equipment after an NBC radio broadcast. (Fred Wostbrock Collection)

Gene's main duty as a page was escorting Madame Toscanini through the complex when she visited, and personally taking her to the dressing room to see her husband. Gene was in awe of Toscanini, frequently staying in the doorway of the studio if he had no other pressing duties, and just watched and listened in fascination as Toscanini led rehearsals. Gene remembered later the sense of amazement when Toscanini heard a mistake during the rehearsal and knew exactly which of the 130 musicians before him needed to be corrected.

> *He was marvelous. He was a genius…He would conduct the rehearsal and he had a remarkable ear. Someone would drop a clinker and he would yell "Basta! Basta! Basta!" (Enough! Enough! Enough!)*
>
> *And he'd pick up the score to make sure he was right, because he was nearsighted. And he looked at it and he'd say "Vergogna! Vergogna!" (Shame! Shame!)*
>
> *I spoke a little Italian, and I was assigned to guard the door when [Toscanini] was rehearsing. He hated when someone walked in to rubberneck and sightsee, so we kept all the doors guarded. But during the Toscanini concert, which was a big event for NBC… I mean, General Sarnoff gave him carte blanche, and Toscanini went all over the world and hired the best musicians in the world, and that became the NBC Orchestra…*
>
> *And I was assigned to Madame Toscanini. She sat in the last row in the center aisle. I was quite near her. During the intermission, I would escort her back to the maestro's dressing room, wait for her, then take her back to be seated. But it was a treat for me to see, to hear this great music performed by Arturo Toscanini.*

There was one other benefit to the job, which Gene explained:

> *It was a good place to meet girls.*

Confidence had never been a problem for Gene. He was an outgoing, good-looking clown with plenty of smarts to back up his jokey demeanor. But as an NBC page, he was a force to be reckoned with among the ladies. The uniform for NBC pages was a navy blue suit adorned with brass buttons and braided shoulders. As entry-level jobs go, it was probably the most eye-catching, flattering uniform ever designed, and Gene felt a surge of brashness whenever he wore it. Gene was wearing that uniform on September 27, 1939, when he got a surge of brashness that changed his life.

> *When you were a page at NBC, you had to do other things too, sit at a desk somewhere, handle tickets... That's what I was doing one day when my boss walked by with a beautiful woman... I called the page boy downstairs from the office I was sitting in. I told him that when this woman gets off the elevator—I described her—to put her on the telephone, which he did. I said, "Your seams are crooked." She laughed.*

Her name was Helen Ticknor. Born in Banff, Canada in 1915 and raised in Gary, Indiana, Helen would later remember that she and Gene bonded over very similar childhoods—meaning very unhappy childhoods. Helen had a crazy mother that she didn't get along with, and a brother that she loved dearly. Her brother contracted appendicitis, which was not easily treatable at that time. He battled it for several weeks before dying from complications. When she reached adulthood, Helen moved to New York to become a model. She secured a job modeling hats through John Robert Powers, a powerful and influential modeling agency, in 1923; the agency is still running today.

Helen remembered, "I was a friend of Gene's boss... I had walked into the office to get tickets for a Toscanini broadcast and saw this beautiful young man sitting at the desk. He said he'd absolutely commit suicide if I didn't go out with him."

She and Gene went on their first date the following night and hit it off immediately. Only ninety-five days after their first meeting, Gene and Helen were married on New Year's Day, 1940, at the Little Church Around the Corner in New York City.

Shortly after the wedding, Gene's professional life at NBC began taking major steps forward. He received a promotion and a five-dollar-a-week raise. Not long after that, he was granted a spot in NBC's internal school for announcer training.

Before long, he was getting the necessary experience. The network sent him to station WGNY in Newburgh, New York. Gene lasted there

The newlyweds… Gene and Helen in their first year of married life. (Fred Wostbrock Collection)

> *NBC affiliates would come to New York looking for young men who had some training, but not much experience, and were willing to work for $1.98 a week.*
>
> *Some station called and auditioned a bunch of us who were in the announcing school so I got a job through that vehicle.*

for about a year and a half and remembered it as a wonderful training experience. Since it was a small station, Gene had to fill numerous roles, and he was forced into becoming a versatile, well-rounded broadcaster. He read the news, he provided commentary for sports, he introduced symphonies, and sometimes, he was just a disc jockey.

The experience was good, but the payday wasn't. He had a wife and they had to build a new life together. WGNY paid him twenty-five dollars a week. The money tended to run out before the following week did, so Gene and Helen struck upon a way for Gene to use his job and his skills to stretch that twenty-five bucks a little further. Gene began attending church suppers, and they would see to it that Gene & Helen got all they could eat in exchange for free announcements on the air.

> *That was how I was introduced to my first New England clambake—and it was delicious.*

Meanwhile, Gene and Helen collaborated on a musical together. Gene's new wife was a kindred spirit and a muse for him, and together, they wrote the book for a show called *Sight Unseen*, a musical revue revolving around television. It was an interesting theme to build a musical around because at the time, television was more of a curiosity than anything. Although Dr. Philo Farnsworth had patented his electronic television system in 1924, progress in getting the new medium off the ground had been remarkably slow. A demonstration of television had been part of the 1939 World's Fair, and a number of experimental broadcasts had been conducted afterward, but even after that, television was largely regarded as a novelty. The fact that it was on Gene and Helen's mind this early, and the fact that they considered it a viable enough concept to build an entire musical around, showed remarkable foresight.

Gene (second from right) preparing for a remote broadcast at WGNY. (Fred Wostbrock Collection)

Sight Unseen was performed at The Experimental Theatre of Vassar College on April 18 and 19, 1941, and the show was greeted very enthusiastically. Tickets for both performances sold out in only one hour after going on sale.

Gene climbed the ladder quickly in NBC's radio division. After his 18 months in Newburgh, he was transferred to WITH in Baltimore and then to WFIL in Philadelphia. But Gene had fallen in love with New York City and wanted to get back there.

> *When I thought I had enough experience—because you know, with these small stations, you did everything. The trotting races at Goshen, New York… the Dutchess County Philharmonic… nightclub coverage of big bands, all that. It was good experience to work at these small stations because you did all kinds of stuff. And when I had enough experience, I started walking the streets of New York and ended up auditioning at WNEW and getting a job there.*

In the midst of all that, he became a father. Gene and Helen finally welcomed a daughter, Lynne, into the world on October 5, 1942. They wanted to grow their family, but to no avail. After Lynne, Helen miscarried four times. They ultimately stopped trying.

Gene had locked onto a career that showed no signs of faltering. Things had stabilized with regards to employment and his value & experience as a broadcaster were rising. He had now lasted a full year at WNEW and had no intention of leaving. Everything was going perfectly until a little interruption called World War II.

Like no conflict before or since, World War II inspired a sense of obligation and duty in Americans, and Gene was one of many who stepped forward to join the fight. He enlisted in the Air Force (or as it was known at that time, the Army Air Force) and was stationed in San Angelo, Texas.

Lynne remembers, "I have very sketchy memories of my life during the war. I do remember that we stayed in a pink stucco apartment. I have a memory of my father wearing his uniform and holding me; I have a photo of it. I also remember my dad having long arms. I got that from

Daddy's little girl, Lynne. (Fred Wostbrock Collection)

him too. I always reach up to get items for little old ladies at the grocery store now. My dad had a 15 ½ neck and a 37 shirt sleeve. He had the longest arms I've ever seen."

Gene trained as a bombardier at San Angelo Air Field. His training involved six classes taught over the course of eighteen weeks. For the flying exercises, Gene and the rest of the cadets had to navigate a series of eighteen target areas that spanned five counties of Texas.

Gene proved to be a skillful pilot under intense training, which probably made it easier for his higher-ups to forgive him for his insolence in the mess hall. Even in the military, Gene saw a meal as a time to relax, no matter how long "relaxing" might take. He simply didn't like to be rushed while he was eating. A fellow cadet remembered that lunch periods almost always included a shout of "Let's go, Rubessa!"

Gene always replied the same way to whoever shouted it: "You'll get ulcers before you're thirty."

And then he'd go right back to eating.

It was like high school all over again for Gene. He engaged in extracurricular activities (The Army Air Force had no drama club, so Gene settled for being on the Yearbook staff) and instead of being

Off Gene goes, into the wild blue yonder. (Fred Wostbrock Collection)

elected Student Body President, he was Squadron Commander of Class 44-7 DR.

Gene's class graduated in 1944. For the yearbook, Gene penned a parody of Edgar Allan Poe's work *The Raven* reflecting on his time as a cadet. For proper context, "Mother Goodwin's" was a tavern located near the base:

> *Once upon a midnight dreary, I released them weak and weary,*
> *Over any and all the targets bombed a*

thousand times before.
Gyro leveled, bubbles tumbled, all my information jumbled.
The instructor gently grumbled,--grumbled, "His procedure I deplore!"
"'Tis some gremlin thing," I muttered, "Gremlins at the bomb bay door,
Only this and nothing more."

Ah, distinctly I remember, the previous night had been a bender,
Now this student air crew member sought to lower his high score.
Eagerly he clambered forward—tumbled through as pilot glowered--
Slowly to the sight he lowered; as his head throbbed to the core,
To his mind came last night's picture-- Mother Goodwin's dusty door.
It shall happen never nevermore.

Deep into the darkness peering, target blurred and at him leering,
Wondering, doubting that this ghastly, ghoulish thing could be South Four.
But the stillness gave no token, and the silence was unbroken
'Til these welcome words were spoken, "Drop the first one on South Four."
Now he quickly raised the trigger confident a shack he'd score.
Shack for him, ah, nevermore.

"Bomb away," he cried, unbending, but for him no happy ending.
For, his trigger locked kept sending others

Portrait of a poetic pilot… Gene poses in his flight suit for the Class 44-7 DR Yearbook. (Fred Wostbrock Collection)

out the bomb bay door!
Ovie D. then put the question, "did 'bomb
away' I hear you mention?"
He replied with nervous tension, "One bomb
left the bomb bay door."
"One bomb, hell, my gay ranchero, on that
target you dropped four!"
"But you'll drop them nevermore."

*Hearken all ye eager students, as I speak
these words of prudence.
Take a lesson from the 'gadget' now no
longer with the corps.
If bombs away you'd keep on sending, this
procedure we're commending--
Here in small print is the ending—choose
and worry nevermore;
Choose between C.E. descending—low C.E. and
hits galore, or,
Mother Goodwin's battered door!*

After finishing his bombardier training in San Angelo, Gene received his orders and was stationed in... San Angelo. He had proven so skillful in his training—for a time, he held the Air Force distance record for hitting a target—and exhibited such a knack for leadership, that he was promoted to Second Lieutenant and remained in Texas to train new cadets himself.

In July 1945, Gene was sent to Lincoln, Nebraska for an extended period. Helen and Lynne had moved with him to Texas when he initially joined the Air Force; Helen had family in San Antonio, so it was somewhat comfortable territory for them. But when Gene was dispatched to the base in Nebraska, Helen decided to stay behind along with Lynne. Gene & Helen felt there was no point in moving a second time when they both sensed that the Air Force had something more planned for him. The day after Gene left for Nebraska, Helen typed a letter to some family friends, the Blotzenheimers. She wrote:

> *I truly am sorry so much time has gone by without a note of some kind, but darling I have been spending those last precious days with the man I love. He left yesterday to spend the remaining five days of his delay with his folks and will arrive in Lincoln on the 21st. How long he will be there and what happens after that, only God knows and he is silent on the subject.*

I won't dwell on what that parting meant or how I feel now. I feel chilled throughout and I know that chill will never leave me until he is here again. They say life goes on, but at the present it doesn't seem possible. Thank the gods I have my darling Lynne, but there is a part of life that ceases for you when it cannot be shared with your husband.

Gene's only feeling was such loneliness, he said the days and weeks of loneliness to come were the thing he feared so much. My heart aches for him. Loneliness in familiar surroundings is hard enough, but in a strange place it must be a hell of all hells. As a good friend once said, after a while loneliness becomes a friend and you welcome it. I know now that she was right. I know that in the long months to come, I will feel closest to Gene and nearer to him when I am at my loneliest. Paradoxical, but true.

Squadron Commander Gene Rayburn of Class 44-7 DR huddles with his crew in Texas. (Fred Wostbrock Collection)

In 1945, Gene received his next set of orders. He was being sent into the south Pacific region to do battle. He was scheduled to depart on August 6, 1945.

Lynne remembers, "I don't know if my father meant this literally, but he used to say that he had one foot in the airplane when he got the word that the war was over."

On the day that he was scheduled to depart, he said goodbye to Helen and Lynne, and then received notification that the first atomic bomb had been dropped in Hiroshima. As a result, all orders in the Air Force had been "frozen," and Gene was told to stay right where he was and await further instruction. Thirty days later, he wasn't in the Air Force anymore. Gene, Helen and Lynne uprooted once more, departing Texas and moving into the sixth floor of an apartment complex in Queens, New York.

Lynne says, "This is one of my earliest memories of my dad and the type of person he was. My parents had people over one night to watch a film. My dad had a really nice 16mm projector, but the projector didn't have a take-up reel. My father stuck the projector in the window, so when the film passed through, it just went straight down the back until it reached the ground below."

Gene wanted to find someplace a little more homely for his queen, Helen, and his princess, Lynne. Before long, he found a castle... literally.

Lynne remembers, "After the war, it was incredibly hard to find homes in New York because everybody moved into the area after they left the military. My father finally found a place that was about two hours outside of New York, in an area between Peakskill and Coldspring. And it turned out to be part of a castle. In the early twentieth century, very wealthy people built castles; that was sort of a trend for a while among the richest of the rich. And there was a castle called the Dick Estate; the house that my father found was actually the gate lodge of the castle. I remember it had a very steep, peaked slate roof. And it was massive. In the winter, the only way we could heat the home was to totally close off about two-thirds of it to turn it into an apartment within itself. My bedroom was so big that my dad actually installed a swing. The seat was attached to these two ropes and they were anchored into the ceiling, and I could actually swing back and forth in my bedroom."

For work, Gene returned to New York City and went straight back to WNEW. The family found another home, this one converted from Army barracks, on Long Island's Roosevelt Field. In a matter of years, the Rayburns would relocate to homes in Peter Cooper Village, Larchmont, and Mamaroneck, New York. The frequent moving took its toll on daughter Lynne, and Lynne long suspected that it affected her parents, too.

She explains, "My dad was working in New York but initially the only home we could find was two hours away. And for a long time they moved around but resisted moving into the city. So we were constantly moving and my parents never saw each other because my dad always had to go to New York City for work. So I think that created tension. And as I grew older, that tension had an effect on me. I developed a lot of psychosomatic problems. I developed a rash on both arms for a while that no doctor could figure out. They thought it was an allergy. I wasn't allergic to anything, I just wasn't responding well to what was happening around me."

Although Gene loved broadcasting and came to feel it was a good path for what he wanted to do, Gene quickly became disenchanted with the station. He felt that he and the rest of the staff were underpaid, and he despised his boss, Bernice Judis; "a mean old broad," as he later referred to her.

Gene was so unhappy that for a time, he would go on the air and say "I hate my boss; I feel like a square peg in a round hole." She laughed it off, thinking Gene was kidding. He wasn't.

And one day in early 1948, she gave Gene an order that really irritated him. As Gene recalled, she said, "You have to change that last name of yours, it sounds too eye-talian."

World War II had just ended, and Judis was wary of any air talent whose name sounded like part of the opposition. Gene grabbed a phone book and turned to the R's, and had Helen hold it open for him.

Without looking down, he waved his index finger over the rows of names and said out loud, "From now on, my name is Gene..."

Gene dropped a finger on the book, then looked down to see where he had landed.

"...Rayburn."

(Fred Wostbrock Collection)

Chapter Three
Do You Remember Radio?

Gene may have detested his boss, and he may have resented being told to change his name (he eventually legally changed his name, but clung to his heritage; for the rest of his life, his legal name was Gene Rubessa Rayburn), but he knew an opportunity when he heard it, so when WNEW fired their morning radio host and asked Gene to replace him, he said yes.

Gene had an idea for what he wanted to do on a morning program, but he needed a little help. He didn't think he would do well acting as solo host, so he told his bosses he wanted to be part of a team and asked them to give him a co-host. WNEW obliged and paired him up with Jack Lescoulie.

Born and raised in Sacramento, Jack Lescoulie was the child of a pair of vaudeville performers, and audiences loved family acts, so by the age

Jack Lescoulie & Gene, the hosts of *Scream & Dream with Jack & Gene*. (Fred Wostbrock Collection)

of seven, Jack was performing regularly. When he finished high school, he became a radio announcer to pay the bills while he studied acting at the Pasadena Playhouse. He had a brief career in western films and Broadway before World War II, but after the war, he passed up acting for straightforward broadcasting.

The marvelously titled new program, *Scream & Dream with Jack & Gene*, was a combination of music and irreverent, ad-libbed commentary between the tunes. *Scream & Dream with Jack & Gene* lasted only about six months before Lescoulie departed. Publicly it was said that he left to pursue other opportunities, although Gene's personal recollection later was that he had been fired for some reason. Rather than appoint a new co-host, the WNEW bosses told Gene to make the selection himself. Gene selected a member of the WNEW staff named Durwood "Dee" Finch.

> *The same woman manager, the mean old boss called us in the office and said "You're startin' the morning show on Monday. Try and do it well!"*
>
> *So we began working together. We had been social friends, our wives were friends, and we were at ease with one another, and he had a wonderful quality. He had a warm, rich laugh. He'd laugh at any slightly humorous thing I said. And we had fun. It was all spontaneous and ad-lib. And in those days, I used to do voices… and I'd use them in commercials. I was a mimic. We had a great time together, and that spontaneous fun really took New York by storm… Everybody listened to Rayburn & Finch. It was really the springboard to my career.*

The show was officially and appropriately titled *Anything Goes*, although most of the listening public just referred to it as "Rayburn & Finch." Rayburn & Finch quickly figured out the elements that they wanted in their program. WNEW had given them three and a half hours of programming time to fill every morning, starting at 6 a.m. They'd play records, read the news, sports, and weather, and they'd interview guests in the studio. And between that, things got zany.

> *It was four hours of a.m. mayhem. I was a mimic and we ad-libbed the whole show six days a week, and we spun records and did the news and weather in between.*

Occasionally, sometimes, the mayhem was too much. One morning, boss Bernice Judis called them during the break and groused, "Listen, you big fat geniuses, remember that a little joke goes a long way at this hour of the morning."

Neither one of them was really a morning person; Rayburn and Finch, the kings of New York radio in the late 1940s. (Fred Wostbrock Collection)

Dee Finch usually played straight man for Gene, whose act would alternate between grouchy and lively. The personas were a rather careful bit of connecting to the listeners. Dee Finch's persona represented "a morning person," while Gene was supposed to come off as somebody who resented having to be out of bed so early. Gene, at least, didn't have to deviate too far from reality for that role. He had to be at work every morning at 4:15, which meant that getting a full night's sleep would have required going to bed at around 7 pm. Gene couldn't do that, so he usually arrived to work unshaven and disheveled.

> *This is no time of day for a decent citizen to start earning a living, so you can draw your own conclusions. Either we aren't decent or we aren't earning a living. Maybe it's both.*

Gene and Dee Finch prepare for a ride aboard Gene's private plane. (Fred Wostbrock Collection)

The two of them would do bizarre songs, typically with lyrics that were incongruous with the sound of the music—for example, a low-key, gentle ballad, with lyrics like "Ah, Hedy, let me take off my shoes and run barefoot through your hair." They did a rather high-tech bit by the standards of the time that stymied other folks in radio who couldn't figure out how they were doing it; they would "mix" sounds with the records they were playing, making it sound like a cow or a duck was singing by syncing the moos and quacks in perfect time with the singer's voice, or synchronizing a crying infant with the song "Melancholy Baby."

And those were the songs that they played all the way through. Sometimes they would interrupt a record to heckle it, sing along with it in a burlesque style, or if they just flat out didn't like the song, Rayburn & Finch thought nothing of yanking the record off the turntable, putting the record on the floor, and smashing it.

They would incorporate co-workers, pulling their engineer, Miles Crosby into some bits, with Miles' shtick being that he was a "long-suffering" employee who was merely putting up with Gene & Dee. And with an uncanny ability to make lemons out of lemonade, Rayburn & Finch made a recurring segment out of phone calls from station manager Bernice Judis, who would berate them on the air.

It was arguably Gene's lasting contribution to broadcasting. For more than three hours every morning, two funny guys, joined by various co-workers, ad-libbed their way from comedy bit to comedy bit between the news, weather, sports, time, and music. Gene helped invent morning drive time radio. In the beginning, 6 o'clock in the morning just seemed far, far too early to listen to the sounds of laughter, merriment, screwy songs, and two guys chit-chatting with the staff, but it worked so well that seven decades later, it's still the most common format for morning radio. Wherever two guys are joking around at the crack of dawn, Gene's influence is showing.

Listeners and newspaper columnists were jarred by the combination way back in 1946, but the fan mail and ratings suggested that they were on to something.

> *We owned Manhattan.*

Gene knew what the true secret to success was. In later years, Gene wouldn't talk about the complex musical gags, the sketch comedy, or the other details of what made the show work. In Gene's eyes, the popularity of *Anything Goes* was because of one basic element.

> *We were a couple of guys having a good time, and the show became enormously popular.*

Nobody likes the blare of an alarm clock ruining the peaceful slumber in a warm bed, the idea of navigating nightmarish traffic for a job that you're only working to pay the rent. Bombarding the audience with comedy as soon as they woke up made the experience a little more bearable, and it became a little easier to walk into work smiling after spending a morning listening to two guys who had it slightly worse than you (they did get out of bed about three hours earlier, after all) having a great time at their job.

New York couldn't get enough of Rayburn & Finch, and the two disc jockeys felt that they were entitled to a little recognition for their success. They went to Bernice Judis and requested a raise.

The persistence of Rayburn & Finch. They were determined to keep New York in stitches with publicity stunts and annoying music until they finally got their raise. (Fred Wostbrock Collection)

> *We revolutionized the style for early morning radio and we were widely imitated. We were really rolling along and feeling our oats when we hit the boss for a raise. The boss... said we didn't deserve a raise, for one thing, and for another, we were overestimating our pulling power.*

Gene and Dee struck upon a unique way to prove their appeal and, hopefully, put Judis in her place. They were confident that they were responsible for the strong sales that some songs were experiencing around the time that they had been played on *Anything Goes*. To prove their point, they contacted a music publisher and asked him to turn over the worst song that he had.

> *We decided to track down the worst recording in the history of human accomplishment, the worst sound since man invented music.*

The publisher gave them a song called "Music! Music! Music!" Gene and Dee introduced it one day by announcing, "Look, gang, this is a song that's bad enough to be a hit."

And then they played it again and again for five straight days.

> *I remember the song began with these lyrics: "Put another nickel in the nickelodeon." I tell you it was nauseating.*

So nauseating that, sure enough, sales of the song increased and twenty different record companies released their own covers of it. Having sufficiently proven their drawing and selling power, Rayburn & Finch requested a raise from WNEW. Request denied.

In the meantime, Rayburn & Finch responded to the increase in sales by commissioning an orchestra and finding a fresh voice, a singer just out of high school, to record a new version. The singer was Teresa Brewer, known as "the little girl with the big voice." She proved to be deceptively versatile, making a name for herself with pop hits like "Choo'n Gum" and "Till I Waltz Again with You," but then went on to release a number of albums consisting of swing and jazz tunes. All in all, she would record nearly six hundred songs, and became a fixture on variety and talk shows for decades after.

Rayburn & Finch went back to Bernice Judis' office and requested a raise again. They had proven their drawing power twice with the same horrible song, and they launched a new star's career in the process. That was enough, right?

> *Wrong... The boss lady said it was a fluke.*

Rayburn & Finch eagerly set out to prove that the success of "Music! Music! Music!" wasn't a coincidence and sought to release another corny song. At the height of the show's popularity, Gene teamed up with Billy Whitlock and Carl Sigman to compose a tune called "Hop Scotch Polka." Not wanting to mess around with their successful formula that worked for their first hit, Gene later acknowledged that he and the other composers deliberately set out to write an annoying song. The song made its debut on *Anything Goes* and in time, the sheet music was released, adorned with a goofy cover photo of Rayburn & Finch in bedshirts and nightcaps.

> *Oh you hop a little on your little left shoe,*
> *You hop a little on your right one too,*
> *You kick a button like the Scotch kids do,*
> *That's the HOP SCOTCH POLKA.*
>
> *Oh you hop a little on your little left shoe,*
> *You hop a little on your right one too,*
> *You don't mind bouncing like a kangaroo*
> *To the HOP SCOTCH POLKA.*
>
> *It's in and out among the maple trees,*
> *It's up and down and then you wave your knees,*
> *Your head goes bobbing in the morning breeze*
> *To the HOP SCOTCH POLKA!*

The Matchless Gene Rayburn

Oh you hop a little on your little left shoe,
You hop a little on your right one too,
You kick a button like the Scotch kids do,
That's the HOP SCOTCH POLKA.

Let your lassie come along,
As off you go to the hop scotch song,
Sing-a-ligh and sing-a-lee,
It's the hop scotch melody.

Let your lassie come along,
As off you go to the hop scotch song,
Sing-a-ligh and sing-a-lee,
It's the hop scotch melody.

Oh you hop a little on your little left shoe,
You hop a little on your right one too,
You kick a button like the Scotch kids do,
That's the HOP SCOTCH POLKA.

Hop, hop, hoppity,
Hip, hip, hippity,
Hap, hap, happily on your way

Hop hop, hoppity, hip hip hippity
Hop to the HOP SCOTCH POLKA.

Oh you hop hop hoppity,
Hip, hip, hippity,
Hap, hap, happily on your way

Hop hop, hoppity, hip hip hippity
Hop to the HOP SCOTCH POLKA.

As popular as the recordings were, Rayburn & Finch had a top-selling hit with just the sheet music for their annoying tune. (Fred Wostbrock Collection)

The song grew popular very quickly, and numerous artists, including Ray Block, Bob Crosby, Guy Lombardo, and Billy Whitlock recorded versions of it. Gene's recollection later was that a total of twenty-eight different artists recorded "Hop Scotch Polka," and Guy Lombardo's version alone sold 600,000 copies.

Bernice Judis still wasn't impressed. Raise denied.

Gene had a bit of a flair for poetry and songs and composed a few more pieces, including a nostalgic tribute to the medium that made him famous, a charming tune called "Do You Remember Radio?"

When I was a child,
I rushed home at five,
To see if Jack "Ahm-strong"
was still alive,
And oh! What miracles
life could bring,
With my Captain Midnite
decoding ring.
It seems like only a ye-ahh ago,
Do you remembah radio?

When I grew old
and stayed up 'til nine
Lum and Abnah
were friends of mah'n.
I still can see that
Jot 'Em Down Store
And Inner Sanctum with its
creaky door.
It seems like only a month ago,
Do you remembah radio?

I remember "I Love a Myst'ry"
And also Vic and Sade,
It was "Hi-Yo Silvah!"
And time to eat

*Quakah Oats and
Cream of Wheat
Let's pretend, and meet Corliss Archah,
My special friend.
Fibbah McGee always
got the blame
And I knew Yehudi
as well as my name.
It seems like only a day ago,
Do you remembah radio?
La dah dah dah
dah dah dah dah,
La de da dah de dah,
Now all that's left are the souvenirs,
Do you remembah radio?*

    Gene also did his fair share of covering other artists. He frequently performed popular tunes on *Anything Goes*. There were the song parodies and sound-effect mixes that they were known for, but sometimes, Gene just played it straight and treated listeners to his own performances of "Ol' Man River," "The Old Music Master," "Way Up in North Carolina," "That Old Feeling," "What is This Thing Called Love?" and "Tenderly."

    Rayburn & Finch also eagerly shared their airtime with an emerging pair of comedians who were delighting audiences in Boston with an afternoon comedy show. The comedy team of Bob & Ray (Bob Elliott and Ray Goulding) made a name for themselves with numerous comedy routines in which a reporter interviewed an eccentric or a dullard. They had a distinctive style of interrupting and "cross-talking" during their routines, giving them an immediately identifiable voice among comedy teams. They were in a different city in a different time slot, so Rayburn & Finch happily welcomed them to their own program numerous times, showcasing signature characters like O. Leo Leahy, Wally Ballo, and the Piel Brothers, Harry & Bert, who plugged fictitious Piel's Beer in a series of phony commercials. In time, they had a national television show, numerous record albums with their routines, and even a two-man Broadway show.

At the peak of their popularity, they sent Gene a certificate making him a charter member of the Piel Brothers Fan Club. In addition to influencing a generation of comedians, Bob would create a comedic dynasty. His son, Chris Elliott, launched his career by showcasing his own eccentric characters on *Late Night with David Letterman* in the 1980s before starring in the cult classic sitcom *Get a Life!* and the film *Cabin Boy*. Chris' daughter Abby went on to become a cast member on *Saturday Night Live*.

If the record's not a smash, Gene and Dee will smash it on *Anything Goes*. (Fred Wostbrock Collection)

The popularity of Bob & Ray ended up making Rayburn & Finch feel like Dr. Frankenstein, threatened by his own monster. As Bob & Ray emerged as stars, a competing station in New York signed them to air against Rayburn & Finch. They chipped into the ratings.

Anything Goes also made stars of its listeners. For Valentine's Day, listeners were encouraged to create and send in original Valentine cards. More than 1,500 listeners mailed in their silliest, gooiest-sounding proclamations of love, and, showing a degree of savvy about how to get extra attention, most of the submissions included mentions of WNEW's commercial sponsors. Rayburn & Finch selected twelve winners and presented them with corsages.

In the late 1940s, there was a glut of game shows—or giveaway shows, as they were known in that era—on radio. With hosts of other radio shows showering contestants and audience members with prizes, Rayburn & Finch turned the tables on their listeners, giving an address and providing an ambiguous instruction: "Mail us a thing."

Listeners headed to the post office in droves to send "a thing" to Rayburn & Finch, and for several mornings, the duo would sort through all the odds & ends on the air and announce what they had received. The most creative "thing" sent into Rayburn & Finch came from a Manhattan woman, Edna Norton. The thing she sent in was... Mr. Norton.

Her husband Charles showed up at the studio one morning, bringing a note from Edna: "He'll clean your studio, shine shoes, run errands, aid the sound effects man, etc." Gene and Dee were so amused that they rewarded the couple by doing their entire three-hour morning broadcast live on location from the Nortons' apartment.

Gene at the WNEW microphone. At the time, he probably expected to spend his whole career there, but as plans do, plans change. (Fred Wostbrock Collection)

Dee Finch wasn't the only partner Gene had at WNEW. From 1948-52, he served as co-star to Peggy Ann Ellis for a weekend show called *Let Yourself Go*. A regular troupe of singers, along with special guest stars, would perform live songs with the assistance of an orchestra. As television began to take over, radio began cutting back the costs associated with such a lavish production, and *Let Yourself Go* turned out to be one of the station's last live music shows. Even toward the very end, the show managed to attract some big names in the world of music to appear as guests, because live music shows were a genre that came and went quickly on television, and radio gave them an opportunity to do something that they didn't have much of a chance to do on the new medium.

Peggy Ann Ellis didn't have a comic mind the way that Gene did, so Gene was pretty much on his own to whip up jokes and comedy bits. By his own admission, he began to "run dry," so he went to WNEW management and asked them to hire a writer for him. Bernice Judis complied, but said it couldn't be an outside hire, only somebody who was already working at WNEW. Gene hired a commercial writer named Bob Stewart to write comedy skits for he and Ellis to perform between songs. Gene would cross paths with Bob Stewart again a few years later.

Although he was there to make the audience laugh, Gene took his work seriously and was committed to making himself and his fellow performers secure. In 1946, he was elected to the board for the local New York chapter of the American Federation of Radio Artists (later renamed AFTRA as television's influence grew, the union later merged with the Screen Actors' Guild and is now named SAG/AFTRA). He would eventually be elected president of the New York chapter. Later, he was also elected to join the union's national board. During his time on the national board, the union created its pension plan, still heralded as one of the best pension plans for any union in America.

Gene gently began tiptoeing into television. In 1948, he was involved in the production of a variety show pilot for ABC. He remembered that his first foray into TV wasn't a great experience.

I had various people who wanted to do shows with me. Mildred Fenton was one of them. And we did a show… in a theater on 48th Street that ABC converted into a broadcast facility. And I'll never forget, it was my first TV show. It was a variety show. And I went to the director and I said, "Listen, I've never done a TV show. What can you tell me? I need help."

He says, "Well, don't make any broad gestures."

I said, "What?"

He said, "Don't make any broad gestures because your hand will go out of the frame."

So I did the show, and I said, (Puts hand against chest) "And now here's the singing chicken… (he points without pulling his hand away from his chest) And here's our baritone who has a beautiful voice…" (he brings his other hand against his chest and uses it to point in the opposite direction). That's the way I did the show. I was a big hit.

Your first appearance on television is a trauma for you, because man inherently fears the unknown. None of us knew what television was. It was very difficult. I got over it in twenty minutes, but I've seen other people… I'll never forget Bing Crosby's first television appearance. I felt so sorry for him. He was so nervous. And the people around him, the floor directors and others really did him a disservice. They were standing right there [next to him], and giving him signals that he couldn't quite see, so he was (eyes darting back and forth) doing this, trying to get what the signal was. He looked just awful. I could have corrected it just like that, but he couldn't. Because when that happened to me on television, I just said "Hold everything!" [to the home audience] and turned around and said "You're trying to tell me something, say it out loud so I can hear you." I wouldn't tolerate that.

His generosity didn't stop with the AFTRA pension package. He also created a broadcasting scholarship at Columbia University, offered specifically to members of the NBC Page staff.

> *I know how hard it is to get started. I wanted to go to school, but couldn't afford it. So I thought I could help someone else by establishing this scholarship.*

Away from the studio, Gene kept himself occupied. Although out of the Air Force for several years, Gene was still flying. He bought a Piper Pacer and flew quite often. He did it mostly for relaxation; he rarely spent more than an hour in the air after departing from Teterboro, and Teterboro was almost always his destination. He did occasionally do some genuine travel in the plane, venturing to Nantucket, Wilmington, and even Alexandria, Virginia. When his popularity put him in so much demand that it ate into his free time, he sold the plane, although for the next few years he would still rent a plane every now and then. He flew a Cessna 140 most often, though he also had access to a Piper J-3 and a Sea Bee.

For a time, the Rayburns spent their summers in Nantucket, along with a circle of friends who stayed in the surrounding cottages. Dee & Betty Finch came along. So did Gene's former fellow page Dave Garroway. One of Gene's childhood pals, Burr Tillstrom, also joined the group. When Tillstrom started attending the University of Chicago in the late 1930s, he took a job setting up a marionette theater and then found himself transitioning into standard hand puppets. One of the first puppets he worked with was a plain-looking character with a bulb-shaped yellow head and ordinary black dots for eyes. The puppet had no name until Russian ballerina Tamara Toumanova saw it one night and referred to it as a "kukla"—the Russian word for "doll." Tillstrom paired up Kukla with another one of his puppets, Oliver J. Dragon, and by 1947, they had their own daily series on a local station in Chicago. Joining singer/comic actress Fran Allison, they starred on *Kukla, Fran and Ollie*, a sly kids' show that was just off-the-wall enough to attract a large following among adults, too. By 1949, it had gone national, remaining in Chicago but airing coast to coast on NBC.

An endless summer: The Rayburns, Dave Garroway, Don Sahlin, and Burr Tillstrom in Nantucket. (Fred Wostbrock Collection)

Gene even flew back home to Chicago to appear on the program once, doing the WNEW radio show before hopping on a plane and heading to the Windy City for the broadcast. On *Kukla, Fran and Ollie*, he was introduced, with a wink and a nudge, as an old friend of Ollie's, who's in town for the homecoming festivities for their alma mater, Dragon Prep. Gene strolled out onstage, more confident than he had been on that ABC pilot the previous year. Introduced by Fran as "a gentleman with a collegiate air about him," Gene sported a beanie, Coke bottle glasses, and a fur coat that Ollie sniffed curiously before barking at it like a dog. Gene mentioned that all of his WNEW listeners were tuning in tonight to see Gene reuniting with his old classmates. He also said hello to his old high school classmates, mentioning that he was a graduate of Lindblom High School, "class of 1886." Kukla ecstatically said that they hadn't seen Gene "since Nantucket." And to top it all off, Gene played peacemaker and resolved a quarrel between Beulah Witch and her sister Phoebe.

Gene's second experience with television was nothing like his first. He chatted comfortably with the characters (he was among friends, after all) and wasn't shy about moving his arms around, even if they went off-camera.

For the summer visits to Nantucket, Tillstrom always brought along his partner, fellow puppeteer Don Sahlin (who would later go on to work for Jim Henson and created the original versions of Rowlf, Cookie Monster, Bert & Ernie, Big Bird, and Emmet Otter, among numerous others). Tillstrom and Sahlin were almost never alone in their cottage. They frequently brought along several of their friends to enjoy the summer in Nantucket. In an era where homosexuality was still taboo, Tillstrom, Sahlin, and their friends were more than accepted by the others.

Lynne remembers, "It didn't matter that they were gay. What mattered was that Burr and his friends were all goofy and crazy, so they had that in common with my parents. They were a wackadoodle group of people.

"There's a story that I remember about them. I need to explain it by giving this much context: When the fog rolled in at night, Nantucket had a wonderfully spooky look to it. All through the town there would be fog and it was very eerie. The houses in Nantucket were built with hatches in the attic so that sea captains' wives could go into the attic and look out the hatch to see if they could spot their husbands coming in. Also, Nantucket had been a whaling center of the world and there was a very prominent early whaler named Jethro Coffin. There's a house in Nantucket named for him. So one night, my parents were with Burr and his friends, and they had too much to drink. And they all went up to the attic, opened the hatch, and took turns yelling 'Jethroooooooooooooo! Jethro Coffiiiiiiiiiiiiiiiiin! Jeeeeeeeeeeethrooooooooooooo!' in these spooky voices. And it was the dead of night with the fog rolling through as they were yelling this, and I remember looking out the window and seeing all the lights in the village switching on, one by one. I was the only child in this circle of friends. My parents were the only ones who brought a kid along, and it's so funny when I look back on it."

The fun wasn't limited to nighttime. During the day, the group formed what they called The Nantucket Ferry Greeters Chorale Society. They would all put on their sowesters and go down when the daily ferry arrived and sing for the arriving passengers.

Lynne Rayburn remembers, "Dave Garroway's mother had sung

professionally as a soprano and they greeted her once as a surprise. Dave's mother didn't recognize any of them and didn't realize it was a joke, so she got off the ferry and just stood there and sang along with them in her best operatic voice for a while."

For the annual voyage each year, Gene would load up his small plane with Lynne and the family cat. Lynne remembers, "We had two scares that happened that caused my father to give up flying. The first time, it was when we were leaving Nantucket. My father only had a VFR rating for flying. He didn't have an IFR rating and I don't think he ever did. But there's a stretch of road that was built right after World War II called the Merit Parkway that stretches throughout Connecticut. There was no I-95 yet or anything like that. At night, all you could see was the light from the Merit Parkway, if you flew low enough. And that's how my father got us home, since he didn't have an instrument rating. He'd follow the lights on the Merit Parkway and the airport was Teterboro in New Jersey. It got dark one night and my father was waiting for clearance to land at Teterboro but something was holding it up, and that was a problem because the regulation was that if you didn't have an instrument rating, you were only permitted to fly for forty-five minutes after dark. My father was looking down for the Merit Parkway lights and the coastline and realized he wasn't seeing any of it because of the heavy fog. Finally he realized he was over the Atlantic Ocean and he was essentially flying us to Spain.

"We had another problem once with *The New York Times*. *The New York Times* at that time was delivered in big wire bundles, and they had a small plane carrying the bundles of papers in a tail-dragger plane that didn't look out. When you pilot a tail dragger, you're looking straight up. Well, they dumped the papers and no one told my father, so as he was taxiing the plane, he turned right into these bundles of newspapers as they were being dumped. The papers got dumped and shattered the propeller, so we had to stay on the island for two days while we waited for the propeller to get replaced. But after the sound of the bundles crashing into the propeller, the cat panicked and escaped from his carrier and was now clinging by his claws to the ceiling, and I got airsick and vomited. And my father said 'Let's chuck it in, I have a cat on the ceiling, a vomiting child and no propeller.'"

Gene's group of friends in Nantucket were actually a bigger part of his life and Lynne's childhood than Gene's family. Lynne remembered that they only saw Gene's mother Mary twice a year, every Easter and Christmas, and Gene's stepfather Milan would come up to Mamaroneck for an extended period every summer just to get away from Mary for a while.

Lynne says, "Mary got really eccentric as she got older. She moved a lot. There came a point where she had lived in three different houses on the same block. She'd live in a house for a while, and then the place a few doors down would go up for sale and she'd move into that house. It was strange."

Gene's hard feelings about his unhappy childhood lingered, as did his painful memories of brother Alfred. When the feelings of guilt became more than Gene could bear, he began pursuing psychiatric treatment.

Lynne remembers, "My father saw a psychiatrist for six years; one who specialized in Freudian therapy. Dad was a big admirer of Sigmund Freud and insisted on receiving that type of treatment, but it really didn't do him a lot of good. Although Freud created psychoanalysis, a lot of the specific methods and theories he used were completely debunked, and for good reason. But my dad was convinced it would work, and he even spent a long time trying to talk my mother into pursuing it. Thankfully, she never did.

"But it wasn't good for my father and it wasn't good for me. Dad was a very absent father. Because of the analysis, he wasn't big on discipline or punishment, and in hindsight, that wasn't a good way to raise me at all. He was never the one to hand down rules or orders, which was unfair to my mother because she was always the one who had to do the hard part of parenting. My dad really didn't know much about how to be a father. And to be honest, he didn't know much about being a husband either. It was tough."

Gene's family experienced a rather traumatic day while vacationing in 1950, when Lynne went to a beach in Nantucket. Lynne was part of a group of nine children and two adults visiting a Nantucket beach as part of a day camp. Lynne and another girl ventured too far into the deep water. The two adults went into the water to pull them out. Lynne got out, but the other girl never emerged.

Lynne remembers, "The water in the shallow end was cold, and the water in the deep end was warm. Most of us made our way to the deep end because we could all swim, and the ones who couldn't swim had water wings or inner tubes. And I just remember suddenly we were all gathered up and brought together in one spot on the beach and everyone is making sure we were all okay. It was very sad."

Today, Gene's name would have been splashed all over the media following such an incident, but in that era, he was able to keep things quiet. Press coverage of the tragedy didn't mention Lynne's famous father, and given Gene's particular line of work, it was probably better that way. Gene's job was to make the audience forget their cares and laugh every morning, and it was easier to do that if the audience didn't know that his daughter had just been through such a troubling experience.

And making the audience laugh was something that Gene still did pretty darn well. Rayburn & Finch were still New York's favorite way to wake up. WNEW was tremendously happy with their success, given that independent stations had to work a little harder against the big guys at the networks, but the problem for WNEW was that the networks were certainly paying attention to what was happening in the nation's number-one radio market.

ABC wanted a piece of the action and in February 1950, the network signed Rayburn & Finch to host a prime-time radio program, Saturday nights at 9 p.m. They were replacing Bob Crosby, who had been filling the time slot in a temporary capacity for several weeks while the network had been searching for something more permanent. Rayburn & Finch launched their new show in a clever way. Bob Crosby opened the show just as he had for the past few weeks. About fifteen minutes into the broadcast, Rayburn & Finch abruptly showed up, and Bob Crosby walked away, giving the air of a takeover by the new hosts.

Rayburn & Finch had trouble getting comfortable in their new network gig, and Dee Finch admitted to the press that it was because of an unusual problem: "We didn't have enough victims to make fun of!"

"We're just feeling our way along on the Saturday night show now," Finch elaborated at the time. "It takes a while to get warmed up especially when we do not yet have the commercials to fool around with as we do on our morning shows. We don't use a script, you know, and when we can't think of anything to chatter about on the morning show, one of our thirty-three sponsors is handy to be picked on. When we get a couple of sponsors on the night show we'll feel more at home."

In the summer of 1951, with their WNEW morning show still going strong, Rayburn & Finch came to CBS with a summer series, featuring Johnny Guarnieri's orchestra and singers Peggy Ann Ellis & Stuart Foster.

Rayburn and Finch are ready for prime time. Here they are in a promotional photo for their CBS summer show. (Fred Wostbrock Collection)

The major networks had particular reason to sit up and take notice in a world where television was starting to take over. As soap operas, variety shows, and game shows began slowly migrating away from radio to television, it was clear that radio couldn't continue existing in the same form. It was equally clear that Rayburn & Finch had established the formula for what radio needed to be to survive. The beauty of the show was that you didn't have to follow it through the entire three-plus hours. You could tune in whenever you wanted, tune out whenever you needed, and be entertained no matter when you jumped into the program. And not only had they set the template, they were undeniably the best at it.

So when the word got out that Rayburn & Finch's contract was up for renewal in 1952, WNEW had to put up a fight. NBC made them an offer to jump ship; so did ABC. WNEW made a counteroffer to keep them aboard. Rayburn & Finch hired a lawyer and had him review each of the offers made. The lawyer's advice: leave WNEW and take either one of the network offers.

ABC had seemed like the right fit for them, given that they already had a history on the network, stemming from their 1950 Saturday night show. But instead, Rayburn & Finch reviewed the network offers and decided initially to go to NBC, where they would be replacing their departing friends Bob and Ray, who had a brief tenure in the morning drive slot. Rayburn & Finch spent several weeks in negotiations before finally getting an offer they were satisfied with. Gene eagerly signed a five-year contract—but suddenly, Dee Finch got cold feet, resisting the switch for some time before finally making his own decision. He renewed his contract with WNEW. NBC was now only getting half of morning radio's most dominant force, and suddenly, morning radio wasn't Rayburn & Finch. It was Rayburn versus Finch.

Gene's departure was a matter of money, but more importantly, respect. He had helped create a new genre of radio broadcasting. It made WNEW enormously successful, it altered the medium permanently, and it made a lot of money for a lot of people. But over the course of six years, every request for a raise had been shot down, with the only explanation that Gene's success had been some kind of fluke. He loved the work he had done and spoke fondly of his years working with Dee Finch and waking up New York.

But time and again, when speaking to interviewers about everything he accomplished at WNEW, he would make the same observation:

I didn't get a raise until I left.

NBC kept Gene in New York and put them on their flagship station, WNBC (which is now WFAN). Although WNBC weren't getting the team they were hoping for, they nevertheless dove headfirst into hyping Gene's arrival at the station. They threw a "record shower" for Gene at the Rainbow Room in Rockefeller Plaza, where record company executives were invited to personally present their newest releases to Gene for airtime on the show.

The recurring theme of WNBC's promotions was "Rayburn Returns to NBC." The network and the station were delighted by the thought that somebody who got his first foot in the door as a page was now going to be the flag bearer for the radio division. When Gene arrived in Rockefeller Plaza for the record shower, he was greeted by all of the pages employed at the network, "falling out" in the style of soldiers. The network even assembled an "honor guard," assembled from high-level executives and other broadcasters, all of whom had started as NBC pages.

Homecoming. Gene returns to Rockefeller Plaza to take over the morning shift on station WNBC. (Fred Wostbrock Collection)

> *"You have a visitor—the new day that's just arrived from the old world after a fast trip across the Atlantic. It's the latest in a long line of a thousand billion days that have come this way ever since the globe under your feet started spinning. Yet this one is different from all the rest, if only because you are living in it and can make something special of it. That young light outside your window is a tiny fragment, a mere sliver of history in the making. It belongs to you as much as to any living creature. Your own diary, no less than the chronicles of nations will be fuller by tonight. May the hours between now and then be all that you want them to be—may good luck be proportionate to the good you invest in the day. And may you be richer for these coming hours by at least a penny, a new thought, a task well done, a moment of laughter, a token of love, both given and received—a grain of contentment, a measure of peace.*
>
> *In other words: Good morning."*
>
> **—Gene, signing on to his WNBC debut with *Greeting to a New Day* by Norman Corwin**

For Gene's first day on WNBC, November 17, 1952, the station made a lavish and pricey arrangement with *The New York Times*, buying up most of the copies of that day's paper in advance. WNBC inserted special advertisements for Gene's new show into the papers, and then handed out the papers for free at the train and subway stations that entire day.

And after all of the heavy hype, how did things work out for Gene's big WNBC show?

> *I fell on my ass.*

Gene was funny, but he wasn't funny by himself. He was funny when he was reacting to someone else, when he had something or someone to play off of. Dee Finch knew which buttons to push to maximize Gene's reactions, and he pushed those buttons often. Gene needed inspiration or else he couldn't work well. And sitting alone in an empty studio, Gene didn't work well.

He tried to repair this a little bit by having a pianist, Stan Freeman, sit in on each show. In addition to playing the piano, Freeman was also a skillful technician who could do a lot of high-concept tricks with audio equipment, similar to the elaborate musical gags that Gene had been a part of at WNEW.

On WNBC, Gene was also frequently joined by "Polly Bradford," a very proper New England girl who spoke in the refined, jaw-jutted accent associated with stereotypical high society, and she boasted quite frequently about her degree in ornithology that she earned from Smith College. There was a little secret about "Polly" that Gene never revealed during his time on WNBC: "Polly" was Helen.

At WNEW, Dee Finch did fine. He rounded up a new partner, Gene Klavan, and they maintained much the same relationship on air that Rayburn & Finch had. Klavan & Finch remained on top, or close to it, in New York for years to come.

Lynne Rayburn says, "I always found it so curious that the station hired a replacement who had a name so similar to my father. In fact, it created a lot of confusion among the listening audience. We found out that there were a lot of people who didn't realize that my dad had even left!"

Finch was the straight man and Klavan was the funny one. Klavan did a variety of wacky characters, like Trevor Traffic, Sy Kology, Victor Verse, and Emilio Percolator. Together, Klavan and Finch continued to thrive on WNEW. They didn't fully dominate the city airwaves the way that Rayburn & Finch had (for six years, they consistently ran second to Bill Cullen's morning radio show on WRCA/WNBC) but they performed quite respectably and lasted until 1968, when Finch retired.

Gene was a good sport about his failure. He freely laughed about it in later years and acknowledged his own shortcomings. His split with Dee Finch had been extremely amicable, and Gene unflinchingly spoke in glowing words about the ex-partner who had run him off the air, telling a reporter that Dee Finch's success was a tribute to his amiability.

Lynne Rayburn remembers, "Dee Finch had a tough life after he and my father split up. His wife Betty used to get up at 4 a.m. to make breakfast for him before he left for the radio station. One morning, a fire started in the kitchen and it killed her, and Dee found her. He became a heavy drinker after that and it caused him to have a series of heart attacks. He actually had to retire from the show and the station because his heart was so bad. He died in 1983. He was in his car, returning from the city, and he sensed that he was about to have a heart attack, so he pulled over to the side of the road without hurting anybody and died. It just always amazed me to think that somebody could be aware that he was about to die and have the presence of mind to do something like that right before it happened."

When it came to the failure of his WNBC program, Gene may have been willing and able to grin and bear it, but NBC wasn't. They were understandably unhappy with the lackluster results that they got with their failed morning show, and decided to fire Gene. The problem for NBC was that they couldn't.

> *My lawyer fortunately signed me to a non-cancelable contract. My show at NBC failed, and they tried to fire me but they couldn't.*

The network heads were, for lack of a better term, stuck with Gene, and had to keep paying him. No company wants to pay an employee to just stay at home, so NBC had to find someplace else to stick Gene. They tried television.

(Author's Collection)

Chapter Four
The Start of Something Big

Gene and the NBC brass didn't exactly have an acrimonious relationship, but it wasn't the relationship that a talent hopes to have with this network. NBC saw Gene as slightly damaged goods that they were now somewhat stuck with, and they had to find something to do with him or else they were pouring money down the drain. Gene, on the other hand, had been hired for a particular job, seen it fail, and lost his bargaining power in the process, meaning that he really couldn't say no to whatever job NBC gave him next. This meant that whatever he did next needed to be a good show, and if it wasn't, he had to at least find a way to try to make it good.

NBC had him host a game show pilot with an odd premise. *Where Are You From?* pitted members of the studio audience against Dr. Henry

Lee Smith, Jr., head of the Foreign Language Training Branch of the Foreign Institute of the State Department. Dr. Smith would listen to the audience members speak for a few moments and then tried to guess what part of the United States they were from. Celebrity guests Joan Edwards, June Hutton, and Hy Gardner also appeared during the show. The premise was a flop and NBC passed on the pilot.

NBC tried giving Gene a daytime series, *Gene Rayburn's Bright Ideas*, in which he dispensed and demonstrated helpful hints for homemakers. It lasted a few months, but fizzled out. The good news for Gene was that while NBC was trying to find something for him to do, he found a gig on another network, and NBC allowed him to drift across network lines for it.

Mark Goodson-Bill Todman Productions signed him to be a regular panelist on *The Name's the Same*, a game they had on ABC's fledgling television network. The game, which had launched in 1951, pitted a group of three (later four) panelists against a contestant whose name was kept a secret. The only hint going into the game was that the contestant's name was the same as a famous person, a famous place, or a common thing. Contestants on the show included people named Frank Sinatra, Ronald Reagan, A. Mattress, Dwight Eisenhower, and Paris France. The panelists had to ask yes-or-no questions to figure out the contestant's name. The payouts were awarded in unique fashion. Each panelist brought their checkbook to the stage, and if they failed to guess the name, they wrote a check on the spot and paid the lucky contestant out of their own pockets. Each week, a celebrity guest visited as well, playing a game called "I'd Like to Be..." which was played similarly to the rest of the show, except that the panelists now had to guess the famous person that the guest said s/he would rather be if s/he had to change identities.

The show's host was Robert Q. Lewis, a young veteran broadcaster who became an overnight star at age eleven on a program called *Dr. Posner's Kiddie Hour*. As an adult, he amassed a long resume as the go-to guy for guest-hosting. He regularly replaced Arthur Godfrey, Jack Paar, Dave Garroway, Perry Como, Faye Emerson, Jackie Gleason, and Garry Moore on their programs over the years. He also had a small but impressive list of roles on Broadway and in films. For *The Name's the Same*, he was a dependable straight man for the panel, giving deadpanned stunned reactions to the double entendre questions that the panelists sometimes asked. Away from the cameras, he acquired a reputation for being difficult to deal with, hot-tempered and perhaps overestimating his role in the success of some of his programs. As a result, work dried up for him to some extent after *The Name's the Same*, and he never really bounced back.

Lynne remembers, "My mom and dad both griped a bit about him. He was a very 'me-me-me' person, they said."

Three years is a respectable run for a game show, but compared to other game shows that Goodson-Todman churned out during the 1950s and 1960s, it almost seemed like a flop. It's a largely forgotten show that had a few problems working against it. Right out of the starting gate, ABC's television division struggled and took years to find its footing.

On top of that, the show had unusual trouble settling on a regular panel. Goodson-Todman's other panel shows over the years had been remarkably fortunate about being able to cast strong panels who played the game well and had chemistry together. *What's My Line?* had a rock solid grouping of Arlene Francis, Bennett Cerf, Dorothy Kilgallen, and Steve Allen. *I've Got a Secret*, introduced in 1952, had the equally formidable foursome of Bill Cullen, Jayne Meadows, Henry Morgan, and Faye Emerson. Later in the decade, they would introduce *To Tell the Truth*, with Peggy Cass, Tom Poston, Kitty Carlisle, and Orson Bean holding down the fort during its most successful years. *The Name's the Same*, on the other hand, was a virtual revolving door of panelists. Abe Burrows, Meredith Wilson, Mike Wallace, Jayne Meadows, Arnold Stang, and Roger Price all came and went during the show's run. They just couldn't hang on.

They couldn't hang onto hosts, either. Robert Q. Lewis hosted most of the run. He was replaced by Dennis James, who was subsequently replaced by Bob & Ray, who were completely ill-suited to co-hosting a panel game. They were replaced by Clifton Fadiman. With the hosts and panelists rotating in and out so frequently, it was hard to build an on-air family, a group that the audience cared about, related to, and wanted to see.

The program's biggest problem, arguably, was that it just had a premise that wasn't built to last. In a matter of time, the show seemingly exhausted the supply of people with odd names who were willing to appear on television, and they had to expand the show's premise to include relatives of celebrities, with the panel trying to guess the famous family member. "I'd Like to Be" was replaced by a game called "Secret Wish," in which the celebrity guest shared something they wanted to do (paint, play a musical instrument) and then the panelists would join the guest and take part.

Despite the rather hollow program he was appearing on—or perhaps because of it—Gene grabbed the attention of Mark Goodson and Bill Todman with how much he was able to add to it, and how simply he did it. On his first night on the show, Gene got distracted by a fly buzzing around. He killed it and, like a mischievous little kid, held it in his hand and asked panel mate Joan Alexander, "Wanna see it?" When a woman with the last name "Flea" was a winning contestant, Gene scratched himself all over while handing her the check. After a game with a contestant named "Pocahontas," Robert Q. Lewis revealed that her full name was "Pocahontas Mankiller," and Gene fled offstage.

Each episode of *The Name's the Same* began with the announcer introducing each panelist one at a time, and each panelist, at the sound of his or her name, would pick up a nameplate bearing their signature and place it on the front of their desk. Gene brought a toy butterfly to the stage one night and rigged it along with the nameplate, so that when he picked up his nameplate, the butterfly fluttered away.

The "Secret Wish" segment one night involved a roasted chicken. Since a cooked chicken might go limp under the hot lights of a television show, and a limp chicken doesn't look right on camera, the stagehands filled it with metal pins so that it would stay upright throughout the segment. Gene, going for a laugh, took a big bite out of the chicken, realizing to his horror what the stagehands had done to it in mid-chew.

Gene would be the first to tell you, though, that you had to work awfully hard at making it look easy.

> *It's not as easy as it looks... There are no real preparations. You walk on that stage and have to be up for it right at the beginning. They say to you, "Okay, go" and you have to be ready. There is a certain talent involved, I think, which is partly congenital and partly developmental. Some people are born with an ability to talk but then it has to be used properly. You have to know how to listen, too. And most of the people you see on panels have been in broadcasting for years. It's their business to make it look easy.*

Goodson and Todman took such a shine to Gene that they saw to it that he got a special gift for Christmas one year. For a bit of publicity, ABC surveyed the stars of the network's shows, asked them "What would you like for Christmas?" and sent out a press release with the stars' answers. Gene's off-beat reply was "a barrel filled with pulverized Guy Lombardo records." When Christmas Day rolled around, Gene was in for a big surprise. Mark Goodson-Bill Todman Productions presented him with a barrel filled with pulverized records.

NBC was taking notice of how well Gene had adapted to television and sought new openings for him. They also had Gene participate in some "cut-in" bits for their ambitious new morning show, *Today*, hosted by Gene's former fellow page, Dave Garroway. In the earliest days of that program, among the news and interviews, *Today* occasionally featured comedy and Gene did his fair share.

By 1954, Gene's contract with NBC was starting to run out. Gene, still with his failed morning radio show in the back of his mind, had every reason to believe that it was time for him to find a new job. An executive surprised Gene by saying that a handful of network brass was hopeful that Gene would stay. They told Gene that they were getting ready to launch a new program and it needed an announcer/sidekick. He was told that he'd be working with an up-and-coming comic named Steve Allen. And there was something rather different about this show—it would be airing very late at night.

Back in 1950, while Gene was still working with Dee Finch, NBC President Pat Weaver created a show called *Broadway Open House*, airing weeknights from 11 to midnight. The time slot alone was revolutionary.

During the golden age of radio, the prevailing presumption more or less was that the entire country went to bed at 11 p.m. *Broadway Open House* found an audience, proving that some folks were still awake—or at least proving that they would stay awake if they were being entertained.

It was a variety show, structured in the style of a vaudeville show, with sketch comedy, music, dancing, and anything else that could be salvaged from the dear departed vaudeville format. Although it was briefly successful, the show wasn't destined to last. The show was supposed to be hosted by comedian Don "Creesh" Hornsby, who died suddenly the week before the show premiered. The show was instead hosted on alternating nights by Morey Amsterdam and Jerry Lester. Amsterdam departed, and Lester carried on. He was subsequently joined by West Virginia native Virginia Egnor, who, renamed "Dagmar," was instructed to just stand there and act dumb. And she unexpectedly rocketed to stardom, to the point that Jerry Lester quit in irritation, leaving Dagmar to host the show. The show went through acts at a breakneck pace. Vaudeville shows toured for months with a consistent package of acts; for the purposes of television, the show had to change night in and night out, and it proved an exhausting task to churn out fresh shows. Combine that with the instability of the on-air talent, and *Broadway Open House* expired after just over a year.

Around the time that *Broadway Open House* was in production, Steve Allen was working a late night shift as a disc jockey at CBS-owned radio station KNX-AM in Los Angeles, but he became restless in the job and took to writing conversational scripts about whatever was on his mind. In time, the station began receiving mail from listeners asking if they could just sit in the studio during the show. In a matter of months, more than one hundred people a night were showing up just to sit there while Steve talked and spun records. Eventually, he stopped spinning records altogether, and the show had grown so popular that the station was able to arrange for celebrity guests to come in so Steve had some folks to talk to during the show. One night, when a guest didn't show up, Steve unhooked his cumbersome radio microphone from its stand, walked into the audience, and just chatted with them to fill the time.

Steve Allen's reputation was growing, and CBS looked for a national spot to plug him into. He moved to New York and was signed to be a regular panelist on *What's My Line?* But no opportunities for him to take center stage seemed to be taking shape at the network. On the other hand, the New York NBC station, WNBT, was searching for a show to compete with CBS' nightly broadcasts of classic movies. Station manager Ted Cott (who had previously worked at WNEW) figured a variety show would work, and sought Steve Allen, figuring that the Steve Allen approach to a variety show—which was drastically less splashy and elaborate than the *Broadway Open House* approach—would be just the thing.

Gene at the microphone for his new job announcing for Steve Allen. (Fred Wostbrock Collection)

For the role of Steve's announcer/sidekick, the station hired Gene, still under contract to the network. Gene said yes, largely because there was no reason to say no. The program, originally titled *The Knickerbocker Beer Show*, premiered on WNBT in the fall of 1953, and aired weeknights from 11:20 to midnight. The show attracted a large audience quickly, generated some buzz in New York, and received overwhelmingly positive reviews from critics.

It was a good job for Gene because it kept him busy, it would hopefully get him back in NBC's good graces, and he got to work with people he liked. He hit it off very well with Steve Allen.

Lynne says, "My mother used to say about Steve, 'When the heck is he going to get married?' Steve was a loner by nature, and I think he was misunderstood by a lot of people. But he and my father got along great because they were both just goofy and very bright. Their sense of humor was very much on the same wavelength. But they weren't friends. My father really didn't have a lot of friends. Most of the people he knew and got along with were people he knew through business. He had far more business associates than true friends. One good friend Dad really had was Garry Moore. They'd go sailing together a lot, and Dad would bring Mom and Garry would bring his wife. They really liked each other a lot."

While *The Knickerbocker Beer Show*—later renamed *The Steve Allen Show*—was thriving on the local level at WNBT-TV, NBC was looking to get back into late night TV on a national level. NBC president Pat Weaver had overseen the launch of *Today* in 1952 and sought to launch a similar round-up of news, interviews, and features to air at the opposite end of the day; since it sought to be a late version of *Today*, the proposal was logically given the title *Tonight*.

> *Pat Weaver... a highly creative man. Created* The Today Show, The Tonight Show, The Home Show Starring Arlene Francis. *He was an amazing guy and very good for NBC. I really loved his attitude and his creative ability.*

Weaver was strongly encouraged by other executives to re-think the plan and instead consider giving the slot to the unconventional comedy/talk mash-up airing on the local station. Weaver came around to the idea, and Steve Allen enthusiastically agreed. On September 27, 1954, the show, now titled *Tonight! Starring Steve Allen* premiered on NBC. On that historic night, the first voice that the viewing audience heard was that of Gene Rayburn:

"From just off the crossroads of the world, Times Square in New York City, the National Broadcasting Company presents... *Tonight! Starring Steve Allen.*"

Gene and Steve, making history with *Tonight!*

Gene had the option to say no to the national version of the show but he was talked into staying with it. The thought of becoming a national star by being another star's sidekick didn't sit well with him, but the network liked what Gene had contributed to the local version and wanted to make sure he came along. They talked him into it with the promise that he would only be the announcer until NBC had found him a vehicle of his own, whenever that was.

> *It was supposed to be temporary, until I got my own show, but I stayed with Steve for five years...*
>
> *When we started* The Tonight Show, *NBC only had seventy-nine TV stations...*

Tonight! was an ambitious project. Steve Allen opened the premiere broadcast by explaining to viewers that the show wasn't going to be a spectacular by any means. But it did deliver a broad and substantial amount of entertainment, both conventional and experimental. In a way, the show had no choice but to be experimental. It was airing live every Monday through Friday from 11:15 p.m. to 1:00 a.m. One hour and forty-five minutes per night, five nights a week, was so much time to fill that it was either take chances and go off-the-wall occasionally, or... well, there wasn't an alternative.

About the only consistent elements of the program: Steve would deliver an opening monologue, ad-lib about this and that, play tunes on the piano, talk to people in the audience, conduct interviews, and perform comedy sketches with a variety of recurring characters (The Question Man, sportscaster Bill Allen, poet Steven L. Stevens, and the Late Night Pitchman).

Although Steve Allen and his crew were later hailed as pioneers for this venture, they really didn't see themselves that way at the time. NBC had essentially given them a blank slate to fill for 105 minutes per night. Allen and his crew did what felt "right" to them, things they thought would be funny, entertaining, or at least somewhat interesting. There was never an attempt to make history with the show, and yet, that's exactly what they did, conjuring up from thin air the elements that created a legendary series.

The guests represented virtually every walk of life. There were the expected celebrities plugging their new projects or singing a song from their new albums, but *Tonight!* also welcomed Mrs. Sparrow, an expert palm reader; Joe Interleggi, the man with "the world's strongest teeth"—he pulled a truck with ten passengers one night; the man with "the world's strongest ears"—he dragged an entire bus; a woman with a sizable collection of chicken wishbones; and countless animal acts.

**Gene's up to something. The announcer amuses himself by making a phone call in mid-broadcast during *Tonight!*
(Fred Wostbrock Collection)**

...[W]e had to do the show live until one o'clock in the morning. We gave the show style and flavor. You do the best you can do with what you've got. At the time, we didn't realize we were breaking new ground and creating a show that was going to become a national institution.

One of the guests who appeared on *Tonight!* was a young comic actor born Dallas Burrows, but who became better known under the stage name Orson Bean. Bean had launched himself to stardom as host of NBC Radio's venerable series *The Chamber Music Society of Lower Basin Street*, a weekly round-up of live blues and jazz acts, interspersed with Bean's pseudo-intellectual, droll remarks (he was billed as "Dr. Orson Bean" on the show).

Bean says, "I personally didn't care for Steve's style of humor. It just wasn't my thing. I adored his wife and her sister, though. I loved the Meadows sisters. But I will say one thing that I liked about Steve Allen was I liked his appreciation for conversation. Late night talk shows today only invite guests who have something to plug. You are only allowed to be a guest if you have a movie coming out, a hit TV show, a new album, or a book. And even then, those guests are out there for eight minutes, tops. If you're invited to stay for ten minutes, you must be somebody really special. But in those days, you were welcome on the program if you could hold up your end of the conversation. Didn't matter if you had anything to plug or not. Steve would have something to ask the guest about, and the two of them would just engage in a good, long conversation. It was wonderful television."

Tonight (the show eventually dropped the exclamation point) also helped launch the careers of many more traditional performers. Steve Lawrence & Eydie Gorme, Andy Williams, Don Knotts, and Louis Nye got some of their earliest TV exposure. And behind the scenes, it helped launch the career of the young pages who, like Gene nearly twenty years earlier, were there in hopes of building a career for themselves. Regis Philbin was one of those pages. Another was Ron Greenberg, who would professionally cross paths with Gene again a few years later.

Much of the comedy presented on the show wasn't so much scripted jokes and sketches, but more aptly, great ideas that happened to be funny. One night, a massive hotplate was built in the middle of the stage, and a number of audience members were given shovels. Together, they made scrambled eggs for everyone in the theatre. On another evening, Steve donned a suit covered with teabags and dunked himself in a water tank to make tea for everybody.

The loose structure of the show made it somewhat easy to do, even with nearly two hours to fill every night. Once in a while, something didn't work, but the show was so chaotic that the audience seldom caught on to whatever went wrong.

And if the audience did catch on to what had gone wrong, they didn't care because they were having a good time. On the premiere broadcast, a scheduled remote segment was delayed because the cameraman driving the car had been pulled over by a cop. On another night, technical problems caused a remote piece to be delayed for fifteen minutes, and Steve filled the time with idle chatter. The TV critic reviewing the show for *Broadcasting Magazine* noted that Steve's chatter was more entertaining than the remote proved to be.

Gene had a signature prop during his time on *Tonight!*, a distinctive cigarette holder. (Fred Wostbrock Collection)

Gene was there, too, largely in the role of straight man. For example, in the Question Man bits (which later inspired Johnny Carson's "Carnac" bits) he would feed Steve Allen "answers" for which Steve already had the questions.

> GENE: *Around the World in Eighty Days.*
> STEVE: *What was the slogan of the airline that went out of business?*

Gene was also the straight man for "The Great Swami Allen," who would answer letters supposedly from viewers, seeking advice:

> GENE: *My husband passed away twenty-five years ago. But when I go into the living room, I can still see him sitting there by the fire. What should I do?*
> STEVE: *Bury him.*

One night, when the show welcomed a hypnotist, the guest put Gene into a trance and laid him as a plank between two chairs, with Gene's head touching one chair and his feet touching the other chair. The hypnotist sat directly on top of Gene, who remained perfectly still and provided an adequate human bench. The following day, though, Gene vocally complained about muscle pains.

Another night, Gene headed up a five-man team for a basketball game that played out during the course of the show. The opposing team was the Harlem Globetrotters. Gene gratefully remembered that the Globetrotters were considerate enough to show their opponents a little mercy.

> *That was one show that was rigged... If they had played hard, they would have killed us. Thank goodness, they took it easy.*

Lynne recalls, "I sometimes got to go to the theater to watch the show from backstage or in the control room. I was still a kid, so, you know, it was exciting to have your dad invite you somewhere and stay up until one in the morning. My mother never came to the show. That's strange now that I think about it. They had enough conflicting times, I guess. I always had this theory that my parents made a deal with each other. 'Let's make sure that we're always happy around Lynne.' And I think bringing me to see *Tonight* was a good way to project that image; they could give each other some space but I got to watch my dad be happy.

"I was the only child they would ever have, and whenever they were together and I was around, everything was always jolly. I think that deep down, they were actually having some problems together. As a rule, if you're a couple and you're having problems, you can't fool your child. But they really played up 'happy family' when they were around me. My friends used to say 'Wow, your parents are great, they're more like your brother & sister than your parents!' But the truth is I didn't have the relationship with my parents that I should have. I became a real loner; I became really fond of dogs & cats at that point. I was never a social person. I'd still rather deal with a dog than a person."

**Gene played a slew of characters for comedy skits on *Tonight*.
(Fred Wostbrock Collection)**

Gene was happy at *Tonight* because he got to be more than a sidekick and announcer. He wasn't just a straight man, he was given an active role in some of the comedy pieces. A recurring piece on the show, simply called "Crazy Shots," saw Steve Allen play jazz on the piano while a series of pre-taped gags appeared onscreen. The gags themselves were almost completely silent (A sweaty man comes to a theater with a sign out front reading "20 Degrees Cooler Inside," the usher tears the man's ticket and then rips his clothes off; a woman sits in a beauty parlor with her hair in curlers, and next to her a shirtless man sits with his chest hair in curlers.) Gene usually appeared in at least one of the gags during each installment of "Crazy Shots," breaking up the audience with his perplexed reaction as he pulled out a pack of "King Size" cigarettes, reached in, and magically removed a cigarette as long as his arm.

> *It may have looked easy but we did work at it... We never rehearsed, except maybe ten minutes for some of those crazy sketches. Everything else was ad-libbed, spur-of-the-moment comedy.*

The Rayburns at home. They had a complex relationship, but they stuck together through it all. (Fred Wostbrock Collection)

Gene had one other job duty on *Tonight*. As a concession to Pat Weaver's original vision that the show serve as a companion to *Today*, Gene did a news report. Not jokes about the news, "Weekend Update"-style; just a straightforward report. It would be unthinkable decades later to see Conan O'Brien taking a five minute break while Andy Richter briefed the audience on current events. But that's exactly what Gene was doing. And even then, it didn't seem to belong. The critic for *Broadcasting Magazine* noted the news report didn't fit in with the rest of the show at all. So Gene began sneaking in his own unique twists to it.

> *I used to do the weather and the news summary. They built a little studio down in the basement of the Hudson Theater for me where I would do the news. It was a five-minute summary. And the news writer I had would always put a funny end piece on it. My audio was always piped to the audience upstairs. Well, when you say something funny and there's a big crowd of people, they're apt to laugh.*
>
> *One of the vice presidents of the news department became incensed. "He's getting laughs! He's getting laughs with the news! The news is serious and sacred!" So they canceled the news and I ended up just doing the weather. But how times have changed...*

Gene wrapped up the news report each night by standing in front of a map of the US and giving a forecast, with one unfailingly consistent prediction: "Snow in the Great Lakes region." Every night, every forecast, with no change, through his entire tenure as announcer/sidekick/weatherman, Gene predicted snow in the Great Lakes region, punctuating his point by turning to the chalkboard map of the USA behind him and pounding the chalk against the map to create the snow.

The home viewers fell in love with his absurdly predictable weather forecasts. He amassed a staggering amount of fan mail (much of which he saved) from the Great Lakes region, usually including a photo whenever a blizzard actually did strike and letting Gene know how much fun it was to watch him give the forecast.

Gene has an impish grin after once again forecasting snow in the Great Lakes region. (Fred Wostbrock Collection)

For example, one night, when Black & Decker provided sponsorship, Gene walked out with some stacks of wood and a pair of Black & Decker saws. He handed one to bandleader Skitch Henderson and announced they would have a wood-cutting race. For a show that regularly featured comedy skits, eccentric guests, and experimental pieces, a wood-cutting race looked no different from anything else on *Tonight*. The only thing that set it apart was that Gene just happened to be repeating the name "Black & Decker" over and over during the bit. Gene believed that not only was the audience more in tune with that than they would have been with a regular commercial, but more importantly, the wood-cutting race was just plain interesting television, commercial or not.

Gene and the rest of the crew took the advertising on the show very seriously, as silly as the finished product may have looked. It was the sponsors who got the bills paid and the *Tonight* crew saw to it that they got some special attention, to keep them happy and keep the dollars coming in. Shortly before the national premiere in 1954, Steve Allen hosted a special closed-circuit broadcast aired only for NBC affiliate managers and prospective sponsors, letting them know what kind of results they could expect from advertising on the new show and emphasizing that they were being treated to a private broadcast. Once the show was on the air, they still gave the sponsors that extra bit of attention. When Johnson Wax signed on to sponsor the show, Steve, Gene, and bandleader Skitch Henderson flew to Wisconsin and drove to Johnson Wax headquarters in Racine to personally greet executives and employees of the company.

Although they were securing their spots in television history, pioneers in any field are rarely in it for the money. *Tonight* was no exception. Nothing like it had ever been done before, and the people involved were being paid accordingly.

> *In my day, they paid nothing. I'm not a wealthy man today because the scale was totally different, even for stars. I don't think Steve made much money, either, but we never discussed it.*

As popular as Gene became as the show's announcer, and as frequently as he appeared on camera, he admitted later that, surprisingly, he was almost never recognized walking down the streets of New York in those early TV years. Late night TV attracted a smaller audience than prime-time TV, and even then, many prime-time viewers were merely passersby who huddled around storefront windows to watch the TVs on display. He never had any doubt about the success of the show, or any doubt about what he added to it, but Gene's life was surprisingly normal for a man whose television career was suddenly taking off.

Gene even got a chance to guest host the show a few times when Steve took the occasional night off.

> *I was nervous and it was difficult. I didn't do enough planning and preparation for it. In the beginning, I didn't do well until I realized I had to meet up with the writers during the day and do all that work. And I'm spontaneous and I'm an ad-lib guy and I thought I could just go in and ad-lib it. But I really didn't pay enough attention to it until I got wise to it after a while, because I'm not that dumb.*

Gene at his makeshift announcer's station for a special week of *Tonight* in Miami. This particular broadcast nearly triggered an international incident because of an elaborate opening in which Steve Allen arrived on the beach by helicopter. Guests at the hotel nearby thought Cuba was invading. (Fred Wostbrock Collection)

Gene was quite active as a straight man, pitchman, and weatherman night after night on *Tonight*, but Steve Allen saw something in Gene and wanted to get him even more involved in the show. Gene declined.

> *I made a lot of mistakes with Steve… He wanted me to do more on the show, but I didn't want to step on his toes. I didn't follow my instincts.*

It was an error in judgment, but it was easy to see Gene's logic. For years on radio, he had been the funny man, with Dee Finch providing perfect set-ups and reactions to everything he did. Gene recognized that a good straight man enhanced everything he was doing. And now, here he was, appearing as a regular on a show that unmistakably had somebody else's name in the title. Steve Allen was the star, and Gene reasoned that he was extending the same courtesy to Steve that Dee Finch had extended to him.

It made sense, but Gene realized down the road that he had cost himself some opportunities with his own good intentions. The star of the show recognized all that Gene had to offer and was absolutely willing to share the spotlight so Gene could be used to his own potential. Gene had positive memories of his years working with Steve Allen, but admitted that he really didn't do all he could have with those years. And that realization seemed to leave a lasting impact on him. For the rest of his career on television, staying on the sidelines wouldn't suit him.

(Fred Wostbrock Collection)

Chapter Five
The Sky's the Limit

Gene was happy at *Tonight* and he knew that he was getting the kind of exposure and fame that money couldn't buy. He admitted later, though, that throughout his time on the show he frequently considered quitting, despite how much he was enjoying the work. He thought back to the pledge that NBC made him that it was a temporary assignment and that he was really only there until the network had a spot on the schedule, hypothetically, for *The Gene Rayburn Show*. The longer he stayed with *Tonight*, the more he realized that he was being strung along, and that the network had only made that promise for the purpose of keeping him with Steve Allen. Gene didn't harbor any resentment when the epiphany came to him, but he seriously considered taking the initiative and quitting *Tonight* just to make himself a free agent and see if another network might take the bait and finally give him a series of his own.

He was reluctant to do that, though, partly because it would have required him to voice frustration or disappointment when giving his notice. And expressing feelings like that didn't always come easily to Gene.

Lynne explains, "My dad didn't let anything show. On an intellectual level, he could talk. He was a very smart man; he could speak Polish, Czech, and Croatian. He was very well-read. Not as well-read as my mother, but nobody was. You could have a conversation with my dad about anything, as long as it didn't go to an emotional level. He never showed any affection, he never showed any disappointment. My mother did. She always showed emotion and always let you know how she felt. And that's why I'm glad she resisted when my father encouraged her to try Freudian therapy. I really think that stunted him in a lot of ways.

"He had trouble expressing emotion and he didn't see the beauty in things. I have home movies that my father shot with his 16mm camera when my parents traveled, and you can tell by the way that my father shot the movies that he really didn't appreciate whatever he was looking at. He shot everything the same way. You'll see something like the Colosseum in Rome, and the shot will pan to the left, then pan to the right, pan up, and pan down. And every shot of the movies looks like that. Pan left, pan right, pan up, pan down. He wasn't really taking in what he was looking at."

While Gene weighed his options in entertainment, he found work as a commercial spokesman outside of *Tonight*, appearing on prime-time shows to do the live commercials for the regular sponsors. In this capacity, he did commercials for Cheer detergent, as well as an extremely popular series of live commercials for Pontiac.

Peter Marshall remembers, "I had actually met Gene a few times before that. I don't remember the first time we ever met, but I had known Gene's brother Jim. I became a page at NBC when I was sixteen. I was the youngest person ever hired for that job, and I got to know Jim because he was a page, too. I then met Gene a few times through Jim… A few years later, I co-starred with Tommy Farrell for a show on WABC, a local station in New York City. The show was called *Two of the Most*. The show was cancelled, and I had three kids at the time and to keep the family above water, I had to move them away from me, so I became separated from my family. I needed money. Gene called me and said 'I'm doing a commercial for Pontiac. They want a guy who looks like me.' I went in, they did some things with my hairline and my nose, and we looked almost exactly alike. It was a great commercial, and Pontiac paid me very generously for that commercial because it wouldn't have worked without me. I made so much money that I was able to bring my family back. I always told Gene how much that meant to me."

> *The Pontiac sponsorship of a show called* Playwrights '56 *was produced by Fred Coe, and directed by him, too, I believe, in a big studio they had in Brooklyn. I did the commercials from 106th Street and Park Avenue, in a large studio that NBC had there.*
>
> *And a year or so after I started doing those commercials, I finally met Fred Coe, and he said to me, "You know, when we broke for commercial, everybody in the studio would rush to the nearest monitor to see your commercial."*
>
> *I said "Why?"*
>
> *He said "Because they were so unusual."*
>
> *They were written by a guy named Mark Lawrence, who was a very creative man. He came out of a great advertising agency. We would have dream sequences. I remember one commercial we did. I was sitting in a chair, and I doze off, and they had a shadowy figure stand up and walk over here… and it was Peter Marshall. They made a hairpiece for him that mimicked my hairline, and we were dressed in identical outfits, and they made his make-up look like my make-up. We looked startlingly alike… It was a very creative commercial.*

Gene could always be counted on as a good friend, if not a good husband. Lynne remembers picking up on the clues. "My parents always gave each other space. My mother had a very good friend named Joan Sullivan who lived in the next town and they spent a lot of time together. And for a long time, I had this memory of being out for a drive with my father. I was a teenager. And we stopped at this apartment building near

Madison Avenue and went into a studio apartment because he said he needed to get something. And for the longest time I thought it was odd and I wondered if I was remembering it correctly. And decades later, I was going through some of my father's papers and I found that he was renting a studio apartment in the city while he was married to my mother. He was probably having affairs."

Gene did get an opportunity to do other shows, though none of them were necessarily "his own" shows. A month after *Tonight* went on the air, Gene picked up another five-night-a-week gig, hosting a local game show, *The Sky's the Limit*, for WNBT.

In 1950, Mark Goodson-Bill Todman Productions, the premier packager of TV game shows even in TV's nascent years, had unleashed a game called *Beat the Clock* on CBS. Each week, married couples teamed up to perform zany stunts, like stacking cups and saucers or throwing pies, with a loud ticking clock serving as the "competition." The couples had to conquer each task before the clock reached 0 to collect the payoffs.

It became so popular that the competing networks and packagers got right to work trying to capture some of that audience. The local NBC station decided to do their own version of *Beat the Clock*. The twist they put on it was having kids do the stunts. Since the stunts on *Beat the Clock* were typically silly and/or messy, it was a natural idea. They called the game *The Sky's the Limit* and it aired live every weeknight at 6:30 p.m.

> *It was successful. People were watching, they were clamoring for tickets and clamoring to get their kids on the show.*

Gene and NBC were relieved to discover how easily he slid into the job of hosting a game show. He had people to play off of—the contestants. The stunts needed explaining or demonstrating sometimes, and they almost always included props. Gene's natural inclination was humor, and he was surrounded by people and things that he could goof around with. It was the right fit for him. The show grew popular enough that it released a board game with Gene's photo on the box cover. Today, it's a

Gene hops in the car… well, hops ON the car to spread the word to New York about his new show, *The Sky's the Limit*. (Fred Wostbrock Collection)

prized collectible because it's a rare example of a board game based on a show that aired locally; it's believed that the game was sold only in the New York City area.

He wasn't completely happy with the show and thought he needed some help. He had to walk kids around the stage as he was giving them instructions throughout the show. Gene was tall and lanky and didn't like the way he looked on camera when he had to take kids by the arm and move them around. He asked the show if they could hire a female model to do that part of the job for him.

The show obliged, but they told Gene to conduct the auditions himself. Gene went in one day and interviewed numerous models. He wound up hiring a nineteen-year-old who had never worked before; her name was Hope Lange.

Gene and nineteen-year-old Hope Lange; discovering her would be one of Gene's favorite achievements. (Fred Wostbrock Collection)

Hope was nervous in her earliest appearances on the show, but Gene, a self-proclaimed free spirit, brought her out of her shell. He was laid back. If she made a mistake, he played it for laughs. If he made a mistake himself, he played it for laughs. She adapted that mindset herself, and Gene said years later that the improvement was visible. With every passing week, she was more relaxed and comfortable, and she easily fit into the mold that Gene had helped create.

After Hope had been with the show for about one year, she got an audition for a one-shot appearance on a TV drama. She got the job, and the day after it aired, she had film and TV offers from the major studios in Hollywood. *The Sky's the Limit* happily released her from her contract to let her pursue her film career. Less than five years later, Hope Lange was nominated for an Oscar for her performance in *Peyton Place*. In 1970, she won an Emmy for Outstanding Lead Actress in a Comedy Series for her role on the sitcom *The Ghost and Mrs. Muir*. Gene admitted years later that he felt personally proud for every one of her achievements in show business.

The producer of *The Sky's the Limit* was a Brooklyn native who was born Robert Steinberg, but worked under the name Bob Stewart. Stewart had served as a writer and producer for many types of programming in radio and early TV, but he showed a knack for game shows. A short time after *The Sky's the Limit* ended its run, he landed a job as a producer with Mark Goodson-Bill Todman Productions. During his tenure, he would create three of the company's most successful shows: *The Price is Right*, *To Tell the Truth*, and *Password*. He would depart in 1964 to launch his own production company and cranked out even more hit shows, most notably *The $25,000 Pyramid*.

Gene's resume during this period speaks volumes about his work ethic. He was an announcer on a popular show that occupied nearly nine hours of network time every week, and he was undeniably being handsomely rewarded for it. But Gene was almost always on the lookout for a second job. With *Tonight* going strong in the summer of 1955, Gene hosted his first national game show, *Make the Connection*.

Make the Connection was a summer replacement series produced by Mark Goodson-Bill Todman Productions for NBC. It premiered July 7 with host Jim McKay (later known for ABC's *Wide World of Sports*) and was slated for a thirteen-week run. McKay departed after only four episodes and Gene came onboard to finish the series.

Make the Connection was a twist on *I've Got a Secret*, which itself had been derivative of *What's My Line?* In 1952, producer and future song parody pioneer Allan Sherman had convinced Goodson & Todman of the importance of stealing from their own ideas as a means of staying ahead of competing producers, and the company adhered to that mindset for decades after. Although still naturally interested in getting original formats on the air, Goodson & Todman would routinely follow up a hit show with one that carried many similar elements. Because the panel shows they produced were always well received in the 1950s, Goodson-Todman Productions just kept churning them out.

Gene rehearses with producer Bob Stewart, a production assistant, and Hope Lange before a broadcast of *The Sky's the Limit*. (Fred Wostbrock Collection)

For *Make the Connection*, each game was played with two contestants who shared a common secret; for example, the vice president of a bank appeared along with one of his employees, and their connection was that the vice president had accidentally locked the employee in a vault for eight hours. For another game, a man and a baby appeared. Their connection was that the baby had fallen out of a hotel window and the man had caught him.

Gene gives a member of the Space Pilots a chance to earn points on *Choose Up Sides*. (Fred Wostbrock Collection)

Gene had a formidable panel joining him each week, a group of four regulars who appeared through the entire run of the series. Gene Klavan, the man who replaced him at WNEW every week, was there. Betty White appeared too, in one of her earliest roles as a game show panelist. Eddie Bracken, who had a long career on Broadway, spanning *The Seven Year Itch*, *Mister Roberts*, *The Odd Couple*, *The Sunshine Boys*, and *Babes in Toyland*; he also had an impressive list of film credits; you might remember him as theme park owner Roy Wally in *National Lampoon's Vacation* or as the toy store owner in *Home Alone 2*. Rounding out the panel was Gloria DeHaven, daughter of two vaudeville performers and something of a late bloomer in show business. At the time she appeared on *Make the Connection*, she had only amassed a small handful of minor film roles. In the years after *Make the Connection*, she appeared onstage in *The Unsinkable Molly Brown*, *The Sound of Music*, and *No, No, Nanette*. On television, she was a regular cast member on *As the World Turns*, *Mary Hartman, Mary Hartman*, and *Ryan's Hope*.

As host of *Make the Connection*, Gene had a similar role to being Steve Allen's sidekick. Gene was the straight man and the panel was supposed to get the laughs. But even with his short time at the helm of *Make the Connection*, one could see Gene's inner funnyman breaking free. He took a pie to the face from Buster Keaton and gave a hammy performance when he did percussion for a Xavier Cugat number.

Gene got even busier in 1956. At the start of the year, Goodson-Todman, a company that was taking a strong liking to Gene at this point, appointed him to host a new game, *Choose Up Sides*. Previous experience got Gene the job. Like *The Sky's the Limit*, it was a game that involved kids performing stunts. The audience, seated on stage, was divided into two teams, the Space Pilots and the Bronco Busters. Kids from each side competed against each other in a series of stunts, with the winner earning points for their team and the loser being forced to perform a penalty stunt, the "Super-Doo," described by Mr. Mischief, a giant wall-mounted puppet with a squeaky, giggling falsetto voice. The voice of Mr. Mischief, almost unrecognizable in the role, was Don Pardo, the baritone announcer known as "The Voice of NBC" and the announcer for four decades of *Saturday Night Live*.

Mr. Mischief looks on while a contestant performs the Super Doo stunt on *Choose Up Sides*. (Fred Wostbrock Collection)

Choose Up Sides was placed in a Saturday morning time slot on NBC, and it would be a live broadcast, as most shows were in that era. This gave Gene a particularly exhausting work schedule. Friday night, he had *Tonight*, as usual. The show wrapped up at 1 a.m., but then Gene got right back to work for *Choose Up Sides* only a few hours later.

Despite the lack of sleep, Gene showed an enviable level of energy during his Saturday morning task. For every walk to talk to Mr. Mischief, Gene would skip and kick his way over in rhythm with the music. When the kids used their foreheads to push inflatable punching bags across the stage, Gene drew a tic-tac-toe grid into the dusty forehead of the winner.

Choose Up Sides lasted only thirteen weeks, but it led NBC to plug Gene into another game show, a daytime series called *Tic Tac Dough*. The game was co-created by Jack Barry & Dan Enright, a duo who first gained prominence in radio and early TV with a panel show, *Juvenile Jury*, in which the home audience was encouraged to send letters about their personal problems. In the summer of 1956, they introduced *Tic Tac Dough* weekday mornings on NBC. For a time, Jack Barry himself hosted the show Monday through Thursday, and Gene hosted the Friday broadcast.

Two months after *Tic Tac Dough* launched, Barry & Enright launched a new series in prime time, a big money quiz show called *Twenty One*. It became a major hit on the heels of a series of victories by a charismatic champion named Charles Van Doren, and turned the production company into a giant.

Tonight was still there to keep Gene busy, and starting in the fall, it would keep him even busier. NBC executives were thrilled with the results that it was delivering, and they thought that Steve Allen and his crew of late night mirth makers could all be the solution to a problem that the network was having: a problem named Ed Sullivan.

Ed Sullivan was a gossip columnist who launched a variety show, *Toast of the Town* (later renamed *The Ed Sullivan Show*) in 1948 for CBS. Although frequently lampooned for his stiff, stone-faced, awkward demeanor in front of the camera, Sullivan, who took an active role behind the scenes in booking each week's line-up, had an eye for emerging talent and a nose for trends in pop culture. As a result, he dominated the Sunday night 8:00 p.m. time slot from virtually the dawn of television, presenting a blend of outstanding acts and celebrity guests that got entire families gathered around their televisions because the show truly would deliver something for everyone on each broadcast.

For the fall of 1956, NBC unveiled *The Steve Allen Show* opposite Ed Sullivan. Steve, Gene, and the crew dealt with the added work by scaling back on their *Tonight* work. Monday and Tuesday's episodes were turned over to a new host, Ernie Kovacs, who brought along his own announcer, Bill Wendell, and his own bandleader. Steve Allen and his gang kept at it Wednesday through Friday.

Steve Allen had established a distinctive brand of entertainment in the late hour: off-kilter, silly, spontaneous, and sly. And though it had delivered tremendous results after 11:00, it appeared to be a form of humor that didn't appeal to the larger, broader audiences of prime time TV. Ed Sullivan continued to dominate in the ratings, though *The Steve Allen Show* was by no means a failure. It ran in a respectable second place during the next four seasons, and it launched the careers of Don Knotts (as the perpetually nervous "man on the street"), Tom Poston, Louis Nye, Pat Harrington, Jr., and Bill Dana ("My name Jose Jimenez"). The show received critical acclaim too, earning a Peabody Award in 1958, for its "genuine humor and frank experiments."

Gene ended up missing out on that fun for several months with a series of mishaps. Early in 1957, he contracted hepatitis and was confined to bed for many weeks. Although he couldn't be a visible part of the fun on the stage, Steve Allen and his crew thought highly enough of Gene to make sure he wasn't left out.

Lynne remembers, "My dad was very sick. He was 6'1" and for most of his life he was 180 pounds. During the hepatitis battle, his weight went down to 127 pounds, so it was bad. He was on doctor's orders to stay in bed. He was only allowed to get out of bed to use the bathroom, but not for any other reason. Other than that, he was in bed for six weeks. What NBC did was send an engineer to our home at 9:00 p.m. The engineer had a rolling tray table that had all of the necessary equipment, and he would set everything up so my dad could announce the show from bed."

Gene made a full recovery, but he didn't stay healthy for very long. The Rayburns took a family vacation to Stowe, Vermont, to do some skiing. It didn't end well.

Lynne explains, "We were all using the beginners' slope. My dad had just learned how to ski and we were all doing really well with it early on, which was a wonderful experience for my father because he was never much of an athlete until his later years. My dad took up tennis later in life and became really very good at it; he was a solid B-club player.

"My mother and I were riding the lift up to the top of the hill and we looked down and saw the ski patrol taking care of an injured man, and we pointed and said 'Oh, look at that poor man!' Well it turned out to be my dad. And we made it down there and my father was completely blue and ashen. We got to the hospital and we found he had broken the tibia and the fibula. The bones in his legs were sawdust.

"We got very lucky, though. Dad had just the right surgeon taking care of him. It was this brilliant Park Avenue surgeon who had moved with his entire family to live in Stowe just so he could practice his craft. He reasoned that if he was working near a ski lodge, eventually, somebody will break something, and that's what happened. So we had an expert surgeon dealing with it. That's not to say it was easy. My mother actually had to sign the amputation papers while my dad was in surgery because in the very beginning, they weren't sure the leg could be saved.

"Thankfully, they were able to save the leg. It wasn't a one hundred percent recovery. For the rest of my dad's life, he had three screws holding that leg together, and he also sort of had to train his body to land a certain way. He could never come straight down on that leg, so whenever he jumped or danced or anything like that, he had to get into the habit of landing a new way."

At the same time, NBC shuffled around its prime time schedule and moved *Twenty One*. It affected creator/host Jack Barry's schedule and suddenly, he was freed up to host *Tic Tac Dough* on Friday, which meant

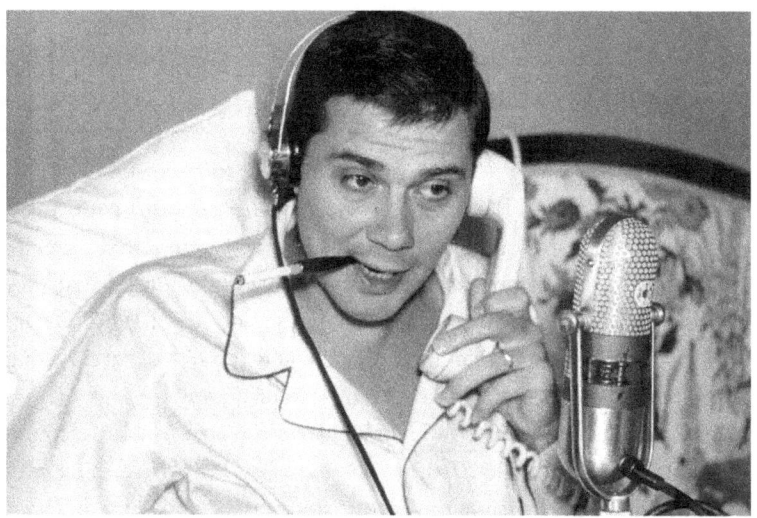

Gene announces *Tonight* from bed during his bout with hepatitis.
(Fred Wostbrock Collection)

Gene skiing in Stowe, just before the accident.
(Fred Wostbrock Collection)

that Gene was losing his day job. The mishaps actually affected Gene's future. He was becoming antsy about staying in place as Steve Allen's second banana for too long and the thought of departing had crossed his mind, but after the sickness and injury, Gene was strapped for cash and stayed right where he was, trading in opportunity for security.

By the summer of 1957, *The Steve Allen Show* still wasn't performing quite up to expectations. NBC and Steve Allen both considered *The Steve Allen Show* to be a greater priority than the late night funfest that they had launched together three years earlier. In the summer of 1957, *Tonight Starring Steve Allen* came to an end. Gene and the rest departed along with Steve Allen; even Ernie Kovacs' crew walked away.

NBC replaced them with Gene's old radio partner, Jack Lescoulie, in a new incarnation called *Tonight: America After Dark*. In keeping with Pat Weaver's original vision, the new version was a companion to *Today*, featuring similar features and news reporting. But the audience turned away in droves. The template had been set for what viewers expected at that hour: They wanted to laugh. Lescoulie and the *America After Dark* format were jettisoned after only a few months, replaced by Jack Paar and a more crowd-pleasing comedy and talk format.

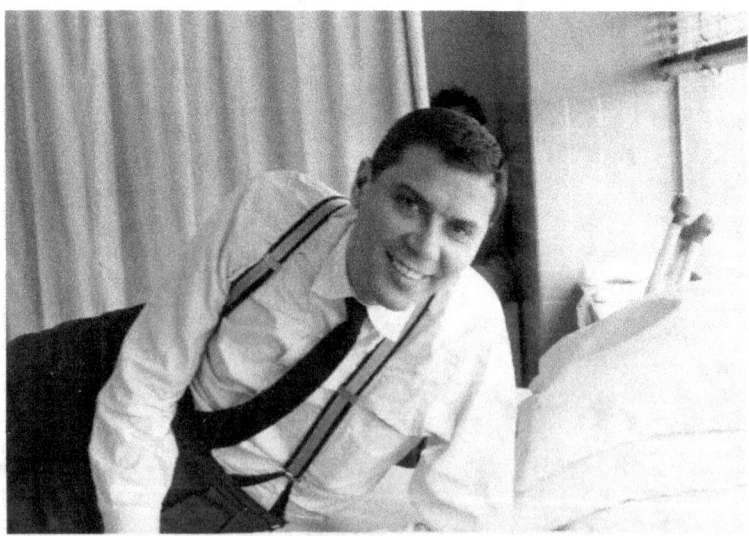

On the mend; Gene gets dressed up for a photo shoot in his hospital bed. (Fred Wostbrock Collection)

> *Steve Allen did* The Tonight Show *in his own style and did it very well. But I agreed with Jack Paar when he took over the show. Jack made one big change when he became the host that I absolutely approved of. When a guest came out and [finished] his interview, instead of being dismissed and leaving the stage, that guest would stay there for the remainder of the broadcast, and was welcome to participate or contribute to the rest of the show. Sometimes the guest sat and did nothing because they had nothing more to offer, but very often, the guest had more to say, so for the rest of the broadcast, instead of interviews, the show played out as more of a conversation. And I thought that was a big improvement on the format of the show, and Steve did just fine without doing it that way. But I think back to some of the shows we did, and if Steve had let certain people stay on for the whole broadcast, it would have really been something special on some nights.*

But the other elements of the Steve Allen version of *Tonight* worked just as they were. That was the mark that Steve Allen's *Tonight* left. In the earliest stages of television, as the rest of the medium was finding its footing, Steve Allen and his crew figured out exactly what worked for late night. A host, assisted by an announcer and a bandleader, working his way through some current, clever comedy and interviews with notable names.

The show even established the look right out of the starting gate: a bandstand, a performance area, and the host sitting behind a desk with a large microphone at the side. The desk and the microphone were set up like that because that's the set-up that Steve Allen was accustomed to from his time doing a radio show. And even today, they're part of the visual language for late night comedy. In 2003, an NBC executive suggested removing the microphone from the desk since it really wasn't necessary, and the suggestion was shot down because by this point, viewers simply expected to see a microphone on the desk. That's how much influence *Tonight* with Steve Allen had. And Gene Rayburn was part of it. He got it off the ground, he made his contributions, and he joined in the comedy and in the sponsor presentations to ensure it would have a long, healthy future. In the span of only eleven years, 1946-57, Gene had helped establish what people did for entertainment when they woke up, and what they did for entertainment as they went to bed.

> **THE STEVE ALLEN SHOW**
>
> GENE RAYBURN:
>
> 1. is missed!
> 2. feels better?
> 3. has bed sores?
> 4. must be in terrific pain!
> 5. 's leg shrank.
> 6. was attacked by the night nurse
> 7. accomplished the only half-gainor on skis.
> 8. hates Stowe now.
> 9. needs new bindings.
> 10. uses "Intracel."
> 11. 's cast weighs 17 lbs., and itches and smells when it gets wet.
> 12. will never be able to take a shower again.
> 13. 's replacement is lousy.
> 14. is missing a lot of confusion.
> 15. will return shortly.

A get-well note from Steve Allen, who simply asked Gene to reply with a number. (Fred Wostbrock Collection)

Chapter Six
Staged

Gene was undeniably happy and successful as a broadcaster, but he did get a bit sidetracked in those twenty years. He had come to New York to pursue a career in acting. That pursuit led to needing singing lessons, which led to becoming a page, which led to becoming a disc jockey, which led to a successful career of going out onstage and being Gene Rayburn for a living. He had an itch that was returning to the surface after two decades... Acting. Gene needed to find a stage.

He did some regional theater in Long Island, co-starring in *The Seven Year Itch* during 1956. Gene began pounding the pavement just as he had twenty years earlier, looking for roles on Broadway, but he found that finding work for an established performer could be just as difficult as finding work for an up-and-comer. With Broadway not showing

(Fred Wostbrock Collection)

any prospects, Gene headed just slightly south to the Bucks County Playhouse in New Hope, Pennsylvania.

Bucks County Playhouse, about a two-hour drive from New York City, was a fitting home for Gene because it had a colorful history and a great producer. The theater was originally a grist mill constructed in the 1600s. In 1939, the building was remodeled into a theater and held its opening night well before it was ready. For its first performance, the seats and the carpeting had not been installed, the restrooms were filthy, there was still construction debris surrounding the building, and for that night's performance of *Springtime for Henry*, pieces of the set had to be hung from trees.

The theater survived and made a number of improvements in the coming years. By the end of World War II, it had a reputation as one of Pennsylvania's premier theaters and began a long history of hosting both established, successful shows, as well as the "test runs" for many shows preparing to make their debuts on Broadway.

It was the perfect place for Gene to seek his fortunes as an actor because the theater's director, Michael Ellis, admitted to *The New York Times*, "I've made a kind of fetish of putting people in plays for the first time... I try to get the best people I can to do the plays I want to do."

And very often, Ellis liked to cast game show personalities in his shows. Allen Ludden starred in plays at Bucks County Playhouse. Merv Griffin's stage debut at the theater drew its highest gate ever to that point. *I've Got a Secret* panelist Henry Morgan starred in a show and people flew in from Maine to see it. *To Tell the Truth* panelist Peggy Cass was already a reputable actress before she joined that show, but the exposure she got as a game show panelist drove Ellis to cast her in a show.

The New York Times writer who interviewed Ellis for a story was baffled about why audiences flocked more eagerly to see a game show host in a leading role than somebody with more "authentic" performing credentials. Ellis theorized, "[Audiences] are simply curious... They feel they know them as people, but they are curious to see if they can act and they are curious to see what they look like from the waist down."

In the summer of 1957, Gene strolled onto the stage of Bucks County Playhouse for the first time, co-starring with Julia Meade in Peter Ustinov's *The Love of Four Colonels* (which Gene later referred to as "a terrible play that Ustinov wrote as a vehicle for himself"). Gene followed that up with an autumn run co-starring in *Will Success Spoil Rock Hunter?* In the process, Michael Ellis and his family became close friends with the Rayburns.

Gene was also able to use his connections at NBC to get a few opportunities performing on dramatic presentations for NBC's anthology shows. He appeared on *Robert Montgomery Presents* in a presentation called "The Man Who Vanished," about a man whose body disappeared any time that he had a pleasant thought. He got a rave review from *The New York Times* for the performance; critic J.P. Shanley noted in his review that Gene's casting in the role was "a coup" and that he performed it with "just the proper whimsical note."

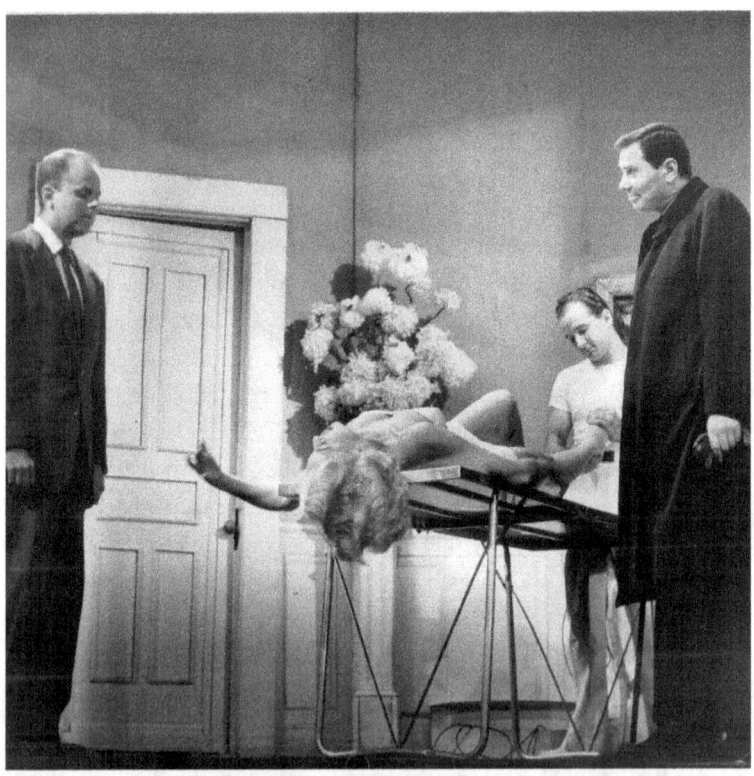

Gene on stage at Bucks County Playhouse, in *Will Success Spoil Rock Hunter?* (Fred Wostbrock Collection)

Gene later remembered the experience as a powerful one, the job that took away whatever reservations he may have had and ensured that he would continue to pursue acting. In December 1957, he appeared on NBC's *Kraft Television Playhouse* playing the role of a subversive, anti-government Russian in a presentation called "Heroes Walk on Sand." He really wanted to make his way to Broadway, but it was still a harder climb than he had anticipated. While Gene continued looking for acting work, he settled into a new job in what was quickly becoming familiar territory.

On February 24, 1958, Gene returned to the game show hosting fold. Although he was trying to veer into acting, it was hard to say no to a game show, particularly in 1958. The genre was white-hot, and the producers overseeing this new game were Jack Barry & Dan Enright, whose games *Twenty One* and *Tic Tac Dough* were drawing millions of viewers. Whatever they came up with was sure to be a hit show. More importantly, it was a live daytime game, which meant it wouldn't take Gene away from any potential stage gigs. Barry & Enright actually gave Gene two auditions for game shows in 1958. He was rejected for *Concentration*; that job went to Hugh Downs. But the company did sign Gene for their other creation for that year.

The new game was a musical quiz, cheekily titled *Dough Re Mi*. Three contestants competed; each was spotted $200 to start the game and heard a series of tunes. For each tune, the live band onstage would play three notes, and an auction would be held for the fourth note. The winning bidder had that money deducted from their bankroll and heard four notes played. Three tunes were played for each game, worth $100, $200, and $300 (changed early in the run to $100, $300, and $500). The high scorer returned to compete in the next game.

Ron Greenberg was a production assistant for the show. He remembers, "I got my start at NBC as a page. I had worked on *Tonight* with Steve Allen. Steve Allen used to do audience participation segments, like 'Stump the Band.' And the prize for the audience member was always a salami. So Steve Allen would talk to the audience member, and I'd be standing just off-camera with the salami, and when Steve gave me the nod, I would hand over the salami. You could never see my face, but my hands were always visible. My parents would always stay up late for

La-dee-dah, what's the name of that song? Gene has the answers on *Dough Re Mi*. (Author's collection)

that, too. They got so excited about seeing their son's hands on national television.

"I really wanted to work in television production, though. I had some good fortune. There was a guy in my apartment building who lived just down the hall from me, named Bob Noah, a wonderful man. He worked for Jack Barry & Dan Enright Productions and he helped me get a job

Gene with some of the staff of *Dough Re Mi*. Ron Greenberg is front and center. (Ron Greenberg Collection)

interview. I got hired. On my first day there, I was greeted by a really young staffer named Dick DeBartolo, who moonlighted as a writer for *MAD* Magazine. And Dick laid out the way that a workday would go and what the duties were for everybody, and as he was explaining it to me, he leaned into the typewriter on his desk and his tie got tangled into the typewriter. So he jerks his head back really hard to pull the tie out and he winds up toppling a stack of books directly behind him. It wound up being this whole comedy routine done for my benefit where he kept knocking things over while explaining the job to me. It was quite a way to start a new job. Barry & Enright hired me to interview prospective contestants and test them. I did that for *Tic Tac Dough* and for *Twenty One*. Then they told me I was being promoted to production assistant for a new game show, *Dough Re Mi*."

No matter what his surroundings, Gene could turn a show into comedy, and *Dough Re Mi* was no exception. While Barry & Enright were known for milking every possible drop of suspense out of their other TV games, *Dough Re Mi* supplied music and merriment.

Actually, it wasn't so much the game supplying the merriment as its goofy, grinning host. The unusual set design had the show's live two-man band (organist Paul Taubman and xylophonist Sal Herman) hidden behind a large screen onstage. Gene played up the barricade by explaining to the audience that the band "is fed twice a week, and relatively harmless."

In the early days of *Dough Re Mi*, Barry & Enright Productions wasn't happy with it. It wasn't that there was anything blatantly wrong with the game, it's just that the finished product wasn't that interesting.

> Dough Re Mi *had been on for about two weeks when Barry came to me and said, "This show is a real dud, isn't it, Gene?" and I said "Yeah, it's a real turkey."*

And that's when Jack Barry did something unusual for an executive producer overseeing a dud. He didn't conduct focus groups. He didn't gather the staff and have a meeting that lasted several hours. No, he decided to give the keys to Gene, trusting his host to find a way to salvage a good show from the wreckage. In a move quite prescient for Gene's future game shows, his solution to the problem was to draw attention away from the game.

> *...I started doing a monologue at the beginning of the show, studio interviews, anything I could think of, and when I couldn't think of anything better to do I played the dumb game. I kept that turkey on the air for three years.*

Gene even got a modification made to the set to add to the fun. He had the show's staff install a small door into that large screen that hid the band. Periodically, Paul Taubman would stick his head through the door and swap one-liners with Gene. Even better, the crew adapted to Gene's eccentric hosting style and joined right in the lunacy. One day, Gene was getting to know the contestants at the start of the game, and a nervous contestant told him she thought she might vomit any moment. Gene looked around the stage and told all the cameramen to keep the cameras focused on him for the entire game, just in case. All of the cameramen instead aimed their cameras on tight shots of the nervous contestant's face, and kept them there as the audience laughed and Gene faux-angrily argued with all of them about not following his instructions.

Ron Greenberg says, "The crew loved Gene. Just loved him. He was a gem to work with and we all got along with him. And I think one of the reasons that the crew loved him so much was because game shows are very much the same day after day after day, and Gene took it upon himself to shake it up so much and make every day different. And that's good for morale. It's funny, if you watch a game show that's been on for a while, you'll see an episode where all of a sudden, there's a really strange camera angle. And when that happens, it means that the director was getting bored and he decided to do something way out of the ordinary just to wake himself up and liven up his job. But with *Dough Re Mi*, every day was already different. That wasn't a problem."

And even though the show had prepared jokes and gags, Gene, spontaneous as always, insisted on having a very "in-the-moment" sensibility about the game. He didn't participate in rehearsals; he sat in his dressing room and relaxed while Ron Greenberg played the role of Gene Rayburn.

Greenberg remembers, "Those rehearsals were almost my big break. There was talk that AFTRA might be going on strike. And the deadline for the terms of the strike to be met sort of coincided with going on the air. So there was a day where Gene showed up an hour before the show but didn't know if he was actually going onstage. If there had actually been a strike, I was going to be the guest host on *Dough Re Mi* that day. But then right before the deadline, the call came in that the negotiations had succeeded and the strike was called off. I came that close…"

Gene's spontaneity extended to the actual playing of the game, too. He didn't want to know the correct answers, so he could play along with the contestants. At the start of each game, Gene opened a large sealed envelope. Inside the envelope was a board with three covered slots; underneath the slots were the names of the three songs to be used for the upcoming game. Gene would open the envelope and then place the board on his podium without removing any of the coverings. The show's crew built a small device that would reveal the correct answers as needed during the game so Gene wouldn't see them until he absolutely had to.

Ron Greenberg says, "I had two very important jobs on the show. I was standing out of sight of the camera but in Gene's line of sight for every show. I did a job that exists only in the game show business called 'working the blackboard.' Most game shows do this. I stood offstage with a blackboard showing how much the reigning champion had already won, every contestant's score, how the bids they were placing would affect the score, and a note of what the score would be depending on if the next answer given was correct or incorrect. And Gene could reference that quickly without doing the math himself and use it to remind the players and the viewers of what was at stake at every step of the game. My other job on the show was to be Gene's laugher. When Gene did any kind of gag, I would let out a really loud, drawn out 'Ha-HAAAAAAA!'"

During the summer of 1958, world affairs caused the live broadcast of *Dough Re Mi* to be pre-empted several times. One morning, the program opened without Gene onstage. Announcer Roger Tuttle stepped in and served as guest host for about ten minutes when Gene suddenly walked onstage, unshaven, shoes untied, and not wearing a necktie. Gene explained that he overslept, figuring that the UN was going to pre-empt the show again.

When Labor Day rolled around, the entire staff took part in a doozy of a prank. Gene opened the show by announcing that everybody was taking the day off and walking off the set. The cameras then caught glimpses of various staff members heading to the exits. The cameramen abandoned their posts, and the studio lights went dim for several seconds, leaving the home viewers watching dead air until Gene finally revealed the gag and actually started the show.

Ron Greenberg remembers, "The audience reacted so well to the bits of comedy that Barry & Enright actually hired a joke writer named Norm Liebmann to come up with jokes and gags for Gene. Norm wound up writing for a lot of different people; Bob Newhart, Jerry Lewis, Dean Martin, Dick Van Dyke… but he started off writing for Gene on *Dough Re Mi*. And he came up with really funny stuff. Not just jokes for Gene to tell, but some more involved comedy. We once had a bit where a vendor

**Jerry Lewis joins Gene on *Dough Re Mi*.
(Fred Wostbrock Collection)**

pushing an ice cream cart walked onstage and disrupted the show, and Gene did some banter with him about the ice cream and about how he was interrupting the program. The actor we hired to play the vendor was Jerry Stiller."

A batch of photos from the series survive today, snapped by an NBC photographer from offstage while games were in progress, and they give some unintentional insight to the Gene Rayburn approach for hosting a TV game show. Like virtually every other game show, *Dough Re Mi* had a lectern onstage for the emcee to stand at and conduct the proceedings.

Gene, however, was almost never behind it. He leaned against it while chatting with the contestants. He'd walk across the stage and stand alongside the players as the game was in progress. He walked to the center of the stage whenever he was addressing the home viewers directly. Gene wouldn't be confined. He explored the space around him and used the whole stage.

Though game shows aren't typically greeted with roses by television critics, *Dough Re Mi* was one of few games to enjoy acclaim from newspaper writers. *Miami News* columnist Arthur Grace said "If we've got to have twelve dozen quiz shows, there ought to be more like *Dough Re Mi*."

Ron Greenberg says, "I'm sure there are purists out there who disliked the show because they wanted to watch the game and nothing else. And when you have a game show, you have to be mindful that you're not drawing attention away from the game. But the thing is, our game was so basic. Here's three notes. Place a bid. Here's four notes. It was so straightforward, if we didn't shake it up a little bit, there wouldn't be much there and the audience, I think, would have become bored very quickly."

TV audiences liked it quite a bit, too; it performed reasonably well in the ratings. It was also popular among the visitors to Rockefeller Plaza who came to sit in the studio audience. *Dough Re Mi* elaborately overhauled Studio 8H, where the show emanated from. Instead of rows of theater-style seating, the audience sat in individual chairs around a series of small tables, cabaret-style. A group of waitresses showed up to serve everybody coffee and cake as Gene Rayburn made his way onstage to get the audience warmed up with jokes, friendly chit-chat, and a short-form version of the game, offering audience members small prizes.

Everything was sailing along just nicely for *Dough Re Mi* in its first few months. Again, it had come along at the right time. The general public was devouring game shows, and networks and producers were happily serving generous helpings of them. And then in the fall of 1958, everything hit the fan.

During the summer of that year, a CBS quiz show called *Dotto* had been abruptly pulled off the air after a standby contestant snooped in a notebook that the returning champion had brought along with her, and

Busting loose. Gene, for the heck of it, wears a football uniform instead of a suit while overseeing a special celebrity game of *Dough Re Mi*. **(Fred Wostbrock Collection)**

discovered that the notebook contained all of the correct answers for that day's episode. Similar accusations began dogging other game shows, most notably *The $64,000 Question* and Barry & Enright's *Twenty One*.

In September 1958, NBC viewers tuned into a conspicuously peculiar episode of *Dough Re Mi*. The returning champion, a Miami postman named Joseph Griffin, returned with $2,700 in winnings, and when Gene was wrapping that day's show, Griffin jumped in and said he could no longer appear on the show because he had run out of vacation days and had to return to his job.

This explanation struck many of Griffin's personal friends as a red flag because they happened to know he actually had a full twelve days of vacation time left. *The Miami News* contacted Griffin, and Griffin gave them a straightforward answer: he was told to leave. Five minutes before the show went on the air, the show's producer, Hugh Branigan, approached him and told him he had to go, no matter how well he had performed on that day's show.

A month later, Jack Barry & Dan Enright relinquished control of their games *Concentration*, *Tic Tac Dough*, and *Dough Re Mi* to NBC. *Twenty One*, which had seen its ratings fall rapidly into the basement in the past few months, was yanked from the airwaves.

Orson Bean, who had begun appearing on Goodson-Todman's *To Tell the Truth* shortly after its 1956 debut, remembered that he wasn't terribly surprised to learn that other companies had fixed their shows. Mark Goodson knew all along.

Orson remembers, "When the big money quizzes were thriving, we were having a conversation about them in Goodson's office, and Goodson very confidently says, 'The fix is in. Those shows aren't on the level.' And we said, 'What makes you so sure, Mark?' And Mark says, 'All the big winners that these shows have, like Charles Van Doren on *Twenty One*… the big winners on these shows are good-looking, charismatic, outgoing. And I hate to say it, but those kinds of people never do well on quiz shows. We hope they will. We pray they will. We wish that they will. But they never do. Our big winners always wind up being the plainer, reserved contestants.'

"I recall another point he made, which was the way the host would ask the question, and the orchestra would play some suspenseful music, and they'd zoom in on the contestant biting his lip and sweating, furrowing his brow, and he'd say, 'Oh, which monarch was that? I believe that was the son of so-and-so who was killed during the uprising… that was the seventeenth century, which means…' And Goodson said, 'If somebody asks you a question, the answer doesn't come to you after thirty seconds of ferreting it out. You either know it or you don't.'

"What was so funny to me when the scandals broke was how enraged the media was about it. They had devoted magazine covers to the winners, they had printed recaps of the previous night's shows in the newspapers like they would report on sports events. The media didn't give a shit that the viewers had been tricked, the media was furious that they

**Not to be confined, Gene avoids his lectern on *Dough Re Mi*.
(Fred Wostbrock Collection)**

themselves had been tricked. That's the funny thing about the media; they really don't care if the country is being lied to. They get upset about something only when they realize 'Hey, they lied to *us*! *We* got tricked!'"

Ron Greenberg said "The scandals were just awful. The mood in the office wasn't very pleasant, and the reason for that was that the accusations against the company were so broad. You'd read what Barry & Enright Productions was being accused of, but in the early going, some people were making accusations without naming names. So you'd say to yourself, 'Well, it wasn't me, I know I wasn't doing it.' And then you'd look up and look around the office at all of your co-workers and think to yourself, 'Was it him? Was it her?' It was a terrible feeling."

A gracious host before showtime. Gene treats the audience to coffee in the cabaret-style seating of the *Dough Re Mi* studio. (Fred Wostbrock Collection)

Dough Re Mi recovered surprisingly well from the scandal. Aside from Joseph Griffin's odd story, nobody else had stepped forward with stories of collusion or chicanery from *Dough Re Mi*. Many of the game show hosts who had overseen shows during this scandalous era were tainted by association, but Gene was able to avoid any residual stench from the controversy. Griffin had even said in his interview with *The Miami News* that he was convinced that Gene didn't know anything in advance. Jack Narz, who had hosted *Dotto*, subjected himself to a lie detector test and stated that although he was suspicious, he was not directly involved in the rigging of the show and had no advance knowledge of what was supposed to take place in any of the fixed games. Monty Hall, who had spent a summer guest-hosting *Twenty One*, referred to himself as "a patsy." Jack Barry himself was aware that his game shows were fixed but insisted on being kept in the dark about how the games would turn out, fearful that he couldn't deliver a convincing performance as host if he knew how the game would end. Given that this was Jack Barry's attitude about his own hosting performance, it would stand to reason that the same policy was enforced for the hosts of other Barry & Enright games. If anything untoward was happening at *Dough Re Mi* beyond Mr. Griffin's experience, it's extremely unlikely that Gene had any knowledge of it.

While most game shows crumbled in the wake of the scandals, *Dough Re Mi* was one of the handful that survived. The only consequence it appeared to suffer was that a planned weekly primetime version of the show was called off. *Dough Re Mi* remained on the air long after the scandals erupted. In the Congressional hearings that followed, plenty of accusations, testimony, and evidence surrounded shows like *Dotto, Twenty One, Tic Tac Dough,* and *The $64,000 Question*… But not *Dough Re Mi*. The odd incident involving Joseph Griffin was virtually the only untoward incident of the entire series. And even though it was certainly untoward, it wasn't a situation where a player was required to forfeit money or throw a game, as had happened on some of the other shows. Griffin was simply told to stop playing. If *Dough Re Mi* hadn't been 100% pure, it was at least a solid ninety. And when NBC seized control of the show and kept a more watchful eye on it, virtually nothing changed. It was still the same lively, funny show with a game buried in it somewhere.

In the late 1950s, westerns were picking up steam on television. ABC introduced one called *Wagon Train*, and suddenly, *The Steve Allen Show* had dipped from second to third place in its time slot—an undesirable spot in a three-channel world. Looking for a way to increase interest in the show, Steve Allen elected to uproot the entire production in 1959 and move it to California. Gene, after six years with Steve Allen, decided to sever ties and stay in New York City.

> *I guess it could have gone on longer, but Allen took off for Los Angeles and I didn't want to go. That place is the worst in the world. I hate it.*
>
> *My wife didn't want to go, either. But it was a mistake. When people see you in California, they know you're alive. They remember you and they cast you. I should have had more of an acting career.*

Gene liked the cozy life he had on the east coast, working in the bustling television business with a steady hit show where he got to take center stage, and then relaxing at his home and devoting his spare time to puttering around in the garage and to gardening; he surrounded the driveway on both sides with corn.

Helen had a comfortable life in New York, too, devoting much of her spare time to organizing fundraisers. She was extremely passionate about the Westchester Adoption Agency, for which she eventually became the head of fundraising.

Lynne remembers, "Her big coup for fundraising was organizing a theater night. She would pick out a show on Broadway and treat a bunch of potential donors to an evening of theater, and then ideally they would enjoy themselves so much that they'd make a big donation. She chose a show that was just opening on Broadway that nobody knew anything about, a completely new show starring two English actors. Well the show ended up being *My Fair Lady*. And that theater night went really well for her."

Gene and Helen; even though they knew Gene might miss out on a few opportunities, they agreed that the east coast was where they would rather be. (Fred Wostbrock Collection)

Gene and Lynne play a game of chess while Bridget & Albert keep them company. Albert was blind; Helen once took him on a walk through Manhattan, and when they came to a crowded corner, Helen yelled "Blind dog!" The people cleared out of the way, and Helen & Albert continued their stride across Second Avenue.
(Fred Wostbrock Collection)

Helen whipped up other lavish fundraisers for the adoption agency. She assembled a garden party for 500 guests, and later a concert by Mary Martin among other events. It was a cause that she was passionate about.

It was also a cause that Lynne found a little odd. "My dad had a favorite expression. He used to say 'Helloooooooooo, Dr. Freud.' And when he said that, what it meant was that there was a deeper meaning to somebody's behavior, and it wasn't really well-hidden. The deeper meaning was obvious. Well, he never used that term talking about my mother, but I do. My parents wanted more children, and yet, after my mother had four miscarriages, they never adopted a child. I thought that was bizarre. If you're financially comfortable enough to bring a child into the world yourself, you have the resources to adopt a child. And for some reason, they didn't. I took that very hard, too. I would have loved it if they had adopted a child. I would have loved having a brother or sister.

My mother worked so hard to raise funds for a cause that she wouldn't personally pursue; I think either she felt guilty or she was trying to get a message across to my dad."

The Rayburns actually nearly lost Lynne in 1959. She had already battled meningitis and encephalitis, and now, only one year before seatbelts became mandatory for automobiles, Lynne was in a serious car accident. She was launched from the vehicle and landed coincidentally near the home of one of Gene's friends, Garry Moore. She was in a coma for several weeks, and required abdominal surgery to remove her spleen and some intestines. When she recovered, she had sustained brain damage and developed a learning disability. Gene, not yet forty-two, had lost enough family already, and he was grateful that he still had a daughter.

Despite staying in New York and steering clear of La-La Land, Gene landed a film role a short time later in *It Happened to Jane*, starring Doris Day as Jane, a plucky widow seeking help from a lawyer (Jack Lemmon) to fight an evil railroad tycoon (Ernie Kovacs) whose underhanded business practices are damaging Jane's lobster business. Gene declined a screen credit for the film, feeling he hadn't done enough work to earn it, but he has a scene-stealing role as a reporter covering Jane's departure by train from Maine to New York. Gene refused a screen credit for the part, feeling personally that he hadn't done enough work to deserve it. And although he predictably shone in his brief comedic turn, he never sought a career in film. He was completely content on television, where *Dough Re Mi* was still prospering with him at the helm. And he loved the theater, too.

Although the comedy bits and Gene's monologues on *Dough Re Mi* did so much to breathe life into the show, Ron Greenberg was working diligently at the office to add some intrigue to the game itself.

He explains, "I was in charge of picking the songs used for every game. I'd go into the office of Hugh Branigan, one of the producers. And I'd sort of play the game with him. I'd whistle three notes through my teeth, then four notes, and then five, to see if he could ever figure it out. We had long arguments about a lot of the songs we used.

"One of my favorite little twists I stumbled upon was when I whistled the first three notes. And he nods his head and blurts out 'National

Gene shows off the tunes that Ron Greenberg has selected for today's game of *Dough Re Mi*. The list of answers was delivered in a sealed manila envelope at the start of each game, with each of the song titles covered by a peel-off tab. Gene preferred to play along with the contestants, and would remove a tab only when cued by a stagehand that the answer a contestant had just given was the correct one. (Author's Collection)

anthem' without hesitation. And I said no. It was a big band song that had been popular a few years earlier, and it just happened to begin with the same three notes. We did it on the show and sure enough, the contestant guessed 'The Star Spangled Banner.' We loved it. From that day forward, we did it for the audience warm-up before every episode. A lot of people who come to TV show tapings are just tourists who are fascinated by the idea of seeing a TV show in person, and you get a lot of audience members who aren't actually fans of your show. So every day before the show, we'd play these three notes and ask our audience members to guess it, and every hand in the studio went up and they'd shout 'Star Spangled Banner.' And they were shocked when they heard the whole song.

"That worked so well that it became sort of an obsession with me. There aren't really very many songs you could do this with, but I would sit in the office and think up songs that had really distinctive beginnings, and then try to think of a song that started with the same notes. It was actually good for suspense because it made the contestants second-guess themselves and play conservatively sometimes, and then sometimes we'd throw a curveball where it actually was the obvious answer but the contestants would spend a bunch of money in the auction to buy the next note. It was a great twist and I tried to use it as much as I could."

And between Ron Greenberg's clever game-building and Gene's contagious antics, the show managed to survive until December 30, 1960, nearly a three-year run, remarkably good fortune for a show that could have suffered a harsher fate.

Peter Marshall remembers, "I was a guest on the final episode. They had me as a special guest and they had me playing on behalf of a contestant against two other folks. Well, my background was in music, so I knew everything. They couldn't stump me. They'd play those first three notes and I'd fire off the correct answer every time. They told me I was the best player in the history of the show. And Gene got such a kick out of it. I was on the last show and I ended the series by draining it of more money than they had ever given away."

One of the harsher effects that the quiz show scandals had overall, though, was that game shows began getting "squeezed out" from prime time slots. A few prime-time games, like *Video Village* and *Password*, premiered during the 1960s, but by 1970, game shows would be off nighttime schedules altogether, relegated only to daytime. Gene was even supposed to host a new primetime game show in 1960. *Head of the Class* was a game conjured up by what was left of the staff of Barry & Enright after the quiz show scandals. On the pilot produced for NBC's benefit, Gene and other performers appeared in comedy skits, and then contestants were asked questions about what had happened in the skit. NBC initially picked up the show, and the June 18-24, 1960 edition of *TV Guide* even has a listing for it to air in a Friday night slot; instead, viewers tuning in at that time saw reruns of westerns. *Head of the Class* was permanently shelved.

But the genre didn't disappear altogether. Television was drifting away from game shows, but they would always drift back. Gene explained why.

> *Game shows were out of favor for a while after [the quiz show scandals], but the people like to watch, and the networks like them because they're cheap and easy to produce.*

Gene continued toiling away in the theater. One of his prouder achievements at Bucks County Playhouse was that he was in the original, pre-Broadway cast for Neil Simon's first show, *Come Blow Your Horn*. Gene played the role of Alan, the swinging playboy who teaches his brother how to be more outgoing with women. He eagerly wanted to go to Broadway with the show, but Simon told Gene that he wanted a more legitimate actor to play the role.

When the show premiered on Broadway, the role of Alan was played by Hal March, former host of *The $64,000 Question*. It was nothing personal against March, but Gene acknowledged later that it was a huge personal blow to him that an actor with roughly equal credentials got the role instead. The wound was salved quite a bit, though, when he got the nod to replace March during a vacation, and when a national touring production of the show was launched, Gene crossed the country playing the role of Alan.

Gene finally made it onto Broadway, and in quite a choice role, too. *Bye Bye Birdie*, a comedy loosely inspired by Elvis Presley's emergence in the 1950s, premiered on Broadway in 1960 with Dick Van Dyke

Gene shows a different side of himself in his theatrical publicity stills. The cigarette holder was a trademark that gave him something of an identity in the 1950s, but ironically, it probably hastened his retirement from the theater in the early 1990s.
(Fred Wostbrock Collection)

playing the role of Albert Peterson, the music agent who eventually gives everything up to start a new career as an English teacher. Van Dyke left the role early in 1961 in preparation for his upcoming sitcom, *The Dick Van Dyke Show*.

Gene was given an opportunity to audition and seized it. The dreams he had as a teenager were alive and well, and the goal he had set for himself a quarter of a century earlier when he arrived in New York was finally within his grasp. He had a chance—just a chance, for the moment—to be a star on Broadway.

> *There's my chance! And boy, I worked my tail off for that job. I rented a rehearsal hall, I hired a vocal coach, I hired a choreographer. I prepared a couple of songs, a ballad and a rhythm tune. I prepared a dance. I had two weeks to do all that, but I worked every day. Five or six hours a day, singing and dancing in this rehearsal hall.*
>
> *And when I went to the Schubert Theater to do my audition, I walked out, and I adopted an attitude for auditions which helped me a lot. I would say to myself, "These people need me more than I need them." And that helped relax me so I could do my best work.*
>
> *It was a formidable job. But I got the part and I loved doing it.*

Kay Cole was a child actress in Los Angeles who landed the role of Amaryllis in *The Music Man* and then made her way to Broadway, where she was cast as one of Conrad Birdie's admirers. She later became an accomplished director.

She says, "Gene had very smart instincts about how to get that part. Hiring a voice coach and a dance coach doesn't mean that you're less. It means you want to be more, and even a seasoned performer would be smart to hire coaches for various skills."

Gene didn't sit back once he had the job. Feeling the need to prove himself now that he was finally realizing his dream, Gene worked even harder at the rehearsals. He threw himself into preparations for the role

Gene's dream finally comes true. He became a Broadway star with *Bye-Bye Birdie*. (Gene Rayburn Archive)

Gene during a rehearsal break. He had walked with a persistent limp after his skiing accident, but threw himself so hard into preparing for *Bye Bye Birdie* that by the time he was finished, the limp was gone. (Fred Wostbrock Collection)

so intensely that it actually finished rehabilitating the leg he had broken while skiing a few years earlier. By the time he was done with rehearsals and finally performing the show for real, he had lost the limp he had been living with for the past few years.

> *I knew I had worked hard to get [the role]. I wanted to do it. Dick Van Dyke is a heck of a dancer. And I had to do all the steps he did, and all the dances he did. And I was proud of the fact that I was able to do it because dancing is not my long suit. But I loved doing it and I was happy to get that chance.*

Cole says, "To take over a role for an accomplished actor can be a little tricky, not just for that one new performer, but for the whole cast and crew. As a director or producer, you obviously want to keep the replacement from altering the show too much. You don't want a carbon copy of the person that's being replaced. For one thing, that's not good for the new actor, and it's not good for the show either, because it draws attention to the fact that the former star is gone. At the same time, you have that show fully developed and you don't want to alter it for anybody. You try to tailor it for the new actor as much as possible without altering anything. You look for nuances in the new performer; their behavior, their way of speaking, their way of moving, facial expressions. And you try to find ways to bring that out without directly touching the material."

Gene had a series of private rehearsals with the stage manager when he arrived. For more crucial scenes in the show, other actors would come to the rehearsals to help Gene practice.

Gene's understudy in *Bye Bye Birdie* was Charles Nelson Reilly, a Bronx-born actor who later broke out as a star with his performance as Bud Frump in the original Broadway production of *How to Succeed in Business Without Really Trying*. As the understudy for the star in *Bye Bye Birdie*, Reilly made a lasting impression on his fellow cast members when Dick Van Dyke became ill one night. Reilly went to stage and gave a memorable performance… memorable mainly because he hadn't bothered learning the songs or dialogue.

"Gray skies are gonna clear up…doo-wah, doo-wah, doo-wah," he sang.

Peter Marshall remembers, "I was in a play with him called *Skyscraper*. I didn't have any scenes with him, but Julie Harris did, and I'll always remember what happened with her onstage one night. My character's name was Timothy Bushman. Charles, at one point, wants to make a phone call to my character, and he says to Julie, 'Get on the phone and get me Mr. Kushman... Lushman, Gushman, Pushman...' Julie says, 'Bushman.' Charles nods and says 'That's the guy!'"

Kay Cole says, "Charles was brilliant. He was a great performer, a stunning director, a brilliant acting coach, and one of the nicest men ever. I worked with him as an acting coach for several shows, and I remember him for his kindness, and how articulate and instinctive he was. When you're working firsthand on a script or scene, and it becomes your work, you don't always see the depth of a character or the depth of a scene. Charles was tremendous and being able to view a scene objectively and immediately picked out what it needed, and he could show it to you."

> *He never had to go on for me. He had to go on for Dick Van Dyke once when Dick was coming in from Long Island and got caught in a blizzard, and couldn't make it to the theater. And I happened to be in the audience that night with Charles performing the role. He did it very well. He's a wonderful, warm actor. He's really quite good.*
>
> *But there were other people in that show, like Paul Lynde. He played the father and had some great lines. Kay Medford was in the show, too. Wonderful actress and she played my mother. It was a wonderful show. I loved doing that show.*

Gene stayed with *Bye Bye Birdie* for the remainder of its original Broadway run. Months after he had joined the show, he went out for a drink with the show's composer/lyricist, Charles Strouse. They discussed how Gene's involvement had come about, and Gene said he presumed he got the role because he had been a well-known television and radio personality and that his name could probably sell a few extra tickets.

Strouse responded, "No. We looked at two hundred guys for that job. You did the best audition."

Dick Gautier played the role of Conrad Birdie, the Elvis-inspired rock star who gets drafted into the army during the peak of his popularity. Gautier says, "If Strouse said that Gene did the best audition, I believe that, but I'm sure that drawing power figured into it. Gene did have a name. This was New York City, so the audience absolutely knew Gene from the radio and knew him from *Tonight*. The daytime game shows gave him some drawing power, too. An audience that might not normally watch Broadway shows may have taken notice because this man that they enjoyed watching every day would be a part of the show. It was better than *Bye Bye Birdie* starring Joe McFlapper, you know."

Kay Cole says, "Gene had a name and he definitely sold some tickets. I was only twelve at the time and I absolutely remember that I already knew who Gene was and that I recognized him as soon as I saw him, so he could definitely sell tickets. But talent had to have played a role in casting him for the show because we were such a hit that we didn't need a big name at that point. *Bye Bye Birdie* was popular enough that it had developed a persona and an identity, and we had a reputation among the general public. The show could sell tickets on its own merit; Gene would have to have been there based on ability."

Still, Dick Van Dyke had helped establish the show as a hit, and as the show's run extended week after week and the cast became better acquainted, the cast had turned into a family. Every Saturday and Sunday, when the cast was performing two shows a day, it became a routine for everyone to go to the movies together during the break between the matinee and the night show. But the switch from Dick Van Dyke to Gene Rayburn was no shake-up. It was barely even a rattle.

Kay Cole remembers, "Gene had no problem fitting in. Anybody who did the type of work he did on radio and television would already have a sense of how to communicate and how to listen. So Gene used those skills to adapt, and he slid right in. He was a nice man and a happy man. When I close my eyes and picture him, all I see is a smile. He was always smiling."

Gene reflected on the end of *Bye Bye Birdie* without regret. After so many years of trying to become a star on Broadway, his big opportunity lasted only a few months. But he was actually glad it worked out that way.

> *I have a lot of variety in my career and I planned it that way because you get stale if you do the same thing over and over. No actor should be required to do a play for more than six months. It becomes a tremendous challenge to make it fresh every night.*

The only part of the plan that went awry was the part where one starring role would lead to another, and another, and another. *Bye Bye Birdie* was the only time Gene ever found his way to a Broadway stage.

Lynne says, "My father loved acting and loved the theater. I think it had to do with the way that he viewed people in that business. He revered people who worked in the theater, and even though he consistently found work in television, I think he felt like the people he worked for didn't really appreciate him. And he saw the attention and praise that stage actors got and I think he wanted that.

"I also think Dad liked the opportunity to disappear into a character. He had an unhappy childhood and I really think my father carried that with him his entire life. He liked the idea that he could lose himself for a few hours and be somebody else every night. I know my dad wished that he had more opportunities to do that."

Dick Gautier remembers, "Dick Van Dyke is a tough act to follow. Light on his feet and a fantastic singer; there's no competing with him. Gene was a good singer and a good dancer, but just good enough to get by."

Peter Marshall says, "Gene was talented. As far as singing skills go, though, he was good. Just good. And to be on Broadway, you have to be a great singer, a hell of a singer. And to be honest, that's why he didn't get the chances he wanted. He was good at singing, but he wasn't great."

(Fred Wostbrock Collection)

Chapter Seven
The Monitor Beacon

WNEW had a problem in 1946: their morning radio show host was gone and they needed to fill a gap, so they turned to Gene. WNBC had a problem in 1953; they needed a boost in ratings and publicity, so they turned to Gene. Just two years later, in 1955, radio as a whole had a problem.

It was dying.

Okay, that's not exactly accurate, but it was clear that major changes needed to be made. Ratings had been dropping for radio broadcasts as a whole since the late 1940s, but the drops had been noticeably drastic in 1953 and 1954. Stars who performed on both radio and television still delivered good results for their TV broadcasts while their radio shows were withering. Genres that had thrived on radio—the soap operas, sitcoms, mysteries, and game shows—were all performing much better on television.

Ratings data indicated that things weren't completely hopeless. For years, radio ratings were measured only with regards to the large radios that families gathered around in their living room. No consideration was made toward portable radios and car radios. When that data was finally gathered, it indicated that radio still had an audience, but they weren't giving their full attention to it. Radios were listened to while hanging out with friends, relaxing in the park, going for a drive, doing household chores; essentially, it had become a companion instead of being the center of attention. Programming had to be altered to fit that usage.

Early in 1955, only a few months after *Tonight* got off the ground, Weaver, executive producer Jim Fleming, and WRCA station manager Steve White concocted an idea for a lavish project, radio's last great program. Weaver jokingly referred to it as "a kaleidoscopic phantasmagoria." The radio audience knew it as *Monitor*.

> *Pat Weaver really had a fabulously creative mind.*

The show premiered at noon on June 18, 1955, heralding its arrival with the soon-to-be-iconic *Monitor* Beacon, a series of dial tones mixed with the sound of the letter M being formed in Morse code. It was used to open each broadcast and each segment of the show. Staffers initially feared that the sound would annoy listeners, but instead, it turned out to be a closely-identified "signature" of the show, an audible calling card that listeners heard to ensure they were tuned to the correct station on the dial.

That opening weekend, *Monitor* aired for forty consecutive hours, as it would every weekend for the next six years. Each weekend, a rotating crew of "communicators" would take turns hosting a few hours at a time. The broadcast was a blend of records, news updates, live interviews, and reports from remote correspondents. With the aid of an elaborate set up of telephones and other equipment, the communicator could contact correspondents and interviewees anywhere in the world. At the push of a button, *Monitor* could take listeners live to a German festival or the Calgary Stampede. The logic of the impossibly vast running time was that none of the features could be burdened by time constraints. There was no reason to restrict a prerecorded news package to only three minutes or hold an interview to ten minutes. The communicators, correspondents, and guests were free to devote as much time to a subject as they felt was necessary.

Pat Weaver didn't last much longer at NBC after launching *Monitor*. He clashed with NBC founder David Sarnoff, who felt that Weaver's ideas, however successful they may have been, weren't cost-effective. Weaver was replaced a few months after the premiere of *Monitor* by Sarnoff's son, Robert. Gene, whose career in television was solidified with Weaver's help, often referred to Robert Sarnoff by punning an Ernest Hemingway work and saying "The son also rises."

For *Monitor*'s first six years, communicators included Hugh Downs, David Brinkley, Clifton Fadiman, Dave Garroway, Bob & Ray, and Monty Hall. In 1961, the show's broadcast time was cut down to a still-impressive sixteen hours, stretching across Saturday and Sunday. Gene joined the program, hosting it for three hours at a time, usually on Saturday. In *Monitor*'s first years, the communicators usually co-hosted segments in pairs, and their conversation was scripted to give each co-host relatively equal airtime. Beginning in 1961, each portion of the show was hosted by a solo communicator, and Gene got the nod because of his past experience with Jack Lescoulie, Dee Finch, Steve Allen, and his handful of game shows made him extremely comfortable with ad-libbing, and he didn't necessarily need a fully prepared script. It was only eight years after Gene "fell on his ass" as solo host of a radio show, but with *Monitor*, the results were quite different. Gene stayed for the next twelve years, making him the longest-tenured communicator of the show's entire run, and arguably the most popular. From the point of view of NBC's advertising salesman, he was certainly the most successful. Gene's three-hour block each weekend sold out all of its allotted commercial spots more consistently than any other block.

The Matchless Gene Rayburn

> *GENE: (Speaking very fast) Andnowhere'sthemanwithoutw homthephrase "Here'sthehostofMonitor" wouldn'tmeanathing, HEEEEEEEEEEEEEEEEEEEEEERE'S GENE! (Normal speed) Hi there, Gene Rayburn here... Monitor promises and delivers the best of popular music every weekend, but one thing you probably will not hear is a new recording mentioned in the Wall Street Journal this week. It's produced by a management association and it's aimed at the corporate market. It claims to be effective in producing better performance from employment even when a pay raise request is denied. We haven't heard the record but we imagine it might sound something like this... (German accent) Dear employees... you will continue to work the same hours or longer. You will receive the same salary or less, and you will really produce! For those of you listening, you will continue to LISTEN... pleeeeeeease... to da Monitor beacon.*

Sound the beacon! Gene has arrived at Radio Central for *Monitor*. (Fred Wostbrock Collection)

As he did with just about anything else, Gene did *Monitor* with humor. One weekend, *Monitor* did a themed broadcast with a number of features about physical fitness. Gene opened his part of the program by jogging in place and playing up how quickly he ran out of breath while introducing the next song. It was a sample of the type of energy Gene brought to the show; even though the audience couldn't see him and even though he had a chair at the microphone, the *Monitor* staff recalled that Gene usually stood whenever he was speaking. It gave more energy to the presentation.

And off the air, Gene's *Monitor* staff remembered that he brought humor to a typical workday, too. Assistant Director Jean Houston told author Dennis Hart, "I adored Rayburn. He was congenial. He was funny. He was terrific."

Producer Bud Drake told Hart, "Rayburn was a great guy. He was very popular with everyone in the building. He was very adaptable and very directable and very easy to work with."

Gene left many lasting impressions on the *Monitor* staff. Few people could forget the day when Gene was interviewing Walter Matthau, who was wearing a suit that had been tailor-made for him by the costume department of his most recent film. He boasted to Gene that everything from the inside out had been specially made for him, and to prove his point, he dropped his pants. As it happened, an NBC page picked that moment to bring in a group of tourists, and the entire group walked in on the sight of Walter Matthau, minus pants, and Gene Rayburn examining the label of Matthau's boxers.

There was also the day when Gene was reading a commercial for Ace Combs, touting their "unbreakable" quality. To prove his point, he held a "no-name comb" from a competitor up to the microphone and announced he would break it in half... then broke into laughter and admitted to the listeners that he couldn't break it.

Gene left a lasting mental image on many co-workers with his hobby of doing needlepoint while playing records. Gene was an expert with needle and thread, and he was mighty proud of it. When a page would bring a tour group through the radio studios, Gene would proudly hold up the piece that he was working on.

But the strongest impression Gene made was on *Monitor* studio engineer Gene Garnes, who told author Dennis Hart about the kindness Gene exhibited once when talking to a fan... who turned out not to be a fan of Gene Rayburn. A woman saw Gene walking through a hotel lobby during a *Monitor*-related trip to Chicago, excitedly approached him, and said, "Mr. Ames, may I have your autograph?"

Gene smiled warmly, pulled out a pen, scribbled a message, and signed it "Ed Ames."

Ed Ames was a popular singer whose dark complexion led to his being cast as a Native American named Mingo on the TV series *Daniel Boone*. He made television history in a wildly unexpected way early in Johnny Carson's tenure on *The Tonight Show*, demonstrating the proper way of throwing a tomahawk, using an outline of a cowboy's body drawn on plywood. Ames threw the tomahawk, hit the cowboy directly in the crotch, and got the longest laugh in the show's history.

As it happened, Ames had a lanky build, dark hair, and a broad smile, and for a time in their lives, he and Gene looked almost exactly alike. Gene told the engineer that he was frequently mistaken for Ames, and that if he had corrected the woman, he would have embarrassed her. He instead chose to sign the autograph "Ed Ames" because she would never know her mistake, and the experience made her day.

There was another look-alike that Gene had a few laughs with. A new skyscraper was opened in New York City, complete with a lavish ceremony for the first day that the skyscraper was open to the public. The master of ceremonies was Peter Marshall, the uncanny double that Gene had sought out for the Chrysler ad years earlier. Gene and Helen attended the ceremony together.

Afterward, they walked to a nearby restaurant for dinner, as did many of the other audience members who had been to the event. When Gene walked in, everybody turned around, applauded, and shouted various compliments to Gene for the great job he did.

Gene calmly replied, "It's not me. He's coming later!"

Gene could even turn good advice into a good laugh. *Monitor* hosts frequently read helpful tips during their segments, covering all areas. In a given weekend, you heard helpful tips about proper grooming, gardening, even what to look for when buying a new rug. One weekend, Gene read

You never know who you might run into at NBC's Radio Central. Gene meets Frank Sinatra. (Fred Wostbrock Collection)

a tip about the importance of looking out for potholes while driving in winter conditions, with his script reading, "You may end up needing a new axle or new springs." Gene ad-libbed, "You may end up needing a new axle, new springs, or new teeth."

Gene could play it straight, though. On the anniversary of the sinking of the Titanic, Gene talked to an elderly pastry chef who had worked in the ship's kitchen. A few years later, he received acclaim for his reverent treatment of the weekend's major news, the death of Dwight Eisenhower. And even from week to week, as lighthearted as the finished product was, Gene treated every interview he conducted as a major undertaking and gave every one of them some serious consideration.

> *I took Evelyn Wood's speed-reading course so that I could do book interviews. I thought it was just insulting to have an author on the show and try to interview them without having read the book. You can do a more sensible interview when you've read the book, so I learned how to speed-read. I did a lot of interviews with a lot of fascinating people. That was a life-saving job for me though, because I had that job when* Bye Bye Birdie *ended and I had it whenever I was in-between other jobs.*

Gene's work in 1961 was largely confined to radio and theater. The following year, he dove back into TV with a new annual gig serving as host of the Miss Universe pageant. Like anything else in show business, though, he had to earn it. And the process of getting hired to host a beauty pageant was an effort that Gene found surprisingly exasperating.

> *Man! The blockades that a guy has to run through to get this job. You have to pass the acceptance muster of the producers of the pageant, the network and the sponsors. And they all say the same thing—'all we want is an emcee who is warm and friendly.'*

Gene kept pursuing theater work. *Bye Bye Birdie* had come to an end on Broadway and Gene found his way into an unusual role—well, not really a role. In the summer of 1962, he was the master of ceremonies for *1962 Aqua Carnival*, a lavish nightly water show in New York Coliseum, featuring champion swimmers, divers, water clowns, and even a few "dry acts," like choreographed roller skating routines, a swimsuit fashion show, and a live orchestra. Gene even stepped in with a little prepared comedy during the show. *The New York Times* didn't care for the exhibition, noting

Gene crowns Marlene Schmidt of Stuttgart, Germany at the Miss Universe pageant. (Fred Wostbrock Collection)

how bloated the whole show was and how they had crammed so much entertainment into the show that it actually made the cavernous stage of the New York Coliseum seem crowded.

Master of ceremonies for a water show wasn't exactly the type of job Gene was looking for, even a lavish, ambitious water show like *Aqua*

Carnival—a *New York Times* article later in the year said Gene "wants to forget about [it]." And though he was busy for much of his adult life, Gene wasn't busy in precisely the way he wanted. Yes, Gene could work all he wanted as a master of ceremonies, an announcer, a disc jockey, a panelist... he had proven himself and then some in all of those fields. And yes, he was happy doing all of it. He loved all the types of work that he got asked to do. But one thing that made him unhappy was that he wasn't a big star for it. Actors got all the fame and prestige, and Gene, the kid who hammed it up as George Washington and paraded around as a king in high school, yearned for that type of recognition.

Producer Howard Felsher, who worked with Gene on *Tic Tac Dough*, told author David Baber in 2006, "He was a very funny man and he was kind of lost because he didn't become the big star that he wanted to be. He was kind of disappointed... He wanted to be a big star like Marlon Brando. Not like a he-man, but he wanted to walk down the street and everybody recognize him."

Gene admitted as much while being interviewed by reporter Ted Holmberg. He said that one of his great hopes for the future was that he could be in the original cast for a Broadway show, as opposed to filling a role that somebody else had already debuted in. He would never get that opportunity.

He did get a bit of vindication, though, in 1962, when Hal March took an extended vacation from *Come Blow Your Horn* on Broadway and Gene, two years after originating the role in previews, finally got to perform it on the Great White Way.

Gene returned to Mark Goodson-Bill Todman Productions later in 1962, and like his work in Broadway, he was stepping in for somebody who originated a role on a New York stage. Goodson-Todman had a popular game show on NBC called *Play Your Hunch*. Originally premiering in 1958, the same year that *Dough Re Mi* premiered, *Play Your Hunch* was a streamlined form of Goodson-Todman's popular *To Tell the Truth*. For *Play Your Hunch*, two married couples would see a series of problems that had three possible solutions; for example, which of three members of a brass band isn't really playing his instrument, or which of three dogs is the father of the other two.

Gene guest-hosts *Today* in 1962, joining newsman John Chancellor for the program. (Fred Wostbrock Collection)

Although the game is really the star on any game show, original host Merv Griffin was the breakout star of *Play Your Hunch*. For segments involving three children, he had conversations with the cute kids. For segments involving music, he almost always sang. He would demonstrate props and play up his own mistakes for laughs. *Play Your Hunch* dominated its time slot and NBC noticed. They signed Griffin to a long-term contract with the network to host a talk show, with the possibility that Griffin might also become host of *The Tonight Show* if things didn't work out with Johnny Carson, who was taking over the show in the fall. NBC guaranteed Goodson-Todman a full additional year of *Play Your Hunch* if they would allow Griffin to leave the show. Goodson-Todman replaced him with Gene Rayburn.

He immediately made a good impression on the producer of *Play Your Hunch*, Ira Skutch. In his autobiography, *I Remember Television*, Skutch said, "Gene's a thorough professional with little of the ego problem that afflicts so many performers. He told me he'd managed to overcome those tendencies through personal soul-searching and psychoanalysis; a good example of the value of that much-maligned discipline. Gene was easy to work with, and in all our time together we had very few problems between us."

Replacing Merv Griffin proved to be a daunting task. Game shows require varying levels of participation from hosts. Long-time producer Ira Skutch once wrote of watching a specific game show with a stopwatch and determined that the host's total participation in an episode came to about three minutes. *Play Your Hunch* was the opposite extreme. Merv Griffin was such an intrinsic part of every puzzle and problem presented that the show really didn't feel the same. In Gene's first month on the job, Nielsen reported a five-point drop in the ratings. NBC panicked and demanded he be replaced immediately.

Gene was fired and replaced by Robert Q. Lewis (whose struggle to find employment after *The Name's the Same* had knocked him down a peg, and producer Ira Skutch recalled that he was then much easier to work with on *Play Your Hunch*). To help Gene save face in such an ignominious situation, Goodson-Todman's press releases announcing the change all referred to Gene as "interim host," to make it sound as though this was the plan the whole time.

Helping Gene save face wasn't a priority for very long. As Ira Skutch remembered later, being abruptly removed from *Play Your Hunch* proved to be the best thing that ever happened to Gene Rayburn. It opened him up to accept another job… one that went a little bit better.

Chapter Eight
Perfect Match

Frank Wayne was a genius.

Frank Wayne was a producer for Mark Goodson-Bill Todman Productions who had been there from the time that the company emerged on television, and his mind seemed to operate at all times with television in mind. During the 1950s, he helped dream up the zany stunts seen every week on *Beat the Clock*. In the 1970s and 1980s, he oversaw *The Price is Right* on CBS and created some of the show's most iconic pricing games, like Plinko, Cliff Hangers, and Hole in One.

And between those two assignments, he created *The Match Game*.

In 1961, Goodson-Todman had unleashed a game called *Password*, in which contestants were teamed with celebrity partners to play a word association game. Panel shows of the past had pitted a panel of celebrities against the contestants, but the idea of having the stars and the players

(Fred Wostbrock Collection)

join forces was a new concept, and the game was an overnight hit. Gene had been in consideration to host *Password*, but creator/producer Bob Stewart said no because he personally felt that Gene was predisposed to putting the spotlight on himself (and even if you liked Gene's style of hosting, it was hard to argue with that). *Password*, he argued, was a strong show, and it needed a more straight-laced emcee who could stay out of the way and let the game be the star. They went with Allen Ludden, who became so identified with the show that he became commonly known as "Mr. Password" among fans of the show.

The success of *Password* led Goodson-Todman down a path they had been down a few times before—ripping off their own shows to stay ahead of the competition. In an instant, Goodson-Todman made a priority out of whipping up new games that teamed up celebrities and contestants.

And then one day, Frank Wayne walked into the Goodson-Todman offices, handed everybody a pen and paper, and gave them an instruction: "Write a fact about elephants."

Afterwards, everybody compared answers, and they found that even though there were many people in the room, they hadn't written a variety of answers. Most had written "THEY HAVE TRUNKS" or "THEY ARE GRAY."

The Goodson-Todman staff collaborated with Frank Wayne's idea and formulated a new team game. But figuring out what worked best was an arduous process. The original game that the staff conjured up was that the contestants would individually wager on each question, but the feeling was that it didn't work. For a time, the staff even discarded the idea of having celebrities play the game, reasoning that there was no point. Next they came up with a game that had six contestants competing individually. Contestants with matching answers remained onstage, while contestants who didn't match anybody were eliminated, somewhat like a spelling bee. That idea got thrown away because the movement of contestants walking offstage was distracting, waiting for them to leave disrupted the game's momentum, and once the game whittled down to three players, waiting for two to match might take a little while.

Finally, the staff settled on something a little closer to their original notion of teams captained by celebrities and simplified the scoring. They pitched it to the major networks and got a deal with NBC. Beginning on New Year's Eve, 1962, the new game would air weekdays at 4 p.m. For a title, they lifted the name of a common bar game, "match game," in which drinkers would split up into teams and grab handfuls of matches, with the opponents trying to estimate how many total matches they had. It was a brilliant title because in addition to being a familiar phrase to at least some potential viewers, it happened to be a perfectly literal description of the show.

The Matchless Gene Rayburn

Goodson-Todman began the search for a host and would have looked right past Gene had it not been for the intervention of Ira Skutch. Gene's firing from *Play Your Hunch* had been a foolish move, Skutch argued, that had been motivated by the network's panic at the sight of a ratings drop that had more to do with Merv Griffin than it did with Gene Rayburn. Gene deserved better. Gene deserved another shot. Goodson-Todman listened.

> *I was in New Hope, Pennsylvania, at the Bucks County Playhouse. Somebody called and said "Would you like to audition for this show?" I said sure. So I went to New York on my day off, did the audition, and got the job.*

There was some concern in the halls of Goodson-Todman about whether or not the show had a sustainable premise. For a show that asks trivia questions, there's a near-infinite supply of question sources in the world, and with a strong enough format, it can go on forever. For a physical game like *Beat the Clock*, props and a couple of imaginative staffers were the only requirements for conjuring up years of stunts. A quick check of the dictionary will find thousands of usable answers for a word association game like *Password*.

But this new idea, *The Match Game*, was a different beast. There were questions and there were answers and yet, somehow, it wasn't what you'd call a question-and-answer show. It was a word game, but you certainly couldn't look at it the same way you'd look at *Password*. As NBC's scheduled premiere date loomed, Goodson-Todman became worried that there wouldn't be enough usable material.

Robert Noah, a former Barry & Enright staffer who had worked with Gene on *Dough Re Mi*, had landed a new job with Goodson-Todman and thought he knew a man who could help. Dick DeBartolo was a Brooklyn-born comedy writer who began writing for *MAD* Magazine as a teenager and briefly worked on the staff of *Dough Re Mi*. Noah called DeBartolo and explained the current problem at Goodson-Todman.

"Listen," Noah said, "Goodson has this new show, and the staff is very worried that they'll run out of material. The show premieres on

Perfect Match

A bird's eye view of the cozy original set of *The Match Game* in Rockefeller Plaza's Studio 8H. (Author's Collection)

New Year's Eve. Between now and then, do you think you can write five thousand questions?"

DeBartolo accepted the challenge and the job offer that came with it. While continuing to write for *MAD* Magazine, he reported to his desk at the Goodson-Todman offices every day to type up questions for *The Match Game*.

"The Goodson-Todman work day wasn't nine to five, it was ten to six, which I loved because I'm not a morning person," he explains. "But I began writing and writing and writing, and I was writing a hundred questions a week. There was no creative process at all, I was just writing questions that I knew could have more than one answer, and then I'd turn them in to Robert Noah. It was a great job because I was the only writer for that show, and I was hired only for that job. No meetings, no appointments, and after a few months, the 10-6 hours were kind of a moot point. I set my own hours, came in and left whenever I felt like it. Nobody cared because I was doing the job I got paid to do."

The Matchless Gene Rayburn

On December 31, 1962, Gene strolled onto the stage of NBC's Studio 8H at Rockefeller Plaza, his arrival heralded by the dulcet announcing tones of Johnny Olson and the pleasant melody of "A Swingin' Safari" by Bert Kaempfert serving as the show's theme music. *The Match Game* was underway. As he started that first day on the job, Gene found something about his surroundings strangely gratifying.

> *It was great because we did it in 8H. That was that great, wonderful, big studio at NBC where Toscanini did his broadcasts and I was a page boy guarding the doors so no one could get in. That was a gratifying experience.*

The game was played by two three-member teams, each team consisting of a celebrity guest and two contestants. Gene would read a series of simple questions, like "Name a breakfast food," or a fill-in-the-blank phrase, like "Paper _____." All six players would write answers on index cards. Afterwards, everyone revealed their answers. When two members of a team matched, the team scored twenty-five points. When all three teammates matched, they scored fifty points. The first team to score one hundred points or more won the game, a dollar per point, and the right to play Audience Match. In Audience Match, Gene would read a series of survey questions that had been asked to one hundred members of a previous NBC studio audience. Each teammate individually guessed what the most popular answer had been, and each match paid $50. Three questions were asked, for a top possible payoff of $450. (Because of the quiz show scandals of the '50s, game shows of the 1960s were typically played for much lower stakes.)

Gene was joined that first week by celebrity guests Arlene Francis and Skitch Henderson. Arlene was a dependable game player no matter what game she was dropped into, and Skitch gave Gene a familiar buddy to interact with. They helped the show get off to a solid start.

Critics weren't crazy about it. Cynthia Lowry's review was a compliment wrapped in a yawn: "[I]f you like *Password*, you'll probably like *The Match Game*, too." Another critic was disgusted with the third episode of the series, in which the contestants were asked to name a city in Asia. Arlene Francis wrote "Vietnam" and one of her partners couldn't even think of one to write.

Oh, well. Critics never exactly threw roses at game shows anyway. *The Match Game* wasn't a blockbuster the way that *Password* was, but it at least found an audience and retained it.

Gene at the podium for what quickly became his signature series. (Fred Wostbrock Collection)

With an incredible lack of foresight, the major TV networks erased the tapes of virtually all of their daytime programming before the 1980s, and *The Match Game* was no exception. A scarce number of kinescopes exist from the series. Many of them are from fairly early in the run of the series and they reveal a surprisingly quiet show. Not a lot of laughs or merriment; just a friendly little game. And Gene stayed out of the way in those early years, not offering much beyond an occasional plug for the home version of *The Match Game*, which, Gene promised the contestants onstage, "will come to you in about six weeks in a plain brown wrapper with no return address." And Gene had a standard response to any answer from a contestant in Audience Match that underwhelmed him: "Do you really think one hundred little old ladies from Upper Montclair, New Jersey would say *that*?"

Robert Noah later said, "It was envisioned as a straight game in which anything funny was merely an outgrowth of the game itself."

And, for a while, that's exactly what it was. In *The Match Game*, Gene had very little to work with. He was confined to a podium across the stage from the six players. The questions were very simplistic; it would take a true comedic genius to get a laugh out of "Name a type of flower." And since Gene didn't have much to work with, he couldn't add much to the game.

Randy West was just a kid in the early '60s when he went into Studio 8H to see a taping in person. "It was very early in the run; I actually saw it in person before I saw it on television. I remember the game being very direct, no-frills stuff. But during the stopdowns, Gene was very, very funny. And I went to see tapings for a long time after that with Gene, and I remember I was always excited if I knew Gene would be a part of whatever TV show I was about to see. Even as a kid, I loved behind-the-scenes stuff, and in those early days of *The Match Game*, it was kind of neat seeing it play out as a very dry show on the air and knowing that during the commercial breaks, the host was cutting loose and doing really funny things. He would do some shtick with Johnny and I remember they had great chemistry, and you could see that Gene and Johnny really liked each other."

But it was all business when the game was actually being played. That's the way Mark Goodson wanted it, and he couldn't stand it when Gene got a laugh. Gene insisted that he was trying to help the show. In Mark Goodson's eyes, Gene was destructive to it.

> *I wanted to do my own thing. I wanted to do it in my own style, and my style is to do it with humor. Humor was part of my nature.*
>
> *And I'll never forget, in the beginning… Mark Goodson used to write these long memos to the producer. "What is Rayburn doing? He's getting laughs! He's getting laughs!" He thought that was terrible because he thought that the most important thing was the game. Well, if you're talking about a thing like* Password, *he's right. But if you're talking about a weak format, like* The Match Game, *you gotta do something to make it fun or light or jazz it up, and so that's what I did.*

As a result, NBC was never completely happy with Gene. In a 2003 interview with game show historian Steve Beverly, Ira Skutch remembered, "…[P]eople at NBC were always wondering why they couldn't get somebody better than Rayburn to do that show. You always had somebody at the network who was never really sure he was quite right for it. I think that was because we never let Gene have enough freedom with the first show."

Probably Gene's favorite environment, a nice bike ride in a quiet part of the world outside of New York City. (Fred Wostbrock Collection)

The Matchless Gene Rayburn

There was one other reason NBC was unhappy with Gene, one that didn't have anything to do with ratings or broadcasting ability. Gene and Helen lived in an apartment near 30 Rockefeller Plaza, so Gene saw no reason to drive to work. He rode his bike to every taping. That was fine, but NBC executives reprimanded Gene in writing several times, because Gene didn't park it anywhere once he arrived, and he liked to ride his bike through the hallways of NBC.

Dick DeBartolo laughs and says "Gene rode his bicycle everywhere. In fact, as good a host as he was, I remember, that was the only real problem we had with him, if you want to call it a problem. The taping was about to start, Johnny Olson was getting ready to introduce him, and you'd have to stop Gene and point out that he still had the bike clip on his pants. He would always forget to take it off."

But Gene did look for ways to breathe life into the show, and he sought help from Dick DeBartolo. DeBartolo explains, "I was always onstage for each taping of *The Match Game*, but you couldn't see me. Normally on a TV game show, the host has all the questions for that day's games stacked on the podium, and arranged in the order that he needs to read them. *The Match Game* did it differently. I sat behind the wall behind Gene's podium. And in front of me, I had a board with a bunch of the questions on 3x5 yellow index cards, all pinned on the board.

"During each taping, I wore a headset, and Jean Kopelman, one of the producers, would be sitting in the control room talking to me. For the most part, I would just grab a question, and I'd hand it to a stagehand, and he would clip it to this small wooden board that had a paperclip on the end, and force the board through a tunnel, and the question card would pop out through a slot on a machine that we had on the side of Gene's podium. And as I recall, the sound effect man would cue the sound of an old crank-style cash register to make it seem like it was really, you know, a machine. But it was just the stagehand forcing the card through that tunnel.

"The reason we did it that way was so I could change up the material based on how well the contestants were playing that day. If it was going poorly and nobody was matching, Jean would say 'Give 'em an easy one,' and I'd look at my wall of questions and grab one that had some really obvious answer that everybody would be inclined to write, and that way a lot of points would be scored. And by the same token, if the contestants were doing so well that it seemed that the show was moving too quickly, I'd grab a card that had a broader range of answers and there wouldn't be any matches made in the next round, and that would slow things down. So that's why I was always in the studio.

"Anyway, one day, the episode we were taping was just falling completely flat. The game wasn't going well, the audience was bored. And we pause for a break and Gene Rayburn comes backstage and says 'Dick, when we come back from the break, come out on stage and do *something*. We're dying.' I don't think Gene even cared what I did, he didn't suggest anything. He just told me to do something. So when we came back from the break, I walked out and walked right up to Gene and said 'Did you see a golf ball in here? I think I lost it.' And it was simple but it got a laugh and it revived the audience. So from that point forward, I began appearing on camera more frequently and that was why. Gene used me as a means of livening up the show when he thought it was dragging."

Gene with the question "machine" on *The Match Game*. Poking through the tunnel is an index card attached to a 2x4, held in place by a stagehand. (Fred Wostbrock Collection)

The show was a modest success in daytime TV. During the 1963-64 season, it was the third highest rated game show on television, which was mighty impressive considering that the top spots were occupied by CBS powerhouses *Password* and *To Tell the Truth*. NBC briefly considered giving the show a prime-time slot but turfed that plan.

Gene had a theory about why the show was a success.

> *For the first time, the audience can participate in the quiz game to the same extent as the contestant on camera. The panelists just represent the viewers by proxy.*

This much was true. *The Match Game* wasn't really a game of knowledge. Sure, they might ask something with factual answers, like "Name an American President," or "Name a state capital." But the game wasn't about knowledge. The game was about intuition and judgment, trying to predict what the other players onstage would write. It was a game that anybody could play, and that's important in a game show because it's easier to make the audience feel as if they're right onstage as a part of it.

Still, it had the daytime slot, if not primetime, and *The Match Game* enjoyed decent ratings for a time before the ratings started to erode, and the show appeared to have run its course. The dip in ratings couldn't have been particularly shocking. Although *The Match Game* was a good show, it really wasn't anything special. NBC canceled it. Ironically, cancellation wound up saving the show.

Dick DeBartolo told Game Show Network in 2006, "The renewal date had come and passed, and so the show was canceled, but we had six weeks of production to go... I went home over the weekend and I thought about it. And I came in and I said (to Ira Skutch), 'Did you ever think about doing silly questions?'"

Skutch asked, "What's a silly question?"

DeBartolo answered, "Mary likes to pour gravy on John's BLANK."

Ira Skutch said in 2006, "It was startling because it just sounds funny. It's just got a dirty sound to it."

And yet, the genius of the question form was that it didn't really alter the game. "Name something you pour gravy on" was the type of thing you would have heard on *The Match Game* up to that point. All DeBartolo had done was stumble on a funnier way of asking it.

They went to Mark Goodson. Goodson was a man who labored over game show formats until they were just perfect. He would hold up tapings of shows if the bell didn't sound in the proper key. And he would re-work and re-work ideas until they were perfect. Some of the game shows that Goodson-Todman got on the air had been meticulously tinkered with in the office for literally years before getting pitched to networks.

On the other hand, *The Match Game* was already on the air, and it had been given the death sentence by the network. As a result, DeBartolo and Skutch caught Mark Goodson on a rare day when he just didn't care.

They told Goodson about the style of questioning that Dick wanted to try and Goodson responded, "The show is canceled. Do what you want."

Just as Dick DeBartolo predicted, it startled the audience without changing the game. The question got a big laugh, and then the players wrote answers like "meat loaf" and "mashed potatoes." But that little change made a big difference. Day by day, as the show's expiration date approached, the ratings picked up. NBC had ceased promoting the show, but the change in the question style had caused incredible word-of-mouth to spread, and audiences rediscovered *The Match Game* and loved what they were seeing… and hearing.

The ratings increased, and *The Match Game* got a stay of execution from the network. Dick DeBartolo began writing wilder questions and getting more creative with them. Pop culture references and puns began working their way into the material. The show's world suddenly opened up.

DeBartolo later told a reporter, "We soon began to find that we could do more with imaginative and creative questions than we could with those that were based on hard fact."

The focus of the show shifted. In the early days, when the show was in line with Mark Goodson's vision of the game being the center of attention, Gene read a question, the players scribbled their answers quickly, revealed them, and then everyone moved on to the next question. Now, the game was more of a framework for creating spontaneous humor. The question got a laugh, Gene would toss in a few jokes, and the players would explain the logic behind their answers, with the stars getting laughs by going off-the-wall with their explanations.

Gene with the team of production assistants hired to assist Jean Kopelman on *The Match Game*. Back row, left to right: Ken Abernathy, who organized the scripts for Gene's live commercials; Lenore Goldstein, who operated the show's scoreboard; Jerry Layne, who conducted warm-up games with the contestants to get them accustomed to playing before they went out onstage. Front row: Audrey Davis, office receptionist; Gene; and Rae Pichon, who acted as the show's judge and helped book some of the celebrity guests. (Author's Collection)

> *We took this rather simple, dull game and began to have some fun with it. We'd talk and joke and fool around, and when that kind of ran its course, then we'd stop whatever we had been doing and turn to this little game and see who could match.*
>
> *I must say to [Mark Goodson's] credit, he finally came around to my way of thinking, and then he helped. He hired comedy writers to write the questions. He was a big help in that regard, but in the beginning, it was extremely difficult dealing with him and trying to keep* The Match Game *light and fun.*

As a comedy show with a game thinly hidden in it, *The Match Game* dominated its time slot, and the longer it stayed in the air, the more prestige it had. It was fun and it was wildly popular, and at its peak, it had no trouble attracting the A-list. Among the big stars who played *The Match Game* in the 1960s: Roger Moore, Lauren Bacall, Lloyd Bridges, Gloria Swanson, Dorothy Lamour, Don Ameche, Mel Torme, Roddy McDowall, David Frost, James Brown, Dionne Warwick, Vidal Sassoon, Ethel Merman, Flip Wilson, Cliff Robertson, Mickey Mantle, Sandy Koufax, Peter Lawford, Dustin Hoffman, Andy Griffith, Bill Cosby, Sal Mineo, Rod Serling, and even boss Mark Goodson.

> *Someone once showed me a single-spaced typewritten list of all the celebrities who have been on* The Match Game. *And it's a formidable list, it really is. Almost anyone that you could name had been on that show.*

Dick DeBartolo remembers, "The celebrity booker for *The Match Game* in New York was a woman named Rae Pichon, and very early in the series, we said 'Let's just try to book every famous person that we've ever wanted to meet.' And so many of them said yes! But that was all there was to the booking process. Rae just tried to book celebrities that we would be excited about meeting backstage."

Sandy Koufax had an interesting motive for appearing on the program. An arthritic elbow had prematurely ended his career and he was beginning a new career as a sportscaster for NBC. He appeared on

The Match Game because he admitted in his first year that broadcasting wasn't coming naturally to him, and he needed some practice.

Gene, to loosen him up, walked into the make-up room while Koufax was getting his face powdered, and instructed the make-up woman to put some make-up on Koufax's elbow to make it feel better.

An all-star Match Game *pitting a team of famous baseball sportscasters against a team of football greats.* **(Fred Wostbrock Collection)**

> *Don Meredith was on the show and he said to me, 'Hey listen, why don't you use my old buddy on the show? We went to college together.' I said 'Who is he?' Don says 'He's the guy who plays the Indian on television. He's Burt Reynolds.' I said 'Who's he?'*

There was one star who eluded Rae Pichon and Dick DeBartolo. DeBartolo says, "We tried desperately to get Mae West. We called her management so many times and she kept saying no to us, which surprised us because we thought Mae would have a great time doing our show. Finally, her agent called me and said 'Look…let me tell you why Mae West will never do your show. She's legally blind, and she only sees people in her living room, because she knows where all the furniture is, and she could correct the problem if she wore glasses, but she's too vain."

Other stars appeared for the usual reasons that stars appeared on game shows: to promote their TV show, to promote their movie, to promote their play, or to promote themselves. Bob Hope didn't even play the game. He just walked onstage one day, bantered with Gene, got some laughs from the audience, plugged his new book (*I Owe Russia $1,200*), and strolled out. Robert Vaughn did a similar walk-on to plug the debut of *The Man from U.N.C.L.E.* Bob Barker showed up to promote *Truth or Consequences* and Monty Hall plugged *Let's Make a Deal*. But even with the incentive for appearing on a daytime game show, it was rare for A-list stars to do so. Supporting players tended to be celebrity guests, not the main attractions. But *The Match Game* was the exception to the rule. A formidable roster of stars appeared time and time again.

Dick DeBartolo explains, "This should give you an idea of why it was easy for us to attract bigger stars than most game shows. When Ethel Merman was booked to be on the show, I came backstage before taping began. She looked nervous so I just said 'Can I get you anything? Cup of coffee?' And she says 'No…this is the stupidest thing I've ever done.' I said 'What makes you say that?' She says 'I don't know why I agreed to do this show. I'm terrified I'm going to give a stupid answer and make a fool of myself.'

"I said, 'Ethel, this is the one game show on television where there are no incorrect answers. You can write literally anything and you won't be wrong.' And she calmed down, she went onstage, and sure enough, she had a good time. But I think celebrities did our show because they knew there was no risk. I mean, there are stars who don't do game shows because they think they're too big to do game shows, that mindset does exist. But there are many, many A-list celebrities who won't do game shows because they're afraid to. They have an image, they have a reputation, they're protective of their spot in the entertainment world, and they're afraid that it'll be damaged if they go on a game show and play poorly. And we were the one game show on TV where that wasn't an issue. *The Match Game* was the only game that didn't have right or wrong answers. And we paid you a thousand bucks and free lunch."

Lauren Bacall, who did the show repeatedly but would not appear on any other game shows, once said, "I will always do *The Match Game* because I love Rayburn."

Unfortunately, the vast majority of the 1960s version of *The Match Game* is gone. Today, a dozen or fewer episodes are believed to have survived. One of the only remaining episodes of the series is one from 1964, featuring guests Jayne Mansfield & Orson Bean.

Jayne Mansfield brings along a little friend to play *The Match Game*. (Author's Collection)

Perfect Match

Bean remembers, "I co-starred with Jayne in a production of *Will Success Spoil Rock Hunter?* I adored her, and I was the only one. Everybody else hated working with her. Walter Matthau couldn't stand being out there with her. She was blonde and beautiful and shapely. Her body was a gift from God, so actors hated working with her because if you had to be out onstage with her, nobody was looking at you.

"What I remember most about working with Jayne Mansfield is that whenever I walked past her dressing room, she would call for me. 'Orsey!' And I would walk into her dressing room and she'd be sitting there naked as a grape. And the amazing thing was how unaware she was, as if she didn't know she was naked. People thought she was arrogant and she really wasn't. And every time she would call me into the dressing room, it was so frustrating because I never knew where to look."

> *Jayne Mansfield was wonderful. I got to know her in the beginning when I was working on* The Tonight Show *at the Hudson Theater, and she was right down about half a block starring in* Will Success Spoil Rock Hunter?
>
> *And someone asked us to be the king and the queen of the Artists and Models Ball, a semi-nude affair that was held in some big ball room... the Waldorf or somewhere... but it was great. I'll never forget Nancy Berg rode by on an elephant, wearing a few beads here and there and not much else. It was a great experience, and Jayne and I were the queen and king of the ball. We sat on thrones, everyone came and bowed, paid their respect, kissed my ring... just the ring.*

Orson Bean remembers, "Playing a game show well is like being a virtuoso musician who specializes in playing the comb & paper. It's a modest skill to be sure, but it's a skill nonetheless, and not just anybody can do it. The first game show I ever did was *I've Got a Secret*. I was a panelist on the first episode of that and I think Goodson-Todman had some intention of using me regularly or frequently, but I didn't know what I was doing and it looked terrible. They fired me after two episodes and Bill Cullen replaced me, and he worked much better.

"A couple years went by and I eased my way back into game shows. I remember once I was a guest on *Pantomime Quiz*, which was a charades game, and my partner was Milt Kamen, a good friend who I was very simpatico with; we were always on the same wavelength. And they had really long sentences and jokes that you had to convey on *Pantomime Quiz*. I remember once, Milt had to convey a sentence to me that started with 'The horse was so swaybacked...' And Milt pantomimed thick, wavy hair and then playing a violin, and I said, 'You're a violinist... a handsome violinist. You're Florian ZaBach... ZaBach... Oh, swayback! The horse was so swaybacked!'

Jayne Mansfield and Gene reign supreme at the Artists and Models Ball. (Fred Wostbrock Collection)

"And after a while, Goodson-Todman began booking me again for their daytime games, like *Password* and *The Match Game*. I loved doing game shows. I was primarily a Broadway actor at the time, which meant my daytime hours were wide open, so you came to a studio, you got free lunch, and they paid you a few hundred dollars per episode to come out there and play a game that was no more complicated than anything you'd play at a party, and as long as you understood how to play the game, they'd keep using you, and I had reached a point where I finally knew what I was doing, so I kept doing game shows. It was an easy gig.

"Career-wise, it's interesting what it does for you. People thought I was famous for being Orson Bean. They had no idea that I was performing on Broadway, that I had released albums, that I did all these other things. They thought I was famous for being famous. The same thing happened to Peggy Cass. She was a gifted actress but most of America only knew her for being Peggy Cass."

Dick Gautier, Gene's co-star in *Bye Bye Birdie*, also appeared quite frequently on TV game shows during the 1960s, 1970s, and 1980s. He remembers, "The reason I started doing game shows was because of a conversation I had with a friend, and we were talking about how there were no preeminent gossip columnists in show business. Dorothy Kilgallen and Hedda Hopper had died, Louella Parsons retired. There were still some gossip columnists, like Army Archerd and Rona Barrett, but they didn't have the clout or the influence. The old generation of gossip columnists had powerful pens. If they mentioned your name, just a mention was good for you. And game shows were a good replacement for that. You were visible, the host said your name... and in my case, pronounced it correctly, which was a big plus... And the audience saw you for five straight days."

But the star who managed to get the most out of *The Match Game* was Gene Rayburn. Gene happily reaped the benefits of the show's spike in popularity. For one, he was happier than ever that he was able to do the show the way he wanted without seeing an angry memo from the boss.

Dick DeBartolo remembers, "I know early on, Goodson got angry if Gene did anything that got a laugh. He wanted people watching his game shows for the games, not the shenanigans. He didn't like it when Gene would make fun of the stagehands or get the stagehands involved in some gag he wanted to do. I certainly don't think Goodson liked it when I appeared on camera for things. But when we changed to silly questions and the ratings went up, the memos from Mark Goodson stopped, because it made the show more free to exploit things for humor. And from a personal standpoint, I'll say this about Mark Goodson. After we changed the question style, and the ratings went up and NBC renewed the show instead of canceling it, Goodson gave me a raise. He paid me an extra hundred dollars a week, which, in 1960s money, was a pretty hefty raise. And when he told me he was giving me a raise, he said 'If it hadn't been for you, we wouldn't have a show right now.'"

Mark Goodson… and I may be wrong about this, but I don't think he ever created a show. But he could take a bad idea and turn it into a good one, he could take a good idea and turn it into a blockbuster. He had that talent. He had good editorial judgment. But he was a cheapskate. He never paid me. Bastard.

Lynne remembers, "It's difficult for me to talk about Mark Goodson. It's hard for me to find the right words. I don't want to call him 'evil,' because that's not right; he really wasn't. I don't want to say he was 'unlikeable' because that's not true either. Mark Goodson thought his big problem in life was that he was short and Jewish. What I think he wanted and what he wished was that he had been a classic white Anglo-Saxon WASP. I think Mark saw that as the privileged class and wanted to be part of it, even if it meant sacrificing his real identity. Whenever I saw Mark Goodson, he always had a new sweater on and he'd wait for a compliment, or he had to show you his new Rolex. There was always a reason that Mark Goodson expected a compliment from you.

"I remember Goodson invited Dad to a party once at his home and he was encouraging everybody to bring their families, so my mother and I came to the party too. I went away for a few minutes to go into the powder room and saw… not a copy, not a poster… an original Picasso painting hanging on the wall. Mark Goodson hung a genuine Picasso in the powder room. And through the whole party, I got that same sense that Goodson needed to have attention and praise lavished on him for the fact that he had all of these possessions. And it's fine to be successful,

Gene leans back and enjoys the ride. *The Match Game* was a hit! (Author's Collection)

and it's fine to reap rewards and be proud of it, but is it really worth it to go so far with that desire that you lose your identity?

"And the reason I've always remembered that party is because I came away from it with a greater appreciation for my mother and father, because I realized that my mother and father were everything that Mark

Gene leaves the razor behind for a trip in the RV. This RV would give Gene an amusing problem that he'd share with friends for years after. (Gene Rayburn Archive)

Goodson wasn't. Mom and Dad were real people. No airs, no pretensions. And that's why I loved my parents so much.

"I'll give you a perfect example of the kind of 'real people' my parents were. My dad liked gadgets and tools and new things. Whatever fun new thing he got, he'd tinker with it for a while and then move on. I was in college when my dad decided to buy a Dodge motor home to do some traveling. It was big enough to sleep six people. Garry Moore had a home in Owl's Head, Maine and invited my parents to Thanksgiving dinner.

"They had Thanksgiving dinner, they stayed for the night. The next morning, my dad goes out to tend to the RV and he tries to drain the septic tank and couldn't. My dad hadn't put antifreeze in it, so my parents were sitting on top of thirty gallons of frozen shit! He had to drive to the local fire department because they had a large enough indoor space that he could drive his RV inside, let it get warm and thaw, and then drain the tank. Garry never let Gene forget that. It was a joke between them for years after.

"The thing about my father is, he'd be the first one to tell you that story. It was a silly story, it was an embarrassing story, it made him seem a little foolish, and he didn't care. I talked about how he didn't let you in or show emotion; that was just his nature, ultimately, it wasn't like he was hiding who he was. But that's the point... he never hid who he was. There were no pretensions. My parents were the least pretentious people I ever knew."

Back at *The Match Game*, DeBartolo recognized another reason that Gene was happy with the show; he should have recognized it, because he made it happen. "When Johnny Carson first started to hit his stride, the 'How hot was it?' bit that he would do with his audience was really taking off, and what was great for our show was that our audience would latch onto it. Gene would read a question that said 'Fat Fred was sooooo fat...' and the audience in our studio would shout back 'HOW FAT WAS HE?' And Gene began really milking it and playing it up.

"When we played the game for laughs, one of the things I began doing was creating characters. We had questions about Dumb Dora, or Weird Willie, or Count Dracula, or Old Man Periwinkle and Old Lady Purvis. Gene loved those questions because he got to act. He would do a Bela Lugosi impression for Count Dracula questions. Old Man Periwinkle, he would stoop over a little bit, and he would do the most decrepit, gravelly voice, and suck in his lips so it looked like he had no teeth. And being able to act made Gene happy. He was a ham."

What made Gene even happier was when stars were as eager about making the game fun as he was. Case in point: Bill Cullen, host of the original version of *The Price is Right* on NBC.

Dick DeBartolo remembers, "Bill was backstage before the taping started, and he rounded up me, Fannie Flagg, who was the other guest that day, and the four contestants. He says 'I have an idea. Everybody write PICKLE for the first question, no matter what it is.' Everyone nods their heads and Bill says 'Now, I'm completely serious, I need everyone to give their word that we're going to do this. If even one of you writes a different answer, this joke is shot. It's only going to be funny if all six of us do it.'

"So the taping starts, and Gene reads the question. I don't remember what the question was, but it was something where PICKLE was just a totally inappropriate answer.[1] Gene reads the question, and the first contestant holds up the card and reveals PICKLE. And then the next contestant says PICKLE, and then Bill says PICKLE.

"And Gene turns to the next player in line and says 'If you wrote PICKLE, I'm walking off this stage and Johnny Olson is taking over.' Contestant writes PICKLE, so Gene walks offstage, and Johnny dashes onstage, and he says to the next contestant, 'If you wrote PICKLE, I'm walking off this stage and Dick DeBartolo is taking over!' Contestant wrote PICKLE, so Johnny walks off the set and I walk out and take over the game. And I announce to Fannie Flagg, 'If you wrote PICKLE, I'm going to stay right where I am.'"

> *Bill and Ann Cullen used to take Helen and me out to a wonderful steakhouse somewhere on Second Avenue, I think. I loved being with both of them. He was a great, funny guy.*

The show's five-episode-per-day taping schedule meant Gene was able to leave New York to be with his family on the cape. As much as Gene might have disliked this thought, getting away from New York was going to be important at this point if he wanted to keep acting. He had tried so hard with his dramatic TV appearances in the 1950s and all the theater

---

[1] According to the official program files that NBC kept for the show, the question was "John said to Mary, 'I think you have the makings of a fine BLANK.'"

credits he had managed to rack up in subsequent years, the fact was that Broadway just wasn't looking at Gene Rayburn.

But he could be a star someplace else. In the summer of 1965, he got to enjoy being the local boy who made good when he headed to Highland Park, Illinois, just 30 miles north of Chicago, to appear in a summer stock production of *Gypsy*.

The following year, Gene returned to Bucks County Playhouse, and this time he brought the family with him. Gene, Helen, and Lynne co-starred in *The Impossible Years*. Lynne had grown up to be a striking young lady with an attractive figure and long flowing hair, and had the right look and the stage presence of a seasoned performer, but ultimately decided that show business wasn't for her. She was a visual artist.

> *It was just like the old days in the theatre. People waiting at the stage door, mostly to meet Helen and Lynne. A lot of them watch[ed]* The Match Game *and said they were wondering who in the world would actually marry me.*

Lynne remembers, "That was my father's idea. I had no interest in acting, never wanted a career in show business. My mother was great, though. She absolutely stole that show. It was my father's idea for us to star in a play together. The play was about a father, a daughter, and a mother, and he figured doing that play with a real family in the starring roles was an interesting gimmick that would get some press, and he wanted to keep his name out there and draw attention to himself as an actor."

The stage was where Gene's heart was, but *The Match Game* was where Gene's fame and fortune were. Gene learned to live with that, although it wasn't always easy. In interviews during the twilight of his career, he would look back on this time of his life and admit quite readily that if his career in the theatre had ever taken off, he would have left game show hosting behind and never looked back. He never got the chance to try. And though he was well paid for his services, he wasn't paid well enough to take a chance.

TENTHOUSE THEATRE | **STAGEBILL**

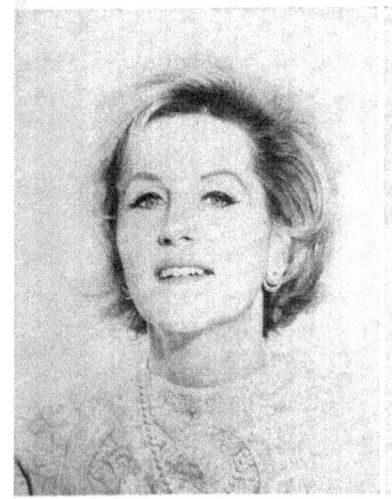 

MARGARET WHITING   GENE RAYBURN

"GYPSY"

The program cover for Gene's star performance in *Gypsy*.
(Gene Rayburn Archive)

> *I just never did get ahead enough to ever be in a position to say "I quit."*

The Rayburns get warmed up for their production of *The Impossible Years*. (Fred Wostbrock Collection)

Lynne remembers, "My mother's side of the family was poor, and there was this expectation thrust upon my father that because he was a big TV star, he should use all of his TV money to care for them. And my father couldn't say no to that, but he probably should have. He was already pretty underpaid by the standards of his field, and the money he did make was gobbled up by his in-laws. It was just an awful situation."

Had Gene been sitting on enough money, he could have walked away from television and made it known to casting directors in film and theatre that he was fully available. But the generous paydays he collected weren't quite generous enough. He needed to keep working and never became secure enough to take the big chance that, in his heart, he really wanted to take.

Dick Gautier explains, "The ability to find work really depends on the nature of the material that's out there for you. I got offers for things like television specials while *Bye Bye Birdie* was still in production, and I wanted to do them, but I couldn't get out of my contract. And dodging typecasting is important too. I was very concerned about being viewed as a rock and roll singer, because that wasn't me at all, but the show was immensely popular. And that was actually part of the reason that I didn't play Birdie when the show got turned into a movie. But if you have the chance to be seen in any kind of role, and if you don't get totally typecast by it, there will always be a role available for you somewhere."

Gene was disappointed, but not distraught, about how things turned out. As Dick DeBartolo recalls, however, there was never a conflict between what he wanted and what he had.

"Every now and then, Gene would read something in the paper about who got cast in an upcoming Broadway show, or even off-Broadway… and I wouldn't use the word 'complained,' but he'd read it and say, 'Aww, geez, why does so-and-so get to do that? I could do that role!' But I don't think he ever would have left *The Match Game* to pursue acting. Hosting that show made him happy; he loved it.

"I know he loved doing the show because he showed it to the people he worked with. If somebody on the staff was having a house party, Gene would always go. And I had a hobby that Gene helped me with a lot. I used to make 8-millimeter films. I kept a camera in the studio and I would film little things with the celebrities in the dressing room. And I got pretty ambitious with it at one point and assembled a bunch of the things I had filmed, and I wanted to put a soundtrack and narration in the finished product. And Gene came to my place on his day off and provided the narration for these movies I made. He actually came over for several recording sessions. And he had a cameo in one the films, too. I shot a parody of *42nd Street*; I called it *242nd Street: The Low-Rent District*. And a member of the Goodson-Todman staff played a character named Ruby Feeler, and Gene was in it briefly. I put a card on the screen that said '**Young Hopefuls Gather Backstage to See Miss Feeler.**' And then the camera pans over and it's a shot of Gene, Betty White, Peggy Cass, and Bennett Cerf standing there. I don't think those films will ever see the light of day, unfortunately. I uploaded some of them to YouTube once and they lasted less than a day before they got pulled. I used copyrighted music, and I can't release them to DVD for the same reason, so I have all

**Gene found the same pleasure in working with his hands that Milan had. He did woodwork during his free time.
(Fred Wostbrock Collection)**

these films that I shot, really just for fun, but Gene helped me make them the way that I wanted, and I really liked that about him."

Gene got other opportunities to spread his wings and veer into other realms of entertainment. He guest-hosted *Today* a few times. When Johnny Carson took a vacation, Gene got the nod to replace him for a week as host of *The Tonight Show*. Like hosting a game show, hosting a talk show is a deceptively difficult job. Being a supporting player for Steve Allen was one thing. Being the host of the show—the one who set up all the comedy bits, performed the monologue, and conducted the interviews—was quite another. Gene later said that filling in for Johnny Carson was the single hardest job he ever did.

Gene and Helen had carved out a comfortable, happy life with the professional opportunities that New York City had provided them. As the years wore on, the rest of New York City—the crowds, the crime, the pollution—began wearing thin on them. Besides, daughter Lynne was grown and living on her own by that point. Gene and Helen decided it was time to move out of their 29th floor Manhattan apartment and head for new digs. Not to a cozier community in Long Island or New Jersey, though; they decided that Massachusetts was the place to be. The five-episode-per-day taping schedule for *The Match Game* was a single lengthy commute that Gene was willing to put up with, so he and Helen began exploring for their new digs.

The Rayburns had spent years vacationing on Nantucket Island and nearly moved there permanently. The problem was that the necessary transportation for leaving the island was unreliable at best. It was really only a desirable home for someone lucky enough to live without any set agenda. Somebody active in television and radio, though, needed something more dependable. They settled down in a small town called Osterville.

> *I started out in the winter of 1965, and I'll bet I met with every real estate broker from the [Cape Cod] Canal to Provincetown, but there seemed to be nothing available. Then one day I got a call in New York from a guy who said he had a place to rent.*

The house the Rayburns saw was actually dilapidated. Gene recalled that among other problems, the back door was hanging from the hinges. But it offered privacy—it was six hundred feet from the nearest roadway—and a beautiful view, right on the water. They rented the home for a year before buying it outright. A beautiful house in a quiet spot of nature, and a job that gave Gene six days a week worth of exposure; what more could a guy want?

Well, there was an urge to be creative, and Gene felt the need to indulge. At least twice in his life, Gene wrote proposals for original show ideas that he had conjured up. One of Gene's ideas was a variety show that used the inner workings of television as something of a gimmick. Instead of a standard host, the variety show was overseen only by the voice of the show's unseen director. For each act, the performer, following the director's instructions, would take some active role in setting up the segment. A dramatic performer might have to move some furniture onto the set to form the scenery. A musician might have to put together the microphone and the stand.

Gene also had an idea for a game show. Among his personal effects that he saved from his career was the memo he drafted describing the game:

1. *Five celebrities, two contestants.*
2. *Before the show the celebrities write answers to questions supplied by the producers. THE OBJECT IS TO WRITE AMUSING ANSWERS. The questions are written so as to elicit personal responses as opposed to factual ones.*
3. *The host reads a question and then reads the answer written by one of the celebrities.*
4. *The first contestant names the celebrity whom he thinks wrote that answer.*
5. *The host asks the designated celebrity to state the answer he had written. If it's the same answer, the contestant scores four points (one for each of the remaining celebrities).*
6. *If the designated celebrity gives a different answer, the host goes to the next celebrity in rotation. If that celebrity had written the answer, the contestant scores three points. The remaining celebrity answers are revealed, one at a time.*
7. *Same procedure continues alternating the contestants until one wins the game at a point score.*

From that proposal, it's easy to glean what Gene liked in a TV game show himself, and the influence that *The Match Game*'s success had on him. The format Gene described was a very basic one, like *The Match Game*. Gene was anticipating that the show would be more driven by comedy and personalities than the actual game itself. Unfortunately for Gene, neither of his ideas ever came to fruition. There's no indication that a pilot or even a run-through was conducted for the variety show or the game show.

Gene pickets his NBC bosses in 1966. He walked out of Studio 8H during a taping and didn't come back until the strike was settled. (Fred Wostbrock Collection)

**Gene is calling a lucky viewer for the Telephone Match.
(Fred Wostbrock Collection)**

As successful as *The Match Game* was, Gene was unfailingly loyal to AFTRA, the union for which he had served on a national level, and done a share of negotiating for. In 1966, AFTRA went on strike, and Gene, along with announcer Johnny Olson honored the strike. During a five-episode taping session for *The Match Game*, Gene and Johnny taped two episodes, and then received official word that the union was striking. They both walked off the set and refused to return until the strike was settled.

At the end of 1966, *The Match Game* celebrated its fourth anniversary. Some game shows endure for years without making any changes. *The Match Game* was a different beast, making minor adjustments to keep the show fresh, but not changing the basic nature of the game that attracted viewers to begin with.

The show livened things up quite often with special episodes. Sometimes, the contestants disappeared for a week while all-celebrity teams competed against each other to raise money for charity. The show frequently did special days with children competing. A Thanksgiving special pitted a team of Marines against a team of WACs. Occasionally, special weeks were presented in which Gene was a guest player, with Ed McMahon and Art James stepping in to act as guest hosts. A special broadcast in 1965 pitted teams of B'nai B'rith Award winners competing against each other, with all the money earned going into a special college fund for black students.

The show got a few facelifts to keep it looking interesting, too. In time, a prettier new set was built, "A Swingin' Safari" was replaced by a peppy original piece composed just for the show.

At the start of 1967, *The Match Game* announced a new daily feature of the program that would involve viewers at home. Beginning on the March 2 program, *The Match Game* featured a round called Telephone Match each day. Gene made a phone call to a random viewer, while an audience member in the studio was selected at random with a ticket drawing. Gene read a blank phrase. If the viewer and the audience member matched, they split a jackpot that started at $500 and grew $100 per day until won.

The hazard of Telephone Match was that the random selection of players meant that none of them had been subjected to any of the elaborate screening techniques that game shows subject regular contestants to. There were no test games played to see if they could play the game well, if they could conduct themselves well on television, or if they even knew the name of the host.

The result was a classic Telephone Match segment, recounted by game show historian Steve Beverly in 1999: "**Gene greeted the telephone player, who promptly answered, 'Yeah. How are you, Raymond?'**

"**The question, for $2,500, was 'BLANK Soup.' When Gene asked the home viewer for an answer, she thought about seven seconds and answered, 'Wellllllllll, I'll say Campbell's Vegg-TAY-bull Soup.' The audience was already roaring at the woman's unique description of the word 'vegetable.' Gene, deadpanning the entire way, looked into the camera and said, 'I'm surprised she didn't say Pepperidge Farm Whole Meat Chicken.'**

"**Gene turned to a rather hapless fellow in the audience who looked like a bald fraternity guy in *Animal House*. The thoughtfully perceptive** answer from the audience was BEAN Soup. Said Gene: 'You must have been slurping too much of her Vegg-TAY-bull Soup.' At the end of the show, Gene said, 'Until tomorrow... Gene Raymond for *The Match Game*... GOODBYE!'"

Although critics as always were cold toward game shows, a few were at least warm to Gene. Dan Sullivan of *The New York Times* referred to Gene and fellow emcee Tom Kennedy (whose *You Don't Say!* aired in the time slot before *The Match Game* on NBC's schedule) as the two hippest emcees on television. The Academy of Television Arts and Sciences was fond of Gene, too. In 1967, he was nominated for an Emmy in the category of Individual Achievements in Daytime Programming.

NBC had a strong line-up of game shows in 1969, with popular favorites like *Eye Guess* with Bill Cullen, *Personality* with Larry Blyden, *You Don't Say!* and *The Match Game* scattered across their daytime schedule. And then, out of the clear blue sky, all four shows were canceled, for no reason other than a new executive taking charge and deciding to build a new schedule from scratch. On September 26, 1969, *The Match Game*, despite still having a large audience, aired its final episode.

Dick DeBartolo remembers, "Mark Goodson broke the news to me about the cancelation, and I remember his choice of words was very optimistic. He said '*The Match Game* is canceled, but it's not dead. We're gonna do something else with it.' Mark already knew this wouldn't be the end of the story. And he even put me to work on some of the other games that the company had in production, but he said to me, 'We're just going to have you work on these shows until *The Match Game* comes back.'"

Although a few of the network's replacement shows were successful—*You Don't Say!* was replaced by the soap opera *Bright Promise*, which lasted about three years, and *Personality* gave way to *Sale of the Century*, which ran five—NBC couldn't recapture the magic of the powerful line-up that they had taken for granted.

Although the end of any series is a letdown for the talent, it hit Gene harder. Normally, somebody who enjoyed a top-rated hit for the better part of seven years would have no problem landing another job, especially when he already came into that seven-year run with some intimidating broadcasting credentials to begin with. Anybody in Gene Rayburn's position could only be leaving television behind by choice. But in 1969,

Gene looked at the television landscape and realized he had a problem. He wasn't leaving television behind, but it looked like television might leave him behind.

Gene takes off the microphone and unbuttons his jacket; *The Match Game* is done. (Fred Wostbrock Collection)

Chapter Nine
Due East

In a 2006 Game Show Network interview, Lynne Rayburn said, "All television in New York died at the end of the 1960s."

Sad as it was, it made good business sense. From a practical standpoint, television productions in California could be more elaborate. The weather was more favorable for an outdoor shoot, and the studios there were cavernous soundstages capable of accommodating sprawling, complex sets, as opposed to New York City, where most of the studios were smaller and had originally been designed with radio in mind.

Television lingered in New York for a while, mostly limited to the news and daytime programming. Game shows like *Concentration* and the original *Jeopardy!* were firmly rooted in New York, but the clock was ticking for the Big Apple. Television wasn't what it used to be, and it could never go back.

(Fred Wostbrock Collection)

Gene opted to stay on the east coast and it was hard to blame him. He had spent so many years impressing the right people, and even with the demise of *The Match Game*, he got plenty of work. Beginning in 1969, the same year that NBC canceled *The Match Game*, WNEW-TV, channel 5 in New York, introduced a local documentary series called *Helluva Town*, a love letter of sorts to New York City. Each week, Gene would visit some of the sites of the city, interview the people who worked there, and discuss each particular site's history and importance to the city. In the premiere broadcast, for example, Gene visited Radio City

Music Hall, a taxi barn, Toots Shors' restaurant, and a soul food eatery on 14th Street. Gene insisted later that, though never seen by a nationwide audience, *Helluva Town* was a pioneering show.

> *"We had the first handheld camera show. I'd get in the car and say to the producer, 'Where are we going?' and he would say 'We're going to Brooklyn to play bocce ball with a bunch of old Italians,' and we'd go and do it. We were the first to go to belly dancing school, and we did all kinds of crazy things."*

Though it would be hard to prove that Gene's reports on *Helluva Town* were a direct inspiration, there's no denying that it predated *Real People*, *That's Incredible!*, Huell Howser's human interest reports about New York, Tennessee, and California, and the glut of cable shows devoted to ordinary people doing ordinary things.

Randy West, the game show fan who attended tapings in the early days of *The Match Game*, remembers a segment of *Helluva Town* that hit close to home. "My father was a golf pro. He used to teach at a place called Galvano Golf Academy, in the basement of a hotel across the street from where Madison Square Garden is now. Gene showed up to do a segment about how it was possible to play golf in a hotel. It was a driving range and my father taught him golf. My father was interested in teaching him, but Gene was Gene. He was interested in shtick.

"I remember my father came in and said 'You'll never believe who showed up today, the hotel didn't tell me this was going to happen.' And I asked him what Gene was like and my dad said 'Boy, what a wiseass he was. I almost felt stupid trying to teach him anything.' And I remember for the rest of the time I lived with my folks, any time Gene Rayburn's name came up, my dad would say 'That show-off!' So Gene didn't have a sterling reputation in my house, but I thought it was funny. I really liked *Helluva Town*. He was so loose, and so funny, and the entire city of New York was a playground for him."

If national television was dying in New York, Mark Goodson-Bill Todman Productions at least made the effort to put it on life support. In the late 1960s, the company was withering. Most of their shows had been canceled and new ideas weren't forthcoming. In 1968, the company reversed its fortunes by putting *What's My Line?* (canceled by CBS the previous year) back into production for a new five-day-a-week syndicated version, hosted by Wally Bruner and featuring regular panelists Arlene Francis (a holdover from the CBS version) and Soupy Sales.

**Gene plays on the pioneering panel show *What's My Line?*
(Fred Wostbrock Collection)**

The CBS version had been presented as a high-brow, elegant affair. The host was erudite South Africa-born newsman John Charles Daly. The panelists were newspaper reporter Dorothy Kilgallen, publisher Bennett Cerf, actress Arlene Francis, and a number of rotating guest panelists, mostly representatives of New York's high society. They played a simple parlor game where the panelists asked yes-or-no questions to a contestant, trying to guess the contestant's occupation, and that was it. The original series ran for seventeen years.

When the series was revived for syndication, Goodson-Todman sought to make it a more freewheeling casual affair. Wally Bruner would usually start the game with a broad hint to move the game a little faster, and with the extra time that allowed, contestants more often than not would demonstrate their unusual occupations. Frequently, the panelists were invited to get involved in the demonstration. Gene was a born ham and didn't have to be asked twice.

Gene's willingness to dive headfirst into the more active, silly version of *What's My Line?* made him an especially valuable panelist, and although he wasn't a regular, he was on the show quite frequently, and tended to leave his mark each time he was on the show. His enthusiasm was apparent from the moment he rode his bicycle onstage and did a lap before settling in his chair at the panel.

Dick DeBartolo, who moved over to the staff of *What's My Line?* in 1969, after *The Match Game* ended, remembered, "Gene was a great panelist to have for that version, not just because he had a great sense of humor, but also because he was a star. It's sort of easy to forget that *The Match Game* had made him pretty famous, so he had this allure and star power that drew viewers. He really did. So it was fun to have him on."

Fred Wostbrock remembers, "I loved it when he did *To Tell the Truth* because Bill Cullen was a regular panelist, and if you were a fan of game shows in that era, that was just a dream team, to turn on a game show and see Garry Moore, Bill Cullen, and Gene Rayburn together on one stage. And Gene was always fun and wild on those shows. I vividly remember one episode of *To Tell the Truth* where Gene got out of his chair, stood up, and climbed up onto the long desk where the panelists sat during the game. And he just stood on top of the furniture while it was his turn. Nobody else would ever think to do that and Gene, I guess, just figured it would be fun."

When a clothing designer appeared as a contestant, the game was followed by a fashion show. One model was supposed to show how a portion of her skirt could be removed to turn a calf-length hem into a mini-skirt. When she had trouble with the removal, Gene volunteered to help, and accidentally destroyed the skirt.

A man who flipped pancakes oversaw a pancake-flipping contest, called a "flip-off" by Wally Bruner (Gene's reaction: "Watch your language!"). Gene played dirty, bumping his hip into fellow panelist Gail Sheldon to slow her down. Gene's flapjacks soared over his head, and Gene, with perfect aim, moved the plate in his hand back and forth to catch every pancake. Once the contest ended, Gene lobbed his pancakes at the audience.

Another day, the panel flipped pizza dough. Gene flipped his too high, and it got stuck in one of the studio lights. As usual, *What's My Line?* was taping five episodes in a single session. The light was so high and the dough was so hard to get to that rather than stop the taping, they just left it there, with the dough dangling high above the panel and the contestants for the remainder of that day's episodes.

The panel was asked to milk cows for one segment. Gene, the Chicago boy who spent his adult life in New York, had never set foot anywhere near a farm, and played up his discomfort for as many laughs as it was worth, cringing, hesitating, and nervously chattering as he milked the cow, who he addressed as "Darling."

After a game revolving around a contestant in the pantyhose business, the male panelists were given inflatable mannequin legs and pantyhose and told to put the hose on the legs. When Gene realized it wasn't as easy as it sounded, he came up with a startling alternate technique, in which he stuck the inflatable legs between his own legs, with one inflatable leg sticking straight out from his crotch. *Line*'s producer, Gil Fates remembered in his memoirs being surprised in the coming weeks when absolutely no angry letters showed up. Gene's unexpected approach had made it a surprisingly risqué segment.

But the segment that Fates remembered more than any other involving Gene was the day that a house painter's game was followed by a race to see who could paint a wall faster. Gene and the other male panelist that day, Alan Alda, accidentally flicked paint on each other's suits. Alan and Gene were a matched pair when it came to going for humor. Before long, "accidentally" went right out the window. Both men were gathering gobs of paint with their brushes and throwing them at each other, and wiping lines of paint all over each other's suits, totally ruining them. The problem was the paint was beginning to spatter the set and there were other episodes to tape that day. Gil Fates hastily gave the signal to stop the race and end the segment. Fates recalled looking at the panelists' faces and realizing that Gene and Alan seemed genuinely disappointed that it was being stopped.

Despite being hired only to write questions for *The Match Game*, Dick DeBartolo was happy to find himself adapting to the new *What's My Line?* as well as Gene.

Panelists Gene, Patti Deutsch, Alan Alda, and Arlene Francis, along with host Wally Bruner on *What's My Line?* Gil Fates later recalled that having Gene and Alan on the show together "was just too much." Together, they nearly ruined the set during a painting demonstration. (Fred Wostbrock Collection)

He recalls, "I helped solve a problem with that show. It had been on the air for seventeen years, we had done a couple of seasons in syndication by this point, and the problem we had was this. Sometimes, we had too much time to fill, but not enough time to play a game. Somehow or another, they had settled on two and a half minutes as the minimum time for a game. If you had two and a half minutes, you could bring out a contestant and get a worthwhile game out of it. But Gil Fates asked us to come up with something that could fill time when we had under two and a half minutes remaining. I came up with a game called 'Who's Who?' I'd go out into the audience before every taping, and I'd look for four people who looked interesting to me, and I'd just approach them and say 'Would you like to be on TV and make twenty-five dollars?' And then, during these five-episode taping sessions, if it came to a point where we needed to fill two minutes, we'd bring these four people onstage, and we brought out a set of cards displaying their occupations, and the panelists took turns shuffling the cards and trying to place the correct lines in front of each person. It worked great."

Gene also became a frequently-seen face on *To Tell the Truth* for Goodson-Todman. The game was created by Bob Stewart, Gene's former producer from *The Sky's the Limit*. Originally premiering on CBS in 1956 with host Bud Collyer, *To Tell the Truth* pitted a panel of four stars against a group of three contestants, all claiming to be the same person; one was telling the truth. An affidavit was read describing some notable facts about the truth-teller, and the panel would interrogate all three contestants before casting ballots voting for who they thought the real person was.

Gene had an interesting personal connection to the program. In 1956, when Goodson-Todman was in the debugging stages with the game, they held a series of run-throughs with staff and friends present. One of the run-throughs was held in Gene's home. And Gene admitted years later that after seeing the demonstration, he predicted the game would never work as a series.

> *Bob Stewart wanted to meet with Mark Goodson because he had an idea for a TV show, and he wanted my help presenting it to Goodson. I said "Sure."*
>
> *So I got Bill Brattar, who happened to be the lawyer for Mark Goodson, and my personal lawyer as well, and some other people in our living room to comprise an audience... neighbors... and Bob Stewart came and demonstrated this show called* Cross Examination. *And Bill Brattar thought it was good enough, so he brought Bob in to see Mark Goodson. They did a demonstration for him... And Goodson had a great talent for taking an idea and improving on it and refining it. And that's what he did with* Cross Examination. *He turned it into* To Tell the Truth. *It had a long run. And so did Bob Stewart.*

The CBS version ran for twelve years, and Gene didn't mind being wrong one bit. He sat on the panel a few times and even served as guest-host. The show ended its network run in 1968, but when the syndicated run of *What's My Line?* became a hit, Goodson-Todman decided to put *Truth* back on the air. It relaunched in 1969 with host Garry Moore (formerly of *I've Got a Secret*) and panelists Kitty Carlisle, Bill Cullen, Peggy Cass, and Orson Bean.

Bean recalled, "I did better than any of the other panelists in the history of the show. I have no doubt that I had the best voting record of anybody that ever played the game. I didn't tell anybody my secret because I figured it would ruin the game if everyone else figured out what I was doing and they did it too. Very early on, I realized that the real person, the one who was sworn to tell the truth, wanted to volunteer as little information as possible, to avoid giving themselves away. The two imposters, on the other hand, had time to think about this. They knew pretty well in advance they'd be on the show, and they knew who they were impersonating. So they prepared, and they thought up all these great-sounding, perfect lies that they wanted to use, so the imposters would talk and talk and talk. When the host, whether it was Bud or Garry, came to the panel and asked for our votes, my vote had nothing to do with accuracy, or who I believed, or convincing answers. All I did was vote for the person who talked the least. And I won't say I was always right, but I was right far more often than I was wrong."

Bean departed after the first season and Gene stepped in for a time to make frequent appearances on the panel in his spot. Gene managed to wring plenty of laughs out of every step of the process, be it the questions or casting votes.

In talking to a woman claiming to be an aquanaut who lived underwater for fourteen days, Gene asked her to tilt her head and smack herself on the ear, reasoning that if water came out, he would vote for her. When voting for a contestant claiming to be a professional heckler who disrupted sporting events, Gene picked the contestant who was going bald, reasoning that it probably happened from being repeatedly pelted with debris.

> *There was a technique to playing that game. If you didn't know anything about the subject, you just did a straight interview and hoped that nobody caught onto the fact that you didn't know anything about the subject. You know who was really good at that? Peggy Cass. She knew a little bit about everything.*

In one of his appearances on *To Tell the Truth*, Gene was one of the victims of a hilarious prank. After Garry Moore introduced that day's panel, he gestured towards the plates of beef stroganoff sitting at their desk. Gene and the rest of the panel chowed down while Garry Moore read the contestant's affidavit. The contestant lashed out at the high meat prices plaguing America in the early 1970s and was living on a new diet in which every meal had the same basic ingredient. The affidavit noted that the stroganoff that the panelists were enjoying so much had that ingredient. The affidavit concluded with the recipe: noodles, gravy, carrots, potatoes… and dog food.

Kitty Carlisle gently spat out the small wad in her mouth back onto the fork. Bill Cullen cringed. Peggy Cass rather smartly hadn't eaten any, suspicious that there was a big gag coming. Gene, with an eye for humor, played up the prank as much as he could, flailing his arms and mugging in horror before picking up his plate and threatening to mash it in Garry Moore's face. Garry's amused reaction to the panel's behavior could very well go down in television history as the first time that a game show host ever said the word "barfing."

Dick DeBartolo was also working on *To Tell the Truth* and used his other job to whip up a memorable game. With Gene sitting on the panel, three contestants stepped forward claiming to be William M. Gaines, founder and publisher of *MAD* Magazine. Garry Moore led off the game by holding up a portrait of the magazine's iconic, gap-toothed, redheaded cover boy and Gene was the first one on the panel to identify him as Alfred E. Neuman.

> *Garry Moore lived near us... and we did a unique thing. There was a wonderful woman scholar at Rye Country Day School, where my daughter went to school. And I got to know this woman. And she came to our house once a week... and Nell and Garry Moore, and Helen and I would read Shakespeare aloud. Garry & I would read the men's parts and Helen & Nell would read all the women's parts. That was a great experience because in this day and age, we're not familiar with all the archaic words that Shakespeare used that were common in his day, and she could explain all that. She was a wonderful Shakespearean scholar.*

DeBartolo explains, "I suggested the spot to Goodson because I said 'William M. Gaines dresses like a slob and nobody would ever pick him as the millionaire publisher of a successful magazine.' So Goodson approved the segment, and sure enough, nobody voted for him, which made Bill very happy. I remember Kitty Carlisle came up to me after the show and said 'I never would have guessed! Look at him!'"

At the end of the game, Dick was invited to come onstage. As the credits rolled, Gene affectionately put an arm around him and held a card toward the camera, reading, **My Writer: Dick DeBartolo.**

DeBartolo also helped orchestrate a memorable game and another memorable prank on the panel. "At the end of most game shows and talk shows, you see something where the host and all the guests stand around having a conversation, and the viewers at home can't hear what they're saying because the theme music is playing and the credits are rolling. Sound familiar? Okay, in television, that's called a mill-around.

"We taped five episodes at a time for each session of *To Tell the Truth*. I walked up to Bruno Zirato, Jr., who was the producer for the show at the time and I said, 'Have you noticed during the mill-around, the panelists aren't really paying attention?' We only gave them a ten-minute break between episodes, so their mind was on having to dash to a dressing room, change clothes, get their make-up retouched, grab some water or some coffee... They really wanted to get off the stage as soon as they could so their minds were never focused during the mill-around.

"So I came up with an idea. For one taping session, during the first four shows, in addition to the six contestants, I sent out one extra guy, a complete stranger, for the mill-around. And we gave him instructions; he had to have a conversation with every panelist during the credits. And then when we taped the fifth episode, we brought out three contestants, and Garry Moore revealed that one of these three people had been onstage four times already, and every panelist had a conversation with him. And we made the panelists question them and try to figure out who they had already met."

A gig's a gig, and Gene certainly liked playing the games he appeared on as a guest, but he always felt that being a mere player didn't suit him very well.

> *I enjoyed being in charge. I enjoyed hosting, I really did, because you had more control over your life. When you're a panelist, you have to sit and wait and wait and wait, and you think, "What is my line going to be? Should I say this? Is this going to be funny?" It's easier running it and being a host than being a panel member.*

Gene was still finding whatever television work was still available in New York City, and he still had his weekend broadcasts of *Monitor*. Professionally, it was nowhere near as bad for Gene as he may have expected at the end of *The Match Game*.

There was one source of employment that eluded Gene Rayburn, though, and he admitted later that it was a big sticking point for him. Gene absolutely could not get hired by Bob Stewart. Gene recalled that he had an extremely positive relationship with Bob during their time on *The Sky's the Limit*. In coming years, Gene had a few guest spots on *To Tell the Truth*, produced by Bob Stewart for Goodson-Todman. In 1964, Bob Stewart departed the company after a falling-out with Mark Goodson over an idea for a game show that Stewart created and wanted to produce, but Goodson disliked. (That game would eventually become *The $10,000 Pyramid*.)

Stewart established himself as a reputable independent game show producer very quickly. He also resisted leaving the east coast for Los

Angeles, preferring to remain in New York for as long as he could. And since Gene had the same mindset, and since he and Bob had worked so well together on *The Sky's the Limit*, Gene figured he'd be getting a call from Bob Stewart at some point.

Bob Stewart created *Eye Guess*, and hired Bill Cullen to host it. He created *Personality*, a game played by three celebrities; he hired Larry Blyden to host and never called Gene to be a guest. He created *The Face is Familiar*, a prime time game with celebrity-contestant teams; he hired Jack Whitaker to host and never called Gene to be a guest. He created *You're Putting Me On*, a game played by six celebrities; he hired Bill Leyden and then Larry Blyden to host it, and never called Gene to be a guest. He created a game called *Three on a Match*, and gave that job to Bill Cullen, too.

Gene never lost sleep over getting passed over for Bill Cullen; Bill was a personal friend and, like virtually everybody who ever worked in the game show business, Gene would gladly tell you that he considered Bill Cullen the best game show host. But even without Bill, there were endless openings for Gene to do something for Bob Stewart, and those openings always went to somebody else. Every week was a new opportunity to appear as a guest on one of the celebrity games that Bob Stewart had created, and those weeks came and went, came and went. Gene tried to take it in stride. Business is just business. But deep down, it actually hurt Gene's feelings that Stewart never wanted to hire him for anything. Gene hired him to write jokes at WNEW. He collaborated with him on *The Sky's the Limit*. He helped Stewart launch *To Tell the Truth*. And none of it seemed to mean anything.

Lynne says, "I'm sure I can guess why Dad wanted so badly to work with Bob Stewart. I came to the studio a few times for *The Sky's the Limit* and I remember Bob Stewart always smiling and always being in a good mood. He was a very warm person. And then there was Mark Goodson, showing off his new jacket, his new shirt, treating Bill Todman terribly—Bill Todman handled the business end of the company and there wasn't much glory for an accountant—and I think I know which kind of boss my dad would want to work for… the kind that most people would want to work for."

> *I guess I did change Bob Stewart's life. Once, we met in the corridors at NBC. And he threw his arms around me and he said "Gene, it's so great to see you! It's terrible how we forget our old friends."*
> *I got ONE booking on one of his shows. That was it.*

The Rayburn family in the late 1960s. (Fred Wostbrock Collection)

Gene and Helen had a life together when Gene wasn't working. Gene loved to cook, Helen loved to read. They loved bicycling and sailing. Gene, despite nearly losing a leg years earlier, fearlessly ventured back into skiing, although he played it safe and stuck with cross-country skiing instead of alpine skiing. They visited Europe several times. Gene and Helen were proud that their marriage had lasted more than thirty years by that point, a particularly rare feat in show business.

> *We were both infants at the time [we got married]. Seriously, we have our little disagreements like every other couple. But we really get along, like the same things, and have a good life.*

Their daughter Lynne stayed close, too. She graduated from the University of Wisconsin. A talented artist who had since become a high school art teacher, Lynne earned a Master of Arts degree from the Rhode Island School of Design.

Lynne remembers, "My father didn't really understand art. That sort of frustrated me because he really was an intelligent man. He read voraciously. He organized Latin nights at our home when I was a kid where one of my teachers from eighth grade would come over and give Latin lessons to my parents and their friends. And it was just fascinating to me that somebody as intelligent as my father could be so oblivious to art and so unable to appreciate my work."

Lynne also worked as a volunteer for VISTA (now a division of AmeriCorps) and the experience led her to become a drug program coordinator for the state of Massachusetts. As a show of support for their daughter, Gene and Helen appeared as guests on the game show *All About Faces* in 1971 and donated the money won that week to Help of Cape Cod, a group that provided aid to teenagers dealing with drug addictions.

As an adult, Lynne's relationship with her parents was firmly cemented. She describes it as an unconventional relationship for a family. "I was intellectually close to my parents but not emotionally close to them. My mother was fun. We joked around and laughed a lot. My mother had a great sense of humor. But my friends were right about what they saw. The three of us were more like friends than parents and a child, and that was difficult for me sometimes. There's no right or wrong way to describe it except to say that, yes, we were a little weird. Things would have been different if they had more children. Being an only child was tough for me."

It's surprising for a fan who only knew Gene as an image on a television screen to hear the assessment. How would a man who could be so relentlessly funny, goofy, and sometimes even blunt on coast-to-coast television be emotionally reserved in his home life?

Lynne explains, "To be honest, I think the reason my father was like that goes back to the Freudian therapy. My father invested all of his emotions into those six years, and the problem was that the guy rubber-stamped my father and said 'You're cured.' And my father walked away and thought, 'I'm okay now' and thought there was nothing left to deal with. I think he had more going on inside him and it was never dealt with.

"My father was very 'hail fellow well met,' but emotionally, I don't think he wanted to get invested in anybody because of his own childhood. He had a mother who was mean and said hurtful things and did hurtful things to him. He had a father that he never knew because his father died so young. He had a brother that he loved dearly, and his brother died while he was a child. And the stepfather that he knew was a very reserved man who kept to himself. And I think my father had a wall around him at all times because he got hurt so badly by the very closest people in his life early on. He didn't want to get hurt by anybody he loved after that, so he just didn't become emotionally invested in anybody."

The early 1970s were a difficult few years for Gene. He was in a car accident that left him covered in cuts and bruises for a short time. Two years later, he and Helen bought a new home in Osterville, Massachusetts, a lavish house designed by Stanford White, the renowned architect of Madison Square Garden and the Washington Square Arch; he was later depicted as a character in the films *The Girl in the Red Velvet Swing* and *Ragtime*. The week before they were to move in, the home was destroyed in an act of arson. The fire marshal who investigated the scene estimated the damage at $150,000. It was a tragedy that hit Gene very hard.

Gene and Helen moved into a small cottage down the street while a construction crew got to work on a new home to stand on the site of the destroyed home. He met one of the carpenters working on the project, and the carpenter described an idea he had for a new exterior finishing product. His idea was that rather than making normal bricks, he would make facia bricks, much thinner ones that were only thick enough to account for what would actually be visible from the outside. Gene invested in a start-up company called Brickover. He later took partial ownership of Plastronics, an artificial brick & stone veneer company.

Helen got a mind for business, too. She opened up a bookstore in Osterville, for which Lynne designed the graphics. It was a success, and it made Helen quite happy.

In 1972, Gene finally began dipping his toes in the waters of the west coast. Merrill Heatter & Bob Quigley, the packagers who had created *The*

Gene on the mod set of *The Amateur's Guide to Love*. Producer Robert Noah later said it was a mistake to put Gene behind a lectern, saying that it tied him down to one spot on the stage.
(Fred Wostbrock Collection)

Hollywood Squares for NBC, had created an ambitious new series that combined a game show with hidden camera pranks. The title of the new show was *The Amateur's Guide to Love*.

Robert Noah, who had worked with Gene for the entire seven-year run of *The Match Game*, had since departed Goodson-Todman and was now working for Heatter-Quigley. This new series would be his first assignment for the company, and with the choice left up to Robert Noah, Gene Rayburn was the first man called for the job of host.

Gene took the call from Noah but said no as soon as he learned the show would be taping in Hollywood and not New York. When Gene lost interest so quickly, Noah tried some gentle persuasion.

Noah told Gene, "There are only about a half-dozen in the country who can do this show, you have to be up there in the top six and you have to be the one."

Gene admitted that the compliments got through to him.

> *I knew I had to go to the coast and do it.*

Gene had one condition, though. He absolutely was not going to move. It wasn't even a matter of being tied down by other obligations. He told one reporter that he "worked on a handshake" and had no commitment to *Monitor*. It just happened that he lasted for a decade on that program because he loved it and the audience loved listening to him. It was simply a personal preference for east coast living. He was staying in Massachusetts and he insisted on a coast-to-coast commute by airplane for taping sessions.

> *My wife didn't want to move to the west. She had a family problem that kept her in the east and she wanted to stay there. She disliked L.A. too, mainly the weather.*

Randy West, Gene's fan who would eventually get to know the man himself over dinner, offers a theory. "Here's my own insight about why Gene didn't want to move across the country. Gene viewed himself as more than a game show host—which was an accurate perception. He

Gene with guest panelists Charles Nelson Reilly, Karen Valentine, and Peter Lawford. Gene and Charles would play many, many more games together in the coming decade. (Fred Wostbrock Collection)

was more than that. Gene had been on Broadway, and Broadway has an interesting psychological hold on anybody who's fortunate enough to perform there. This isn't exclusive to Gene, but there are a lot of performers who, once they have been on Broadway, view Los Angeles as being beneath them. They don't want anything to do with film and television in Los Angeles. Often they even feel that film and television are beneath them altogether, but if they do it at all, they'll only do it in New York. Broadway is Broadway, it's the pinnacle of show business, and I think he held his nose at the idea of moving to Los Angeles.

"Besides that, New York was a comfort zone for him. He had been a wildly successful radio and television star in New York, he had been on *The Tonight Show* and Steve Allen's prime time show in New York, he had hosted a hit show, *The Match Game*, for almost seven years in New York. Anyone with that kind of track record could understandably shudder at the idea of leaving New York."

The Amateur's Guide to Love premiered on March 27. It was a notable series in a few respects. It was the first game show on CBS in four years. The network had been home to some of the great game show hits of the previous decade, like *Video Village* and *Password*. But as the hit game shows disappeared one by one, the network didn't replace them with other game shows. Slowly but surely, the genre simply disappeared from CBS.

The network had a new head of programming, Bud Grant, who didn't like the sleepy daytime line-up that the network had when he assumed office. CBS had a batch of soap operas that were performing well, but the rest of the daytime schedule was a rather thoughtless assembly of prime-time reruns. *The Amateur's Guide to Love* was the network's first attempt to mount a fresh game show for the new boss.

The game was an unusual blend of game show and hidden camera pranks. Gene narrated a series of practical jokes played on unsuspecting victims. All of the gags were in some way intended to be titillating. For example, a woman was brought in for a job interview and was told she'd have to wear a bikini for each eight hour shift. A man came to a barber shop for a hot lather shave and was surprised when a sexy woman showed up to do the job; right as she was about to get started, she told him that it was her first time shaving another person. Gene would offer the panelists two possibilities for what decision the victim would make at a key moment in the tape ("Does she take the job or not?"; "Does he go through with receiving the shave?"), and the panelists made a single prediction as a group. The victim (who had, in the meantime, been let off the hook and was now essentially a contestant) received $200 if the prediction was wrong, $100 if it was correct. Each episode also involved non-game segments called "Sneaky Surveys," in which an interviewer with some distinctive trait asked silly questions (for example, a pregnant woman stopped people and asked for their suggestions for how to revive a stale marriage).

The game was canceled after only thirteen weeks on the air. Robert Noah later spoke to author David Baber about two key problems with the show. First, daytime programs are produced on lower budgets than prime-time programs, and hidden camera gags are deceptively expensive, given the costs of hiring actors, scouting locations, discreetly setting up equipment (the show used a whopping three production vans for their remote shoots), and postproduction. The program showed two elaborate hidden camera gags each day, which meant ten pranks needed to be completed for each taping. The daytime budget required cutting some corners and the product suffered.

> *It would have been a good weekly show, but there wasn't enough to sustain it on a daily basis.*
>
> *I thought it was a good format and I was surprised that it didn't make it. But apparently it didn't get the numbers, or we would have had a longer run. But I thought it was unique, it was not a run-of-the-mill game show, it was different. A lot of effort had to go into it, especially for the crews that were out getting the spots with the people.*

The other big problem was that Gene had almost nothing to do. Noah called the show "a straightjacket" because Gene was limited to narrating the clips and canvassing the panel for responses. And it was hard for a man who thrived on spontaneity to be funny when the best parts of the show were on videotape.

Gene, pedaling his bike through New York City en route to another *Monitor* broadcast. (Fred Wostbrock Collection)

Noah's "straightjacket" observation was very telling. There were many game shows over the year where the emcee had nothing to do. On *To Tell the Truth*, for example, the host read the affidavit to start the game and then asked "Will the real _____ please stand up?" to end the game, but the weight of the show was on the panel's shoulders. But Bud Collyer was happy to stay in the host's chair for twelve years, and Garry Moore stuck around for seven years before getting sidelined by illness. Jim Lange became a household name with *The Dating Game*, even though he had very little to do while the contestants flirted and got all the laughs.

But a game that gave the host little to do just wouldn't suit Gene Rayburn. He was a broadcaster by trade, but a theatrical actor in his heart. He wanted to bring life to a show. He wanted to do broad movements, and broad jokes. He could have won that pancake-flipping contest on *What's My Line?* with a simple toss, but he had to blurt out "Boing!" and flip the pancakes way over his head because that's who he was. He didn't see why he had to walk onstage for an appearance on *To Tell the Truth* when he could easily pedal his way onstage on a bike and get a laugh. Gene needed to break free.

Gene wasn't exactly sad when the show got canceled after only three months. The schedule had been exhausting for him. The show taped five episodes each Sunday, which meant that every weekend, Gene went from Massachusetts to New York, did his three hours of *Monitor* for NBC radio, then headed to the airport and took a 2 p.m. flight from New York to Los Angeles. The next day, he taped five episodes of *The Amateur's Guide to Love* and then took a red-eye flight back to the east coast, landing in Philadelphia and then taking a connecting flight to Massachusetts.

Reporter Ray Benson was understandably blown away to see anybody willing to make such a trek on a regular basis, let alone a TV performer at Gene's age. "At your age" was a phrase that Gene was beginning to hear a lot of lately, and it amused him.

> *Next thing I know, somebody's going to relate Rayburn to demographics. I really didn't care. I got a lot of exercise, I was careful of what I ate and I took vitamin supplements. Listen, I rode a bike to work every day in New York while doing The Match Game, and that was a couple of miles one way. In fact, I rode a bike in Manhattan for years.*
>
> *I had five bikes, two motorcycles, two dogs, and one wife, not necessarily in that order. Our daughter lived in the next village where she works for the Massachusetts Department of Mental Health. We lived ninety feet from the ocean, and I'd get on that bike and ride up the beach to visit my daughter, or ride down... It didn't matter. Going fifty miles in a day is nothing.*

CBS gave up on *The Amateur's Guide to Love*, but Bud Grant wouldn't allow the network to give up on game shows. Despite the setback, Grant ordered three more game shows into production and scheduled all of them to launch on Labor Day. Those games received considerably more favorable reactions from audiences: *Gambit* with Wink Martindale, *The Joker's Wild* with Jack Barry, and *The New Price is Right* with Bob Barker.

Gene returned to LA a few more times for another game show, a revival of *I've Got a Secret*. Goodson-Todman's executive vice president, Jerry Chester, had a few years earlier lobbied the FCC to impose a restriction on television networks that, instead of starting their prime-time line-ups at 7:30 p.m. Eastern, the line-up had to start at 8:00 p.m. Eastern. The logic was that it would encourage local TV stations to produce more local programming and reach out to the larger audiences that prime-time had to offer. Hence, the 7:30-8:00 time slot came to be known as "prime access time." However, most local TV stations didn't have the necessary money and other resources to produce original programs for that slot. Syndication came to the rescue, offering new syndicated sitcoms and talk shows... and game shows. Game shows not-so-coincidentally exploded in the early 1970s, in part because of that new time slot.

Gene didn't know it yet, but the groundwork was being laid for a big move. By appearing on *I've Got a Secret*, Gene rekindled a professional relationship with producer Ira Skutch. He also crossed paths for the first time with the comedian that Goodson-Todman signed to be a regular panelist on this version of *Secret*, Richard Dawson.

Dawson, born in Gosport, Hampshire, England, had a sense of humor that belied an unhappy upbringing. He spent his childhood witnessing bombings and raids near his own home during World War II. When he grew up, he went from merchant seaman to boxer and eventually to actor. He moved to America in the late 1950s and flourished as a nightclub comic and occasional television performer. His big break in America was the World War II-themed sitcom *Hogan's Heroes*, on which Dawson spent six years playing the role of Corporal Newkirk. He followed that with a stint in the final seasons of *Rowan & Martin's Laugh-In*.

Dawson had a knack for simultaneously playing the game and ad-libbing that made him a natural fit for game shows. No matter what the situation, no matter the set-up, Richard Dawson could fire off the perfect punch line at will.

For one dynamite segment of *I've Got a Secret*, Gene was on the panel and so was Richard Dawson. The celebrity guest that night was Gene's old Broadway buddy, Charles Nelson Reilly. The panel was blindfolded while Charles performed his secret: Using body paint, he was creating a still-life painting of a bowl of fruit on the torso of *Price is Right* model Janice Pennington, who was wearing only a bikini.

> *GENE: Charles, is this something I could do?*
> *CHARLES: What was that, Gene? I'm very, very concentrated on this. What is it, Gene?*
> *GENE: Is this something I could do, Charles?*
> *CHARLES: If you're that lucky.*
> *GENE: I take it this is something I'd enjoy doing?*
> *STEVE: You probably would.*
> *CHARLES: Do you like sunshine?*
> *GENE: Would it benefit me in any way physically? Would it contribute to my physical well-being?*
> *CHARLES: I certainly hope so.*
> *GENE: To your knowledge, Charles, and you've known me a number of years, have I ever done this?*
> *CHARLES: No, but you'd better get with it.*
> *(Buzzer sounds)*
> *STEVE: All right, Gene, you may remove your blindfold.*
> *(Gene takes off his blindfold and looks. His jaw drops. He throws his blindfold across the stage, smiles, and stands up.)*
> *STEVE: Down, Gene, down!*
> *(Gene pantomimes clawing at Janice.)*

Despite how well the elements came together, the revival of *I've Got a Secret* failed. Producer Robert Sherman later said that the biggest harm done to the show was that *The New Price is Right* had become Goodson-Todman's top priority, and *I've Got a Secret*, a show which presented a broad variety of demonstrations, performances, and filmed pieces, was a show that required a lot of attention. A half-hearted presentation just wouldn't do.

And even though it wrapped up in the spring of 1973, Gene was about to get handed a new reason to keep commuting to Los Angeles.

(Fred Wostbrock Collection)

Chapter Ten
Re-MATCH

At the end of 1972, Gene turned fifty-five years old. He was becoming reflective about his career, the goals he had set for himself, what he had been able to do and the opportunities that he missed out on. He was a television master of ceremonies and panelist, adored by audiences. He was an immensely popular communicator for more than a decade of *Monitor*.

And then there was acting, the career that brought him to New York all those years ago. Gene once talked of the dream of being in the original cast for a Broadway show, but leading roles for a fifty-five-year-old are hard to come by. Gene knew the opportunity had passed, and he knew why. What Neil Simon had once told Gene still resonated all these years later; nobody saw a broadcaster as a credible actor. Gene didn't regret the choices he had made career-wise, however. He wasn't bitter about the fact that he was identified as a game show host. His venom was reserved for the decision-makers.

> *I enjoy acting… But I'm not going to have any career as an actor because of the stupid attitude of producers. They keep turning me down, saying I'm not a legitimate actor, that I'm 'one of those TV personalities.' So I'm not getting offers… I'm not going to eat my heart out because it's not happening. But I'd like to strike a blow against typecasting.*

Gene wasn't about to give up being a game show personality for acting gigs, though. The plain facts were that he was darn good at the work, and even if critics and casting agents turned up their noses at game show hosts, he was proud of the fact that it wasn't a particularly easy job. He once said that the primary duty for a game show host was "the ability to write a TV show on your feet."

Gene hosts the unaired pilot *Celebrity Match Mates*, with guests Joyce Bowman (Mrs. Alejandro Rey), Barbara Stuart (Mrs. Dick Gautier), and Brett Somers (Mrs. Jack Klugman). (Fred Wostbrock Collection)

Goodson-Todman tapped him to host a pilot for them in early 1973, *Celebrity Match Mates*. The game was one that the company had been tinkering with for a decade. It had originally been an unsold pilot for NBC, titled *It Had to be You* and hosted by Ed McMahon. The premise was that McMahon would announce a category to a group of four husbands. The husbands would ring in to tell a story from married life that fit into that category. The wives, who were in isolation, would then hear a clue based on the story, and tried to ring in when she recognized the clue that came from her own marriage. The husbands and wives would trade places and roles during the game.

In 1969, Goodson-Todman tried the premise again, with a new pilot hosted by Joe Garagiola titled *He Said, She Said*. In this pilot, the added twist was that there was a celebrity couple among the contestants; for this pilot, the stars were Gene & Helen Rayburn. Goodson-Todman tinkered with it one more time, removing the contestants altogether and making it a competition between four celebrity couples. The show ran for one year in first-run syndication. *Celebrity Match Mates* was substantially the same game.

The game didn't sell, but the bad news came with a silver lining. A CBS representative came to Gene and said that the network had said no to *Celebrity Match Mates*, but asked Gene if he could return to Los Angeles one more time, because Goodson-Todman had come to them and revealed that they wanted to make a new version of *The Match Game*.

Dick DeBartolo remembers, "Mark Goodson sat me down and said 'We're bringing back *The Match Game* but I'm moving the show to California. We're going to totally revamp it. And if you want to move to California, I'll pay for it. I'll move you out there.'"

DeBartolo declined. He was still writing for *MAD* (and in fact, hadn't missed an issue since being hired as a teenager) and he was a full-blooded New Yorker. He declined.

DeBartolo says, "Goodson didn't put up a fight at all when I said no. He shook his head and said 'That's fine. Even though everything is moving to the west coast, I'm going to keep the New York office open, so as long as *The Match Game* is on the air, you have a job. You can just come here and write the questions.'"

The pilot for, as Johnny Olson announced it, "The 1973 Edition of *Match Game!*" The pilot panelists: Bert Convy, Arlene Francis, Jack Klugman, Jo Ann Pflug, Richard Dawson, Betty White. (Fred Wostbrock Collection)

DeBartolo remembers that some years later, Goodson-Todman mounted a rare non-game show effort, a reality series titled *That's My Line!*, profiling people with strange occupations. Goodson asked for DeBartolo's help and enticed him by buying a fully-furnished home for DeBartolo to live in while the series was in production.

DeBartolo says of the experience, "The house had a beautiful view, but it made me say to myself, 'What am I doing here?' The house was situated on the edge of a mountain, and I couldn't walk anywhere. That's one of the things I love about New York City. Because of the subway system and the way the city is laid out, everything is within walking distance. You don't have that in Los Angeles. So I had a party for the staff one night, and it was really just because I wanted to show off the view of the house. But I went up to Jonathan Goodson and said 'Listen, there's a Motel 6 near the studio and there's an IHOP across the street from it. Just let me fly in from New York and put me there.' Working in Los

Angeles is one thing. Living there is another. I can see why Gene would rather stay on the east coast."

Goodson-Todman were proud of their own output, but like any good business, they kept a watchful eye on the competition. And in 1973, the biggest competition on the air was NBC's *The Hollywood Squares*, from producers Merrill Heatter & Bob Quigley. Goodson suggested that his own company should try to whip up a game show that somehow involved a panel with many stars. Goodson's staff came up with a new version of *The Match Game*, in which contestants would try to match a panel of stars instead of just matching a couple of teammates.

A pair of pilots was shot on May 19, 1973, with Gene hosting and celebrity guests Bert Convy, Arlene Francis, Jack Klugman, Jo Ann Pflug, Richard Dawson, and Betty White. What Gene may not have realized was that it didn't always look like he'd be the host.

Ira Skutch said in 2006, "I held out for him to do it again. You again had some network people who wondered if somebody else might be better. There were people who did not want him. Everybody has their own favorites. You get a bunch of people together, everybody wants to score. But I can't remember any other specific names who came up. It never got to where there were competitive thoughts or conversations."

Gene gets back to work, reading the questions for a *Match Game* pilot on May 19, 1973. (Fred Wostbrock Collection)

Goodson-Todman staffer Robert Sherman remembers, "We knew the network wanted other people. We didn't. Mark Goodson didn't. So when CBS asked us early in the proceedings who we were looking at for potential hosts, I think Mark Goodson sort of bluffed and said 'Well, we're looking at these folks, we're in talks with this person,' but he didn't mean it. He was only saying it because he knew that's what CBS wanted to hear. We knew from the beginning that Gene was hosting."

The new game pitted two contestants, a champion and a challenger, against each other over two rounds. To start a round, Gene would reveal two questions, labeled A and B. The challenger picked a question and the champion got the other question. For each question, the panelists wrote their answers and the contestant gave a verbal response, scoring one point for every star matched. In round two, the contestants each tried to match only the celebrities that they failed to match in the first round (so the highest possible score was six points).

Top scorer won the game, $100, and the right to play a two-part bonus round, Jackpot Match. For the first part of the bonus round, Audience Match, Gene would read a simple blank phrase, like "_____ RICE", which had been given to a previous audience. Hidden on the board were the audience's top three answers, valued at $500 for the most popular answer, $250 for the second, and $100 for the third. The contestant gave one answer in hopes that it matched one of the top three. If the contestant won any money at all, the next step was Head-to-Head Match. The contestant picked one of the six stars, Gene read another blank phrase, the celebrity wrote an answer, and the contestant gave a verbal answer. If they matched, the contestant won ten times the payoff from Audience Match, for a top prize of $5,000.

Four days later, Gene got the call that CBS was putting the show on the air. Despite the fact that the previous *Match Game* had lasted seven years, the new version was an unknown quantity, a totally new format being plugged into a fading time slot on the network. Gene resisted moving to Los Angeles for the series, instead opting for a seemingly grueling travel schedule, commuting by plane from Cape Cod to Boston and then onto Los Angeles, every two weeks for a weekend visit. On Saturday, five episodes would be taped in the span of about four hours. On Sunday, five more episodes would be taped, and Gene would head back to Massachusetts. While flying out every other weekend made it a slightly more bearable schedule than *The Amateur's Guide to Love*, Gene had to make one sacrifice for the new version of *Match Game*. Since the shows would be taping on Saturday and Sunday, Gene had to leave *Monitor*. He probably viewed it as a low-risk proposition—he likely could have easily asked for his old job back if the new *Match Game* failed—but after twelve years, Gene was done with *Monitor*.

Jackpot Match, as seen—or not seen, really—in the unaired pilot for *Match Game*. (Fred Wostbrock Collection)

The Matchless Gene Rayburn

The new series, officially titled *Match Game '73* to emphasize that it was a new series, began taping on June 10, and premiered on June 25 in the 3:30 p.m. Eastern time slot on CBS. It was supposed to, anyway.

Robert Sherman remembers, "We debuted at the same time that the Watergate hearings began. And that created all sorts of problems for us. We gathered in the office together to watch the first episode. We got pre-empted. So the next day, we gather around the TV in the office, and we're pre-empted again. Our first week did not air. We didn't think we'd ever get on."

The opening week panel for *Match Game '73*: From left, Michael Landon, JoAnn Pflug, Richard Dawson, Gene, Vicki Lawrence, Anita Gillette, Jack Klugman. Landon would never return, feeling that the new game as designed was "unfair." (Fred Wostbrock Collection)

The show finally did go on the air on July 2, beginning with the episode that was supposed to air on June 25, and Goodson-Todman finally got to show viewers version 2.0 of an old favorite. The finished product was substantially the same as the pilot, except that the bonus round was renamed Super Match. Gene welcomed America to the new series hyping that it contained "more money, more action, and more stars."

What Gene didn't mention was that the new version would contain more Gene. It was due to a simple but brilliant omission in the show's set design. There was no lectern for Gene to stand behind during the game. The question machine was next to the contestants, who were across the stage from the celebrity panel. The change required Gene to move around the set for the entire show, and that change couldn't have made him happier.

Ira Skutch told game show historian Steve Beverly, "That was the major change we made. That's what turned it from a serviceable show into a smash hit."

It would be hard to argue with "smash hit." Preceding *Match Game '73* in the time slot had been an ambitious but bloated celebrity game from Jack Barry, titled *Hollywood's Talking*. The show came and went in only thirteen weeks. *Match Game '73* took over the time slot, and six weeks later, it was the number-one show on daytime television.

Robert Sherman remembers, "When we went on the air, our hopes were high but our expectations were low. Finally, we premiered, and things just got worse because the Watergate hearings happened at different times each day, which created problems with time zones. We had a lot of episodes in the first few months that aired on the east coast but not on the west coast, and some days where a show that the east coast already missed wound up airing on the west coast. And we were so upset because we thought that if the show got pre-empted repeatedly, the audience would never get comfortable with it, they'd never be able to comprehend it, and so they'd turn away without giving us a chance. We were amazed that people stayed with us."

It wasn't just a matter of snapping the fingers and saying "hit show!" There was a bit of tinkering required in the earliest episodes, because *Match Game '73*, early on, had taken a bit of a step backward. In the first week of shows, the contestants were being asked to "name something you squeeze." There were mildly suggestive questions ("John said to Mary, 'Your _____ is flat'") but for the most part, the show had backpedaled right back to 1962.

Even though the name of the bonus round had been changed to Super Match by the show's premiere, CBS widely circulated this shot of Gene to promote *Match Game '73*. (Author's Collection)

Robert Sherman, who was brought onboard to help write questions, remembers, "In the original form, half of all questions were 'name something' questions. And I mean that literally. We counted the questions and mixed them so they would work out to exactly half 'name something' questions and half fill-in-the-blank questions. And the fill-in-the-blank questions were always basic. 'John likes to cook BLANK for breakfast.' But Ira Skutch really began pushing for comedy questions like they did in the '60s version. He came into the office one day and just said 'This isn't working, write this kind of question instead.'"

Ira Skutch said in 2006, "What happened was, Mark always was game-oriented. He never really understood the dynamics of a comedy show like this. It really wasn't his forte. He was always trying to hold the reins in a little bit. We kept venturing out. We started out by saying these blank questions are funny and we want to use a lot of them. We could use those as the first round questions and then use questions for the second round with more game-playing. The blank questions just played like crazy. The other stuff was just mundane. We went to Mark and said we ought to do more and more of these. He finally saw how funny the show was and when the ratings went through the ceiling, we made every question a blank."

Gene himself was pushing for more fill-in-the-blank questions and more comedy. In the twilight of his life, when he wasn't worried about upsetting a boss anymore, he didn't hold back. He said he wanted the game played for comedy because, Gene said, *Match Game '73* was "a rotten format."

Michael Landon, who had been on the NBC *Match Game* plenty of times, appeared as a member of the panel for the first week of programs on CBS. After the taping, he confronted Ira Skutch backstage and said "This is a terrible program; it's unfair."

The main problem with the game was the rule that each panelist could only be matched once by a player, which put all panelists on equal footing. A strong player couldn't really make a significant impact on the game because once he or she had matched, that was it. The contestants had to depend on the weaker panelists for more of the game. And even casting aside the rules of the game, there was the futility of having six celebrities gathered for a game if it wasn't being played for laughs. When Gene read a straightforward "name something," the panelists wrote their answers in silence. No laughter, no chatter, no reactions. Just a momentary look of puzzlement and the squeak of a magic marker on a 5x7 index card. If the questions were naughty and suggestive, the stars could mug and exaggerate their reactions; they'd laugh; they'd make jokes. The game came to life when the game came to laughs. And inch by inch, those laughs began seeping into the early weeks of *Match Game '73*.

"Though Sam was 80 years old, he still liked to (_____)."

"Mark Anthony said, 'Cleopatra has the biggest (_____) in Egypt.'"

"The Jolly Green Giant has a giant green (_____)."

Gene explained why the game needed the funny lines, and why the funny lines needed a game.

> *We use the game as a hook, [and] the funny lines and ad-libs make it work.*

The other important element when assembling a panel game show is, obviously, the panel. This is trickier than it sounds. *The Name's the Same* ran for four years without settling on a stable group of panelists. *What's My Line?* was on the air for more than two years before finding a group of panelists that the staff and viewers were completely happy with. It took the original version of *I've Got a Secret* about a year. But Lady Luck was on the side of *Match Game '73*. They found the right panelists almost immediately.

Richard Dawson was signed first. The 1972-73 version of *I've Got a Secret* had been a bust, but virtually everyone who saw it would have agreed that Richard Dawson was a saving grace. Before even one episode of *Match Game '73* had been taped, Dawson signed a contract with Goodson-Todman to be a regular panelist for the new series.

Orson Bean says, "Richard Dawson's seat on the panel was actually supposed to be mine. I had been a regular panelist on *To Tell the Truth* in New York for seven years or so, and then CBS canceled it. Goodson-Todman introduced a new version for syndication, and I did a season of that and then I quit. I was becoming incredibly paranoid in 1970 because I thought the country was going to turn fascist and I moved my entire family to Australia to escape the USA before that happened. And then I started to notice that America was still there, and it hadn't gone fascist, and I returned to America and settled down in California.

Re-Match

The anchor of the *Match Game* panel, Richard Dawson. Viewers loved watching him and contestants loved winning with him. (Fred Wostbrock Collection)

"I had done the original *Match Game* at NBC a lot and I got along wonderfully with Gene, so the production staff called and explained that they were doing this new version that would include a whole lot of celebrities on a panel and asked if I wanted to be a regular panelist. I was all for it. But Mark Goodson was pissed off as all hell at me because I had walked away from *To Tell the Truth*. When he found out I had been made this offer, he handed down the order. I was allowed to be a guest. I was allowed to appear on the show sometimes. But I was absolutely not allowed to be a regular panelist for anything. Goodson and I had a decent relationship, but he never completely forgave me for quitting *To Tell the Truth*, and he wouldn't use me as a regular for anything else after that."

Robert Sherman explains, "Dawson was great because he had a comedian's mindset and a writer's mindset, and he could see where we were going with some of the questions we were writing. After we were on the air for a while, we began writing some of the questions a certain way. We never dealt in right and wrong answers because we weren't that type of game, but we would write a question and say 'There's one great answer for this.' And we might sneak in a hint by phrasing a question a certain way or putting a key word in there, and Richard would always pick up on it and write the answer that we had in mind.

"The great thing was how often we could count on him and how right we were to count on him. We didn't write questions with him specifically in mind. But we kept doing things with that 'one perfect answer' approach. Question writing really turned into a science for us. And the end result was so great on the air. We had so many contestants who were just average people off the street—little old ladies, housewives, no show business background—who picked up on it too, so here was the situation that would play out. An ordinary contestant would give the perfect answer that we had in mind. Gene would pretend he was shocked and act like there was no way these six sophisticated, high society celebrity panelists would ever say it, and he would sort of lightly chastise the contestant for saying it. And then he'd go to the panel. And the first four panelists would give good answers but not matching answers and Gene would sort of speak to the contestant with that tone like, 'See, I told you that answer wouldn't work.' And then Richard would hold up his card and match, and Gene would feign shock, and the contestant would let out a scream and jump up in her seat, and it would get a huge round of applause from the audience."

The next regular panelist signed was a happy accident named Brett Somers. Born Audrey Johnston in 1924, in New Brunswick, Canada, she ran away from home when she was seventeen years old and arrived in New York's Greenwich Village. Seeing her arrival as a new start in her

Re-Match

Brett Somers gives another ridiculous explanation for her answer, while Charles Nelson Reilly puts that in his pipe and smokes it. (Fred Wostbrock Collection)

life, she called herself Brett Somers, cobbling the name together from the lead female in *The Sun Also Rises* and her mother's maiden name.

Brett joined the Actors Studio and from there, she began building a steady body of stage credits including *Happy Ending*, *The Seven Year Itch*, and *The Country Girl*. After a failed first marriage and bringing a daughter into the world, she wed actor Jack Klugman in 1953 and together, they had two sons. She began acting in television and racked up a number of one-shot roles on TV shows, not landing any regular work until the early 1970s, when her husband was cast as slovenly Oscar Madison on the TV version of *The Odd Couple*. Brett was fittingly cast as Oscar's ex-wife Blanche.

The Odd Couple was at the height of its popularity in 1973 and Jack Klugman was booked for the premiere week of *Match Game '73*, hoping that his star power would give the show an extra boost. After the taping ended, Jack Klugman approached Ira Skutch with a request.

"Listen, would you do me a favor?" he asked. "My wife is dying to do something. It would really help me a lot if I could get her out of the house and get her something to do."

Skutch was grateful to Klugman for his help getting the new show off the ground and, even though he didn't know anything about Brett, he figured that it probably wouldn't do any harm to put her on the show for one week. And Brett, from the day she arrived, just seemed to belong there. She joked around with Gene, teased the other panelists... it was a new show and yet, Brett looked and sounded like she had been there for years. She brought humor and a sense of comfort to the new game. She was brought back for a second week when the next taping session rolled around, and after that, she was signed to a contract and made a full-blown regular panelist.

GENE: *We're at the end of the show and I have to fill thirty-five seconds. What can I do?*
BRETT: *The same thing you used to do in thirty-five minutes.*

GENE: *Lois Lane said "Superman flew over New York City last night and got BLANK."*
BRETT: *Huh?*
GENE: *Lois Lane said "Superman flew over New York City last night and got BLANK!"*
BRETT: *That is the worst question in a year and a half I have ever heard on this show, ever!*
GENE: *Now wait a minute, just think about it. Read it to yourself now.*
BRETT: *Does that make sense to you?*
GARY BURGHOFF: *It makes perfect sense to me.*
BRETT: *Can I see your answer?*
GARY: *No.*
GENE: *There are many good answers here! Now use the tiny brain God gave you and think of one of the answers.*

GENE: *Betty White, do you think Bob (the male contestant) is cute?*
BETTY: *Yes!*

Re-Match

Orson Bean looks on with amusement while Brett explains her answer, and Charles Nelson Reilly just isn't impressed. (Fred Wostbrock Collection)

BRETT: If you were married to Allen Ludden, you'd think almost anyone was cute.

BRETT: I love it when Betty White acts like a female dog, know what I mean?

The last regular panelist to join the series was Charles Nelson Reilly. After a few sporadic guest appearances, he finally began appearing full-time in the final weeks of 1973. His show-stealing spot on *I've Got a Secret* had caught Goodson-Todman's attention and he provided the same type of command performance on *Match Game '73*, positioning himself as a lovable nuisance. He criticized the question-writing, he would chew Gene out for his delivery, he would nitpick answers, he would complain when other panelists—particularly Brett Somers—talked too much. He had such strong chemistry with Brett, in fact, that it actually affected the way the panelists were seated. Brett, in the early months of the series, tended to it on the bottom tier of the panel, but she and Charles played off of each other so wonderfully that they were seated side-by-side on the top tier to maximize their interaction.

Dick DeBartolo remembers, "What cracked me up to no end about those two was that Charles absolutely would not address Brett by the correct name. He would always say 'Listen to Sheila!' if she said something snide, or he'd say 'Gene, can we do something about Susan?'"

GENE: Tarzan is getting really weird. In his new movie, he swings on a vine, beats his chest, goes "Aaaaah-ah-ah-ah!" and makes a funny face and BLANKS his loincloth.
CHARLES: This is the only question we've ever had that requires an intermission.

GENE: Joe said to Mike, 'What's green and pink and wobbles like a huge bowl of Jell-o?' and Mike said 'I don't know,' and Joe said 'I don't know either, but it's oozing all over your BLANK.'... Are you finished writing, Charles?
BRETT: No, he's asleep as usual... I have never disliked a question more than I dislike that one. I hate that one!
CHARLES: Does that mean you're leaving?

The Audience Match question is (_____) Stick.
GENE: Let's see the $100 response. (Answer is revealed on the board.) LIP Stick!
BRETT: I thought that said 'Up Stick' when I read it and I was about to ask what in the world an Up Stick is.
CHARLES: I'll show you.

GENE: Norman said to his wife, "Doris, stop treating me like a baby!" And Doris said "Shut up and get back in your BLANK."
CONTESTANT: Crib.
CHARLES: You know, when Brett was young, they didn't even call it a crib.

Re-Match

BRETT: What did they call it?
CHARLES: A manger.

In 2007, writer Rob Hoerburger summed up the relationship between Somers and Reilly thusly: "Somers and Reilly provided a mid-afternoon snack of comedic pas de deux that was sometimes bawdy, sometimes puerile but somehow never cheap. The repartee was hardly the stuff of Mike Nichols & Elaine May or even Sid Caesar & Imogene Coca... but with Somers and Reilly what mattered more was not what was being said exactly but who was saying it.

"Many viewers were introduced to Somers and Reilly on *Match Game*, as if they'd sprung straight from the Spiegel catalog, the Paris Hiltons of their day, famous for being famous. But both were already accomplished veterans of stage and screen... And that acting talent could be why on *Match Game* they weren't just panelists but characters. Somers was the middle-aged man-hungry 'dumb brunette' with the lefty chicken scrawl, Reilly, the fussbudget forever disparaging her answers, her wardrobe, her decorating skills. In that sense they were forerunners of Will & Grace, the gay man and his gal pal with a bitchy, loving disregard for each other."

Likewise, Brett isn't all that impressed by Charles' answer. Quite frequently, the game took a backseat to the bickering.
(Fred Wostbrock Collection)

The Matchless Gene Rayburn

Orson Bean remembers, "They always sat me on the top tier along with Charles Nelson Reilly. I remember when Johnny Carson retired, some magazine published a list of the ten most frequent guests of *The Tonight Show Starring Johnny Carson*. The list said I appeared as a guest ninety-two times. I was, you'll pardon the expression, under Charles Nelson Reilly."

Charles Nelson Reilly had a great deal to offer in show business. He was an award-winning actor on the Broadway stage, as well as an experienced writer, director, television performer, film performer, acting teacher (his students included *M*A*S*H* cast member Gary "Radar" Burghoff and *Lou Grant* co-star Robert Walden) and even a television advertising producer. Despite all he had to offer, Reilly would be remembered primarily for *Match Game*, something that he had mixed feelings about. He was openly gay, in a more conservative era, but said that his career was actually more harmed by becoming known as "a game show fixture," and like Gene Rayburn, he found that he was missing out on work that he was perfectly qualified for because he was tied to a genre that the show business world didn't respect very much. Nonetheless, Reilly stuck with *Match Game* because, frankly, it was a cushy gig.

Dick DeBartolo remembers the way Reilly described the role of a game show panelist: "This job is like stealing. I come in for a four-hour workday. I play a very simple game with people I like, we're joking around almost the entire time. In the middle of it, they stop everything to feed you. And then they actually send you a check for it!"

Gene, countless times through the remainder of his life, was fond of telling interviewers about what Charles said about *Match Game* during a dinner break: "This isn't a job. It's a social engagement."

> *Charles Nelson Reilly worked on Broadway in a play called God's Favorite. He wrote his own program notes on his bio. And the last sentence was "Mr. Reilly is twenty-nine years old and totally adorable!"*

When Ira Skutch wrote his autobiography in 1989, he seemingly couldn't find enough encomiums for Reilly. "Charles Nelson Reilly [is] a true professional; dependable and concerned for his fellows. Although he's had a long and distinguished career and is respected by all as an actor and director, he knew that *Match Game* was good for him, so he was good to *Match Game*. His zaniness and unfailing good humor brightened both the show and our dinner breaks. Sometimes he panicked us when he was late for his studio call, but he always appeared before his introduction on the air."

Robert Sherman adds, "Charles was another one that we could count on as writers. He was very broad, and flamboyant. His training was in the theater, so he was prone to very theatrical mannerisms and delivery. We'd write a question about a tough biker because we knew Charles would do a deliberately unconvincing tough guy act when we called on him. Sometimes he'd yell his answers, or he'd nitpick the phrasing of a wordier question. It was a lot of fun."

Suggestive questions and a wild, sassy panel could have overwhelmed the show if it hadn't been for the delicate art of conducting the proceedings as Gene did. He had to cut off the celebrities if they got too chatty. He had to rein them if they got so caught up in the fun that they weren't writing. He had to make sure that attention was still paid to the game, even if it was a weak game. He spoke on numerous occasions with interviewers about what a tricky job game show hosting truly was, and what the hardest part of it was.

> *...Well, being an instantaneous editor. You are constantly called upon to make a value judgment on time. You've got to use good taste in that you edit everything you say, or do. You have to make sure there is no lagging, that there is a pace, a regular tempo to the show. The pace is supposed to be in the writing, but it doesn't necessarily happen all the time. When that happens, that's when the instantaneous comes in.*
>
> *The essential ability is to write a show, in a sense, as it happens. It's like most extremely difficult things—the harder you work at it and the better you get, the easier it all looks. But it never really gets all that easy.*

Contestants, he acknowledged, were the biggest challenge of all.

> *Sometimes they freeze, sometimes they get traumatized when the red light goes on. You have to be sensitive to the way non-professionals are in public. Garry Moore does it beautifully. So does Bill Cullen. They make it look so easy.*

Gene clowned around as much as anybody on the panel, but he also understood the value and appeal of the stars, and when one of them had a funny line, he knew his place. Being a sidekick to Steve Allen proved to be unexpectedly invaluable for a job like hosting a game show with a six-star panel.

> *It's my responsibility to set them up. I'm an actor, basically, [and] I understand the make-up of the show. I'm playing it straight for the stars.*

One of the things that helped the stars of *Match Game '73* have fun was that the show wasn't totally bound by the clock. *Match Game '73* was designed to "straddle." The game as-is wasn't enough to fill thirty minutes. An episode might start with two contestants playing a new game. After they had played their two rounds and the Super Match, there was enough time to bring out another contestant, do a brief interview, and start a new game. They might have had enough time to play Round 1 before the half-hour ran out, so on the next day's episode, the show would start with Round 2. Since nobody had to worry about making sure that certain elements of the game were crammed into every half-hour, Gene and the panel were free to explore anything they thought was worth pursuing for a laugh.

Not everybody was laughing, though. The big boss, Mark Goodson, was unhappy with what he was seeing each day. And in his eyes, that laughing and carrying on was going to be detrimental to the show.

Robert Sherman remembers, "Mark Goodson was in the studio one day for a taping fairly early in the run of the show. We taped an episode that we thought was hilarious, and we thought 'Wow, this show is really hitting its stride quick!' We were really happy with it. We got word afterward that Mark Goodson wanted to see me, he wanted to see Ira Skutch, and he wanted to see Gene in his office the next day. And we walked in expecting a pat on the back.

"We walked in there and absolutely got the riot act from Mark. As I recall the episode, we only managed to play two complete rounds—four questions—in the entire half-hour, and the game ended in a scoreless tie. And Mark wanted to know how we planned on improving the show and he wanted answers, you know, right now! And I can't remember the exact dialogue of who said what in response, but we all told Mark, 'Well, the reason it moved so slowly was because it was such a funny show.' The contestants weren't matching because they had given imaginative answers, but too imaginative for their own good. So the contestants were getting a reaction. The panelists were writing a variety of answers, and they all had little stories or joke explanations to justify their answers. And it was funny, and it was interesting and very engaging TV.

"And I do remember one specific thing we said to Mark. I think it was Ira who said, 'Mark, if laughing and making jokes and giving a variety of imaginative answers is a problem, there's an easy fix. Gene can ask the panelists, 'Name a type of pie.' And everyone will think of 'apple' immediately and write it without discussion. And the contestant will say 'apple.' And then when Gene goes back to the panelists and says 'What did you say, panel?' everyone is going to say 'Apple, apple, apple, apple, apple, apple.' And then you'll have a fast-moving, high-scoring game, but Mark, is that better TV than the slower-moving show we did?'"

Even though the show had risen to #1 quickly, Goodson was initially convinced that the game alone had drawn viewers in, and that the panel's antics would be the death of the show in the long run. But with every passing week, ratings data came in, and the results were unmistakable: daytime viewers adored this show.

Robert Sherman says, "Mark Goodson very admirably kept his distance from us after a while. When it's your company and your name on it, and you're the big boss, having your employees tell you that their way is better than your way, and their way actually works, that can be a bit of a blow to the ego. But Goodson was pragmatic enough to say 'You know what? This works, and I don't understand why. It just does.' And he sort of held his tongue and left *Match Game* to run itself. He really didn't offer very much input after that."

The holiday season of 1973 rolled around and the #1 show on daytime TV got a remarkable present: Even more viewers.

Robert Sherman says "We were already tops, we were already, obviously, thrilled with our ratings. But for whatever reason, during Christmas 1973, the show exploded. And we actually managed to retain those viewers, which was amazing."

At the end of 1973, Gene waved bye-bye to the big *Match Game '73* sign that filled the stage at the start of each episode. Confetti and streamers flew across the set, a brand new sign, reading *Match Game '74*, flew down from the ceiling and lit up for the first time, and Gene wrapped up the show and the year with an expression of gratitude.

"I want to say a word of thanks to all of these lovely people and all the people behind the scenes who kept us going this time, and are gonna keep us going through *Match Game '75* and '76."

It was an optimistic proclamation, in an era where any show's future in daytime television went up for scrutiny every thirteen to twenty-six weeks. But Gene's hubris and optimism were justified. He was on a show that just worked. For whatever flaws the game had, however "rotten" the format may have been, all of the right pieces clicked, and the show was #1. Gene wasn't going to be doing anything but hosting a game show for a while. And for a man who craved exposure and stardom, that suited him just fine. *Match Game '74* was underway.

Chapter Eleven
The Match Makers,
On Stage and Off

It was, as usual, a five-episode taping session at CBS Television City in Hollywood. Gene read the question: "Ed Sullivan said, 'Tonight right here on this very stage, King Kong will BLANK the Lennon Sisters!'"

Louisa Moritz filled in the blank by writing the answer "rape." Fellow panelist Kaye Stevens laughed riotously, the audience screamed in shock, Gene nervously looked off-stage at producer Ira Skutch, and Richard seemed to speak for everybody when he said he didn't want to follow that. The CBS standards & practices representative objected to the answer and insisted that Moritz write something else. When the show aired, viewers saw an alternate take, with Moritz revealing the answer "ravage." An alert viewer could figure out something had gone wrong just

The Matchless Gene Rayburn

Fred Wostbrock Collection

from the sight of Gene, who looked visibly flustered for a few moments after seeing Moritz's answer.

Later in the same taping session, Richard Dawson helped a lucky contestant claim $5,000, and the time had come to welcome a new challenger and start another game. Her name was Karen Lesko. Gene would never forget her.

Gene introduced her and she smiled at the round of applause that the audience offered. Gene noticed the dimples forming at the edges of her mouth and tried to pay her a compliment. It went horribly wrong for him.

As he would recall many, many times in the years after, he gestured toward her and said "Doesn't she have pretty nipples?"

She laughed, the panelists laughed, the audience absolutely howled, and director Marc Breslow zoomed in on Gene in an uncharacteristic state: absolutely mortified.

> *I wanted the earth to open up and swallow me whole.*

The standards and practices representative objected again. A second take of Karen's introduction was done, and that's what CBS viewers saw. Gene's blunder was saved for a blooper reel, and much later in his career, it was easier for him to laugh at as he brought the tape along for interviews on whatever talk show was doing a game show retrospective that day.

As the five-episode taping continued, a visitor was wandering through the halls of CBS Television City. He heard that *Match Game '74* was taping that day, and decided to drop in for a surprise visit. Gene was wrapping up a segment and threw it to a commercial break. During the two-minute pause, Gene went to the edge of the stage and answered questions from audience members. Out of the corner of his eye, Gene saw a familiar figure walking through the side entrance, out of view of the audience.

Angrily, he shouted, "Excuse me, sir! We're taping a TV show!"

The audience was stunned by the disruption and wondered how a stranger made his way to the stage. He kept walking toward Gene and once the stage lights hit him, the audience was shocked to see Burt Reynolds warmly greeting Gene. Gene carried on a conversation with Burt and lost track of the time signals from the stage manager. The show faded in on Gene in mid-conversation with Burt. Gene hastily did an introduction once he realized that the tape was rolling, but that was an indicator of how "real" things were kept on the show. Nobody instructed Burt Reynolds to walk off-stage so Gene could welcome their very special guest to a prompted round of applause. The audience was seeing the surprise exactly as it played out.

The Matchless Gene Rayburn

Gene and Helen had their share of ups and downs during their marriage. In 1974, they rebuilt their home and their lives. (Fred Wostbrock Collection)

It was just another day at *Match Game '74*.

Moments like this were bountiful on *Match Game '74*. The wheels fell off during other TV game shows and provided memorable moments, but what made *Match Game* such a treasure is that the wheels were never bolted on very tightly to begin with. It was a weak game, Gene would do anything to get a laugh if it helped mask that weakness, and the stars, following Gene's example, felt uninhibited. If you missed a hilarious moment on *Match Game*, there was no need to worry. The next one was never far away.

Dick DeBartolo remembers, "*Match Game* was the first game show that I can remember that made fun of the contestants. Not that they were dragged out there to be humiliated, but it was the first game show where contestants were held responsible for playing the game poorly. If somebody gave a terrible answer, it was addressed and it was dealt with. I remember a day where they had two terrible contestants, and they had each given two really bad answers in the first round. We get to the second round, and one of the contestants gave another awful answer, and Brett just looks at Gene and blurts out 'Gene, are there absolutely no qualifications for being a contestant on this show? Did you walk out onto the sidewalk half an hour ago, point to two people and yell 'You! You're on television'?"

In 1974, Gene and Helen took a final step toward righting a terrible wrong from a few years earlier. They built a new home on the land they had purchased a few years earlier, where the home they had planned on moving into was destroyed by arson. They had their dream house in the quiet, private spot of land that they had fallen in love with. And though his hit show required him to commute every two weeks, Gene wouldn't dream of trading in that inconvenience for a permanent home somewhere closer to CBS Television City in Hollywood.

> *[On the east coast,] life's more peaceful, the water's much warmer, the air's a lot cleaner... Whenever I fly to California and look down on Los Angeles during the descent, I see that green guck and I say, 'God, I'm going to be breathing that.'*

Gene and Helen's custom-built house included a corner-to-corner glass wall on the south side, giving them a panoramic view of Nantucket Sound. Gene had a flower and vegetable garden in the backyard, framed by rows of Japanese pines; on the other side was a swimming pool.

Gene occasionally flew from Massachusetts to New York City for a five-episode taping session of *What's My Line?* or *To Tell the Truth*. It was a short flight, the tapings rarely took more than four hours from start-to-finish, and Gene was right back and sleeping in his own bed that night.

Most days in Cape Cod, Gene would stroll up and down the beach and enjoy the scenery. He would also gather the seaweed that washed ashore and turn it into a mulch for nourishing the massive garden that he tended to. He devoutly believed in the value of seaweed mulch, saying that because man evolved from the sea, elements taken from the sea contained all the nutrients man needed to sustain himself.

He spent plenty of time with Helen. Most of their chores and errands were treated as a team effort, and when it came time to relax, they swam, bicycled, or played tennis. The Rayburns did a bit of sailing, often with Walter Cronkite, who had a house on the other side of the sound.

Every two weeks, Gene headed to Logan Airport. He paid his own way every time. Goodson felt that asking him to move to Los Angeles had been a reasonable request and wouldn't accommodate him by adding an air commute to the company's expenses.

Robert Sherman remembers, "Gene complained about it sometimes. I'd hear about how his ticket was too expensive, about how he was too old to travel this much. But… Gene must have loved hosting that show an awful lot if he was willing to spend a couple hundred dollars every few weeks and fly across the country and put himself up in a hotel to do it."

Gene departed on Friday for a noon flight. He brought a book and a needlepoint project with him. Often, he said he liked needlepoint because he got tired of reading on long flights, but Gene admitted to at least one reporter that there was another reason he preferred it. Being in the public eye, a frequent hazard to the job was being seated next to a fan who recognized him. He did his best to be gracious to the fans—they were the ones who indirectly paid all the bills for him, after all—but the problem was they tended to ask the same questions over and over again. Gene, being only human, got tired of answering them eventually. But for some reason, busying himself with needlepoint seemed to throw a "do not disturb" signal to anyone sitting around him, and he could be alone. During all of his coast-to-coast flights, Gene made belts, pillows, and sneaker decorations. Eventually, he had a gallery exhibit showcasing his needlepoint work.

Once Gene landed in Los Angeles, it was off to the hotel; later, he just started renting an apartment on Wilshire Boulevard. Gene didn't bother adjusting his body clock for just two days at work, and that part of it was a little troublesome. Gene would look for ways to keep himself occupied until 9:30 p.m. (half-past midnight back in Cape Cod) and then head to bed. He would sleep for a few hours but had a bad problem with waking up at 2:30 a.m. He'd pop a sleeping pill and sleep for a few more hours.

The next morning, he went to the Bel Air Country Club, played some tennis, and then headed to CBS Television City. He got a haircut and make-up and then pulled out one of the forty custom-made suits from the rack in his dressing room, and then the fun began.

From Gene's point of view, taping ten episodes of fun and games had exactly one hard part to it.

> *What's most important is to be able to maintain that sharpness, the edge. Remember, my job is to keep things appearing fresh and spontaneous. Except for the questions, nothing is written for the program, and whether someone's watching in the studio or at home, no one wants to see an emcee standing around looking all worn out. For most of the audience, this show is original, and there's no reason we should let on that it might well be our fifth of that day. That's the challenge.*

Gene plays tennis with Bill Cosby at a fundraiser called Raising a Racquet. Together, the two of them looked like a version of *I Spy* that any game show fan would have loved. (Fred Wostbrock Collection)

The Matchless Gene Rayburn

But if that's the hardest part of the job, most people could agree that Gene had one great job. He got to give away other people's money and laugh it up with six witty, charming celebrities. And during his breaks, free food and spirits were laid out for everyone.

The magic of television, though, is making it look like it's always this much fun. But to make a show that happy and that entertaining, a lot of very talented people had to work very, very hard.

Despite being a Mark Goodson-Bill Todman Production, the man that most of the *Match Game* staff viewed as the boss was Ira Skutch. He had arguably the hardest job of anybody on the show. His job was to make everybody else's job easy. Lynne remembered him as a very smart and very gracious man.

Robert Sherman explains, "Ira was good at working with people. Any people, even difficult people. Some of the stars felt that being on a game show was beneath them, and Ira was very good at working with them and talking to them, and encouraging them until they finally had a good attitude about what they were doing and we were able to handle them. He dealt hands-on with Gene and if there were ever any problems with Gene, I didn't know about them. And that's Ira's doing. They had a friendship away from the show and Ira just had a good feel for him and knew exactly what to say if anything ever bothered Gene or upset him.

"Ira was also great with politics, and with a hit show, a producer has a lot of politics to deal with. He has to deal with network censors, business people, advertisers, executives at Goodson-Todman, executives at the network. And he had to listen to every one of them make suggestions. 'Do this, don't do that. You're not doing this enough. You need to cut back on this.' And he was able to keep the show from getting bogged down. He could take that feedback, come up with something that made everybody happy, and didn't let the show get tied up with all of those accommodations. He was able to keep the show going in a productive direction."

Randy West says, "Gene adored Ira. The respect was personal and professional. Personally, they were great friends. They played chess together. Ira started his career as an NBC page a few years after Gene, so they had a lot of shared experiences on their way up the ladder and they connected with that, and Gene just thought Ira was a fantastic producer.

He felt Ira had a good head for what a show needed, what worked and what didn't."

The show had a staff of freelance writers. Dick DeBartolo remained in the Goodson-Todman offices in New York City. In Los Angeles, Robert Sherman, Joe Neustein, Patrick Neary, Marsha Morris, Elliott Feldman and Jake Tauber wrote questions, too. Aside from DeBartolo, the writers collaborated on the questions, polishing and refining them like the team that crafted a late night talk show monologue might do.

But despite the fact that the show was played for laughs, "Naughty and silly" wasn't good enough. Writing a question for *Match Game '74* was a delicate art.

Gene amuses panelists Dwayne Hickman, Brett Somers, and Carol Lawrence with another fill-in-the-blank. Viewers at home had no idea how much care went into the silly questions that the panel responded to. (Fred Wostbrock Collection)

Dick DeBartolo explains, "The important thing about the question is that it has to steer the contestants into some kind of area. A bad question is something like 'John is very ____ during the day.' Far too vague. There needs to be something that tells the contestant that there's a category that the possible answers could fit into."

Ira Skutch went into greater detail while talking to author Maxine Fabe. "'The millionaire Japanese dwarf came to the United States and bought a BLANK.' There, you have too many elements that can affect the answer. The question should lay a field for funny and amusing answers, but not so wide that there is no chance for a match.

"The material we have selected is then tested around the office to see whether the answers we think we're going to get are actually the answers we do get. Then we arrange the questions to avoid conflicts in subjects."

Robert Sherman says "Ira Skutch was very, very good at editing and anticipating. He'd read a question that began with something like 'Fat Frieda is dating a one-hundred-year-old man…' and he'd read the whole question and say 'The way the question is phrased, it's more about the one-hundred-year-old man. A fat joke doesn't really figure into it, so there's no reason to use Fat Frieda. Just use an ordinary name and say 'Susan is dating a one-hundred-year-old.' And we'd sit in that office and read questions to each other, and there'd be a very informal thumbs up or thumbs down vote."

Dick DeBartolo explains, "We really tried to have a broad range for each taping session, so it wasn't the same joke over and over again. There were times when I'd sit at my desk and I'd write a Dumb Dora question, but then I'd think 'Well, no, I already have a Dumb Dora question,' so I'd put it aside and write something else."

Robert Sherman explains, "We used pop cultural references in the questions quite a bit, but we were very careful about what we were referencing. Even though we had the highest audience overall, we also knew that a sizable chunk of our audience were women, so we were very careful to keep questions involving sports to a minimum. We also tried not to use references to rock music because male or female, the audience that watched daytime television wasn't an audience that knew rock music. So that was a touchy area, you had to know what you could write that the audience could relate to and would want to play along with at home.

"When the questions started to take shape, we would look at 'should the key word be here or here? Would it be better if we phrased it like this?' There was always that 'perfect answer' that we looked for when we wrote questions, but we would write based on what panelists might say. Charles was very theatrical and flamboyant, so we might write a question because we expected Charles to say some grandiose remark when it was his turn to talk. So it was a great panel to write for.

"And honestly, Gene was helpful when we wrote questions. Old Man Periwinkle was good, of course, but we'd write questions a certain way because we knew he'd do a certain voice for it, or he'd know to emphasize a certain word, or he'd act drunk if it was a question about drinking.

"The important thing though, was that we had to keep pushing ourselves to try new things. Even though we wrote based on what we anticipated Gene and the panel would do or what we knew for sure they would do, we couldn't keep doing the same thing every day, so we had to keep finding things to do. And as we explored new things to do, we had to make sure that we were moving the show forward and not going into nonsensical or unplayable questions.

"We spent up to one hour on a single question sometimes, which was fine because in a given episode, we only had five questions or so, we didn't really go through that much material, so we had the luxury of being able to take our time and perfect it, so we could really do our part to make every show the best that we, the writers, were capable of making it.

"After we had weeded out the bad questions, we went to Ira. Ira would still vote down some of our questions or suggest re-writes, and we would always die a little inside because Ira's suggestions for re-writes were always correct. No matter how much experience we had or many questions we wrote or how long the show stayed on the air, Ira always knew the best way."

Once the questions had been written and re-written, and tested around the office, they still had one more hurdle before getting on the air. CBS required them to be submitted for approval by the network censors.

DeBartolo says, "We sort of played games with the censors to get questions on the air. If we only submitted the material that we were satisfied with that we absolutely wanted to get on the air, the censors would have rejected a few of them and we would have lost usable material. So what we did for each writing session was we came up with questions that were just wildly inappropriate and dirty that we knew the censors would reject. We had no intention of putting those questions on the air, but we submitted them because that way, the censors would reject those, and the questions we really wanted to use wouldn't seem so bad by comparison and the censor would approve them.

"Every now and then, we did wind up getting a question rejected that we genuinely did want on the show. I remember one in particular that I wrote that the CBS people absolutely did not like. 'Whenever the Six Million Dollar Man runs out of energy, he sticks his BLANK in an electrical socket.'"

Just holding up a card and declaring your answer wouldn't do. The panelists almost always explained their train of thought leading up to each answer, usually getting more laughs with their explanations than with the actual answers. (Fred Wostbrock Collection)

Robert Sherman remembers, "We wrote fall-back questions leading up to the meetings with the censors. Fall-back questions were questions that we liked, but we didn't want to use them unless we had to. But to be honest, we weren't the censors' top priority."

The CBS censors kept a watchful eye on more than just the question writers. There was a Standards & Practices representative from the network present at every taping to keep a watchful eye on what everybody was saying and doing. Spontaneity could be dangerous, after all.

Considering how frequently and eagerly the show pushed the envelope, *Match Game* was rarely censored over the years. Every now and then a celebrity would write and reveal an answer that wasn't fit for broadcast. Since an answer that merited censoring would virtually never match, and therefore wouldn't affect the game, a star who gave a dirty answer would sometimes be told after the taping to write a different answer, a re-take was done with the star revealing that answer, and the program would be edited.

Charles relieves the CBS censors when he reveals his answer of "makes love." It was the only euphemism that they approved. (Fred Wostbrock Collection)

On one episode, Gene read the question, "Janet said, 'I've got good news and bad news. The good news is I found a new place to live. The bad news is it used to be a BLANK.'" Gail Fisher wrote "Whorehouse," but when the episode aired, home viewers saw the answer "Red light district" written on her card.

Robert Sherman remembers, "We almost never censored a regular panelist. The problem we had by and large was this. We would give the non-regulars a briefing before the taping. 'Here are the words you can give for answers, here are the words you can't give.' And it was never, in my eyes, malicious when this happened. What would go wrong would be that a panelist just outright forgot what word they were allowed to use. So for a question, the 'perfect answer' we had was 'boobs,' and a panelist would write a word that meant the same thing but one that the CBS censors didn't like. That was our biggest problem."

Kay Henley was in charge of rounding up the panelists for each taping. Previously a celebrity coordinator for *You Don't Say!* and *Password*, Henley was hired to book the stars for *Match Game* from its CBS inception in 1973. And it was more than a matter of calling up the stars on her rolodex and seeing if they could drop by for the next taping. Putting together a *Match Game* panel was a particularly complex task.

Producer Ira Skutch for many years would refer to the process of assembling a game show panel as "casting a play." Even though they were all there to play the same game, it was ideal to have stars filling a variety of roles and put as many types of personalities among the panelists as possible. The network naturally wanted cast members from CBS shows to get extra airtime. The show wanted to showcase stars from other networks, too. A hit show is a hit show no matter where it was airing, and featuring those stars would help give *Match Game '74* a little added luster. Goodson-Todman liked giving a spot on the panel to the hosts of their other game shows now and then, too.

Little by little, the show assembled a strong roster of semi-regulars. Brett Somers, Charles Nelson Reilly, and Richard Dawson were there day after day. But there were also stars who popped in about every month or so.

Patti Deutsch, a former classmate of Lynne's from Carnegie Tech, was a Pittsburgh native with thick red hair and a broken vocal cord that left her with a distinctively lilted little-girl voice. She became the only female member of the Ace Trucking Company, an improvisational comedy troupe, where she caught the attention of the producers of *Rowan & Martin's Laugh-In*. She joined the NBC show as a writer and performer for what proved to be the show's final season, beginning in 1972. The following season, CBS signed her to a contract, and she began appearing semi-regularly on the new *Match Game*. She typically opened each episode by staring into the camera lifelessly as Johnny Olson said her name; it was a ruse. She gave some of the most marvelously left-brained answers when she played the game.

GENE: Shirley said, "I just found out where my butcher gets those unusual cuts of meat. I walked into the meat locker and saw his BLANK hanging from a hook!"
PATTI: "Competition."

GENE: Superman lost his BLANK in a telephone booth.
PATTI: His "S".

GENE: The jungle doctor said, "These patients are really mean. I get nervous every time I ask one of them to BLANK."
RICHARD: "Bend over."
PATTI: I just want to say for the record that I didn't realize this answer would follow that answer. "Open wide."

(Gene notices Patti is wearing a form-fitting top.)
GENE: It's lovely to have your bodies here on the stage... Oh, you're beautiful. I mean you've really got it.
PATTI: Well, you were discussing bodies, and since I only have mine for a couple more months...
GENE: I guess we've got to explain that. You see, Patti recently became a mother. And, uh...
PATTI: Mothers get neat stuff.
GENE: That's right. And let me tell you, the kid ain't complaining either.

Patti Deutsch smirks as she gets ready to reveal another oddball answer. (Fred Wostbrock Collection)

Joyce Bulifant was born in Newport News, Virginia, but really didn't have any place in the world that she called home. Her family moved twenty-one times by the time she reached 7th grade. When she reached adulthood, she tackled acting, spending a few years on Broadway before moving to television. She was passed over for the role that went to

Florence Henderson on *The Brady Bunch*, but she did find her way to a role on *The Bill Cosby Show* and a recurring role as Murray's wife on *The Mary Tyler Moore Show*. She had a perpetually sunny disposition that made her a natural foil for the sarcastic regulars on the panel.

GENE: For $5,000, "Panty BLANK."
CONTESTANT: Hose.
GENE: Okay, her answer is Panty Hose. Joyce, for $5,000, would you show us yours?
JOYCE: I beg your pardon?
(Joyce stands up and pulls up her ankle-length skirt to show her panty hose.)
GENE: Okay, in that case, for TEN thousand dollars...

Joyce Bulifant has to defend another answer.
(Fred Wostbrock Collection)

Fannie Flagg, born and raised in Alabama, won "Miss Congeniality" in the 1961 Miss Alabama pageant, and the title came with a prize, a scholarship at the Pittsburgh Playhouse. Told that she would never make it in show business because of her thick southern accent, her career benefited from remarkable timing. Texan Lyndon Johnson was the new Vice President of the United States, and his wife Ladybird was now in the public eye, and Fannie was able to build a career in comedy because she could do a pitch perfect impression of the Second Lady. In a matter of years, she became a frequent face on *Candid Camera* and *The New Dick Van Dyke Show*. As a panelist, she and Brett played up what would now be known as a "frenemies" relationship. They snapped at each other throughout the show, always smiling and laughing through each barb. Fannie was also famous for the distinctive, form-fitting and form-emphasizing sweaters that she wore, often with glittering pictures or messages splashed across them.

FANNIE: I have something I'd like to say. For years, Brett Somers keeps making fun of me because I never receive any fan mail, and I received some fan mail. And I'm so thrilled, I wanted to read it. "Dear Fannie Flagg, I watch Match Game every day. Do you know Brett Somers? I love her."

Sitting on the bottom tier are Elaine Joyce, Richard Dawson, and Fannie Flagg.
BRETT: Do you know that from up here, the only person who doesn't have dark roots is Dickie Dawson?
FANNIE: I'd like to say something. If Brett wasn't such a good friend, I'd go right up there and snatch that wig right off her head.

BRETT: Did you see Fannie's new hairdo? She's got Little Orphan Annie hair now!
FANNIE: As you know, I went to the doctor with Brett a few days ago and they brought out the report on her liver, and when I looked at it, my hair went straight out like this.

GENE: *The Big Bad Wolf said, "I just came from a house where this old lady had the biggest BLANKS I ever saw."*
CONTESTANT: *Boobs.*
GENE: *Speaking of "bazooms"… Fannie, would you show us yours?*

GENE: *Chiquita the flamingo dancer said "I forgot my castanets, so at tonight's performance, I'll be banging my BLANKS together.*
BRETT: *I said she knocked her "Knockers" together.*
GENE: *I guess I have too logical a mind for you people. That's the last answer in the world that I'd give. (Shakes his torso) You could do that all day and you wouldn't make a sound! I wouldn't anyway.*
FANNIE: *You wouldn't make a sound but you'd get a lot of bookings.*
CHARLES: *I said "boobs."*
FANNIE: *I take this game very seriously, I really do. And I was thinking in terms of "If I was Chiquita, what would I do?" Now logically, I would take off my earrings. Listen carefully. (She puts her earrings on her fingertips and taps them together several times.) I said "earrings."*
CHARLES: *That's great, but now try it our way.*

Marcia Wallace was bitten by the acting bug as a teenager and moved to New York City the day that she graduated from college. She worked as a substitute English teacher throughout The Bronx before forming an improvisational troupe with some friends. She caught the eye of Merv Griffin, who featured her as a guest on his talk show seventy-five times before moving production from New York to Los Angeles and convincing Wallace to make the same move. Once there, she was cast as Carol the receptionist on *The Bob Newhart Show*—a role that was created specifically for her. Despite rarely matching (the audience gave her a standing ovation the first time that she actually did so), she had the right attitude about doing the show, consistently laid back and sardonic.

GENE: Hello, Marcia. Try to stay calm, cool, and collected.
MARCIA: It was between this show and Celebrity Bowling, *and I'm starting to think I made the wrong decision.*
MARCIA: I figured this show out. The perfect answer is always either "boobs" or "Howard Cosell."

"HHHHA!" Marcia Wallace enjoyed watching the game as much as playing it. (Fred Wostbrock Collection)

Betty White, wife of *Password* host Allen Ludden, actress, and avowed animal lover, came to the show with the thickest resume of any panelist. She had been a co-star on multiple radio shows in the 1940s before signing in 1949 to co-host a live daily variety show, *Hollywood on Television*. She followed that with two sitcoms, *Life with Elizabeth* and *A Date with the Angels*. From there, numerous bit parts and commercials followed. In 1973, her career was abruptly revitalized when she was cast as Sue Ann Nivens, the Happy Homemaker, on *The Mary Tyler Moore Show*. And on *Match Game*, she was a utility player, acting as a foil to the rest of the panel or scoring with her own lines.

GENE: *Fred said, "I've had it with my wife! She doesn't believe in sex after BLANK."*
CONTESTANT: *"Marriage."*
BETTY: *On-the-job training and all that... Well, being married to Allen Ludden, a lot of things came to mind. After breakfast, after hours, after Freshman year...*
BRETT: *I want to let Betty White know that before I came to the studio today, I killed seven flies.*
BETTY: *She talked them to death.*

Betty White sat on the panel, but not next to husband Allen Ludden. Betty was such a strong panelist that the show simply wouldn't allow her to sit anywhere but the sixth seat. Even some dedicated viewers may have picked up on the fact that there was a strategy to the way that the panelists were seated. (Mike Klauss Collection)

But you would rarely see any of the regulars on the same panel. The show would never book, for example, Betty White and Fannie Flagg together on the panel during a given week. Casting the panel, again, was like casting a play, and the show would never book multiple panelists who brought the same strengths to the show.

Amazingly, there was even a science to the way the guests were seated on the stage. Gene canvassed the panel for their answers from the top tier, left to right, and then the bottom tier, left to right. The first seat on the top tier was always occupied by a "leading man," somebody like Ed Asner or Leslie Nielsen, who had been booked primarily for star power. Since their star power was more valued than game-playing ability, this star sat first on the panel because if they gave a poor answer, there were five other stars to talk to next, and a bad answer could be forgotten easily.

Next on the panel were Brett Somers and Charles Nelson Reilly. For each question, they could bring the audience back around if the leading man on the panel was a dud. And they were seated side by side because as funny as each of them was, they were infinitely funnier when they were in close proximity. Brett complained to Gene and the audience about how Charles almost never wore socks. Charles would complain about how Brett took too long to write her answers, and that her answers were in bad taste, they were badly spelled, or they were just plain bad answers.

The first seat of the bottom tier was rather dismissively referred to as "the dummy seat." This was another seat usually reserved for a guest star, always female, usually from a current prime-time series, and more often than not, she brought sex appeal to the show. Stars like Joan Collins and Suzanne Somers sat here, although a handful of guests like Elaine Joyce—a bubbly blonde who turned out to be deceptively bright—wound up becoming semi-regulars when they proved surprisingly strong in the role.

As on the top tier, the guest player had somebody to "save" her if she proved to be a subpar player. Richard Dawson was always in the next seat, quick with a quip and a strong answer. In the sixth position was one of the semi-regular women. It was the toughest spot on the panel because the game, more often than not, would be decided by that panelist's answer, so it was important to have someone who not only played the game well, but somebody who was liked enough by the audience that they could "forgive" her when the inevitable happened and she cost a contestant the game by failing to match.

Joan Collins, in the "dummy seat" for *Match Game*. (Fred Wostbrock Collection)

Robert Sherman says, "Goodson-Todman never had a fully-stocked regular panel for *Match Game*, which was actually a big departure from the way they had traditionally done panel games. *To Tell the Truth* and *I've Got a Secret*, for years, had the same group of people on every episode. *What's My Line?* was the same thing. The same people week after week, and even if it was a guest panelist, it was somebody who had been on the show before. You almost never saw 'a new person' on *What's My Line?* Oh, sure, once in a while, somebody would take a vacation and there would be a guest, but by and large, when you watched a Goodson-Todman panel show, it was the same people every single time.

"For *Match Game*, on the other hand, we always had our three regulars, the sixth seat was a semi-regular, but Seat #1 and Seat #4 were always guests, and honestly, it worked best that way. There was a certain magic to that because it kept the show fresh and it kept the game from getting repetitive. Imagine if we had a panel of six regulars. If we did that, and Gene reads a question about Tarzan… well, with six regular panelists, everybody has heard a Tarzan question before, so all six of them write 'loincloth' and there's no surprise. Always having guests meant always having a fresh set of perspectives and a sense that you were seeing something new."

When taping day rolled around, contestant coordinator Diane Janaver gathered all of the contestants to be used during that day's episodes and gave them a briefing far different than the contestant coordinators for other game shows had to do.

In 2006, she told GSN, "I had to stand up there and say, 'Here are all the words that you can't say on the show... Please do not say 'urinate.' The *Match Game* word is 'tinkle.' If you can't bring yourself to say that, say 'wet.' Those are your two alternatives for 'urinate.' Please do not say 'fornicate.' We say 'make love.' Please do not say 'lay' or 'laying' when talking about making love. If you're talking about hens, then you can say 'laying.' No mention of genitals. Even if you think you have the cutest euphemism in the world, do not use it. And remember, there are questions where that's going to come to mind. The answers are 'nose,' 'toes,' and 'ears.'"

With the contestants, Gene, and the celebrities all assembled, the CBS page staff let the audience into Studio 33 of the Television City complex. The taping didn't start immediately. There was one more piece of business.

Music, often Motown or disco, would start blaring over the audio system, and announcer Johnny Olson would boogie his way down the aisles, dancing with some audience members, kissing a few others, and whipping everyone into a frenzy. Johnny would whip out a stack of $1 bills, read his own fill-in-the-blanks ("I knew it was TV star Jimmy Dean when I saw the size of his BLANK") and then pay out the dollar bills to audience members who matched each other. He'd give silly instructions ("Don't burp, and fix your zipper"). He'd have conversations with some other audience members ("Are you married?... Well, don't worry, your ship will come in. Of course if your ship doesn't come, your pier might collapse").

Robert Sherman says, "Johnny worked amazingly well for the show. Our show really was a different animal in the world of game shows, but he got the audience in the right spirit. They laughed at everything because they wanted to laugh. Johnny just got them so loose and they were in such a good mood that they were up for anything. And Johnny kept them motivated. He made them feel like friends, he made them feel like they were at a party. The audience gave such great reactions to everything, and Johnny helped make that happen."

> *Johnny Olson was a dear man, and absolutely suited to what he was doing. He could warm up an audience better than anybody. And one of the reasons he was so good at what he did was because he was a tenor. Somebody with a deep bass voice can't stimulate an audience the way he did. But with the pitch that his voice had, when he yelled "Come on down!" for* The Price is Right, *it just went right through you.*

With the audience ready to laugh and cheer their heads off, the panelists made their way onstage, Johnny went to his spot at the announcer's booth, and the taping started. During the taping, Johnny would draw out stronger audience reactions by pantomiming reactions to the questions. If Gene read a risqué question, Johnny would feign shock and stare at the audience with mouth agape. If the question was just silly, he'd slap his knee hard. He'd thrust and swivel his hips and wave his fingers as he pointed at the audience.

This might seem like a lot of effort for a silly daytime game show, but the results justified the effort. *Match Game '74* was the highest-rated daytime TV series… ever. It averaged a 15 rating each day (meaning about 15% of all homes with televisions were watching *Match Game '74* each day; considering the percentage of the population that was still at work at 3:30 p.m. each day, that's an astronomical figure). Today, that 15 rating still stands as the record, the gold standard for a daytime TV show's rating. Commercial breaks for *Match Game '74* became a gold mine for CBS, which was charging $18,000 per minute for commercials during the show. (For perspective, a CBS soap opera, *As the World Turns*, was charging $20,000 per minute, which at the time was a record for daytime TV advertising.)

CBS was so happy with the show that it canceled *The Secret Storm*, the fading soap opera that followed *Match Game '74* on the daytime lineup, and gave the slot to Goodson-Todman. The network, better late than never, picked up the *Celebrity Match Mates* pilot that Gene had taped the previous year. The show was retitled *Tattletales*, and Gene was replaced by Bert Convy.

In the original form of *Tattletales*, Bert would read a category and the husbands would ring in to tell a story from married life that fit that category. Bert would then tell the wives the category and announce a key word from the story. If the correct wife rang in, the couple won $100. Halfway through the show, the husbands and wives switched roles. The high-scoring couple at the end of the day received an additional $1,000. Later, the game was changed to one similar to *The Newlywed Game*, with the couples trying to match answers to hypothetical situations and questions about their home lives. The studio audience was divided into three colored sections, each one a designated "rooting section" for each couple. All of the money won by each couple was divided among the audience members in their rooting section.

Many of the same stars that appeared on *Match Game '74* also made their way over to *Tattletales*. Bobby Van & Elaine Joyce appeared frequently. Betty White brought along Allen Ludden. Patti Deutsch was joined by her husband, comedy writer Donald Ross. Richard Dawson played with his girlfriend, Jody Donovan.

And even though he was understandably replaced as host, Gene popped in quite frequently, too. Goodson-Todman became very fond of having Convy and his then-wife appear on the show as players while Gene or another emcee served as a guest host. And every now and then, the lovely Helen would join Gene for his bi-weekly commute, and they'd stay an extra day for a *Tattletales* taping. Although Helen started off as a model, she largely faded from the spotlight after marrying Gene. Appearing on *Tattletales* revealed to the viewing audience what a truly perfect couple the Rayburns were for each other.

BERT: You're in the middle of making love when the room begins to shake. It's an earthquake. Do you think you'd stop or do you keep going?

HELEN RAYBURN: Sure as heck aren't gonna stop, we need all the help we can get.

The Match Makers, On Stage and Off

BERT: Ladies, you're introduced to a Supreme Court justice at a party. You notice that his fly is open. Would you tell him about it?

HELEN: I would go up to him and I would say, "Your honor, your court is open, and your jury is out."

BERT: A world-famous sculptor offers to pay Gene to pose for a statue. The catch is, it would be a nude statue. Would Gene pose for it?

HELEN: Are you kidding? Not only would he do it, he'd demand that the statue had to be 400 feet tall.

Match Game '74 and everybody involved in it eased into a comfort zone. The show aired new episodes all year, no reruns; that was the standard at the time for daytime TV. And as they cranked out episode after episode, the show developed its own language, its own inside jokes, comforting and entertaining rituals that connected with the viewers who tuned in every day. Richard Dawson would insult other panelists by calling them "Huckleberry Dillinger" or doing a Paul Lynde impression as he called them "Hamburger." Brett would demand compliments for the wig she was wearing that day and make a formal announcement if Charles Nelson Reilly wasn't wearing socks again.

Gene had his own habits and quirks, too. When welcoming a female panelist who had never done the show before, he would always lead off the week by whipping out some breath spray, giving himself spritz, taking her into his arms, and planting a big sloppy kiss on her. He demystified the show's elaborate set; when it was time for the sliding placards on the Audience Match board to magically whip away and reveal the winning answers, Gene would yell "Slide it, Earl!" to the stagehand crouching inside the board. If all six panelists managed to write six different answers, he would declare it a "gallimaufry." Gene did a Bela Lugosi impression for all of the questions that involved Count Dracula, and for no particular reason, he would lead off the impression by saying the non-sequiter word "antipasto." For questions involving The Godfather, Gene would sometimes cram a wad of tissues into his mouth to imitate Marlon

Brando's garbled delivery. Gene chewed the scenery harder than ever for "Old Man Periwinkle" questions. He did the distinctive stoop and voice that he had always done, but, free to move around the set on the CBS version, he added a ridiculous walk, shuffling his feet with tiny steps.

Gene briefs the panelists on the latest antics of Old Man Periwinkle. (Fred Wostbrock Collection)

The Match Makers, On Stage and Off

The zaniness was contagious, and even the show's crew looked for ways to squeeze out extra comedy. When Brett Somers began complaining about how annoying the sound of the buzzer was, the sound effects man placated her by signaling her non-matching answers with a ridiculous variety of sounds, like a Bronx cheer, a car horn, a cuckoo bird, or a mooing cow.

Director Marc Breslow took a very standard, staid element of every game show—the ticket plugs—and found a way to give *Match Game '74* some of the most memorable in the business. A ticket plug was a rather unremarkable announcement by Johnny Olson ("If you're going to be in the Los Angeles area and you'd like to join us for a taping, send us your request along with a self-addressed, stamped envelope to **Tickets, *Match Game '74*, CBS Television City, 7800 Beverly Boulevard, Los Angeles, California, 9-double-oh-36**") with the address superimposed on the screen, usually on a plain shot of the set or an extreme close-up of a set piece.

Under Marc Breslow's watch, the ticket plug sometimes got some of the biggest laughs of the show. Breslow used some very elaborate camera tricks to make extremely memorable bits. He fixed one camera on Richard Dawson, duplicated the shot five times, and superimposed the duplicates on a wide shot of the panel, making it appear that every panelist was Richard Dawson. He placed panelists' heads on the bodies of more buxom contestants, who would cheerfully oblige by striking a pose while the panelists did a series of seductive faces. With two very carefully arranged camera shots, McLean Stevenson appeared to be holding the severed head of a contestant. The beautiful woman sitting in the fourth seat on the panel would find herself smiling through a bushy moustache because a man's mouth had been placed over her jawline.

The show was a hit, and everyone involved had found their groove. And for Goodson-Todman at that point, the next move was undeniable. A daytime slot couldn't contain *Match Game*. It was time for the show to see a new audience.

(Fred Wostbrock Collection)

Chapter Twelve
Match Game After Dark

One thing that must be said to Gene's credit was that even as host of the hit show on daytime TV, his mind was always on ways to improve his performance as host. And going into 1975, he stumbled upon an unexpected, seemingly odd key to what would help him do a better job hosting the show. Gene decided that he needed to get a new microphone.

Gene started the series wearing a lavalier microphone before switching to a bulky handheld microphone. He later switched to a Sony ECM-51, a very distinctive-looking pencil-thin microphone that was widely used for TV game shows in the 1970s. TV viewers would instantly recognize it as the same model of microphone that Bob Barker used for more than three decades of *The Price is Right*.

One day, Gene noticed a feature of the microphone that he had never noticed before. It telescoped. Pulling on the tip of it would cause it to expand, like the antenna on a radio. And Gene immediately discovered how much freer he felt when he kept that microphone extended. Normally, Gene had to keep his arm elevated and his fist close to his chest to talk into the microphone. Gene found that with the microphone extended, he could move his arms around as needed and still hold onto it, which meant he could put more of his body into his characters or the spontaneous shtick that broke out on the show. He could even use the microphone itself for comedy. He held it sideways against his mouth and pretended to play the flute. When a panelist teased him, he would say "Turn to dirt!" in a feminine voice and wave it like a magic wand. When a question mentioned the Olympics, Gene pretended it was a javelin and aimed it at the audience. He'd wave it around like a sword. Gene had a mind for theatrics, and the long microphone allowed him to add more to his performance. In time, he went to the technicians at CBS and asked for a custom microphone just for his use; a special model based on the design of the ECM-51, but without the telescoping function. Gene's microphone was simply made to be that long.

Gene's trademark microphone. (Fred Wostbrock Collection)

Match Game After Dark

It's never enough for a hit show to be a hit show. When enough eyes are drawn to a television series, writers step forward to ask the same question: "Why?" And plenty of folks were willing to step forward to elaborate on the enormous success of *Match Game '75*. A reporter named Donald Davidson was particularly intrepid about rounding up interviewees and trying to zero in on the secrets to the show's appeal.

Veteran host Bill Cullen, who, like Gene, travelled from the east coast a few times to appear as a guest panelist for *Match Game*, felt that, weak as the game itself may have been, it deserved some of the credit. He explained to Davidson, "Certainly, it is more of a comedy show than any other game show on the air… Game shows take an amount of participation by the viewing audience. They need to make a good stab at the game to stick with it. *The Match Game* is simply a vehicle to derive from."

In other words, yes, the comedy was a major attraction, but viewers also liked conjuring up their own answers and seeing how they would have done if they were actually in the studio trying to earn a shot at the big money. Gene had his own opinion of what made the show work.

> *…[T]he key element is the spontaneity. Our panelists need what I call a 'fey' sense of humor to be panelists, because nothing is written for them, unlike some shows that are striving for comedy.*

Dick DeBartolo maintained that the success came from the fact that it was the only game show on TV that viewers could watch without feeling dumb because a question stumped them. What on *Match Game '75* could stump any viewer?

"The attraction of *The Match Game* is that people are not bolted into hard-set answers," DeBartolo said to Davidson. "I think people want to enjoy themselves. I think people want to laugh. It is a simple game that almost anyone can relate to… The fact is that you can play along and be silly. Even if people won't admit that they're being silly, I'll admit it and I like it… I've always thought that *The Match Game* is the *MAD* of game shows… We've made it so that the answers themselves elicit comedy."

The *MAD Magazine* of game shows. Sitting on the panel this week: Dwayne Hickman, Brett Somers, Gary Burghoff, Carol Lawrence, Richard Dawson, Marcia Wallace. (Fred Wostbrock Collection)

Ira Skutch agreed. "This is the type of game the audience enjoys and wants to play along with... and that is a very strong element in any game show: the participation of the home audience. We start with that. Then we add in this party atmosphere and the comedy element that grew out of it... *The Match Game* is unique for its time, because it brings together a lot of things."

Brett Somers weighed in with her thoughts, too. "The success of this show above all the competition is its spontaneity. Out of all the others, this is the least predictable."

Skutch added, "The *Match Game* celebrities are a group of people who all get along very well together and enjoy what they're doing, and it comes through on the tube. People can sense it."

Somers agreed. "People can look at us on the screen and think to themselves, 'Are those people having a good time?' The answer is 'yes.'"

Kay Cole hadn't seen Gene since they appeared on the Broadway stage together for *Bye Bye Birdie*. But she still enjoyed looking in on Gene and his friends during the 1970s. "I loved *Match Game*. There was something about that show and other game shows of the era. They all had a sense of spontaneity. These people carried on a conversation together, and they joked around and had a good time together, but there was an audience looking in on them. Being a part of that audience made you feel like you were in on something special. They had a great rapport and they were giggling and enjoying themselves, and they made you feel like you were a part of it."

New York Times writer Virginia Heffernan wrote a 2006 piece remembering her childhood fandom. "I was 7: it came on after school, was broken up by ads for bicentennial memorabilia, and its mysteries — 'John always put butter on his BLANK' — stayed with me long after my parents had appeared with cocktails as the face of CBS dissolved from Gene Rayburn to Walter Cronkite. The snickering, lascivious ways the regulars interacted — always hinting that the others were more depraved or druggy than they admitted — was more than a little scary to a kid. It was certainly a direct counterpoint to the after-school parables elsewhere on television."

Singer-songwriter Paul Williams, who was still a few years away from appearing on the panel himself, referred to *Match Game* as "the Algonquin Roundtable of the air," invoking the revered New York City high society group that met for lunch at the Algonquin Hotel every day throughout the 1920s, swapping jokes and observations that got printed in newspaper columns around the country.

Orson Bean remembers, "For better or for worse, all of us who appeared as panelists on *Match Game* contributed to the coarsening of America. In the 1950s, I did shows where everything was censored. I remember I wrote a joke for a show in the fifties. 'My great great grandfather owned a bar in Harvard Square during the American Revolution. He poured The Shot Heard 'Round the World.' Couldn't say it; I wasn't allowed to reference liquor.

"I had another joke where I'd be reading the paper and I'd say 'The gossip columnist is asking if Debbie will say yes to Eddie Fisher. I guess that depends on what the question is.' They wouldn't let me say that! They said it was too racy.

"And then you look at television decades later, when David Letterman is saying that summer is so hot in New York City that the squirrels in Central Park are putting ice on their nuts. How did we get from the uptight censorship of the 1950s to jokes like that being permitted on television? I honestly think *Match Game* helped a little bit. Because we began to break that down very slowly. There were suggestive words in the questions, and we very delicately would handle it by writing answers like 'tinkle' and 'doo-doo,' and we just kept pushing and pushing it. I'm not sure television is better for it, but at the time, we had a lot of fun playing the game."

Dick Gautier adds, "We behaved ourselves. Most of us kept it as tasteful as possible and the vast majority of the panel already worked in television, so we knew what you could get away with and we managed to avoid crossing the line most of the time. In my entire career, I got censored on a game show exactly once, and it wasn't *Match Game*, believe it or not. I got censored on *Tattletales*. I was appearing with my then-wife, Barbara Stuart, and my friend Bert Convy asked the question to the husbands. The question was 'Which of these TV wives does your wife's personality resemble most closely: Edith Bunker or Maude Findlay?' And I answered 'Well, most of the time, she's Edith Bunker, but once a month, she's Maude Findlay.' They edited that! Can you believe that?"

Brett Somers did acknowledge that being a *Match Game* panelist came with a mild emotional toll. She admitted that she felt sad for any contestant who didn't win the big payday in the Super Match. She got over it fairly quickly if the contestant was in her age range, but she said she felt particularly terrible whenever a very young contestant missed out on the cash. She said she remembered what her life was like when she was in her late teens and early twenties, and she knew how much five thousand dollars would have meant to her in those days.

Bob Noah was still working at Heatter-Quigley Productions when he spoke to Donald Davidson. Heatter-Quigley was still delivering big ratings for NBC with its own hit comedy game, *The Hollywood Squares*, but Noah wasn't shy about addressing the contrasts between the two games.

The name might be *Game*, but the appeal was in Gene's chit-chat with the stars. On the panel: Orson Bean, Brett Somers, Charles Nelson Reilly, Lynda Day George, Richard Dawson, Patti Deutsch. (Fred Wostbrock Collection)

Noah said, "A party is exactly what I'd call [*Match Game '75*]. The program is amusing and puts a smile on your face, and it's all spontaneous… You simply have a feeling of people having a really good time. The important thing in *The Match Game* is the interaction. You almost can't get that on *Hollywood Squares*."

This was true. Although *The Hollywood Squares* was played for laughs, it was a tightly run show. That game saw host Peter Marshall asking trivia questions to nine celebrities seated in a giant tic-tac-toe grid. The star would usually fire off a joke (the show's official term was "a zinger") before taking a legitimate crack at the answer, and the contestants earned the squares by correctly agreeing or disagreeing with the star's answer. As funny as the show was, a sense of spontaneity was virtually non-existent. In the early weeks of the series, way back in 1966, the stars did improvise and clown around, but it didn't work as well for that particular show. Heatter himself noted that a single episode of *Squares* "seemed endless" when the stars had free reign.

After those shaky early weeks, the show ran under much stricter guidelines. The "zingers" were fully scripted by a team of writers, and Heatter instituted a policy that each episode had to have a minimum of twenty-two questions, even if it required heavy editing afterward to meet that guideline. Though the finished product played much better this way, it serves to illustrate the key differences between the two shows: For *Squares*, the humor was largely scripted and came almost entirely from questions and answers. For *Match Game*, the humor was spontaneous, and the questions and answers were the jumping-off point, not the principal source.

Bob Noah observed one drawback about the *Match Game* way of doing things, though. "They are funny without being quotable... You would never hear of anyone calling up a neighbor and saying 'My God, did you hear what was said on *The Match Game* today?'"

That was a valid point. Because *The Hollywood Squares* was tightly written and tightly run, and because each question and zinger were prepared to be contained laughs, it was the more quotable show. A *Hollywood Squares* record was released, featuring forty-five minutes of rapid-fire questions and zingers taken from the show. A series of books was published too, printing Peter Marshall's questions and the stars' wacky reactions.

On the other hand, you couldn't do that with *Match Game*. Gene might read a question that got a laugh, grow impatient with Brett for taking too long, and reprimand her. Brett might respond by making fun of something Gene said earlier in the show, which would lead to Charles taunting Brett. Brett would chastise Charles for not wearing socks as Gene went to the contestant for an answer. The contestant would give a bad answer, and Richard would make a joke playing off that. It was funny to watch, but that kind of humor required so much context and so much personality that it didn't always work if you tried to tell your friend what was so funny about *Match Game*.

Although comparisons flowed when discussing the two shows, *Match Game* and *Hollywood Squares*, star-studded games from rival producers on opposing networks, coexisted quite peacefully.

Squares host Peter Marshall says, "We were happy for the success they were having. We didn't have any kind of rivalry. You know, in show business, there are people who root for the failure of others, and that's

Gene takes questions from the audience during a commercial break, while announcer Johnny Olson looks on. (Fred Wostbrock Collection)

a dumb mindset to have. For example, on Broadway, I know for a fact, there are actors who audition for a role in a show, and when they don't get the role, they root for the show to fail. That's stupid. If the show is successful on Broadway, that leads to regional productions and a national touring company, which means you get about a dozen new opportunities for work because that show was a success.

"Well, it was the same thing for our shows. *Match Game* was #1. But maybe there were viewers out there that said 'Wow, I like this celebrity game show, maybe I'll watch this other celebrity game show that I've never looked at.' And then *Hollywood Squares* gets a few new viewers who had never looked in before. And maybe a local station manager is looking at *Match Game*'s ratings and says 'Well, I can't get my hands on that, but there's this other celebrity comedy game called *Hollywood Squares* that offers two episodes a week for nighttime syndication. I could buy that show.' And so we pick up a new station and that's more viewers for us. See what I mean? If *Match Game* did well, we were completely happy for them. And by the same token, I'm sure that our success created opportunities for them."

The comparisons were more for the sake of reporters who brought it up whenever they were doing a story about game shows. Both shows concentrated on doing their own thing. *The Hollywood Squares* did what worked for *The Hollywood Squares* and didn't really try to duplicate the other show. Meanwhile, *Match Game* did what was best for *Match Game*.

Peter Marshall smiles and explains, "The only things that *Match Game* and *Hollywood Squares* had in common is that they were both well-produced, they were both clever, and they both had pretty good MCs. And they were both pretty good little games. *Match Game*, I thought, was a pretty intriguing premise. Here's this sentence with a blank, and you have to fill in the blank with something that's clever, but you also have to be clever in the same way that these celebrities are trying to be clever. And the object of the game is to be on the same wavelength as these people."

The cordial attitude of Heatter-Quigley wasn't completely shared by the competition, though. Orson Bean remembers, "Mark Goodson made it known that he didn't want the celebrities who did his shows frequently to do *Hollywood Squares*, and he didn't want *Hollywood Squares* celebrities to do *Match Game*. Obviously, you wouldn't see the regular panelists on the other show because they had contracts, but for example, people like Vincent Price never did *Match Game* because Vincent did *Hollywood Squares* so much, and Goodson didn't want a *Hollywood Squares* guy doing his game show. And Mark liked to use his favorite celebrities for multiple shows, so most of us adhered to that. I never appeared on *Hollywood Squares*, even though I really wanted to. I thought Paul Lynde was one of the funniest men who ever lived. Peter Marshall asked him 'Paul, what is a pullet?' And Paul smiled and said 'A little show of affection.' I knew that they wrote the line for Paul but he delivered it so well. I loved that."

Robert Sherman gives his input on the success of *Match Game*. "For its time, it was a very interesting combination of approaches to humor. It combined sophisticated humor, like wordplay and jokes about public figures, with very broad, naughty, slapstick humor. We had questions that teased references to body parts, bodily functions, and sexual acts. *Saturday Night Live* wasn't on the air yet. Sonny and Cher had just started doing slightly edgier jokes about that kind of stuff. And it was just amazing at that time in TV history to see a show that aired at 3:30 in the afternoon and see the kind of humor that, if it was ever done on television at all, was usually only done on late night TV."

And there was one other element that many people were quick to point out when discussing the success of the show: The man who had put so much of himself into each program that he seemed almost to become one with the program.

Bill Cullen said that *Match Game* wouldn't be the same without Gene. Millions of viewers would agree. (Fred Wostbrock Collection)

Bill Cullen said, "I think Gene Rayburn is a sensational emcee… I think Gene is very, very important to *Match Game*. That show would not be the same if Gene left it. Now none of the shows that any of us do would be the same if any of us left them, but Gene's would be more different. That show would be a completely different-type show without Gene."

Robert Sherman remembers, "Gene was great at taking the written material he was handed and making it as good as possible with his delivery. And he was great at being able to use anything that happened. With another emcee, we might have to stop tape with a technical problem.

But if we were taping *Match Game* and a scoreboard broke down, or a sound effect went wrong, or if a cameraman fell over, Gene could keep going, and more often than not, he would draw attention to it and make a moment out of it. He would show the audience what was broken, or he would sort of mug at the camera when the sound did something wrong. It was fun to watch and it took away the need to stop tape and edit the show. We didn't want to get rid of mistakes because Gene could make the mistakes the best part of the day."

Gene stayed calm even when the audience was part of what was going wrong. Gene made his way onstage and the audience let out an uncharacteristic roar. Gene looked offstage and realized there was a commotion. An audience member was excitedly running onstage for an autograph and had to be restrained by Johnny Olson. With tape rolling, Gene let out a laugh, grabbed a card from panelist Gary Burghoff, and scribbled an autograph for her. The entire incident made it on the air.

Chris Clementson, a research staffer who worked for several Goodson-Todman games in the 1970s, adds, "The funny thing about the CBS version of *Match Game* is that if you were to peel away the suggestive questions, the comedy and the panel's antics, it was a very staid, tame show. Read a question, the panel writes, get the contestant's response, poll the panel, repeat. The questions and the panelists brought levity to the proceedings. Gene's job was to keep it all on track. He had to move the game along while getting into the festive spirit and at the same time maintain order when the celebrities got unruly. He was extraordinarily adept at doing these things. Some people think the humor originated with Gene the way it did with Groucho Marx on *You Bet Your Life*... but Gene largely played off the antics of the panel and the material. Gene was a seasoned broadcaster whose experience stood him in good stead on *Match Game*."

Orson Bean remembers, "I loved Gene. He could be funny on his own, but he would let you be funny too, and he freely laughed when you got in a good line. I remember once, I was booked on the show in an unusual way. I was a standby panelist. Gary Burghoff was scheduled, but his wife was a full nine months pregnant and she was apt to go into labor any minute. So they booked Gary Burghoff, but they called me too, and they had me sit backstage just in case Gary's wife went into labor, and he could leave the stage immediately and I could run out, Gene could introduce me, and I would take over for the rest of the taping. Well, they ended up not needing me. She didn't go into labor that day, but since I had shown up, Gene brought me out to take a bow. So I came out and Gene says 'What are you doing here, Orson?' And I said, 'I'm standing by because Gary's wife is pregnant and they're expecting the baby any minute, and they're asking me to stand by. And I agreed to do that because I felt it was only right, inasmuch as I had performed the same function for Gary at the conception.'

"And I loved the way Gene reacted to the line. He gave me a bit of a slap on the shoulder and did a very broad 'Get outta here!' He yelled it and he waved his arms while he was yelling at me. And that was pure Gene to do it that way, but the great thing was, it gave the joke I had made more punch. It seemed even funnier because of the way Gene reacted to it. He didn't interrupt, he didn't try to top the joke, he let me deliver the line and then reacted like that. He was Bud Abbott to my Lou Costello."

Instead of walking onstage after Johnny Olson's intro, Gene stayed right where he was and read the newspaper while the audience applauded. Why not? (Fred Wostbrock Collection)

The Matchless Gene Rayburn

Fred Wostbrock elaborates, "Gene took risks. If he was a movie star, he'd be Steve McQueen. He'd walk through the audience; not in the aisles between the sections of seating, but literally through the audience. He'd climb over them and step on the chairs. He did barrel rolls down the stairs when he made his entrance, he broke through the walls. Gene was wild, and full of energy, and it made him different from all of the other game show hosts. That's not a knock on other game show hosts; Bob Eubanks and Monty Hall and Tom Kennedy and Jack Narz were all just great, but Gene was such a free spirit, and he would act on total whims and do all of these silly things, and it made him fun to see just because you knew Gene would do things that another game show host would never do."

Gene would sometimes pry the doors open or pull the ropes himself during his introduction. Just for the BLANK of it.
(Fred Wostbrock Collection)

Match Game After Dark

Gene and *Match Game '75* were on top of the world, but in 1975, being the number-one show on daytime TV wasn't the ceiling for success. There was still one more step that the show could take.

Television's Number One daytime hit is now available for prime access! Gene Rayburn heads a star-studded cast in this greatest comedy game show of all! Goodson-Todman's Match Game '75. –Ad in *Broadcasting* Magazine

Even merely announcing that they wanted to do a prime-time show had been the end of a long battle that Goodson-Todman had been waging with CBS. Ever since the FCC instituted prime-access time, the major broadcast networks had written up all of their contracts with daytime programs to include the same clause. Any show that wanted to syndicate episodes for prime-time slots had to get permission from the network.

Virtually from the moment that *Match Game '73* had reached number one in daytime, Goodson-Todman wanted to launch a prime-time version, but CBS emphatically said no, fearful that overexposure would kill the daytime show. CBS had also denied permission for Heatter-Quigley to produce a prime-time version of their CBS game, *Gambit*, for the same reason. Meanwhile, over at ABC, Monty Hall was fighting a strange battle with his network bosses. The network had no problem allowing Hall to syndicate *Let's Make a Deal* for prime access time, but for some reason, it repeatedly denied permission for him to syndicate the other game he created and produced for ABC, *Split Second*.

It wasn't a completely unfounded concern. Every time the argument came up between a network and a production company, the network pointed to the same precedent: *The Hollywood Squares*. NBC's game was still unmistakably a hit series, and a force to be reckoned with for any show that opposed it, but the network number crunchers all noted that when *Squares* introduced a prime access time series, the daytime version's numbers were dented.

The first ad ran in mid-February, but Goodson-Todman had already gone to work, pitching the show to stations. It wasn't a hard sell. Before the ad had even ran, the new prime time version already had commitments from stations in New York, Los Angeles, Chicago, San Francisco, Detroit, Philadelphia, St. Louis, Miami, Baltimore, Cincinnati, Albany, and Portland, Oregon. By May 9, thirty-nine stations had signed up. By the summer time, that number had doubled to seventy-eight stations.

It appeared that local stations had been waiting for a nighttime *Match Game* for as long as Goodson-Todman.

Dick DeBartolo remembers, "There was a lot of excitement in the office because we went into it knowing that it would be a hit. We were at our peak, so we knew the audience we already had would want to see an extra episode every week. And since it was prime time, we had a chance to reach a new audience and we knew we would reach them because we automatically had tremendous word-of-mouth advertising. People who worked during the day would be curious to tune in and see this show that their wives and kids loved."

Gene and the panel would light up the night with a new prime time version, *Match Game PM*. (Fred Wostbrock Collection)

Because the show was syndicated, it couldn't have any continuity with the daytime version. In those days, syndicated shows were sent to local stations through the mail in a process called bicycling. A videotape of an episode would come with a checklist of local stations' mailing addresses. After a station aired the episode, it would mail the tape to the next station on the checklist. Because of this, the nighttime show couldn't feature champions from the daytime version, and games couldn't straddle. Instead, each week's episode had two new contestants. The game would be fundamentally the same, except that the Super Match would involve two Audience Matches instead of one, which meant that the Head-to-Head Match could be worth as much as $10,000.

It also necessitated a minor change to the title. Since mailing a tape from station to station was obviously a slow process, it wasn't a smart idea to put a year in the name of the show. An episode mailed out in 1975 wouldn't necessarily air on every station during 1975. Accordingly, the prime-time show would be called *Match Game PM*.

The nighttime show started taping in July 1975, with a large group of celebrities assembled to tape twelve episodes over the course of a few days. The show quickly switched to a more practical method of taping; for each taping held for the CBS daytime version, a sixth episode was taped with the same panel.

Taping six episodes instead of five led the staff to adjust the way the show was taped each day. Even though they had always taped five episodes in a single day, asking an audience to sit through five episodes might have been asking a bit much, so they taped three episodes with one audience and two episodes with another. With the advent of *Match Game PM* and a six-episode taping day, they switched to three audiences per day, watching two shows apiece.

The nighttime version had other logistical issues to work out. Nearly every panelist who appeared on the show was a member of AFTRA, which had an established minimum fee for performers appearing on television shows. AFTRA also had different standards for daytime and nighttime programs, so panelists had to be paid more for nighttime episodes. Gene, as host, commanded a bigger payday too. Similarly, the show's technical crew included many workers who were members of numerous unions and likewise required higher pay for working on shows that aired at night. All totaled, a single episode of *Match Game PM* was about as expensive as three episodes of the daytime show.

There was one other issue that had to be worked out. The daytime version had a CBS censor present for every taping, but that wasn't sufficient for the nighttime show. It was syndicated and it would be airing across the country on some CBS stations, some ABC stations, and some NBC stations. Because of this, *Match Game PM* was required to have three censors present, one on behalf of each network.

Robert Sherman elaborates, "The CBS censor was still the one who reviewed the questions for each taping. By 1975, though, we had been on the air for two years, so by that point we had 'figured out' the censor. We had a good feel for what we could get away with and what got rejected so almost nothing got rejected anymore in regards to written material.

"As far as the tapings go, we were on the air at 7:30 p.m., and you know, the average person's reaction was 'You must have really cut loose because it's nighttime.' It was actually completely the opposite. At the time, standards were tighter for nighttime shows than daytime shows. 7:30 p.m. to 9:00 p.m. was deemed 'family time,' and the networks wanted to make sure that the programs that aired in that time frame was very safe for viewing, so we actually had to have a little restraint, which could be a challenge for the panelists because it was the last show taped each time, but they were all professionals and they understood what we needed and they didn't give us very many problems.

"What gave us problems was that the censors all had different standards for what we could say and do. I don't remember which networks had which specific rules, but off-hand, I remember that one of the networks had a rule that you couldn't say the word 'pregnant.' You could say it on the other two networks, but not that one. Likewise, one of the censors objected to the word 'virgin.' And I remember even the other two censors thought that was odd. One of them actually said out loud, 'What's wrong with *virgin*?'

"So at the end of every taping, we got three sets of notes. Here's what we can't do on CBS, here's what we can't do on ABC, here's what we can't do on NBC. And we would edit the show and make three versions of it, one suitable for each network, and we mailed each copy out with the list of stations printed out so only affiliates of the same network got the same tape. So here was the funny thing about *Match Game PM*. Across the country, viewers were seeing the same episode, but depending on where in America you lived, you were seeing a different version of that episode than viewers in another part of the country were seeing.

"To be clear, though, the edits were rarely drastic. Editing the same show three times could have been a very long, frustrating process, so at

**The sparkling set was already fit for a nighttime show.
(Fred Wostbrock Collection)**

the start of the series, as a time saver, we printed up a graphic with the word **OOPS!** against a black background so it could be superimposed on the screen, and we had a sound effect of a slide whistle. So when we got to whatever the censor objected to, we would just mute the audio, insert the slide whistle, and show the **OOPS!** across the bottom third of the screen so that the written answer wouldn't be visible."

During the two breaks in taping, Gene and the panel enjoyed dinner together backstage. The *Match Game* dinner breaks became the stuff of legend because the alcohol flowed quite freely. And according to one staffer, pills were a common sight too.

Stage manager Joe Harwood told Game Show Network in 2006, "Getting them to get in their seats became a large problem, especially after lunch."

Music supervisor Michael Malone remembered, "If you watch a week of episodes now, you can tell which episodes were taped right after dinner. It got a little looser, usually."

Dick Gautier remembers, "The dinner breaks were great. It kept it from feeling like work. You and the other celebrities sat around and BSed each other about what you were planning and what you had done in the past. Told jokes, told stories, got a free meal, they gave you a thousand or so for taping multiple episodes. And all you had to do in exchange was play this game where the host would say your name over and over again while the camera was fixed on your face. What a deal!"

Orson Bean adds, "My favorite memory of the dinners was a night when I asked Richard Dawson something that I had always wondered. He was formerly married to Diana Dors, the British sex symbol. There was a famous story that a church in her old hometown was holding a festival and she was going to appear as the guest of honor. The story goes that her name at birth was Diana Fluck, and you can see why you'd change that name as soon as you had a chance. Well, the vicar of the church was reminded that she had grown up as Diana Fluck and decided to introduce her to the crowd by her real name, and the vicar went up there and made his speech and said something like 'Ladies and gentlemen, please welcome our star guest, our local girl, the very lovely Diana Clunt.' And I asked Richard about it and he laughed and said 'Yes, it's true, and if Diana was here, she'd tell you that story herself. She thought it was so funny.'"

A former CBS page who dealt with the audiences for *Match Game* tapings remembered, "Some magazine or some tabloid paper published an article about the show mentioning these meal breaks where the stars and Gene would drink between the tapings. So it kind of became the worst kept secret in the game show world that everyone on *Match Game* was consuming alcohol during their breaks, and the funniest thing happened once that got out. We would do three tapings a day, and when audience members showed up at the entrance at the start of the day, we would divide them up according to which taping they had tickets for. And there would be days where you had five or six people who had tickets for the first taping, five or six people who had tickets for the second taping, and then the line for the final taping of the day would stretch to the end of the block and around the corner. Everybody wanted to see the *real* show, I guess."

The nighttime show, in accordance with everyone's expectations, was a success. Granted, it wasn't as easily quoted as the zinger-driven *Hollywood Squares*, but it drew many eyes and ears with its more organic comedy. The following transcript is the Super Match from the seventh episode taped for the nighttime show. While it may lose something in the written word, it's a good demonstration of what drove *Match Game*.

GENE: We polled a recent studio audience and we asked them to give their best response to this…(phrase is revealed on board)…"BLANK Ben." Now the answer that audience gave the most often is worth $500 if you match it, if you match the next one you make $250, and the bottom one gets you $100. Three of our celebrated, gifted, charming, beautiful people may help. Whom do you choose?
CONTESTANT: I'd like to have Brett.
GENE: You'd like to have Brett?
BRETT: Aww, thank you. I'll write down my number.
GENE: Just a simple answer is all he wants here.
BRETT: How about Big Ben?
CONTESTANT: Charles?
CHARLES: Gentle Ben.
GENE: Gentle Ben, that was the name of the bear on that series, right?
CHARLES: No, that was what Brett said to her date last night. "That was very gentle, Ben."
CONTESTANT: And I'd like to have Richard.
RICHARD: Has Ben…I don't know a third one.
GENE: Third is a tough position.
RICHARD: I'll say "Little Ben." If there was a Big Ben, there might be a Little Ben somewhere. I think from "Bonanza."
GENE: Okay, so you got Little Ben, a terrific answer…you got Gentle Ben, and you got Big Ben. Want one of those?
CONTESTANT: "Big Ben."
GENE: May we see the $100 response…Uncle Ben.
PATTI: Who is Uncle Ben?
RICHARD: He's the uncle of Little Ben from "Bonanza," and he's now a Has Ben.
GENE: Big Ben is the one we're looking for. Let's look under the $250 response…Gentle Ben!…Last chance for Big Ben, here comes the big number. Go!
(Big Ben is the $500 answer.)

GENE: Okay, so now, you've won $500, which means the least you'll be playing for is ten times that amount, or $5,000. Now let's see how much more you can win with our second Audience Match. Here we go….Slide it, Earl! (Phrase is revealed on board) "Burns and BLANK."

CONTESTANT: I'll have Brett again.

BRETT: How about Burns and Allen?

CONTESTANT: I'll take Charles again.

CHARLES: You can say "Burns and Allen" when you're sitting next to Burns and who?

(Camera pans to Avery Schreiber, half of the comedy team Burns and Schreiber, sitting on the panel that night)

BRETT: Schreiber?

CHARLES: Of course, Burns and Schreiber.

CONTESTANT: Charles. Gotta stay within the group.

GENE: No, Charles just gave you an answer.

CONTESTANT: I'm sorry, Richard! I meant to say Richard.

RICHARD: No, make Charles give you the third one!…Well, there's Burns and Little Ben, who are a wonderful act.

GENE: They were on vaudeville, weren't they?

RICHARD: Yes, but I'm going to go for an act that you've probably never heard of.…Uh…excuse me, your teeth are okay, but your gums are gonna have to come out…Burns and Cuts. It's what happens when you're in the Towering Inferno and you fall. You get burns and cuts. Is that correct?

GENE: You're crazy! You're out of your cotton-pickin' mind!

RICHARD: Okay, then put me up there and you answer number three!

GENE: There isn't a third one…You got Burns and Allen, Burns and Schreiber, and Burns and Cuts.

CONTESTANT: I'm gonna take Burns and Allen!

GENE: All right!

RICHARD: Then why ask me?!

GENE: We're gonna reveal the $100 response.

(The placard that's supposed to reveal the answer doesn't budge. Gene walks up to the board and knocks on it.)

GENE: Earl, I am talking to you. Earl, are you in there?

EARL: I'm here!

GENE: Well, then slide it! Do what I tell you, I'm the star of the show, Earl!

(Earl slides the placard and reveals the $100 answer…Burns and Cuts. Richard stands up and takes a bow to thunderous applause.)

$5,000 for a nighttime show? That just won't do. *Match Game PM* **offered the <u>big</u> dough for Super Match winners. (Fred Wostbrock Collection)**

Richard triumphantly accepts the round of applause after the "burns and cuts" argument. (Fred Wostbrock Collection)

Gene, talking to reporters, freely opined that *Match Game PM* was stronger than the daytime version, owing to the fact that it was taped last during each session. By the time *PM* was taped, the stars were firmly in a groove from having already played the game for two and a half hours, and the two taping breaks gave them plenty of time to get... well... lubricated and uninhibited.

The joking around once had an unintentionally positive outcome. The Audience Match phrase for one episode was "Trench BLANK." The first two celebrities chosen gave the obvious answers "Trench Coat" and "Trench Mouth." When the contestant asked Richard to suggest a third answer, Richard froze and then blurted out "Trench Hand."

Gene asked what Trench Hand meant, and Richard explained, "It's when you have Trench Mouth and you cough." He demonstrated covering a cough with his hand and finished, "Then you have Trench Hand."

Gene never heard anything so ridiculous in his life, and it turned into a running joke for the remainder of the episode, with Richard giving updates on the money being pledged for a non-existent Trench Hand telethon. He wrapped up the show by imploring viewers to give all they could. "Together, we can stamp this out."

A few weeks later, Gene and Richard happily discussed the unexpected result of the fake pledge drive. Viewers enjoyed the gag so much that they had mailed the show very small amounts of money, mostly just a few cents. But so many of the viewers enjoyed the gag that those cents added up to several hundred dollars, which Gene & Richard donated to the Muscular Dystrophy Fund.

Gene got a hefty raise in accordance with his stature as the host of America's #1 TV game show and now a hit prime time series to boot. He and Helen used the money to buy a vacation home in Jackson Hole, Wyoming. Like their Massachusetts home, it was isolated from the world of show business and allowed Gene to enjoy stardom without any of the burdens that sometimes come with it. And while Gene enjoyed biking and swimming on the Massachusetts coast, Wyoming appealed to him because it allowed him to go cross-country skiing.

Allen Ludden and Betty White on the *Match Game '75* panel. Thanks to them, the Rayburns would strike up a nice friendship with Fred Astaire. Also on the panel: Brett Somers, Charles Nelson Reilly, Dolly Reed Martin, and Richard Dawson.
(Fred Wostbrock Collection)

Gene and Helen were enjoying a quiet evening in Jackson Hole when they got a phone call from Allen Ludden, asking "Why are you in Jackson Hole?"

Allen and wife Betty White were throwing a lavish dinner party for many friends. They sent an invitation to Gene and Helen, but the Rayburns had already bought the plane tickets to Jackson Hole and didn't want to change their plans. There would be other dinner parties.

Allen explained, "We have one guest who says he won't come unless you're there, Gene."

Gene asked, "Who?"

"Fred Astaire."

Gene and Helen went straight to the airport the next morning, bought a ticket, and went to Los Angeles only to attend Allen & Betty's dinner party. Gene and Helen arrived at the front door, stepped inside, and looked for Fred Astaire. Astaire made eye contact with Gene from across the room, and moved forward to greet him. Gene delightedly remembered the way that Fred Astaire moved toward him: stooped over, and slowly shuffling his feet in tiny steps toward Gene.

> *He came up to me as Old Man Periwinkle... He was doing me! Fred was a big fan of* Match Game. *We talked a lot. Helen sat with Delly, Fred's sister, who told her, "You must visit me at my castle in Ireland."*
>
> *Helen thought she was kidding, but she had married the second son of the Duke of Devonshire, Charles Cavendish. She really did have an 11th-century castle with one hundred rooms, and we did go and visit her there. But she always said "You can only stay seven days; those are all the menus I have for the cook."*

Gene had fans in high places, but not in one high place where it counted. After all these years, with *Make the Connection, Choose Up Sides, Play Your Hunch,* the original NBC *Match Game,* the current *Match Game,* and his occasional turns on the panels for other game shows, Gene Rayburn still had not been given a seal of approval from Mark Goodson.

> *Once, as we were going to commercial, I walked to the edge of the stage, into the audience, and climbed the backs of the seats all the way to the back of the house and finally put my hand to the front of the lens. I thought it was a great bit. [But] Mark Goodson was a problem. "Jesus, play the game! The game's more important than anything!" And he was* so wrong *about that.*

Randy West, who met Mark Goodson several times at the Goodson-Todman offices while participating in run-throughs of new formats, remembers, "Mark Goodson, I think, wanted to be viewed as professorial. He always had a pipe and he would hold onto it while he was thinking about something. He always dressed to the nines. He was preening. He wouldn't let anybody call him Mark. He was Mr. Goodson; he insisted on that. Demanded it

"I was finally invited into his office and he absolutely made it a point to tell me as soon as I walked in there that the painting on the wall was an original Picasso, and that the desk in the office was one that had once been owned by Napoleon. I actually blurted out 'Bonaparte?' because it was just beyond me that he could have possibly meant that. At the time, I had never heard the term 'Napoleon complex,' but boy, how much more literal could you be with that term? He actually went out and bought a desk that belonged to the man. You know, when Mark Goodson walked into a room, everybody stopped what they were doing. When he spoke, everyone would shut up and listen. He had that much authority. I was already impressed with Mark Goodson, but that's what jumped out at me in his office; that compulsion he had to try to impress me. He felt that he had to. He looked for respect that was due him anyway, but he felt it wasn't forthcoming."

**Fast friends. Fred Astaire and Gene at dinner.
(Fred Wostbrock Collection)**

Robert Sherman says, "Gene and Mark did not have an overtly hostile relationship. They were very cordial to each other, but they were very distant. I think the issue was this. In Mark Goodson's head, he had a very narrow definition of who or what made a great game show host. To Mark Goodson, the great hosts were Bill Cullen, Garry Moore, and Bob Barker. And Goodson liked those guys for what they did, and for their sensibilities and their approaches to the job. And then Goodson watched *Match Game* and he saw a guy who would do a scenery-chewing, exaggerated smooch with the female panelists. Bill Cullen would never do that. And Gene did silly voices when he read the questions, and Garry Moore wouldn't do that. And Gene would walk straight off the stage and step on the armrests of the audience seats and climb over them and go to the camera situated behind the audience for wide shots, and he would grab that camera and shake it. Bob Barker wouldn't do that. Gene did pratfalls. He danced. And Goodson thought that kind of behavior was beneath a master of ceremonies, and I think he had a lower opinion of Gene for that.

"On the other hand, when Gene looked at Mark Goodson, he saw a stubborn guy who was out of touch, who thought he was infallible when he really wasn't. He regarded Mark Goodson as a guy who had the nerve to hand down orders to people whose jobs he didn't understand. And I think Goodson may have gently, or not-so-gently, a few times, suggested that Gene hold back on all that stuff that he found irritating. And I think Gene's attitude toward Mark was 'Shut up, leave me alone and let me do my pratfalls.'"

Fred Wostbrock elaborates, "Mark Goodson and Gene Rayburn coexisted fairly well. They had dinner together a number of times. But their professional relationship was tough for both of them. Mark Goodson said time and again that there was a certain way that he wanted the show done. And Gene, every time, would push back and say 'No, we're going to do it my way and we're going to be funny, and I have an iron-clad contract and you can't get rid of me.' And he ended up being right. So you had a guy who didn't like being told what to do versus a guy who didn't like it when his demands were ignored."

But there was one star on *Match Game* who met Mark Goodson's approval: Richard Dawson. At the peak of *Match Game*'s success, Dawson signed a new contract with Goodson-Todman entitling to host a series of his own at some point. In 1976, Dawson exercised that option, and was about to become the star of his own game show. It should have been a proud moment for all the friends he had made at *Match Game*. And it was… at first.

(Fred Wostbrock Collection)

Chapter Thirteen
More Games

The Danny Thomas Show begat *The Andy Griffith Show*, which gave birth to *Gomer Pyle, USMC*. *All in the Family* led to *The Jeffersons*; it also led to *Maude*, which later brought us *Good Times*. But daytime game shows aren't exactly a genre that lends itself to spin-offs.

Match Game was the exception. In 1974, the Goodson-Todman staff began bouncing an idea off the office walls for a *Match Game* spin-off that fused both incarnations of the series. It would use the same type of questions seen in the early days of the '60s version ("Name a fruit you squeeze before you buy it" or "Name a book that you might own, but you wouldn't read it cover-to-cover") with the '70s Super Match element of ranking the answers by popularity.

The game was originally to be titled *On a Roll*, with two contestants competing against each other and trying to name the most popular answers in a survey. The problem that they discovered early on was that virtually every player played the game the same way. They'd be able to give two or three answers, but then run out of gas and not give any answers for the rest of the round. Goodson-Todman determined that *On a Roll* should be a team game. Before long, the idea of families competing against each other was brought up, and the game was retitled *Family Feud*.

Goodson-Todman initially planned to go the traditional route with casting a host. They first approached Geoff Edwards (*Jackpot* and *The New Treasure Hunt*). In what proved to be an unfortunate miscommunication for Edwards, he was given a fairly inaccurate description of the new game's premise and thought it sounded very similar to *The Neighbors*, a recent ABC game which had bombed. In reality, the two games couldn't be more different, but Edwards didn't know that until it was too late to change his mind.

Next, they turned to Jack Narz, a veteran emcee with an extensive history at Goodson-Todman (*Beat the Clock*, *Now You See It*, *Concentration*). And Narz was almost certainly a lock to host the show until Richard Dawson turned up at Goodson-Todman's offices.

Dawson had that clause in his contract giving him a chance to host a game show, and when he heard the earliest rumblings about *Family Feud*, he immediately jumped on it. And honestly, as good as Jack Narz was, casting Richard Dawson had a certain extra layer of logic to it. The game was derived from *Match Game*, so why not have a *Match Game* personality hosting?

Peter Marshall remembers, "Richard Dawson was the only guy who ever got Mark Goodson's goat. Mark Goodson always got what he wanted, always had final say, and Richard was the only one who always won out over what Mark Goodson wanted. When Richard wanted to host *Family Feud*, there was tremendous resistance from Goodson-Todman and ABC. At the same time, I did a pilot called *The Numbers Game* for ABC, and I said I wanted to book Richard for this pilot and I wouldn't do it without him. The show didn't work, but Richard did. So Michael Eisner, who was the head of ABC daytime back then, agreed, and he saw Richard and fell in love with his performance. So Richard completely won over the network, and Goodson didn't have a choice, he had to give it to Dawson, and that really irked Goodson."

Richard Dawson, in early 1976, was getting ready to host a show of his own. Nobody realized how much of an impact it would make. Also on the panel: Avery Schreiber, Brett Somers, Charles Nelson Reilly, Jo Ann Pflug, and Fannie Flagg. (Fred Wostbrock Collection)

Robert Sherman remembers, "Once Richard got the nod to do *Family Feud*, we all noticed that his behavior changed a little bit around Gene, and we picked up on what he was doing. He viewed Gene very analytically. If something went wrong, or Gene was dealing with a contestant who had frozen up or was giving bad answers, Richard's eyes were on Gene. He was trying to learn from Gene, which was smart."

Dawson hosted a pilot for ABC. The network picked up the game, and oddly enough, plugged it in on their daytime line-up to replace *Rhyme & Reason*, a poetry-driven knock-off of *Match Game*. *Family Feud* starring Richard Dawson premiered on July 12, 1976. Like *Match Game*, the show was a near-overnight smash.

On the day *Feud* premiered, Gene strolled out on *Match Game '76* and congratulated Richard on his new series, encouraging the audience to tune in. Every now and then, he would ask Richard how the show was going and Richard would even mention families who had won big recently. At the start of the show, when Johnny Olson announced the names of the six panelists, he was now introducing "From *Family Feud*,

Richard Dawson!" *Feud*'s success, by all rights, was a reason for *Match Game* to celebrate. *Feud*'s success was their success. After all, they had taken what Gene had rightly called "a rotten format" and found ways to sustain two different shows with it.

Robert Sherman says, "In the very beginning, Richard worked very hard at not letting *Feud* get in the way of *Match Game* and we appreciated it, and we were very happy for him."

Match Game '76 had success of its own to celebrate. It was still number-one in daytime TV and *Match Game PM*, which drew impressive ratings among women ages 18-34 (a very lucrative audience for advertisers) got the nod to come back for the 1976-77 season. For the third straight year, it got nominated for a Daytime Emmy (it would never win one, though).

The best part, for Gene, was that at a time when television was rapidly changing, and not always for the better, he was the host of a TV show that he felt genuinely proud of. Daytime soap operas were pursuing more shocking storylines, daytime talk shows discussed controversial subjects, and even game shows weren't safe from the changing tide. Producer Chuck Barris drew huge audiences with shocking games like *The Gong Show* and *The New Treasure Hunt*. Critics and even some angry letter-writing viewers used words like "cruel" and "humiliating" to describe Barris' shows and the way they treated contestants.

Gene told a reporter at the time, "Game shows have gone through a lot of changes… but the only one I'm not proud of is this vulgar stuff produced by Chuck Barris. I'll never be party to anything where people are humiliated. On *Match Game*, we walk a thin line, but we stay respectable. What Chuck Barris does is a freak show."

Gene was one of a handful of game show personalities who publicly stated in interviews that he would never work for Chuck Barris. He kept that vow.

Gene didn't need his contestants to be victims. Laughing with the contestants was more fun for Gene than laughing at them. A little old lady complained that Gene only kissed new girls on the panel, but not new contestants, and Gene made a show out of giving himself another sprits with the breath spray and planting one on her. When a contestant was struck by stage fright and couldn't stop giggling, Gene did a comical breathing exercise, making a bizarre noise when he exhaled that caused the nervous player to keep giggling more. Another contestant talked about how she had married the father of her son's new wife, leading to an incredibly convoluted explanation of her family tree, while Gene frowned in mock-frustration at the camera.

It was expected that Gene would get laughs from interacting with the stars and the contestants, but Gene was even willing to wander off-stage and get the show's off-camera personnel involved in the wackiness. One day, Gene got ready to read a question when he glanced off-stage and started to announce a commercial instead. Stagehand Joel Hecht was supposed to give him a cue to go to a commercial break, but Hecht missed his own cue and forgot to hold up the cue card to get Gene's attention. Gene smirked when he realized what had gone wrong and found a way to make a moment of it.

"You were late in holding the sign up, weren't you?" Gene asked Hecht while grinning devilishly. "I'll show you what we do when people are late holding the sign up!"

Gene walked off-stage as the camera hastily followed him to where Hecht was standing. Gene snatched the cue cards away from Hecht and whacked him over the head playfully, but repeatedly, with them. He grabbed Hecht's arm and warned him not to forget again.

Roger Dobkowitz was a production assistant who also had some duties involving cue cards. For each question, he would write the contestant's answer on a cue card as a reminder for Gene while he canvassed the panel in search of matches. Roger occasionally misspelled the answers—when he wrote "**ACCORDION**" on a cue card, Charles snatched it from him so he and Gene could give the audience a quick lesson on the proper spelling of what called "the most frequently misspelled word in the English language" (it should be an "a" near the end, not an "o"). Gene cracked up one day when a contestant answered "a parachute" to fill in a blank, and Roger's cue card read "**A PAIR OF SHOES**." Roger was, at the time of *Match Game*'s heyday, a young single man, and occasionally he would be seen on-camera holding a sign that read "Dad—Send Money!" For another show, Roger was giving some last-minute instructions to the panel right as the tape was about to stop rolling. As the taping started, Richard Dawson grabbed Roger by his leg, and Brett Somers and Charles Nelson Reilly each grabbed an arm. When Gene walked onstage, he was treated to the sight of Roger, helplessly trapped onstage and unable to leave.

Although Roger enjoyed being part of the fun, a personal encounter with Gene during one taping left him with decidedly mixed feelings about the show. He explains, "Gene was an ass to me once, and I never forgot it. Now to set this up, there's one quick thing I need to explain; in television in those days, cue cards were sometimes referred to as 'idiot cards.' Now… we were shooting promos for the local stations that aired *Match Game PM*, and Gene had these lines he had to deliver for each promo, and I was holding the cue cards for him. And Gene bungled his lines over and over again, and he kept blaming me for it. He said I wasn't holding the cue cards right. I was. I knew I was. And, you know, Gene was the star of a number-one show, he had a contract, he was popular… it's not like he had anything to lose if people thought he was bumbling a line on a cue card, but it just really bothered me that he was blaming me. And he tripped up on the line on the next take and he said I was holding the card wrong again, and I couldn't take it anymore. I threw the cards down and said, 'Oh, it's my fault? Well, I guess we know why they're called idiot cards now, don't we?'

"And I know the sight of a production assistant mouthing off to the star shocked a lot of the people in the studio. If I had been anybody else, I probably would have been fired, but I was personally fortunate because Mark Goodson himself had hired me. Goodson didn't directly hire a lot of the people in his own company, but he hired me, so because of that, I had this invisible hand on my shoulder at all times, and that probably saved me.

"And there were a couple of other things that bothered me about Gene. At Christmas time, it's sort of a longtime custom for the host of the show to get a small gift for the members of the show's staff. And there are a lot of us, so it's never a major gift. Just a small token, like a pen & pencil set or a box of chocolate or something. But some sort of gift. And for the handful of shows that I worked on in my career, Gene was the only host that never gave the staff gifts. Truth be told, that didn't bother me so much. I don't care if I get a present or not. But when all the other hosts give you Christmas presents, you do sort of notice the one guy who doesn't get you one. And there were all kinds of rumors around the office that Gene was cheating on his wife. I do want to say in fairness that Gene was the perfect host for that show and I can't say enough about how important he was to the success of *Match Game*. That show wouldn't have worked with any other host. They needed Gene. But… that was my own experience with him."

A new season of *Match Game PM* means a new round of publicity photos and promos to send to the local stations. (Fred Wostbrock Collection)

The Matchless Gene Rayburn

Orson Bean remembers, "I only met Gene's wife once. Gene and I went out a lot when he was commuting here to California for *Match Game*. We liked to make each other laugh and we would go out to restaurants and hang around together, make each other laugh until Gene found a woman. And once he began talking to a woman, I would quietly show myself out while Gene pursued whatever romantic vision he had in his head… And Gene liked to fool around. Women are attracted to power. And Gene, as a game show host, had this job where every day on national television, women saw him in a position of authority. He was the one running the game. And the show was a big hit. So Gene's job gave him an air of power, and because it was a success, he actually did have that power. And women loved that. And Gene loved women."

Elsewhere in 1976, *Match Game PM* got renewed after a stellar rookie season and began work on year two in prime time. The nighttime show made one minor change to the rules that made Mark Goodson an extremely happy boss, although he didn't realize why right away.

**As part of the rule changes in its second season, *Match Game PM* introduced a new tiebreaking round. The contestants would write their answers to a final question and the stars gave verbal responses. The first contestant to score one match was the winner.
(Fred Wostbrock Collection)**

Robert Sherman explains, "We did have a lot of working viewers who couldn't watch *Match Game '76* and they were only seeing *Match Game PM*, so to give them a little more show, we began playing three rounds instead of two, so the main game had six questions instead of four.

"What made this possible was that we had started editing the daytime show to make it move a little faster without actually changing it. As much as we had banter and jokes and antics on the daytime show, we also had a lot of occasions where the stars would just hear the question and sit there, think of an answer in silence, and write, and that was it. And there's nothing fun about sitting through that, so we decided that we would just start removing moments during the show where nobody was talking, and we tended to gain about two minutes on each episode by doing that. So the daytime show had the same rules that it always had, we were just editing it. But for *Match Game PM*, we really made use of the extra time that we gained and gave the home audience more game by adding the third round."

Because the nighttime show was reaching a bigger audience, with the potential to reach even more, the material was an important consideration. At the writers' meeting, once Ira Skutch and his team had finalized all the writing, and determined which questions would definitely make it onto the show, they tried to use the funniest questions for the nighttime show. At the same time, they didn't want to make sacrifices at the expense of the daytime show so they still tried to put some of the best material on the daytime show, but the daytime version's audience was pretty loyal by that point and besides, ho-hum questions wouldn't affect the show too much when Gene and the regular panelists could make some magic by riffing about how bad the question was. By and large, though, the strongest questions were used in prime time. So with more questions, with all the lulls edited out, and with the writers' best material, *Match Game PM* became a very strong show, and consistently strong, week after week.

Mark Goodson sent out a memo to his entire staff one day. Having recently watched several episodes of *Match Game '76* and *Match Game PM*, he told his staff that he had very different feelings about the two programs. He was extremely unhappy with what he was seeing on *Match Game '76*, but thought that *Match Game PM* was a wonderful show.

"The difference between night and day." Gene's mind is on the game for *Match Game PM*, and that was how Mark Goodson liked it. (Fred Wostbrock Collection)

A Goodson-Todman staffer responded to the memo by sending a note to Mark Goodson that read, "That's the difference between night and day."

Robert Sherman remembers, "The funny thing was Mark Goodson didn't understand what the staffer meant. The staffer was actually disagreeing with him completely about show quality, but the way he phrased it confused Goodson. Goodson took 'the difference between night and day' to mean what most people usually mean when they say it, that it was two opposite extremes in terms of quality. The staffer had to go into his office and explain that he meant it literally, that the difference between the two shows was literally night and day. In other words, we had to do the show differently for day and night, and we weren't going to change anything because what we did in daytime worked best for daytime and what we did at night worked best at night. Mark Goodson expected us to repair what he saw as broken and the staffer kind of surprised him by disagreeing."

It wasn't the only disagreement happening at *Match Game*. There was another one brewing, arguably far more consequential. *Family Feud* had grown so successful so quickly that it was putting Richard Dawson in more demand than he had ever experienced in his career. He was guest-hosting *The Tonight Show* on Johnny Carson's nights off. He appeared in a made-for-TV movie, *How to Pick Up Girls*. He competed in an NBC prime time special, *Us Against the World*, which pitted American stars against foreign-born stars in a series of competitions. And Goodson-Todman was not only getting the nod from ABC to produce a prime access time *Family Feud* for 1977, ABC had actually signed Goodson-Todman to produce a series of *Family Feud* one-hour prime time network specials, with the stars of prime time shows competing against each other for charity.

Dawson had enjoyed his time on *Match Game* and there was no doubting the show's importance to his career, but new doors were opening for him and he felt that it was time to move on. He asked to be released from his *Match Game* contract. Request denied.

Nobody wants to mess with success, especially something as wildly successful as *Match Game*, and Richard was a major cog in the machine. But, by 1977, so were Brett Somers, Charles Nelson Reilly, Dick Martin,

The Matchless Gene Rayburn

For the moment, Richard was still having fun as a panelist. Also on the panel: Brett Somers, Charles Nelson Reilly, Joan Collins, and Patti Deutsch. (Fred Wostbrock Collection)

Bill Daily, Gary Burghoff, Fannie Flagg, Marcia Wallace, Debralee Scott, Joyce Bulifant, Patti Deutsch, Patty Duke, Avery Schreiber, and Nipsey Russell.

Dick DeBartolo says, "Looking back, I don't think letting Richard leave would have had any effect on the ratings. The audience wouldn't have even asked 'Where's Richard?' I mean, Richard had a show of his own, and the audience would have just drawn a conclusion that seemed perfectly logical—'Oh, Richard has his own show, so he won't be on this show anymore'—and that would have been the end of it. As much as Richard helped build that show, I think they were at a point where they could have functioned without him."

Robert Sherman explains, "I don't think *Match Game* at that point made him unhappy. I think more accurately, the issue was that he felt a little awkward doing the show once *Family Feud* had become a success. He had this wildly popular show where he was the star, and he was the man in control, he was the man who ran the game. And then he had to go from that to *Match Game*, where he always had to defer to Gene and cede control to him. And you can see how that would be a strange dynamic for someone."

Richard took the denial in stride and that seemed to be the end of it. In fact, he almost seemed to be having as much fun as ever. On a daytime episode of *Match Game '77*, the entire upper tier of the panel matched in Round 1, leaving only the second tier to play Round 2. Gene knelt down and peered over the lower tier as if talking to the panelists on the upper tier. The lower tier embraced the gag as fully as possible. Richard and Fannie Flagg borrowed some accessories from Brett Somers and Charles Nelson Reilly, and together they pretended to be the upper panelists. Richard lowered his voice an octave, asked Gene time and again to repeat the question, drank, and used multiple cards to write a single question. Fannie fussed, complained, and referred to Richard as "Susan." The bit worked so phenomenally that a few months later on *Match Game PM*, Gene noticed the same situation presenting itself and knelt down in front of the lower tier so they could do the bit over again. This time, Betty White played the role of Charles, taking a very counterintuitive approach to the role by dropping her voice and talking about going out cruising for chicks after the show.

Meanwhile, Gene was still looking for ways to capitalize on his own successful role on *Match Game*, but he didn't get the same opportunities that Richard got. He hosted an instructional film in which a female instructor demonstrated some basic self-defense techniques and he hosted a PBS prime time special in which marching bands competed against each other with their best routines and songs. But that was really about it. Make no mistake, Gene loved *Match Game*, and nothing would have pulled him away from it, but it bugged him that the show's enormous success didn't create any ancillary opportunities.

> *My basic bag is acting. I'm a trained actor. That was my original ambition... I may still get a chance to do it. In order to keep what I'm doing now fresher, I'd like to do something else, such as, oh, I don't know, maybe a film series or just some acting jobs. Maybe a CBS movie of the week or something like that.*

Did it frustrate Gene that he wasn't getting more frequent opportunities to act?

> *You bet! I think that's why so many of us, who are serious about our craft and don't get the chance we'd like to use it, are always going to school. There is always a class we're attending. You know the ballet dancer goes to the bar and practices every day, and the musician practices on his instrument every day, but the actor... we're lazy. We don't have a monologue at home. We've got to have a school or a class to practice our craft.*

The other thing frustrating Gene was his paycheck. There were a number of emcees throughout the history of TV game shows who fell into the job by accident. John Daly hosted *What's My Line?* for seventeen years, primarily frustrated and disappointed at how it came to totally overshadow his work as a journalist, but he was paid generously for the show, and the show's director remembered later that money gave him comfort. Gene didn't have that comfort. He was definitely making more than the average guy riding the subway to his office job, but by TV standards—particularly by hit TV standards—he wasn't getting much.

Peter Marshall says, "He worked for Goodson-Todman! They were the worst. Goodson was a terrible man. He was awful to his hosts. Bob Stewart worked for him for so many years—I never worked for Goodson or Stewart professionally, but I became friends with Stewart later... And I heard stories about what Goodson paid his hosts. Bill Cullen never got paid all the money he should have seen from *The Price is Right*. Bob was producing it at the time, and he knew what Cullen was getting paid and couldn't believe it. Gene was in the same position. Bob said Gene was getting paid $3,500 a week, tops. For the ratings *Match Game* got and as integral as Gene was to the program, he should have been getting $10,000 or $15,000 a week, because that's what I was getting for *Squares*. Gene was always complaining that he never made much money.

"And I never understood why he didn't play hardball. He should have gone to Goodson and said 'This is what I want,' and if Goodson said no—which he would have been crazy to do—Gene should have walked away. Somebody else would have hired him for something if he had. As much as Gene complained, I don't understand why he put up with it. He should have demanded more money."

Gene hams it up with an audience member during a break in the show. (Fred Wostbrock Collection)

Lynne adds, "It's a hard subject for me to talk about gracefully. When I think of the money that Mark Goodson made from my father's work and what my father got paid for it, I want to throw things across the room."

When the CBS version of *Match Game* arrived in 1973, it attained rapid success and hung onto it almost effortlessly for the next four years. Coming down from the top of the mountain and withering away proved to be a slow, sometimes painful process that began in November 1977.

(Fred Wostbrock Collection)

Chapter Fourteen
No Smiling

"BRIGHT NEW DAY!" was the slogan seen in the *TV Guide* ad that ran at the beginning of the month, but that wasn't how the folks at *Match Game '77* took the news that they were moving to a new time slot: 11:30 a.m. Eastern. Gene, a company man with a rebellious streak, hyped the time slot change on each episode for a few weeks, making it a point to roll his eyes, stare stone-faced, or even frown a little bit to make sure the audience knew how unhappy he was about the change, and for good reason. On the last day in the 3:30 p.m. time slot, Gene signed off by giving the viewers one final reminder about the new slot, and then pretending to pass out and collapsing on the floor.

Dick DeBartolo remembers, "I was never privy to ratings data or anything else on that show. I was only there to write questions, nothing else. But when you're getting history-making, record-breaking ratings for a TV show, and the time slot is 3:30 p.m., it doesn't take a genius to figure out that a big chunk of your audience must be kids."

Lynne says, "Through the years, people have told me that as soon as they got home from school, they got a bowl of tomato soup and turned on *Match Game*. I don't have a clue what the connection is to soup, but that show and that food together were a ritual for so many kids all over the country."

Match Game had been a popular after-school habit for kids. After a long day at school, what could possibly be better for unwinding than a game that was lively and simple? It was TV's version of a peanut butter and jelly sandwich. And this put *Match Game* in a painful predicament. They were losing the largest chunk of their audience. And it wasn't because there was something better on in the new time slot, and it wasn't because the show itself had made some change that the viewers hated. *Match Game '77* had been moved to a time slot where it was impossible for their largest audience to tune in.

The decision to move the show came from Mike Ogiens, a network executive who had previously been a producer for Chuck Barris Productions. He was fired from that company after a bizarre incident in which he invited Barris to a costume party, and then kicked him out because the boss had shown up not wearing a costume. Barris was ultimately forgiving of Ogiens; in his book *The Game Show King*, Barris recalled that while he stood by his decision to fire Ogiens, he at least wrote a letter of recommendation for him.

Ogiens wouldn't receive that kind of forgiveness from Gene Rayburn. Gene never forgave him for changing the time slot. In later years, when Gene talked about his career, he almost never even referred to Ogiens by name.

No Smiling

> *Our time slot was changed by a guy at CBS who had the IQ of a shoe size. What a dummy! What a dummy!*
>
> *In the beginning, I didn't think* Match Game *would last that long, because I had no way of judging, but as long as the numbers were good, we'd last. But when they moved the show, and the ratings went down the drain... that was the dumbest thing that could have been done with that show.* Match Game *should have had a much longer run than it did have, but that didn't happen thanks to this genius vice president.*
>
> *He moved the show around, our ratings never came back, and then he canceled the show. Good thinking. Network vice presidents are brilliant men. Brilliant.*

The ratings sank like a stone, as virtually everybody connected with the program expected them to. The drop was so far, so drastic, that *Match Game* was taken out of the 11:30 a.m. time slot after only six weeks and moved back to the afternoon. So, problem solved, right? Not quite. The show wasn't moved back to its old 3:30 p.m. time slot, it was moved to 4:00 p.m., and the changing nature of television made that a very crucial distinction.

When *Tattletales* was introduced in 1974, the 4:00 p.m. time slot was a boon, allowing the show to soak up a massive lead-in audience that ensured it would be a hit show. At the end of 1977, a glut of syndicated programs, like talk shows and situation comedy reruns, were generating big profits for local stations in a finite number of available time slots. Local newscasts were also becoming a popular way for stations to generate money, because the station got 100% of the cash flow. Station managers began taking the matter of limited schedule space into their own hands. A number of managers at CBS affiliates had started dropping the 4:00 network broadcasts to air a syndicated show. So *Match Game '77* still wasn't getting back the giant audience they had enjoyed so much, because yet again, CBS was putting them in a position where their most devoted fans were incapable of watching the show.

And for the fans who could still see the show, there was yet another problem to deal with. Ironically, that problem was named Richard Dawson.

As Peter Marshall succinctly put it, "Richard became worse than Mark Goodson. Richard was crazy."

Then. Richard has a blast during *Match Game PM*. (Fred Wostbrock Collection)

It was hard to pinpoint exactly when the change happened. Once upon a time, Richard was the glib, quick-witted anchor of the panel who always gave, if not a matching answer, the best and smartest answers. At the opening of every show, when Johnny Olson announced the names of the panelists, Richard would punctuate his own introduction by holding up a card with a cute pun, a message, or even sometimes a greeting to a fan. He was doubtlessly the funniest, lightning fast with quips that usually got the biggest laughs of each episode. He was the best-looking, drawing eyes with his good looks and hanging onto them with the charisma that he had shooting out of every pore. He always got picked for the Head-to-Head Match, and it was hard for viewers not to be charmed about his approach to the big money portion of the show. When Gene asked a contestant to choose which celebrity would play, and the contestant invariably chose Richard, Richard would react by holding up his fingers and crossing them for luck. He wrote his answer, and then the contestant would give an answer. If he hadn't matched, Richard would let the contestant off the hook quickly, apologize, and usually commend them for giving a good answer. If he did match, Richard would deadpan a sad tone as he explained the logic leading to another answer, and then shock the contestant by revealing that he had actually written a match. If the contestant was a lady, he would congratulate her with a kiss on the lips, and it was sometimes difficult to figure out if the big winner was excited about the cash or the kiss. And Richard would usually wrap up the victory celebration by signing a congratulatory autograph on the winning card and passing it over to the winner for a souvenir.

But as *Match Game '77* rolled into *Match Game '78*, that wasn't the same Richard Dawson sitting on the panel anymore. The Richard Dawson of 1978 sometimes opened the show, as Johnny Olson announced his name, by turning his back to the camera, or looking down, or turning to the side, or by just staring emotionlessly. When the rest of the panel was bantering or joking around, Richard sat there silently. When Gene called on him for his answer, Richard would hold up the card and mutter his answer, nothing more.

> *He stopped participating… [I]t appeared that Richard was trying to kill the show.*

Robert Sherman says, "I disagree with that. I don't think Richard had malice toward the show. I don't think he walked into the studio and said 'I'm going to act like this because it will repel viewers and that will kill this show and I'll never have to deal with it again.' I don't believe that was his mindset. I think what viewers were seeing from Richard on *Match Game '78* was just a very, very long hissy fit. Richard was walking into the studio and doing only what absolutely had to be done. He sat down, wrote an answer, and when Gene came to him he held up his card and said his answer, because that was literally what he had to do. He would not do any more than that."

"Richard was just sitting there like a lox most of the time," remembered Dick DeBartolo.

Randy West says, "I don't think Gene took Richard's attitude problems personally. I don't think he saw it as 'This is my show and my show is being ruined by this man.' He didn't see it as an affront to himself. I think Gene was more offended as a professional. Whether or not you want to be there, you have signed a contract to do this job. You go into it knowing exactly what you want to do, what you have to do, and what you're expected to do. And I think Gene was put off by the sight of somebody who had a contract but behaved unprofessionally just because he didn't want the job anymore. If you're there, you have to perform. Gene didn't understand showing up and not performing."

Ira Skutch elaborated in his memoirs, "Because high ratings are ephemeral, and nobody knows for sure where they come from or what makes them disappear, there's a deep fear of change, a reluctance to tamper with success. As a result, everyone catered to Richard and treated him with kid gloves. Then, as *Feud* became a bigger and bigger hit, Richard seemed to become infected with the same virus that infected Robert Q. Lewis: the belief that he alone was responsible for success. As Dawson became increasingly successful on *Feud* he became more and more withdrawn at *Match Game*."

Peter Marshall says, "It was completely out of line. Completely unprofessional. Goodson was the one who developed the show, and even though I don't have a high opinion for Goodson, you're there to do a job that you were hired for. Goodson had Dawson there for a reason, and Dawson should have respected that."

Robert Sherman says "In my eyes, things began to get really bad when *Feud* superseded *Match Game* and became the highest-rated show on daytime television. *Feud* was #1 and *Match Game* was #2 and I think that totally changed Richard's attitude toward *Match Game*. I think it made him see *Match Game* as an annoyance. Being a panelist paid less than being a host, so Richard had to come in every two weeks to tape this show where he wasn't the star, where he had to take orders from Gene even though his show was a bigger hit… that really rubbed Richard the wrong way. He participated less and less."

To Richard's credit, though, he still played the game to the best of his abilities. One would think that an unhappy panelist who didn't want to be on the show would just, for example, write "potato" for every answer to every question whether it made sense or not. Richard, however, had enough human decency to realize that whatever was making him so unhappy, the contestants had nothing to do with it. Richard was still playing to the best of his abilities, writing the best answers and trying to win money for the players.

But even though he was still putting forth the effort, his unhappiness was palpable. Those wacky incidents, those fits of spontaneity that made *Match Game* such an unpredictable kick, just didn't happen anymore. And that was a major problem, because if nobody was kidding around, all that was left to do was play the game. And, again, it was a rotten format that didn't work unless there was a lot of kidding around to sidestep how weak it was. Seemingly day by day, the fun was disappearing from *Match Game '78*.

Now. Richard, showing signs of detachment later in the run. Also on the panel, Greg Morris, Brett Somers, Charles Nelson Reilly, Roz Kelly, Joyce Bulifant. (Fred Wostbrock Collection)

Confrontations in television tend to happen backstage. If there's an issue with the on-air talent, the standard procedure is for a producer to try to handle it to everyone's satisfaction, as privately as possible. Ira Skutch tried to do that; when Richard began keeping to himself during the between-taping dinner break, Skutch tried to boost his morale by playing backgammon with him. This went on for several weeks with no discernible change in Richard's blackening mood. Gene couldn't take it anymore and decided to handle Richard's dampened morale in his own way: very publicly, on the air, during an episode of *Match Game '78*.

GENE: We have a request from someone in the audience. Will you repeat your request?
AUDIENCE MEMBERS, IN UNISON: Give us a smile! Do it!
GENE: Now look at your friends out there screaming at you.
RICHARD: What do you want me to do, smile or do it?... Say goodbye, Gene.
GENE: No, I'm not going until you smile.
RICHARD: All right, then, we'll be back tomorrow here on Match Game. Bye-bye.
GENE: No, I'm not going! Smile! Smile!
Gene hooks his arm around Richard's head and grabs at Richard's face to try and "force" a smile. The credits start rolling. Richard finally smiles.

And then, along came a newfangled contraption called the Star Wheel, and that's when the simmering pot finally boiled over.

Introduced in the summer of 1978, the Star Wheel was a tweak added to the Super Match. After the contestant played the Audience Match, they were escorted to a large wheel divided into six wedges, each labeled with the name of a panelist. Each wedge also had a row of gold stars above the star's name. The contestant spun the wheel to determine who their partner would be for the Head-to-Head match. As a bonus, if the wheel came to a stop on a gold star, it doubled the potential payoff

The Star Wheel; Richard took it as a direct insult, while the staff maintained that it wasn't personal. (Author's Collection)

for Head-to-Head match, for a possible top prize of $10,000 (or $20,000 for *Match Game PM*).

Dawson himself admitted in an interview years down the road, "I took that as a direct slight at me."

Ira Skutch put it less delicately during a phone conversation with Dick DeBartolo: "Richard is so pissed off about the Star Wheel."

Dawson was the go-to guy for contestants who made it to the end of the rainbow and had a shot at the big money. The contestant was free to choose whomever they wanted for a Head-to-Head partner, but within mere months of the show's debut five years earlier, the "choice" became a formality. It was almost always Richard Dawson. In 1975, the show had even tried instituting a rule that a returning champion couldn't pick the same celebrity twice for consecutive Head-to-Head Matches, but the rule had proven wildly unpopular with the audience and done away with after only a few episodes, and the Head-to-Head Match went back to being the domain of Richard Dawson. And audiences liked it that way. To introduce a new element that put Dawson on equal ground with the rest of the panel struck him as a hostile act.

DeBartolo explains, "Richard could not be convinced that the Star Wheel was devised for any reason other than to knock him. Here was the logic behind the Star Wheel. In the first part of Super Match, the Audience Match, we'd ask the contestant to choose three celebrities for suggestions, and sometimes they would choose a guest, but very often, the three celebrities they chose were Brett, Charles, and Richard, the regulars. And then you go to Head-to-Head Match and they always chose Richard. So you had this chunk of five minutes on every show where the guest stars sat there quietly and didn't do anything. The Star Wheel was devised as a way to get the guests involved in the end game, that's all."

In a moment that doubtlessly made Richard happy, on the episode in which the Star Wheel debuted, it actually landed on his name. The rest of the panel stormed off the stage in mock frustration, and for just a brief spell, it felt like old times. Everybody—even Richard—was smiling and making a memorable moment out of thin air. But before long, everything was back to "normal." Richard was unhappy and everybody just went through the motions, albeit with a wheel involved now.

Three weeks later, *Match Game '78* took another crack at breathing new life into the show by unveiling a glitzy new set. The earth tones of the set that the audience had seen for the past five years were gone, replaced by a glittering white and blue set, with the panel area backed by an array of blue beams and white lights against an orange backdrop, which looked quite attractive to some viewers' eyes and just looked like an enormous Confederate flag to others. Gene's question machine, which malfunctioned so often that it created an unintentional catch phrase, "Nobody do anything!" (blurted out by Gene every time it broke down), was replaced by a sleek new motor-operated question machine, which malfunctioned slightly less frequently. The show even had a distinctive new logo.

**Gene with the distinctive logo on the new set.
(Fred Wostbrock Collection)**

But a few fresh coats of paint couldn't conceal the gloominess permeating the set. Everyone still held out hope that something could be done about Richard Dawson. And one day, a six-episode taping session rolled around and Richard showed up wearing sunglasses. Nobody backstage thought anything of it… until he walked onstage and wore them through the entire taping. Richard had also worn sunglasses during the *Family Feud* tapings that week, telling the studio audience that he had scratched his eyes and would be sensitive to bright light for just a little bit.

That was a completely understandable explanation, but the problem was that even though one was a spin-off of the other, under the same production company banner, *Match Game* and *Family Feud* didn't share staff. Richard just wasn't talking to anybody at *Match Game* anymore and didn't care badly enough to explain to anyone why he was wearing sunglasses. To the *Match Game* staff, it just looked like a guy partially covering his face on the air to isolate himself even further from the show surrounding him.

Ira Skutch saw the sunglasses as the point of no return. During the taping break that day, he approached Richard Dawson backstage and told him, at long last, that he was free from his *Match Game* contract and that he didn't have to stay on the show if he didn't want to. Richard accepted the offer and stayed in the studio to finish out the remaining episodes of the taping session. No mention was made on the air during that week that Richard was leaving, save for a cryptic declaration by Richard himself. As the credits rolled on the final *Match Game '78* of that session, he held a card over his face, reading "Fare Thee Well."

After the taping, Richard Dawson, who had been there even before the show was on the air, who had been an anchor for the panel from the original pilot in early 1973 and hadn't missed a single episode yet, walked out of the studio without saying a word to anybody, got in his car, and left. For the following week, *The Price is Right* host Bob Barker held the distinction of being the first person to fill Richard's seat on the panel in the "post-Dawson" era. Gene made some remarks about Richard's departure, which were removed from the show in post-production. The editing crew did, however, leave in a wisecrack from Barker, who noted that the message "The sun never sets on the British empire" was scribbled on the desk.

A few weeks later, McLean Stevenson appeared on the panel, sitting in the middle seat of the bottom tier. He casually quipped, "Richard's not going to show up in mid-broadcast and demand his seat, is he?"

Gene replied, "Richard who?"

It could never be the same show again, but at least the dark cloud hanging low over the set for the past few months was cast away. *Match Game '78* was a somewhat happier place to be. The show adapted rather easily.

Robert Sherman explains, "We were already in trouble because of the time slot change, so the ratings were not what they used to be in general. But when the word got out that Richard was done, we were all a little bit nervous about the effect it would have on the show. And I do remember looking at the ratings and seeing that for the first week that Richard was gone, our ratings were down just slightly, but then the week after that, the ratings went back to what they were for the last week that Richard was there, and things sort of stabilized. Richard really did not have an effect on the ratings."

As Sherman remembers, there was one other area of the show that Richard didn't really affect. "Richard always being picked for the Head to Head Match didn't really have anything to do with how well he played the game. It was a self-fulfilling prophecy. A handful of people picked Richard and they all won. Future contestants saw it on TV so when they made it onto the show, they picked Richard. And the cycle repeated. Richard's popularity in the Super Match was a perfect example of circular logic. The reason Richard always got picked was because people always picked Richard.

"Once Richard was gone, we became very curious, so we checked our files from previous episodes and we kept detailed track of the Head to Head Match results. Guess what we found out. Absolutely every other panelist on the show performed exactly as well as Richard. There was no difference. We had winners with anybody else as often as we had with Richard."

Unfortunately, they had only solved one problem. And truth be told, getting Richard Dawson to leave was the easiest of all of the issues hampering them. They were still trapped at 4:00 p.m., and they had now been in the time slot so long that at this point, moving back to the 3:30 p.m. slot that had been so fruitful to them in the first place wouldn't solve the problem. The viewers who had loyally watched the show had, by this point, found other shows to watch or other things to do after school.

Match Game '78 held on through the end of the year and the show celebrated one more New Year's Eve, with Gene, Brett, and Charles ringing in the new year by unplugging and removing the "78" from the massive logo on the set, unpacking a "79," and hooking it up to see it illuminate for the first time. Gene rang in *Match Game '79* by thanking the viewers the show still had left for their unwavering support.

As the show limped along, Robert Sherman remembered recognizing another problem that he felt was hurting *Match Game '79*, and it wasn't a departing panelist or a lousy time slot. He felt that the show's biggest enemy was time itself.

Sherman says, "Going into 1979, we had been on for five and a half years. Statistically, that makes you an oddity in the world of TV game shows. If you look at the whole history of the genre, maybe one percent of all game shows are on the air as long as we were on the air. And we were also an anomaly in that we were doing a very different type of game show and we stayed on that long. If you look at the game shows that get long runs, most of them are very traditional shows.

An interesting mix of stars showed up in 1978 after Richard's departure opened up an extra seat on the panel. Here's Raymond Burr coming in for a week of games. Also on the panel: David Doyle, Brett Somers, Charles Nelson Reilly, Elaine Joyce, Joyce Bulifant. (Fred Wostbrock Collection)

"And the other thing is, even though we dominated the ratings for a few years, our ratings weren't that high. It's true that we got the highest ratings in the history of daytime television and that the record still stands, but honestly, that makes our ratings sound higher than they really were. We weren't destroying the competition. When we were number one, if you took the ratings of shows two, three, and four and added them together, we'd be swamped.

"By 1979, the standards for comedy on TV had changed. *Saturday Night Live* was the standard bearer for television comedy, and they broke all kinds of barriers on that show. And the result of that was that we weren't special anymore. In 1973 and 1974, we were the only show on television where you heard people joking about the things we joked about. 1979, doing exactly the same show with the same type of humor… we were still funny, but we weren't special. We lost that extra luster that we had early on."

Unfortunately, the fate that the show had eluded for a year and half couldn't be swatted away anymore. In late March, 1979, CBS dropped the bombshell on Goodson-Todman. *Match Game '79* was going off the air. And not only was television's biggest daytime hit of all time done, but it was getting a "don't let the door hit you" send-off from the network. CBS aired *Match Game '79* for the final time on April 20, 1979… despite the fact that there were fifteen episodes taped that hadn't aired yet.

(Fred Wostbrock Collection)

Chapter Fifteen
Coming Unbuttoned

Mason Randolph boarded the Pacific Princess for a relaxing cruise when he bumped into an enchanting redhead named Alicia Finch. Their pleasant conversation was interrupted by a high-pitched "arf" from Alicia's purse. Alicia ran into her cabin and pulled out her Yorkie, Cricket, and lovingly brushed her fur, and fed her. She headed out to the pool, where Mason was thumbing through a copy of Dogs' World Magazine. It turned out that Mason was a dedicated dog fancier. He talked about the purebred Great Dane that he had taught to sing. She talked about her not-quite-purebred Yorkie. Mason was immediately enchanted and asked for a date.

That night, over dinner, Mason admitted to missing his dog, to the point of nearly crying, and vented in frustration over not being allowed to bring his dog along for a cruise. Alicia invited Mason into her cabin, explaining that she wanted to cheer him up by showing him something. Mason, misreading the signal, took her out for dancing and a drink, fearful that things were moving too quickly. Mason entered the cabin, quivering with excitement until he laid eyes on Cricket. Cricket angrily barked and snapped at Mason until he finally walked away for the night, disappointed.

The next morning, Alicia apologized. Mason was quick to forgive. He was a dog lover and knew how protective they could be of their masters. Alicia casually mentioned her approach to taking care of a dog, keeping her healthy with a good diet and occasionally treating her to Swiss cheese. A few hours later, Mason showed up with a box of chocolates for Alicia and a chunk of Swiss cheese for Cricket. Cricket still snapped at him.

Mason asked Alicia out to another dinner but had trouble concentrating. All he could think about was trying to swipe lobster tail and caviar to feed to Cricket. He was convinced that he couldn't win over a woman whose dog didn't like him. Alicia, determined to prove him wrong, invited Mason back to her cabin for an overnight stay. As Mason placed the "Do Not Disturb" sign on the doorknob, Cricket made her escape, running in circles all over the deck of the Pacific Princess while Mason and Alicia frantically chased her. Cricket ran into the pool and doggy-paddled around in a panic. Mason, thinking nothing of the expensive tuxedo he was wearing, dove in and rescued Cricket.

A short time later, Mason returned to Alicia's cabin, wrapped in a heavy towel, hoping to pick up where he left off. Cricket angrily bit the towel and Mason couldn't stand it anymore. He told Alicia that Cricket was probably just trying to give them a sign that it wasn't meant to be. He walked out disappointed, and she stayed in the cabin, heartbroken.

The next morning, they both returned to port in Los Angeles and walked off the cruise ship. Mason, with a cooler head, presented Alicia with a silver dog whistle, as a memento from their little adventure the previous night. Mason greeted his butler, who had brought along King, the Great Dane that Mason had missed so badly. Cricket rushed away from Alicia's arms and eagerly sniffed around King, getting to know him and making an obvious new friend. Cricket was so excited that she didn't seem to notice Mason anymore.

Mason, feeling a spark, told Alicia, "Two dogs can live as cheaply as one."

Mason and Alicia kissed passionately. True love had prevailed, as it often tended to do... on *The Love Boat*.

Alicia was played by Fannie Flagg. Mason Randolph was portrayed by Gene Rayburn. And he couldn't have been happier. He had been away from theater far too long. He was finally getting a chance to act. He had a kissing scene. He got to cry. He got to do broad physical comedy. He loved *The Love Boat* for giving him an opportunity that nobody else would.

Although grateful for the opportunity, he acknowledged that he didn't particularly care for the way that *The Love Boat* was shot. As feature films did, *The Love Boat* shot multiple takes of a single scene using one camera. Gene wanted to do a sitcom.

> *One-camera shooting is boring, hard work. I prefer three-camera style shooting where you rehearse for a week and then tape in front of a live audience. It's more like stage; it has some validity.*

Gene never got an opportunity to appear on a three-camera sitcom in front of a live studio audience. But *The Love Boat* was at least giving him an opportunity that no other show on television was giving him, so he appeared on a few more episodes. The following season, he was right back on board the Pacific Princess, wooing Gopher's mother (played by Ethel Merman).

Gene wanted to get back into acting as much as he could. At the end of 1978, he turned sixty-one years old and he already had spent a career watching opportunities to act slip through his fingers. He didn't want to give up on acting for good. At the same time, though, he was hopelessly in love with the job that he wound up in by accident while chasing his acting dreams, and this looked like it might be a problem, because the cancellation notice from CBS wasn't going to be the end of *Match Game*.

Goodson-Todman's winner is back with all-new production for first-run syndication. Markets are closing fast! So don't dawdle. Act now if you hope to play Match Game *on your station in the fall.*

The Matchless Gene Rayburn

Break time's over! Gene and the panel get back to work on *Match Game*. Sitting on the panel: Bart Braverman, Brett Somers, Charles Nelson Reilly, Eva Gabor, Bill Daily, Fannie Flagg. (Author's Collection)

During 4 seasons at 3:00 and 3:30 on CBS, Match Game *ranked as the Number One daytime show for 3 years! The Number One daytime game show for 4 years! And the Number One CBS daytime show for 3 years! When* Match Game *wasn't Number One, it was Number Two. You can't score much higher than that!* —Ad in *Broadcasting* Magazine, May 21, 1979

History was repeating itself. In 1969, NBC cancelled the original *Match Game* and Mark Goodson prognosticated that it wasn't the end for the venerable show. It hadn't run its course. It had been mistreated by the network and still had more life in it. A decade later, Goodson's prognosis was the same. It was CBS' fault that the show died. And it was a blame that had some merit. As the ratings for the CBS daytime version eroded, *Match Game PM* was as strong as ever. In New York City, the #1 television market, it tied the nighttime version of *Family Feud* for the top spot in prime access program ratings.

Glad to be back. Gene is having a good time with the contestants on the syndicated *Match Game* in 1979. (Mike Klauss Collection)

Back to normal. Everyone is having a good laugh during *Match Game*, the way they did before. (Mike Klauss Collection)

Goodson-Todman was now offering local stations two syndicated versions of *Match Game*. The once-a-week *Match Game PM*, designed for the prime access time slot, and a five-day-a-week version that could air at any time (with the provision that the station couldn't air it in direct competition with *Match Game PM*). Stations enthusiastically signed up in a narrow window of time. Syndicated programs often get pitched to local stations as far as one year in advance. CBS cancelled *Match Game* in March 1979, and to have a syndicated version on the air in the fall, tapings would have to start at the end of June. Goodson-Todman had just under three months to get the show sold to enough stations to justify continuing production. They pulled it off. They had already managed to sell the show to nineteen stations before the ad ran in *Broadcasting Magazine*, and more stations just kept signing up.

Robert Sherman says, "There's a story in the television business about Bob Stewart, and it's probably apocryphal but the story goes that he was anticipating that *The $10,000 Pyramid* was about to get dumped by CBS and he was already talking to the other networks. And the story goes that while he was sitting in the office, two phone calls came in at the same time. And Bob Stewart takes the call from CBS telling him that they're cancelling the show, and he puts the CBS guy on hold and on the other line, it's the ABC guy telling him that they're picking up the show. That didn't exactly happen to us but it was almost just as fast.

"What helped us get the syndicated version off the ground was that the cancellation didn't exactly blindside us. For the last year that we were on CBS, there were a few thirteen-week renewal periods where we were really on the bubble and we didn't know one way or the other, so we were kind of anticipating that we'd be off CBS in due time. So we sort of talked to Jim Victory Television, which was the company that distributed *Match Game PM* to the local stations and Jerry Chester, who dealt with the local stations on behalf of Goodson-Todman, was already putting out feelers while we were still on the network. So as soon as we got the word from CBS, everybody sprang right into action. And what sort of helped us and kept our hopes high was that the profit margin was really low. I remember the accounting department did the math and figured out that we only needed fifty stations to air a daily syndicated series for us to turn a profit. Anything beyond fifty stations was bonus money. So we were excited and optimistic."

And while Gene was happy to see that his beloved game looked like it was going to survive, he decided it was time to have a talk with Mark Goodson, and a talk with Helen. Gene loved *Match Game*. He loved the exposure he got, he loved the paycheck that came with it, and he loved the job itself. Just one problem—he was sick of flying.

The daily syndicated version of *Match Game* wouldn't produce episodes year-round. That part was already set in stone; most syndicated shows didn't go year-round. *Match Game* would only produce thirty-five weeks in the next season, with seventeen weeks of reruns. Gene would drastically cut down the coast-to-coast commuting. Instead of the hotel rooms he had been staying in for the past six years, Gene started renting a housing cooperative in Los Angeles. He would live in Los Angeles for six months out of the year, and during that six-month window, Goodson-Todman would make a genuine effort to tape as many of the thirty-five weeks as possible. After that six months, Gene would return to Massachusetts, and do the bi-weekly commute to tape two weeks of episodes at a time until the rest of the season was taped.

Gene's resistance to the west coast was remarkable given the direction that television had taken. ABC's *The $20,000 Pyramid* was the last remaining network TV game show taping in New York City in 1979. Prime time television had virtually abandoned the city altogether. Soap operas were still active in the city, although that obviously wasn't a good fit for Gene Rayburn, the stage actor who wanted to do a three-camera sitcom. As good as Los Angeles had been to Gene in the 1970s, it appeared that the city itself hadn't made a good impression. Gene and Helen couldn't stand Los Angeles.

> *Hollywood is the no-taste capital of the world... New York is the only place to be, I love New York.*

That wasn't entirely true. The Rayburns admitted that, despite going to the west coast kicking and screaming for part of the year, there really were some parts of California living that agreed with them. They enjoyed the long strolls along the Venice coast, usually going there early in the morning and taking a three-mile stroll near the ocean. They also frequented a roller skating rink in Reseda where Cher was known to hold lavish parties on Monday nights.

On June 30, 1979, the daily syndicated version went into production. The long-standing custom of sticking the year in the title was done away with. Going forward, the show was only called *Match Game*.

Gene and the panel say goodnight... except for Charles, who already went to bed. Also on the panel: David Doyle, Brett Somers, Debralee Scott, Dick Martin, Patty Duke (Mike Klauss Collection)

Dick DeBartolo remembers, "Well, for one, syndication was still being done through the mail, so it was the same issue as *Match Game PM*; you didn't know when it was going to air so you didn't want a year in there. And with seventeen weeks of reruns a year now, I think Goodson-Todman realized that a show had more rerun value if you didn't draw attention to a year in the title of the show."

Goodson-Todman found other ways to make the syndicated version more rerun-friendly. Each week of episodes was designed to be self-contained. There were no returning champions; two contestants would compete against each other in two full games. Regardless of how they did, both contestants left after those two games. Exactly six complete games and six Super Matches were played in each week. If games ran short, Gene would go into the audience and play a special game, reading simple blank phrases and offering fifty dollars to audience members who could match the stars. If tiebreakers had to be played or the games ran long for any other reason, the shows were heavily edited so that Friday's episode ended cleanly on the sixth Super Match of the week.

Typically, all that was edited from the show were the moments of silence. The stars were frequently chatty and would talk to Gene and each other while writing their answers, but if all that was happening was six people scribbling answers without conversation, that wound up on the cutting room floor. On the other hand, if Gene made a mistake during the show, it stayed in the final cut. And believe it or not, he liked it that way.

He told reporter David Nicolette, "A lot of the people who have become used to taping think in terms of 'Well, if we goof, we can do it again.' But I don't think that way... I go into every show with this attitude that we have one shot at it and that's it. We play our show that way. If we make mistakes, they stay in, unless someone says something really offensive."

Gene did goof occasionally. Once, during the Audience Match, the contestant canvassed the panel for three possible answers and Gene excitedly said "Let's see the $100 answer!" without asking the contestant to give her answer. The contestant corrected Gene about the possible procedure. Gene, without missing a beat, handed the contestant his microphone and traded places with her. Gene gave his own answer and she called for the answers to be revealed one at a time. When Gene's answer proved to be worth $500, Gene jumped and screamed in celebration along with the contestant, who had wound up with top dollar because of Gene's error.

Sometimes the contestants goofed on Gene.

GENE: Do you want A or B?
CONTESTANT: Well, I have a blue-eyed boy named Brendan, so I'll take A.
(Camera cuts to Gene, revealing that he's already pulled question B. Gene hastily puts it back and gets question A.)
GENE: Good luck anyway.

The Matchless Gene Rayburn

Sometimes, the contestants just plain goofed. A contestant named Ginger bewildered Gene and the panel with her bizarre answers. For one game, Gene read the question, "That caterpillar must be an athlete; he just bought one hundred sneakers and a BLANK." Ginger, for some reason, answered "Accordion."

Despite that, she won the game and had a chance to win $2,500 in the Head to Head Match with Robert Walden. Gene read the phrase, "Cuckoo BLANK." Walden wrote his answer quickly, and Ginger smiled and confidently gave her answer, "Cuckoo, Fran and Ollie," shrugging her shoulders and looking puzzled when the entire panel broke into fits of laughter and Gene staggered away from her, almost speechless.

Gene and a happy winner; one of hundreds over the years on *Match Game*. (Mike Klauss Collection)

And Gene was still finding ways to make a lot out of a little. Lynne remembers, "I came to the studio one day with my dog, Trotter, a medium-sized black pup. And because Trotter was completely black, I would always put a red bandana around her neck. And my dad saw me with my dog backstage and he decided to bring Trotter out with him. He went to the dresser at the studio and asked him for a red pocket square, and the dresser had one, so my dad and Trotter matched. Betty White was on the panel that day and she loves animals, of course, and Trotter went right to Betty and laid down next to her and fell right to sleep as the show was going on. We didn't plan it, my dad just thought it would be fun to bring the dog onstage."

Match Game began airing that fall, with many airing it in the 4:00 p.m. time slot. It was a funny fate for the show. Because local stations were pre-empting the 4:00 p.m. hour for syndicated programming, the final year or so of *Match Game* on CBS couldn't be seen at all by most viewers. But now, because *Match Game* itself was a syndicated show, the very time slot that had helped kill the show was the perfect time slot for it. And a handful of stations that had been carrying the 4:00 p.m. slot were now bumping it to show the syndicated *Match Game*, so for some viewers, it just seemed like they had taken a long summer break.

**Gene, Betty White, and Trotter on *Match Game*.
(Fred Wostbrock Collection)**

Robert Sherman said, "It was great. We made some changes to the show, but all the changes were so minor that everybody adapted immediately. We had the same set. We were in the same studio; we remained at CBS and kept using Studio 33. Same staff, same stars. It was easy."

Match Game was back, and it was alive again. Gene deliberately misstepped and shuffled around while reading a question to trip up the cameramen one day. A contestant pointed out that a bolt had fallen out of his seat, and Gene stopped everything to repair the chair himself, as the cameras kept rolling.

And the audiences who had disappeared in droves at the end of 1977 seemed to be eagerly rediscovering the show. Though not the record-breaking hit it had been on CBS, *Match Game* had a respectable and loyal audience watching in late 1979 and early 1980 in syndication. More importantly, it was the right audience. Women aged 18-49, a very lucrative group for advertisers, loved the show. A trade ad in February 1980 for *Match Game* reported that the station airing the show in Tampa had seen its 18-49 female audience increase 180% since the show premiered. For the Minneapolis station, it was a whopping 271% increase.

The ad gushed, *When popular host Gene Rayburn brings his celebrity-packed* Match Game *to town, he zeroes in on a station's target audience: 18-49 women. He did it when* Match Game… *became a young woman's favorite and the <u>highest rated daytime network game show</u>… He captivated young women again when* Match Game PM… *joined the top ranks of all syndicated programs. Now… he's winning the allegiance of young women for a third time in* Match Game's *first season as a syndicated strip. What's Gene Rayburn's secret? He's an established all-star host with enormous appeal… Gene Rayburn needs no introduction.*

So the target audience was happy with Gene. The ad copywriter in charge of selling the show was clearly happy with Gene. There was one person, however, who was very unhappy with Gene: Mark Goodson.

About halfway through the 1979-80 season, Mark Goodson circulated a scorching memo to his staff complaining about the quality of *Match Game*. Among his complaints: the "unbuttoned" hosting style of Gene Rayburn.

Chris Clementson elaborates, "[Goodson] was concerned that Gene and the other cast members had become too 'unbuttoned' and predicted the show didn't have much of a future because of it. Thinking back on it, Goodson should have dealt with Rayburn directly rather than sending a memo to the producer and expecting him to deal with it."

Patty Duke cracks everyone up by interpreting a confusing question in sign language. (Mike Klauss Collection)

By 1979, *Match Game* had seen ups and downs and numerous changes from the day it first arrived in 1962, but after two separate, successful runs, it was unmistakably a broken-in show. Even if it was still funny and spontaneous, it was hard to be surprising. The show had been around long enough for the unexpected to be expected. And on many game shows, the host's performance tends to change as years go by. Often, a host dives right into the game without pausing to explain the rules or the mechanics, and comes across as more relaxed than he did earlier in the series. Gene wasn't immune to that, and given that his approach to hosting the show was already rather laid back in the first place—Gene himself half-jokingly said that they only played the game when they had run out of funnier things to do—it appeared to Mark Goodson that Gene was completely on cruise control.

Robert Sherman says, "It didn't matter how long we were on the air, Goodson could never shake that mindset of 'the game's the thing.' Most of the time, that's true, but in the case of *Match Game*, it was all about Gene and the panel joking around and having fun, and the game was just the framework for it. And Goodson never really accepted that, even after all that time."

Although his relationship with his boss was starting to cool, Gene still got approval where he felt it counted most. The fans loved him. In 1979, Gene was particularly gracious to Fred Wostbrock, a young fan who had written him a rather impressive fan letter a short time earlier.

"I guess he was impressed by how much I knew about his career. There's a line where you can know a lot about a celebrity's career and it makes them think 'crackpot' or 'stalker' but I was good about not crossing that line. He was flattered. And in the summer after my first year of college, I traveled to Los Angeles for a vacation; paid my own way out there, and Gene invited me to see a taping of *Match Game*. And he came out into the audience area after the taping was over and met with me and we had a good long conversation. And he found me intriguing. I think I was the first person he ever met who was heavily into game shows, and he was intrigued by how much I knew about every game show and every host he named. And I showed him the photos I collected of him and he got a big kick out of the idea that some kid had paid a buck apiece for every photo of him that anybody had ever taken. But in my experience, he was the same person off the air as he was on. He was funny; he did odd, random things as we talked. We went out to dinner and he loved it when people recognized him, he was very gracious to other fans."

A happy life away from the show was keeping his morale up, too. In 1980, he and Helen celebrated forty years of marriage. Helen, who was now channeling her love of books into a job as a book critic for the *Boston Herald American*, reflected on her marriage during an interview with reporter Cynthia Robins.

She said, "For a marriage to last, I think you have to understand what commitment means... The most difficult thing about being married to a man as well-known as Gene is an invasion of privacy. Many times I resent it, but he's one of the kindest people I know about fans. He's never been rude and has learned to turn them off quickly. Fans are a strange

Gene graciously greets a fan after a taping in 1980, little realizing that it's his future agent. (Fred Wostbrock Collection)

brand of people who get very proprietary with people they like. Often, they'll come to the door and ask for an autograph. That's too much sometimes."

Daughter Lynne had a different view of their marriage. "In the beginning, I'm sure there was something there. When I was a child, my mother got out of bed at 3:30 in the morning, cooked breakfast for my father, saw him off to work, and then went back to bed for another hour and a half, and then got up again to get me ready and off to school. So there was love there. You wouldn't do that if you didn't love the man you were doing it for.

"When I reached adulthood, I didn't see the commitment anymore. Now that's not to say it was an unhappy union. My parents were always affectionate and kind to each other, and I believe they cared about each other, but there was no passion there. My mother had wanted to become a writer, and for reasons that she never elaborated on with me, she became very close to accomplishing that and then it fell through. And I think she stayed with my father for the security. And likewise, my father had certain goals that he had his eyes on and didn't really see through.

I don't think my parents had a bad relationship, but I do think that if certain things had turned out differently, especially if my mother got into a position where she had her own income to depend on, they would have gone their separate ways."

Gene and Helen, celebrating their fortieth anniversary. (Fred Wostbrock Collection)

Match Game wrapped up the 1979-80 syndicated season and for the first time, Gene excitedly realized, he was going to get to take a few months completely off. He took full advantage, going back into acting with regional theater. It wasn't Broadway, but it would do. He took to the stage of the Alhambra Theatre and starred in *Lovers Leap*. He followed that up with another regional production, *Prisoner of Second Avenue*, Neil Simon's dark comedy about a middle-aged man who loses his job and suffers a nervous breakdown.

The 1970s was the decade when entertainment and social issues had first collided. Sitcom producer Norman Lear unleashed programs like *All in the Family* and *Maude* that tackled controversial subjects like rape and abortion head-on. Performers like Ed Asner and Jane Fonda began fearlessly expressing their personal views about hot button topics. Going into the 1980s, Gene began rather fearlessly expressing liberal viewpoints about major issues. In 1980, the game show *Card Sharks* featured a special three-week tournament featuring TV game show hosts playing for their favorite charities. Gene played for Planned Parenthood, explaining at the beginning of his game that he felt the major problems that the world was facing were all rooted in overpopulation, and that population control could prevent many crises. Gene won $8,475 for Planned Parenthood during his appearance. When the organization was paid, Gene kicked in $30,000 of his own money.

Lynne, meanwhile, had focused her graphic design skills on a campaign for the National Organization for Women and their push to get the Equal Rights Amendment passed. She asked her father for help, inviting him to host a rally on the steps of Boston's City Hall to raise money for the National Organization for Women.

At the time, Gene told reporter David Nicolette, "Women never have been on an equal footing with men and they should be... They should be paid the same as men for equal skills, and they should be given the same opportunities. It just has to happen. People forget that in World War II, women had to step in and do the jobs, physical and mental, that men who were off to the wars had done. They were marvelous. They can do anything as well as a man, and some things better."

Unfortunately, recalls Lynne, he wasn't as eloquent during the actually rally. "It made me cringe. My dad did a very generic speech. 'We need to pass this amendment. It's a wonderful thing and everybody should work as hard as you can to help pass it. It wouldn't hoit.' I cringed. I couldn't believe that. He didn't really understand the women's movement. He wanted to look like he understood it, but my parents both came from a different era. And my father was a womanizer by nature, and I think he saw women a certain way. It frustrated me. Someone else might justify it by saying 'Well, he's from another generation.' I couldn't justify it that way. But I didn't even bother saying anything to him afterward about it because I realized he didn't get it in the first place.

"What really lingered in my mind was that I had also worked adamantly for animal rights over the years and I got my mom and dad to 'make the quantum leap,' so to speak, with that cause. They learned about it, they became educated, and they became involved. And I thought it was odd that they were more interested in the rights of animals than fellow humans."

On the other side of the fence, a growing conservative movement was gathering steam. Censorship would become one of the major issues of the new decade. Song lyrics were heavily scrutinized for hidden messages and magazines were removed from newsstands. Religious groups like Rev. Jerry Falwell's Moral Majority were leading the charge to exert more control over what Americans were seeing and hearing. Gene found that disturbing.

The discussion of censorship led to the discussion of content. Gene actually agreed somewhat that outrage was justified about some television programming, but believed it was repairable without censorship.

> *I think that most of the stuff is just plain vulgar. And most of that stuff is out of Los Angeles. They're putting out awful stuff. We'd correct a whole lot of the problems if we'd get the television industry out of there, spread it out around the country. Have the shows reflect the morals and culture of the rest of the country. It's just too centered on Los Angeles and the result is sickening. I think the greatest thing that happened to TV is when Chuck Barris and his horrible* Gong Show *[which ceased production in 1980] were thrown out. There's an example of how you can control what goes on. TV stations just decided not to buy the show. I think they just got too embarrassed. It was degrading to humanity. Just a terrible show.*

In the summer of 1980, Gene returned to Los Angeles and got to work on another season of *Match Game*. He was still enjoying himself, but the concern was starting to mount that the show was running out of steam. Gene told one reporter that he had asked the writers to come up with fresher ideas for questions and stop going for "boob" jokes because it had run its course. Goodson-Todman's salesman expressed concern to Mark Goodson that after the 1980-81 season wrapped, he might not be able to sell the show for a third season unless something was done to spruce up the show. The problem was that when Mark Goodson shared this concern with his staff, nobody could come up with any ideas for how to change the show.

Charles, Brett, and Gene get ready for one more go-round in syndication in 1981. (Fred Wostbrock Collection)

The 1980-81 television season proved to be the final season of *Match Game PM*, after a respectable six years. Ironically, *Family Feud* had been the death of it. In 1980, Goodson-Todman expanded the prime access time version of *Feud* to five nights per week. It was the first prime access show to do so, and because the daytime and nighttime versions to that point had been so immensely popular, stations eagerly signed up at the expense of other prime access time properties. Numerous stations dumped *Match Game PM*, so at the end of the season, Goodson-Todman Productions itself reluctantly dumped *Match Game PM*.

And that wasn't the only reason that *Family Feud* was a sticking point for Gene. During the 1980-81 season, Richard Dawson had an aggressive contract renegotiation with ABC and Goodson-Todman, threatening at one point to quit *Feud*. Goodson-Todman actually considered letting him leave. Dawson had been a combative figure backstage, frequently clashing with *Feud* producer Howard Felsher, frustrating the crew by going on tangents during taping that caused the shows to run long and required more editing, holding up tapings for simple reasons like empty seats in the audience or burned out light bulbs on the set... but ABC was afraid of what *Feud* would be without Dawson. As Ira Skutch remembered while explaining his own personal issues with Dawson at *Match Game*, nobody can pinpoint the precise reasons that a show is a success, so when a program is drawing big ratings, there is tremendous reluctance to change anything about it. As long as *Feud* was dominating the ratings, Dawson held all the cards, and ABC eventually agreed to a $300,000-per-year contract for Dawson.

News of Dawson's new deal, to say the least, annoyed Gene. *Family Feud* was number one. It had been number one for a few seasons now. But even at its very peak, *Family Feud* had never averaged a 15% rating. *Match Game* had. Although *Match Game* was now fading, it had been a bigger hit than *Feud*, and Gene began wondering where his $300,000 payday was.

While Gene would hate to admit it, he had to take part of the blame for his own problem. Years earlier, he made a questionable business decision by switching lawyers and choosing to be represented by the same firm that represented Mark Goodson. Although on the surface it seemed like a good idea to share representation with the boss, it created a conflict of interest any time that Gene's contract had to be discussed. Who would those attorneys be looking out for; the man who was receiving the money, or the man whose company generated the money?

Match Game went away for a nice long break in 1981. The show managed to finish taping the entire 1980-81 season before 1980 ended, and taping wouldn't resume until July. Gene needed a breather from being a game show host for a little while and headed to Dallas (where none of the local stations carried *Match Game*) to star in a play for a little while. *Tribute*, written by Bernard Slade, had opened on Broadway in 1978 with Jack Lemmon in the lead role as Scottie Templeton, an actor who spent his entire life avoiding responsibilities, choosing instead a cushy life of parties, pranks, and joking around. When he is diagnosed with leukemia, Scottie contacts the son he's neglected his entire life and invites him to Manhattan, where they finally comes to grips with their strained relationship and learn to bond.

The original Broadway production was so overwhelmingly popular that by 1980, it was a movie, with Jack Lemmon reprising his role. So Gene had a big pair of shoes to fill when he made his way to Dallas to step into the role of Scottie Templeton.

> *That doesn't ever cross your mind… Comparisons are inevitable, but I'll do it my way. He did it his way. I came up against the same thing doing* Prisoner of Second Avenue. *Someone said, 'You do it different from the others.' But I've lived in New York, and I know what Neil Simon had in mind.*

Gene got the star treatment when he arrived in Dallas; a restaurant near his hotel had to put an employee in charge of chasing off autograph seekers while he ate. He also talked to the press while he was in town. *Dallas Morning News* reporter Diane Werts described Gene as slouching and looking irritated when she asked a question that he seemed to get every time he performed in a play: "What is a game show host doing performing in such a demanding play?"

> *[She was] making the same mistake producers make—typecasting me. They think, all he can do is what he does well. But the basic fact is, my training is in acting.*

Gene had been a master of ceremonies, a disc jockey, a songwriter, he sang and danced on the Broadway stage, he had been an announcer, he acted in skits for six years with Steve Allen. When he looked in the mirror, he saw a very versatile performer. When the rest of the world looked at him, all they seemed to see was a game show host. Gene couldn't understand that, and it exasperated him when people were surprised to see him doing any other work.

The Matchless Gene Rayburn

> *As a big corporate structure divides, I think it's more interesting for an individual to do different things. It keeps life interesting for me, to do different things.*

Peter Marshall weighs in on the barriers that a game show host faces when trying to do different things. "My situation was different because by the time I began hosting *The Hollywood Squares*, I had already been on Broadway. I had done films. I had done a bunch of things. So I had a reputation that allowed me to keep working. But to be honest, it's not casting directors or anybody on Broadway who hinder your career, and here's why. By and large, Broadway doesn't give a shit about television and television doesn't give a shit about Broadway. People who watch game shows have no idea that I've done Broadway. But there are people in the theater who refer to me as 'Peter Marshall from *Skyscraper*.' I did *La Cage Aux Folles* in the 1980s, after *Hollywood Squares* ended its run, and I worked with people who had no idea that I had ever hosted a game show.

Summer stock always gave Gene a home where he really wanted to be: the stage. (Fred Wostbrock Collection)

"The times that hosting a game show really harms your prospects are, well, for example, a singing career. Other television, too. Television executives view you as a game show host. And honestly, they're not narrow-minded in doing that. They're making decisions that reflect what the general public is thinking. The general public ties you completely to the game show that they see you on, so executives don't want to make you the star of a prime time sitcom because the audience will think 'He's a game show host. Why would he be on a sitcom?' I love my fans, I love the audience, but it's the audience that ties you down, not the decision-makers."

The show was being held at the Country Dinner Playhouse. Gene admitted that he would have shuddered at the idea of doing dinner theater in the past, but he agreed to the *Tribute* engagement just because the role was so different.

> *Normally, I would not do a dinner theater, because, frankly, they don't have enough seats to afford me. But I wanted to do this one to get it under my belt. I think my agent is on the right track. I've got to get a part where I'm cast against type, play a villain or a killer or something.*

Gene also spent part of 1981 in Denver, playing writer's block-plagued screenwriter Herbert Tucker in Neil Simon's *I Ought to Be in Pictures*. His co-star was Valerie Lansburg, later known for the role of Doris Schwartz on the TV series *Fame*.

Although Gene sought to break the chains of typecasting, he made it very clear that he didn't regret the jobs that trapped him. Television had been good to him, and he knew it.

> *You can reach maybe 20-25 million people. How many performances would you have to do at the Shubert Theater to reach that many people?*

And he didn't regret game shows a bit. Twenty-five years earlier, Jack Barry & Dan Enright gave him free rein over *Dough Re Mi* and Gene was able to make it his own. When *The Match Game* faltered, the solution to it, through lucky happenstance, catered perfectly to Gene's strengths, and he was able to make that show, likewise, a vehicle for Gene Rayburn. It wasn't exactly the fate he wanted, but he did get to be a big fish in a small pond. And though his heart still belonged to the Broadway theaters that never had any room for him, he admitted that he had become a much bigger star by doing something else. It didn't hurt that the job that he wound up in was one that carried a significantly smaller workload.

Gene himself told the reporter in Dallas, "I'm having so much fun doing what I'm doing and getting paid for it. Hell, in this business you really have to live day to day."

A few nights later, *Tribute* premiered and Diane Werts printed an unintentionally profound review of it. She wrote, "Life is just one big game to Scottie Templeton... But it's much more than games to Gene Rayburn... Rayburn hasn't met his match in Scottie, he's found the perfect outlet for the wild humor he displays in his emceeing chores—and for the acting skills he honed thirty-five years ago. Scottie could very well take Gene's place on TV's *Match Game*. He's doing much the same shtick, taking off from whatever's said to him, leaping into character and doing a number, seizing on a word here or there and following it up with a homemade punch line. Always 'on,' he's dedicated his life to being the life of everybody else's party. Only now life's running out for him, with some business left unfinished."

And with that, Werts locked in on a hidden truth without realizing it. Gene Rayburn claimed that the role was a challenge that he was up for, but the reality is, he was giving more of his honest self in that performance than the audience realized. Gene, now sixty-three years old, had experienced several colossal successes, but not the specific form of success that he had been shooting for when he was a cocky nineteen-year-old strolling into New York City for the first time. Like Scottie Templeton, he was the life of the party, his own life was running out, and he had unfinished business.

Dick Gautier says, "I'm surprised to think that Gene wanted to be an actor, because he didn't have an actor's chops, at least in my eye. We would talk about acting sometimes, and he didn't seem interested in discussing technique, or schools of thought."

Gene got his wish to play a villain, albeit one who reforms by the end of the show. He was cast as Ebenezer Scrooge for Boston's regional production of *A Christmas Carol* in the Charles Playhouse. Gene was so excited about the opportunity that he accepted the offer without reading a script, and had a wigmaker in California make a customized wig of wispy, flowing white hair (he also wore it for a taping of *Match Game* to finally give a face to Old Man Periwinkle).

Gene received less-than-favorable reviews for his performance as Scrooge. *The Boston Globe* critic observed that as purely evil, black-hearted Ebenezer Scrooge in the first part of the show, he did just fine. But Scrooge's gradual breakdown as he discovers the ill will toward him from family, business associates, and even strangers, and his eventual redemption required a level of complexity that Gene just didn't seem to have in him.

The critic tersely finished with "If he can't act Scrooge, he can't act."

> *You can't really let those knocks affect you in any way.*

Ebenezer Rayburn, in a Boston production of *A Christmas Carol*. (Author's Collection)

Game shows didn't get rave reviews either. Gene insisted that critical response didn't mean anything to him, but on the other hand, he still prized his clipping of *The New York Times* from the day that they gave him a positive review for *Robert Montgomery Presents*.

Gene got some small consolation in that he got a unique opportunity to perform *A Christmas Carol* in front of a very special audience. On opening night, the show was attended by Charles Dickens' great-granddaughter, Monica Dickens Stratton.

In July, Gene returned to Los Angeles to kick off tapings for the 1981-82 season of *Match Game*, with two slight changes on personnel, off and on the camera. Lynne went to work on the show as Gene's personal dresser, coordinating his wardrobe for him. It was actually an unofficial duty that she and Helen had been handling for years.

She says, "My mother had a built-in sense of style, which I probably picked up from her. My father, by nature, was clueless about how to dress. He had two companies that supplied him with suits on *Match Game*, Rubin Brothers and Palm Beach. And the suits looked good and the regular dresser at CBS did fine with the job before I got hired there. My father had a reputation in television for being a very well-dressed man. He always dressed really well on camera, and that was because, by and large, he avoided fads and trends in clothing and wore very traditional, very timeless outfits. So year after year, everything he wore looked great on him. But he didn't have any sense for what tie went with what suit, or if it was separate jackets and pants, which pants went with which jackets and what tie you could wear with that combo. And what my mother and I actually did was we got tags like your mother would put inside your clothes for summer camp. We put labels inside absolutely everything that my father would ever wear on television. We labeled all of the ties with numbers and we labeled the shirts with letters of the alphabet, and we made notes for my father that said things like 'Wear 4 with J.'"

The on-camera personnel change was on the bottom tier of the panel. Three years after Richard Dawson's departure, his seat was finally being filled on a permanent basis by a new regular panelist, McLean Stevenson.

> *Lynne Rayburn put this outfit together for me! The last year we were on [in syndication], she was my wardrobe specialist. She has a talent for that; she learned it from her mother, who had wonderful taste in clothing. I remember in the early days of television, Helen always laid out my clothes for me. And Lynne has a great ability for that. And she's a sweet, darling person and I love her.*

Colonel Blake, front and center. McLean Stevenson finally got the nod to replace Richard Dawson in 1981. Also on the panel: Robert Pine, Brett Somers, Charles Nelson Reilly, Dolly Martin, Fannie Flagg (Fred Wostbrock Collection)

Stevenson had appeared only sporadically on *Match Game* during its years on CBS. Stevenson had worked a variety of odd jobs, including managing his cousin Adlai's presidential campaign, before settling into acting. He struck gold with the role of Colonel Henry Blake on the CBS sitcom *M*A*S*H* in 1972. He stayed with that show for three seasons before departing in 1975. Stevenson's departure was and still is regarded as one of the all-time bad career moves in the history of television. His subsequent shows, *In the Beginning* and *The McLean Stevenson Show*, came and went in a matter of weeks. His biggest post-*M*A*S*H* success was an NBC sitcom, *Hello Larry*, which lasted only a season and a half.

He took the failure in stride, even laughing it off on one episode when Gene introduced him to the audience as "the man responsible for the death of more TV shows than anyone else in the history of the medium."

Robert Sherman explains, "McLean had done *Tattletales* and *Password Plus* and always brought that right combination, where he played the game really well but he was incredibly funny while playing it well. But when he appeared on *Match Game*, one of the things we noticed was that he had the same knack for anticipation that Richard had. He could anticipate questions and see what the writers were going for and give us exactly what we were hoping for. And he was outstanding at filling a lull and making everything more fun. So we thought McLean would be a good choice to fill that gap and be our new Richard."

Though McLean Stevenson was filling Richard Dawson's chair, nobody could have mistaken the two. Stevenson got more immersed in the shenanigans breaking loose around him than Dawson. Dawson typically remained seated at all times, even if some sort of shtick had emerged in which everybody was running around or milling about the set, and he typically didn't instigate anything.

Stevenson was more willing to cause trouble, or get caught in the middle of it. For one episode, he wrote "antelope" for the answer to every question. On another day, Gene and Charles got into an argument about the miniseries *Shogun* while the panel revealed their answers. Charles had disliked it and Gene was singing its praises. Charles, as a joke, lifted his stack of index cards and smacked Gene across the face. He meant to be playful about it, but used too much force, and Gene dropped to the floor. McLean reacted by reaching down, snatching the microphone from Gene's hand, and taking over the show. Gene rose, revealing a cut lip, and went along with it, taking McLean Stevenson's seat on the panel. McLean excitedly applauded when attractive contestants said they were single, he would get up and hug the more shapely contestants when they matched, even if he hadn't been the one who matched them. For somebody who hadn't really been a part of the show for the previous eight years, McLean Stevenson looked like he had been there all along, and he did revitalize the show somewhat.

The problem, though, was that it didn't revitalize the show quite enough. The news was trickling in from the local stations that ratings were faltering across the board. It wasn't a matter of time slots. This time around, it was a matter of, well, time.

A strong format for a game show, like *The Price is Right*, *Wheel of Fortune*, or *Jeopardy!*, can, with proper care from the people overseeing it, go on for years and years. Weaker games are more prone to having an expiration date. No amount of "proper care" can hold off the demise for a weaker show. Gene would be the first one to tell anybody who would listen that *Match Game* was a weak game. That's why they played it for laughs and goofed around. It offset the show's shortcomings.

Ira Skutch, in a 2006 interview, noted that by the 1981-82 season, the game played for laughs had run out of things to laugh about. *Match Game* grabbed the public's attention by pushing the envelope with the naughty double entendres and by slyly hinting at dangerous words. By 1981, cable TV, soap operas, daytime talk shows like *Donahue*, and public figures like Dr. Ruth Westheimer, were peeling away taboo after taboo, making it harder for a simple game show to shock the audience.

And even if they hadn't made it harder to shock the audience, the other problem was that the element of surprise is required to shock people, and nothing that happens on an eight-year-old show can be particularly surprising. As Skutch succinctly put it, "Once you've said the word 'boobs' so many times, it stops getting laughs."

Robert Sherman remembers, "We began looking for changes to make. Not necessarily changes to the game itself, but ways to make the show surprising again. Changes to the content, finding a new envelope to push. And when we sat around the office and talked about it, what we found was that none of the new extremes we were considering felt like things that would work within the show. And that was a tough realization to come to. To stay alive, we had to make a change, but every change we thought of felt wrong."

The time had come, and no writer, no panelist, and no host could fight it off. In January 1982, *Match Game* taped its final episode. No acknowledgement was made of the show's impending demise. Gene ended the show with a simple goodbye, no different from any other goodbye that he had offered in the previous nine years. It was going to be mailed out and circulated along with all the other batches of tapes that been taped for that season. And while the writing was on the wall, there was an off-chance that the show might get renewed and saying a final farewell would amount to egg on the face. The following month, the official word came in that *Match Game* was canceled.

Gene reflected on the end of the run with mixed emotions. On the one hand, being a game show host for so many years had tied him down and taken him away from the stage work that he dreamed of. But on the other hand, he couldn't have asked for a happier distraction.

> *A couple of times, I'd say, "What the hell am I doing here? I've been here 18,000 times."*

Gene took it the same way he had always taken the news of a lost job: He got out of the house and went looking for work.

Chapter Sixteen
Saturday Morning Fever

Disappointed as Gene may have been by the cancellation of his signature show, he saw the demise of *Match Game* as a new opportunity. He got rid of the apartment in Los Angeles and began chasing acting jobs on both coasts. He did yet another episode of *The Love Boat*. He also popped up on the soap opera *One Life to Live* and a game show–themed episode of *Fantasy Island*. He was also master of ceremonies for the annual Massachusetts Junior Miss Pageant.

And when Gene didn't have those gigs, he just sat in the yard at his house in Osterville, breathed in the ocean air, and enjoyed the good life. He had a motorcycle that he took for a ride when he didn't feel like pedaling the bicycle. He kept doing needlepoint, too. Staying fit was becoming important to him as he reached his mid-sixties. Years earlier, he had quit his two-pack-a-day smoking habit. With *Match Game* and

(Fred Wostbrock Collection)

the between-show dinner breaks out of his life, he drastically cut back on drinking. He still swam and played tennis regularly. Although Gene was probably missing out on potential gigs, he resisted leaving Osterville. He still didn't care for Los Angeles, frequently invoking two favorite quotes whenever anybody asked him why he refused to move there.

"Once you get there, there's no *there* there." –Gertrude Stein

"Los Angeles is fine, if you're an orange." –Fred Allen

He appeared on *One Life to Live* because it taped in New York, and he declared that, as unlikely a fit as it may have seemed to viewers, he truly wanted a regular role on a soap opera. It used the three-camera taping structure, the same way that sitcoms did, which meant that it was similar to the type of stage acting that Gene preferred. And again, the very idea of doing something different, something that no viewer could have expected from him, appealed to him.

But Gene didn't hold his breath. He openly spoke of his desire to do three-camera sitcoms, soap operas, and stage acting, but he was at a point in life where he was bracing himself for disappointment. He was coming to grips with being identified as "Gene Rayburn, game show host."

> *They cast you in whatever you've done last. I resent people saying "Well, he can't do that because he's a game show host." I think that's hardening of the arteries of the skull… I think we should all diversify our lives.*

Gene sought other ways to diversify his life. He was doing more and more volunteer work, assisting non-profit causes, like Planned Parenthood, United Way and United Cerebral Palsy. Gene also had a for-profit cause that he was actively involved in: a roller skating rink in Hyannis.

Gene loved roller skating. He even skated around the stage of *Match Game* for his entrance on one episode. The skating rink he invested in had an organist providing live music every Monday night and Gene showed up every week for music and skating. Word that the TV star in the neighborhood liked to hang out at the skating rink was very good for business. There was usually a massive crowd there every Monday night and Gene signed a few dozen autographs before the night was done. It didn't irritate him at all. It was obvious that his presence was good for business, and he was happy to be bothered by autograph seekers at every turn as he circled the rink.

Local television proved to be a friend to Gene. The local ABC affiliate in Boston hired him to host a believe-it-or-not series called *It Happened Right Here*. And Gene brought his career full circle by returning to New York City every weekend to host a show for local independent station WNEW-TV. That series was *Saturday Morning Live*.

Saturday Morning Live was a service/talk show. Gene interviewed guests, the usual mix of celebrity guests, authors, and musicians. The show also had a regular "family" of guests who appeared on every program with Gene. Chef Annemarie Huste cooked something with Gene. Joel Rapp was a plant care expert. Ruth Katz demonstrated arts & crafts projects. Handyman Mike Gallagher did home improvement projects. For regular segments about animal care, the show hired a pet trainer named Warren Eckstein.

Eckstein explains, "I never planned on having a career in radio and television. I'm shy, the thought never crossed my mind. But I had been a trainer-for-hire in the New York area for a couple of years. I would go to people's homes and train their pets for a fee. Well, I wound up getting a reputation from that. Local newspapers began calling me a lot when they were writing articles about animals and I would be the expert they quoted. And then I began working behind the scenes for TV shows. I worked for David Letterman for a while, training his dog. I worked at *Saturday Night Live* a few times when they had skits that involved live animals.

"And then I got a call from a producer explaining that WNEW was starting a new show called *Saturday Morning Live* that would involve a lot of demonstrations and educational segments, and the producer asked if I would come in and just talk about animal training. And by the way, that's a way that television has changed over the years and not for the better. A lot of what you see on television now is actors who are delivering a prepared script about the information, instead of legitimate experts talking about the information. Anyway, before the show premiered, I came to the studio and we did a demo tape where the producer just talked to me about my work. And they liked it and hired me. So from day one, I was there, and I was on every episode of the series."

Warren Eckstein became a television regular with the launch of *Saturday Morning Live*, and a self-described "shy guy" would be sharing the stage every week with a natural born ham who never met a camera that he didn't like. At first, it seemed like it would be an oil-and-water relationship between Gene and Warren. At first.

Warren remembered, "I was a big fan of *Match Game* and I was genuinely star-struck the first time I saw Gene. I was also intimidated from watching the show backstage. I was a little surprised by how knowledgeable Gene was about a lot of subjects. They had done a

Gene with Warren Eckstein and a four-legged visual aid during a segment of *Saturday Morning Live*. (Author's Collection)

cooking segment already and Gene really knew a lot about cooking. He had interviewed a few guests and he knew so much about what they were talking about. He was really a renaissance man. I didn't get a chance to talk to him backstage before the show, so walking onstage and seeing him the first time, I became very nervous.

"For that first show, I brought a Staffordshire terrier, which is one of the breeds of dog that people commonly call a pit bull. And I remember being amazed at what Gene did as soon as I came out. He immediately got down on his hands and knees so he was face-to-face with the dog. And he greeted the dog and made friends with it. I had just written a book called *Pet Aerobics*. So I was talking about exercising with your pet, and I demonstrated puppy push-ups, jogging, and jumping jacks, and Gene jogs around the stage with the dog, he does the push-ups, he does jumping jacks. Meanwhile, I'm talking about aerobics and how to go about getting your dog started on this, and Gene is actually doing the things I was talking about and showing the audience everything I'm describing, and he's being funny and clowning around, but the way he's doing it is just completely drawing attention to everything that I'm saying.

"And Gene begins asking me questions, and I came to realize that Gene respected knowledge. If Gene determined that you knew what you were doing and you knew what you were talking about, he would do everything he could to promote you and put the spotlight on you."

Gene viewed himself as Warren's helper, rather than viewing himself as the star of the show. For one show, Warren chatted with dog owners who were having problems with their pets. Warren took the microphone in hand, spoke to the home audience, and spoke to the pet owners, asking them questions and giving his insight. As Warren did that, Gene, silently standing in the background, simply opened cans of dog food, filled a few bowls, and placed them on the floor to set up a demonstration of how to handle a finicky eater.

"That was so great," Warren said. "Gene did that for everybody. He let the expert do their job. If you were knowledgeable, he let you do it."

Sharing the knowledge wasn't just enough, though. Warren knew the value of entertainment, and he knew the value of being joined by a host who wanted to entertain. For a segment about puppy care, Warren brought thirty puppies to the stage with him. Thirty puppies were far more than he could handle, and that was exactly why he did it.

Warren explains, "It's important to be fun because people don't like being preached at. You don't want it to just be a lecture because it'll go in one ear and out the other. You can be interesting and you can just present the information, and the viewer might listen to it, but they don't remember it. If I had brought out one puppy, and held onto the puppy for the whole fifteen-minute segment and said 'Here's how you care for this puppy,' the audience would have listened, but they wouldn't have learned anything. I brought out thirty puppies. One's running all over the place, one is peeing on the floor, one is chewing on something, some of them are rolling around and play-fighting. One is climbing up on Gene and licking his face, and people will remember that. Things are getting out of hand while I'm talking about all the puppy behavior you're seeing. It's great television."

It wasn't what producers had in mind, and even after seeing the way the audience reacted to the puppy overload, a few staffers suggested to Warren that things might go more smoothly if they used a professionally-trained dog for the segments.

Warren adamantly disagreed, telling the producer, "If you want a perfect dog, go to Radio Shack and get a dog with batteries."

He clarifies now, "I don't want perfect dogs on television with me. I don't want professionally-trained animals, because the average viewer, the average pet owner, can't relate to that. Pets aren't perfect, so I wanted animals that weren't immaculate. I wanted mistakes to happen. I wanted some things that didn't go right, because a viewer who actually has a problem with his pets will watch that and say 'Yeah, that's exactly the problem that I'm having!'"

And through it all, he had the perfect helper, both for letting everything get out of hand, and for making sure that the chaos always had some substance to it. "Gene was so great; he would allow himself to be made fun of. He actually ate dog food one day when I was discussing nutrition. He never said 'I won't do this,' he never refused to do anything. And he trusted me. I did a segment with snakes once. And I could tell that Gene wasn't enthusiastic about it at all. He didn't like snakes. But he held them for the segment and went along with everything.

"And he always made sure that we made the most out of every segment, as far as being informative. We got into a routine off-camera every week. Before the show began, I came up to him and I said, 'Here's what I absolutely need to cover and what I need to say while I'm on,' and I gave him four or five things that I really wanted to tell the audience. So while I was out there, we'd have an interview, a conversation. Sometimes we'd get off-track, but Gene loved hearing the information that I had to share, and so even when we got off-track, it was always worthwhile and important. If I may say so myself, that's why animals are great for talk shows. A cooking segment is step A, step B, step C, step D. Home improvement is the same thing; here's a way to do this, and now we've done it. But an animal segment doesn't go exactly as planned. Eventually, something happens that causes the subject to change, but anything that goes wrong is still worth your attention.

"But as we went along each week, I would try to mention all the talking points I had in mind. And during the course of the segment, if I forgot to make one of those points, Gene would ask me a question, and what he was doing was structuring his question so that the answer would be my talking point. He remembered what I wanted to say, and without letting the audience in on the fact that I forgot, he always had a way of making sure I said everything I wanted to say. And he managed to do that all while he was running around the stage rounding up all of the puppies that were running away."

Gene wasn't ready to pass the baton yet. He still had a lot of work to do in 1982. (Author's Collection)

He did more than wrangle puppies. He cleaned up after them, too. Warren got a little more ambitious for one show, bringing llamas and goats to the set. The llama relieved itself. Gene unhesitantly drew attention to it, feigning outrage at the rudeness of the llama, the danger that he was putting other guests in by making the floor slippery. Gene walked offstage, returned with a broom, and cleaned the set himself while Warren continued talking.

Gene, invoking a famous old joke about the circus janitor who hated his job, but refused to quit, looked at the camera and yelled, "And leave show business?!"

Warren remembers, "Gene was hilarious. I brought a gecko to the show once, which is a very small lizard, and it does bite sometimes, but… you know, it's so tiny. Even if it does bite, it might not even break the skin. But Gene lets out this big gasp when I show it to the audience, and he begins warning the audience to stay clear and give the creature plenty of space. It could bite, it might get violent, and we're all in a lot of danger. The urgency just looked and sounded so ridiculous."

Warren did get himself into some danger once. It was away from the show on a Friday. He was dealing with a mongoose and he got a serious bite on his hand. He had to go straight to the emergency room, and for just two fingers, he received a total of 115 stitches.

The show must go on, though, Warren arrived at the Metromedia Studios in New York the next day. "My hand looked like a football, swollen and covered with stitches. I walk up to Gene before the show and I said 'I'm going to be keeping this hand away from the camera because it looks so bad.' And I told him what had happened the day before.

"So my segment begins and the lights haven't even finished coming up on set and Gene grabs my bad hand and yanks it into view of the camera. And he says 'Look at what happened to this guy. This is our animal care expert. This man wants to tell you how to handle animals, and look at him!'"

Gene didn't need a camera or a show if he wanted to joke around with Warren, though. Warren remembers, "Gene returned to Los Angeles for some kind of business and he invited me to join him. I came to Los Angeles and he says 'Come on, let's go to dinner!' I was and still am a vegan. And Gene takes me straight down to the most famous hamburger stand in Los Angeles. And we're in line and I say 'Gene, just tell them I want lettuce, tomato, and mayo on a bun.' And Gene shoots me a look and I say 'Gene, when have you ever seen me eat anything besides vegetables? When have you ever seen me eat meat?' I honestly believe he knew. I really do. And I think he just wanted to see the look on my face if he took me to a hamburger place."

It wasn't just Gene clowning around. Warren fondly remembers one *Saturday Morning Live* segment where a friend dropped in for a visit. "Charles Nelson Reilly was a guest once and he stayed beyond his own segment and he was onstage when I came out. And I brought more puppies with me to demonstrate how to train them to come on command. Gene and Charles both get down on hands and knees, rolling around, barking, whimpering, panting… I swear to you, I thought I was going to pee myself right there on the air. I was laughing so hard I could barely get through a sentence. It was so great. And years later, people would meet me and mention that segment. People thought that watching me train these two grown men was just so funny. And it was."

Eckstein just thought of it as goofing off with a purpose. As usual, Gene was generating laughs while Warren educated the audience, and the result was an enlightening segment that happened to be really funny. It wasn't until much later that Warren realized what Gene was doing f or him.

"In the beginning of that show, I was so nervous and so shy. As time went by, I became comfortable in front of the audience, in front of the cameras, around Gene. And when I began getting comfortable, Gene began trying to trip me up. During the commercial break, I'd walk onstage and take my place for Gene to introduce me when the show returned. And once I was standing next to Gene, he'd say 'Don't look at the woman in the second row, her skirt's really short and you can see right up it. Very distracting.' He'd say 'Oh, don't look at the front row, there's a bald guy blowing his nose into his hand. That's awful.' Just something like that to catch me off-guard right as I'm about to go on the air. He got into this habit of talking to me about the previous segment. I'd be talking about a cat and he'd say 'Boy, how about that rabbit you brought last week?' And he'd just talk about rabbits and try to get me veering off-track, but I'd stay right on the subject and I wouldn't get distracted.

"And after months of this, Gene takes me to dinner, and while we're eating, he said 'You can't be selfish about your knowledge. I want to make sure you understand how much good you can do.' And I said 'What do you mean?' He said, 'If you just want to be a private trainer and make yourself available for hire to people with pets, that's fine. But think about how many people you can reach through television. Millions of people, some of them just want to be entertained, but some of them really need help. They have a problem pet, or they want a pet but they're not confident that they can care for it. You can really use television to do something important for a lot of people.'

"And… you know, again, television never would have occurred to me as a career path. That wasn't me, that wasn't something that I considered a skill… and in the years after *Saturday Morning Live*, I became a semi-regular on *Hour Magazine* with Gary Collins, I've been on *Today* so many times, I did *Regis and Kathie Lee* a lot, I was the Creature Keeper on *The Mickey Mouse Club* for the Disney Channel, I've had a radio show for thirty years now. And that came from being onstage with Gene Rayburn. He taught me how to handle broadcasting, and how to make it work to suit my abilities."

On his own time, Gene got together with the *Saturday Morning Live* staff and cobbled together a fifteen-minute highlight reel of Warren Eckstein's appearances on the show. It was an informal pitch tape. In the long run, Gene was hoping to get Warren a series of his own and help produce it. The planned series never came to fruition. Away from television, Gene continued bonding with Warren.

Warren remembers, "We went bowling a few times, had dinner a few times. He listened so much; rarely talked about himself. He was always in 'learning' mode with everyone he had a conversation with. He wanted to know more. He always challenged what you said, but when I say that, I mean 'challenged' in a very positive way. You'd make a statement and he wanted you to clarify it, and he wanted to know what you were basing it on, and what it was rooted in. He wanted to know why I thought these things and why I believed them. He was infatuated with the world around him, and if he felt you had something to share or something to offer, he treated you with the ultimate respect. In the time that we worked together, thankfully, I never went through a time of crisis. My private life, my personal life was completely fine. But I remember Gene made me feel like he would be there if I ever fell apart. I felt like I could have called him and told him what was going wrong and he would have said 'Okay, let's work this out for you.' I never had to, but I could have."

"Gene was my mentor, and I can't say that enough. If you look back at your school years, and you think of a teacher who made a difference in your life, a teacher that you put on a pedestal… that's the way I look at Gene Rayburn. He taught me to be comfortable and he gave me a chance to help more people than I ever could have. And I picture Cher's eulogy at Sonny Bono's funeral. She wrapped up by talking about reading *Reader's Digest* when she was a girl and there was a feature called 'The Most Unforgettable Character I've Ever Met.' When I look back at my own life... it was Gene Rayburn."

The *Saturday Morning Live* experience left its mark on Warren Eckstein, who went into a broadcasting service career that took him from show to show, spreading his knowledge of animal care, and his knowledge of how to present it.

Eckstein remembers, "I did *Live with Regis and Kathie Lee* once. And I talked to Michael Gelman, the producer, before the show. I told him what I wanted to do, and he said 'No, do this instead.' And I said 'It'll work better if I do it this way.' And he said, 'No, you need to do it this way.' So I went onstage with Regis and Kathie Lee and I just ignored everything Michael Gelman told me, and I did exactly what I wanted to do. And Gelman walks up to me after the show and says 'See, I told you it would go well.'"

In a matter of months, *Saturday Morning Live* was consistently a ratings winner and it was generating positive buzz. It looked for a time that it could fill a void for stations across the country. *Today* and *Good Morning America* were raking in big profits for NBC and ABC affiliates, but independent stations across the country were left out in the cold, without a service program to call their own. Discussion began mounting of turning *Saturday Morning Live* into a national show through syndication.

A highlight reel was assembled to show stations across the country what this local morning show in New York had to offer. It was a chance to compete with the big networks, with a show that had forged its own identity. The show had a live (and lively) studio audience. Gene didn't look like the typical morning show anchorman. For *Saturday Morning Live*, he often sported a plaid shirt or a sweater, along with blue jeans and sneakers. If things were going to be a little more physical than usual, he dressed down even more, hosting the show in a cotton jacket and sweatpants.

The guests were an eclectic mix. Gene and Edward Asner modeled hats together, while a flea market shopping expert showed off several hundred dollars' worth of Christmas gifts that he had rounded up for only a few bucks by knowing what to look for. A yo-yo artist put some coarse material on one end of the yo-yo while Gene stuck a kitchen match in his mouth. She swung her yo-yo and lit the match without touching Gene's face. A female self-defense expert startled Gene one day when he lunged at her for a demonstration and she reacted by grabbing and squeezing his genitals. The show's fashion expert demonstrated how to change from a business outfit into an evening gown by dressing in layers. A homemaking expert tried to demonstrate a kitchen tool that would peel a hard-boiled egg with the push of a button, but mistakenly used a raw egg, causing a small mess. To commemorate the fifteenth anniversary of Dr. Martin Luther King Jr.'s death, James Earl Jones recited King's "Drum Major Instinct" sermon.

The host himself was an eclectic mix. Gene hosted an episode while taking a bubble bath, and spent another episode wearing a mud mask. For another episode, Gene was asked to bring his night wear to the show. Gene walked out wearing his pajama top and a tightly-cinched bathrobe, and sheepishly explained that he didn't bother keeping the bottoms. For a physical fitness segment, Gene walked out dressed for a workout, wearing gym shorts with puffy white cloth sticking out all over. He explained to the audience that he preferred boxers to briefs and flat-out forgot he was going to be wearing gym shorts that day. During a cooking demonstration with Annmarie Huste, Gene observed that the bananas she was using weren't quite fit for cooking, and justified it by singing the old Chiquita banana jingle ("When they are flecked with brown and have a golden hue/bananas are the best and are the best for you"). He got a shiatsu massage during one episode. He brought some old knick-knacks to the studio, encouraged viewers to phone in and describe the junk they had around the house, and had a swap meet live on the air. He even poplocked one day after a lesson from a breakdancing troupe.

Though New York was treating him extremely well after the demise of *Match Game*, Gene frequently returned to Los Angeles to appear as a guest on a few game shows. He appeared on the second-to-last week of NBC's *Password Plus* as well as the new version of *Tattletales* on CBS. As a favor to friend Betty White, he appeared as a panelist on the new game show she was hosting, an oddball series called *Just Men!* for NBC.

It came and went in thirteen weeks, but White wound up claiming a Daytime Emmy Award in the category of Outstanding Game Show Host; she was the first woman to win that accolade.

One game show where Gene didn't pop up: *Family Feud*. The invitation was extended, though. *Family Feud* was preparing for a special week of episodes in which ten game show hosts would compete for charity. Gene was invited to participate. One team, named The Magnificent MC's, would be comprised of Bill Cullen, Betty White, Nipsey Russell, Bob Eubanks, and Jim Perry. Their opponents, the Heavenly Hosts, would include Tom Kennedy, Jim Lange, Leslie Uggams, Peter Marshall, and Gene.

Gene quite emphatically said no. Time had not healed all wounds. Despite a combined sixteen-year run, Gene maintained for the rest of his life that *Match Game* could have and should have had a longer run, were it not for the damage done to it by other people. Realistically, time slots probably harmed *Match Game* more than any other factor, but the memories of Richard Dawson—in Gene's eyes—actively causing harm to the show with his off-putting on-air behavior lingered. Gene never forgave Richard and had no desire to be in the same room with him under any circumstances.

Gene and nine contestants, during a rehearsal for the unsold pilot *Party Line*. (Fred Wostbrock Collection)

And though Gene wanted to continue acting, he knew that game shows were still a viable career move for him. Reg Grundy, a prolific Australian producer, had started making strides in the United States by overseeing an NBC game, *Sale of the Century*. He mounted a pilot for a new game, *Party Line*, produced by Robert Noah. Gene was cast as host.

The pilot pitted a team of five men against five women. A member of the team was shown a word while his teammates wore headphones and couldn't hear anything. With a forty-second clock ticking away, the teammate who saw the word tried to convey it to one of his partners. Once his partner had guessed it, that player attempted to convey it to the next partner in line, and so on, with the catch being that no key words in any of the clues could be repeated. The challenge for the players further down the line was that their headphones had precluded them from hearing clues already given, and using a clue already given stopped the clock and their progress. The series eventually went to air in 1986 for ABC, under the title *Hot Streak*, with Englishman Bruce Forsyth hosting.

Gene also took part in a loving tribute to his best-known line of work at the 1983 Emmy Awards ceremony. Gene, along with fellow game show hosts Monty Hall, Peter Marshall, Alex Trebek, Art James, Art Fleming, Jim Lange, Dennis James, Bert Parks, and Geoff Edwards, sang a cute tune called "Game Show University," a song about an "institute of higher earning" in which graduates received their GHDs ("doctor of game show-ology," according to Alex Trebek's line in the song). Gene was one of the few trained singers among the emcees and mugged at the camera after belting out the line "The farmer's daughter said I've got the nicest fill-in-the-blank!"

Back at WNEW, Metromedia was still waiting to give everyone the word about whether or not the national *Saturday Morning Live* would become a reality. As they waited, Gene got a call from Mark Goodson Productions (Bill Todman died in 1978 and the company had just changed its name) about an unusual new project. Mark Goodson wanted to revive *Match Game* in a way that had never been attempted with another game show. Gene was intrigued by the idea that Goodson described and agreed to return to Los Angeles and shoot a pilot for NBC.

A few weeks later, Gene got bad news and good news. The bad news on the east coast was that while *Saturday Morning Live* would continue on WNEW, there wouldn't be a national version. Not enough stations had signed on. The good news on the west coast was that NBC had picked up this strange new game show idea that NBC had talked Mark Goodson into putting together. Gene decided that it was time to leave *Saturday Morning Live*, and revisit *Match Game*. On paper, it seemed like the right move.

Chapter Seventeen
Hour Without Power

The title was cumbersome, but there was no denying the ability it had to grab a game show fan's attention right away: *The Match Game/Hollywood Squares Hour*.

Robert Sherman shares the unusual genesis of an unusual game. "I think I was the first one to hear about it. An NBC executive contacted us at the office and he talked to me. NBC was going through this bizarre problem that doesn't come up very often in TV. They had just picked up a new soap opera, but they wanted it to be a state-of-the-art production, very high-tech and very complex by daytime soap standards. And it was such an elaborate production that even though they picked it up, they were estimating that it would be about two years before this soap was ready to go on the air. The problem it gave them was that it would go into the 3:00-4:00 afternoon slot on the line-up, and in the meantime,

(Author's Collection)

they had nothing to plug into that slot. That was a big problem, because the concern from NBC was that if they left that time slot empty, affiliates would just pick up syndicated shows and drop the hour altogether, and then by the time the soap opera was ready to go, the soap opera would be a bust. They absolutely needed a show for that slot so they wouldn't lose the affiliates.

"NBC needed a new series to be, essentially, a placeholder for the soap opera. And game shows are cost-effective and they thought an hour-long game show would be a cost-effective solution. And the first thing they had to assure us of was that we weren't just going in for a temporary capacity. They made it very clear that we were in the 3:00 p.m. time slot as a placeholder, but if this new game show was a hit, they would reconfigure the schedule so they could have their soap opera and hang onto us. Obviously, they would. It costs money to put a show on the air, so there has to be a commitment there and a desire to make it a hit, but they wanted to make sure we understood we weren't just a quick fix.

"Here's what was strange about NBC calling us. They weren't calling us asking us for formats, they called us and flat-out told us what the show had to be. What this executive told me was that they had already held a series of meetings about it. And the NBC executives had initially decided that they wanted a one-hour *Match Game*. But they kept talking it over and they decided that *Match Game* wasn't strong enough to sustain one hour. So then they discussed doing two game shows, *Match Game* and *Hollywood Squares*, but they were concerned that the affiliates might carry only one show but not the other, and plug in a thirty-minute syndicated show. They were adamant that whatever filled that hour slot had to be a single, one-hour show. And then instead of doing *Match Game* and *Hollywood Squares*, they came up with the idea of doing a game show that combined both. Both games were comedy games with big panels, so they figured there was good parity there and they would go together. But they hadn't fully fleshed out the idea. So the conversation was, NBC came to us and said 'We want you to come up with a game show that runs a full hour, that combines elements of both shows into a single game. Can you get the rights to *Hollywood Squares*?'"

At the peak of the success of *The Hollywood Squares*, creator/producers Merrill Heatter and Bob Quigley sold the show to Filmways,

Inc., arranging a deal to continue producing the network and syndicated versions of the show for as long as they remained on the air. The NBC *Squares* came to an end in 1980, the syndicated run ended in 1981, and with that, Heatter-Quigley Productions no longer had any connection to the wildly popular show that they had unleashed in 1966. In 1982, Filmways was sold to Orion Television. There was another co-owner who needed to be dealt with in brokering the deal, however: original *Squares* host Peter Marshall.

And Peter Marshall delves even further into the origins of *The Match Game/Hollywood Squares Hour*. "I actually owned a piece of *Hollywood Squares*. There was a year when Heatter-Quigley gave me a share of it when I renewed my contract, and even though they sold off what they owned, I still had my piece and I was in a position where I could do things with it. What I really wanted to do was get two shows back into production at NBC. During the '60s and '70s, *Hollywood Squares* aired back to back with *Jeopardy!* It was the original version with Art Fleming. And we got great ratings and I thought we still could. *Jeopardy!*, I had no control over. That was a different company, different people, and I couldn't do anything about that. But I was completely serious about pitching this even though *Jeopardy!* wasn't mine. I wanted to talk NBC into putting both shows back on the air. I met with a man at Orion Television and negotiated a deal where I would sign over my rights to *Squares* and in exchange they would help me get both shows back on the air.

"I pitched the idea first to Grant Tinker, who was chairman of the board for NBC at that time, because Grant and I had a relationship outside of television. We were friends. And Grant liked the idea. The guys running NBC daytime at that point were incensed because they felt I went over their heads. I didn't go over their heads! Grant was my friend! So the NBC daytime guys found out I had signed over my share of *Squares* to Orion, they did business with the people at Orion, and Grant Tinker wound up being the one who called and broke the news to me that NBC was picking up *Hollywood Squares* but that they didn't want me involved. They screwed me. And I immediately knew the show was going to be a disaster because they weren't going to hire anybody who had worked on the original show. They were going to hire an entirely new group to run it and that was a horrible idea."

Together, Orion leased the rights to the format to Mark Goodson Productions. From there, Goodson's staff began fleshing out a format as prescribed by NBC.

Gene, on the unaired pilot for *The Match Game/Hollywood Squares Hour*. (Fred Wostbrock Collection)

Robert Sherman remembers, "From the beginning, I had reservations. It was 1983. And I still felt the way I felt a year ago, that *Match Game* was a product of its time and its time had passed. So reviving the show a year after I felt that way really bothered me."

The format originally conjured was that three contestants would compete against each other in *Match Game*, with a panel of six celebrities as always. The low-scoring contestant was eliminated and the two players remaining would compete against each other in *Hollywood Squares*, with three more celebrities joining the game. The winner of *Hollywood Squares* would then play a Super Match round.

The game was lightly retooled by the time NBC put it on the air on October 31, 1983. In the finished product, *Match Game* was scaled back to the standard two contestants, with the winner playing the previous day's returning champion in *Hollywood Squares* (a default champion was randomly selected for the premiere broadcast). The winner of *Hollywood Squares* would go to the Super Match.

In the Audience Match portion, the three most popular answers were worth $1,000, $500, and $250. In an added twist, the contestant won $100 for giving an answer that didn't rank among the top three. The Star Wheel was eliminated and the contestant was once again free to select any panelist they wished of the nine sitting onstage for Head to Head Match. A new wrinkle was that all nine celebrities had envelopes containing multipliers; four stars were hiding a 10, four stars were hiding a 20, and one star of the nine was hiding a 30. The star selected would reveal their number and determine the grand payoff for Head to Head Match; it could potentially be $30,000.

So far, so good. Two proven hits that both had long runs in daytime and prime time to their credit. Lots of funny celebrities, and the hour would end with a shot at the biggest cash prize on television that year. It was the biggest can't-miss prospect the game show world had ever seen. "Miss" was exactly what it did, however.

The issue of casting a host was the first sign that something was wrong with this format. Given what exactly the show was, there was seemingly only one logical choice: Gene Rayburn. But it wasn't; NBC had their own host in mind. And they suggested that their host should share the show with Gene.

Hour Without Power

Ira Skutch remembered later that he vehemently argued against that proposal, saying it would make the sixty-minute extravaganza look like two separate shows.

Robert Sherman remembers, "A lot of us—not just Ira—were vocally speaking up in favor of having Gene host the full hour. And knowing Gene, he would have been delighted to do it. But for some reason, there was tremendous insistence from the network that we needed two hosts."

In fairness, there was an inspired bit of logic in place here. Gene Rayburn could host *Match Game*, with the other host sitting in as a regular panelist every day. When *Hollywood Squares* rolled around, the co-host would take over, and Gene would sit on the panel and be a regular panelist for that portion of the show.

Jon Bauman, Gene's co-host who would run *Hollywood Squares*. (Fred Wostbrock Collection)

NBC wound up selecting, to say the least, an unlikely candidate to join Gene every day: Jon Bauman, a/k/a Bowzer. Jon Bauman, born and raised in Queens, had grown up a quiet, nerdy kid who loved classical music and carried a briefcase to school instead of a backpack. Inevitably, a tough kid would kick the case away from him. He channeled the childhood bullying into something surprisingly productive and successful. After graduating from college with a degree in musical theory, he joined a singing group called Sha-Na-Na, which specialized in '50s-style tunes. Bauman greased down his bushy hair, dressed in leather and jeans, and created a stage alter ego for himself, "Bowzer," based largely on the bullies that had kicked his briefcase.

The group became a wildly successful nostalgia act. They performed at Woodstock, appeared briefly in the movie *Grease*, and starred in a syndicated prime access time variety show for four seasons. Bowzer was more than a character for Jon Bauman, he was a full-blown alter ego. He was almost never seen in public as himself. Like Cliff Arquette's Charley Weaver and Paul Reubens' Pee-Wee Herman, the character seemed to take on a life of its own. Bauman even appeared numerous times on *Match Game*, always in character as Bowzer.

And then suddenly, he began escaping from Bowzer. He hosted a hidden-camera pilot on ABC, *We Dare You*, as Jon Bauman. He hosted a short-lived rock music-themed game show called *The Pop and Rocker Game* as Jon Bauman. And Mark Goodson hired him to co-host *The Match Game/Hollywood Squares Hour* as Jon Bauman.

As everyone moved forward with the new project, it became clear that there were serious problems with it, and Gene was already regretting the departure from *Saturday Morning Live*.

Announcer Gene Wood later told interviewer David Hammett, "Rayburn was dragged kicking & screaming into that hour."

Robert Sherman counters, "I'd say 'kicking & screaming' was a little bit of an exaggeration. I'm sure Gene wasn't happy about leaving his local show in New York, but it was national exposure, and Gene truly loved *Match Game*, so he was going back to a job that made him happy. And I'm pretty sure that the paychecks that NBC and Mark Goodson gave him for hosting the show made him kick & scream a little less. To be very blunt, I'm pretty sure that Gene needed the money. Gene enjoyed living the good life, and he liked to spend money. And I'm fairly certain that for most of his career, he was spending more than he should have. And the money he made from CBS in the 1970s allowed him to live the good life. Local TV in New York, not so much. So when Goodson told him what they were willing to pay, I think Gene was all in. At the very beginning, I think the only thing that Gene was unenthusiastic about was the notion of having to share the job of hosting. If he had a say in it, I'm positive that he would have wanted to host the full hour."

From virtually the day that it premiered, *The Match Game/Hollywood Squares* fell to pieces, and to the day it met its end, almost nothing got fixed. It was a peculiar mountain of failures and oversights from a company heralded for its meticulous attention to detail for every new format. The audio/visual elements were certainly handled with care. Edd Kalehoff whipped up a dynamic music package combining brass, strings, and synthesizers. The main feature of the set was a dazzling marquee spanning almost the entire studio, which flashed the names of the hosts and panelists for the beginning of every episode, and then split apart so that the co-hosts could make their entrance. The celebrities sat at an ingeniously designed cluster of desks and boxes that could adequately accommodate two different game shows. And the series seemed to have a perfect time slot: weekdays at 3 p.m., just like old times. Maybe the after-school crowd would discover this show, too.

The first problem with the show was that Gene never had a chance to develop a rapport with the panel. It was determined in the developmental stages that *Match Game* wouldn't work with nine celebrities on the panel and that they'd leave it at six. That meant that for half of every episode, there were three celebrities sitting in the green room, doing nothing. To make it a little more fair, Goodson had the panel rotate seats for every episode (except for Gene and Jon, who always occupied the bottom left chair). As discussed earlier, *Match Game* had made a science of how to seat the panel to maximize the entertainment, but that had gone out of the window in the interest of being fair to everybody, and it meant that Gene had a slightly different group of people to deal with every program.

Other than that, *Match Game* was the same as it had always been, even retaining most of the same writing staff, and it felt almost if not quite like old times. And then at the halfway point of the show, a cluster of chairs and lighted panels swung in from offstage, in walked three more stars for *Hollywood Squares*, and things went completely wrong.

Once upon a time, Peter Marshall asked Charley Weaver, "How many balls are on a billiard table?" And Charley Weaver replied "How many guys are playing?" A fan of *Hollywood Squares* loved those famous zingers and expected them on every show. With *The Match Game/Hollywood Squares Hour*, though, the fans were in for a big disappointment. And Mark Goodson wanted it that way.

For the first half of the show, Gene hosts *Match Game* on a very faithful-looking update of the 1970s set. (Fred Wostbrock Collection)

Goodson despised the zingers of *Hollywood Squares*. They had been prepared by a team of writers for the stars, who were briefed on what jokes to make before each taping. Goodson once referred to this as "actionable fraud," holding it in the same regard as briefing the contestants with correct answers on the rigged quiz shows of the 1950s. It really wasn't the same thing because the stars' answers didn't have sole bearing on whether or not a contestant claimed their square. After giving an answer, the contestant had to say "I agree" or "I disagree." A contestant captured a square by agreeing with a correct answer or disagreeing with a wrong answer. Goodson didn't see it that way. And now placed in charge of a game that he despised, Goodson saw to it that the stars went into the game blindly.

Robert Sherman remembers, "Mark Goodson hated the original *Hollywood Squares*, and I mean it when I say that word. He hated it. He wrote an essay for some newspaper about how terrible it was that the show briefed the celebrities about the questions for each show, and how the show tried to justify it by putting a disclaimer in the end credits explaining what they had done. But Goodson argued that the disclaimer ran far too long and they only flashed it on the screen for a few seconds and the audience didn't have a chance to take it in or understand what it meant. So if he was going to do *Hollywood Squares*, he was going to do it Mark Goodson's way, even though the Heatter-Quigley way worked. So we had to re-invent the wheel."

This created a couple of problems. The first was that *Squares* just wasn't funny. Bauman was asking straight questions and the stars were giving straight answers. To bring the show to life, Mark Goodson Productions tried to repair it the same way that they had repaired *Match Game*. *Squares* still used trivia questions, but now they were *Match Game*-style trivia questions, small stories with characters and humorous situations. ("You're eating dinner at Liberace's house. Should you light a cigarette on his candelabra or does Emily Post say this is tacky?" "Minnie Mouse is throwing a party; should she freeze her cheeseballs before serving them to her guests?") The idea was that it would get a laugh from the audience and inspire some panel banter.

The problem with this was one that had actually been solved nearly seventeen years ago. Merrill Heatter had already figured out that *Hollywood Squares* didn't work with banter, just quick jokes. Questions were terse and straightforward, giving extra weight to the funny lines that the stars fired off. And the show had its policy in place that twenty-two questions had to be asked for each show. On the premiere of *The Match Game/Hollywood Squares Hour*, twelve questions were asked.

Robert Sherman adds, "We were applying the *Match Game* science of question-writing to *Hollywood Squares*-style questions. And one of the things we tried to do was anticipate reactions, the way we used to for

At the halfway point each day, an extra tier would whisk onto the set and transform it into *Hollywood Squares*. Sitting on the panel: Richard Kline, Lilibet Stern, Leonard Frey, Fred Travalena, Bill Daily, Barbi Benton, Gene, Tom Poston, Alison Arngrim. (Fred Wostbrock Collection)

the regular panelists on *Match Game*. Okay, so Goodson doesn't want us briefing the celebrities on the questions and he doesn't want us preparing jokes for them. He insisted that we not do that or come anywhere near that. So we began slipping cues and key words into the questions. We would think of a really funny joke that somebody might give in response to the question, and then we'd re-write the question ever so slightly to include a word or a phrase that would steer the panelist into thinking of the same joke that we had thought of. Once in a while, you'd get a really good panelist who picked up on all of the hints we were dropping and fire off all of the jokes, but the vast majority completely missed what we were doing.

"What was unfortunate for us was that Goodson slowly realized the problems we were having, and as time went by, I think Goodson really began to regret ever saying a bad word in public about *Hollywood Squares*. I think deep down, he wished we would switch to writing the jokes and briefing the panelists, but doing that would have essentially required him to admit a mistake and risk losing face, because down the road, a reporter interviewing him might say 'You said this about *Hollywood Squares* and now you're doing it yourself,' and Goodson would have to address that. And that was just the worst part of the whole experience. Everybody in the company from Mark Goodson on down knew how we could repair this, but we couldn't do it."

On top of that, there was the issue of Jon Bauman, a talented musician with a character that he knew so well he could play it in his sleep… but not a game show host.

> *Mark Goodson made a mistake in hiring Jon Bauman… He took him out and bought him a whole wardrobe for the show, then ended up spending an hour after each show telling him what he did right and what he did wrong, and most of the time, he did something wrong.*

Announcer Gene Wood told Hammett, "Instead of being looked up to, he was doing shtick… and it didn't fit."

In his autobiography, *Backstage with the Original Hollywood Square*, Peter Marshall recalled the advice that an agent, Noel Rubaloff, gave him about how to go about hosting a star-studded game show. "Peter, there are going to be a lot of stars on your show—don't let them intimidate you. Just imagine that you've invited them all to a party at your home. Treat them as you would an honored guest, but always remember—it's *your* party."

Bauman, on the other hand, would let the stars talk and talk, without stepping in. Occasionally, he would even step into character, doing his Bowzer voice. Week in and week out, Bauman never really made the show his own, never took command of *Squares*. At best, he came off as a guest host.

Lynne locked onto another problem with Bauman. "The idea of *The Match Game/Hollywood Squares Hour* wasn't such a bad idea. It was an intriguing thought to take these two popular shows and mash them together. But Bauman had been 'Bowzer' to the public for years. He performed at Woodstock and he was always in that character any time he was in public, so that's over a decade of Bowzer but no real familiarity with Jon Bauman. So even though Bauman had been a performer for years, he had no identity outside of that character. For the viewers, it was like a total stranger was hosting *Hollywood Squares*."

Gene had his own problems. Robert Sherman explains, "Gene felt very uncomfortable doing a dual role in the show. Going into it, it didn't seem like a problem, but once the series actually went into production and Gene had to do this for every show, you could see how awkward it was, having to be host and panelist. As host, you're the 'boss' of the game and you're in charge. As panelist, you defer to somebody else onstage. It was the same problem that we had with Richard Dawson a few years earlier, but in a way, Gene had it worse because he had to make that transition every day on one show. In a single hour, he had to be the boss of the show and then demote himself to being part of an ensemble. And making that adjustment, show after show after show, was more awkward than we thought it would be."

There was another strange problem with the show, in that there were no regular panelists. The show lacked an on-air family for the viewers to become attached to. Charles Nelson Reilly, Fannie Flagg, and Bill Daily made occasional appearances. Two old favorites from *Squares*, George Gobel and Abby Dalton, appeared as well. But those were occasional visits. The only regulars to speak of were Gene and Jon, who had absolutely no chemistry together. Whereas Gene would happily banter or go into routines with the regulars on *Match Game*, there were times when Jon Bauman would make a joke and Gene would reply with a nearly impatient-sounding "Right…" and then move onto the next panelist.

Robert Sherman adds, "There was one more really bad problem with the show. Even though *Match Game* and *Hollywood Squares* were paired up by NBC because of their similarities, they were two very different shows, so we had panelists who played one of the games very well but then they were just awful at the other. And we had the same problem with contestants. The contestants could play *Match Game* or they could play *Hollywood Squares*, but most of the time, they couldn't play both. We had so many episodes where only half of the game was any good and then the other half was just dismal."

Jon and Gene during the *Match Game* half. Although they had interacted well when "Bowzer" appeared on the '70s *Match Game*, they didn't seem to have any chemistry together when they became co-hosts. (Fred Wostbrock Collection)

If all of this sounds like a rather unpleasant show to sit through, well, it was. And even Mark Goodson's own staff couldn't help thinking that. Dick DeBartolo remembers, "It just didn't make sense to me. It just seemed like such a silly mash-up. I remember being in the office one day and they came to me and said '*Match Game* is coming back.' I said 'Oh!' And they said 'And it's going to come back as part of a show with *Hollywood Squares*.' And I said 'Oh?' And the show just didn't look right. I wrote the *Match Game* questions but that was all I did. I watched it a few times and it just seemed like such a bizarre show to me."

After a rocky nine-month run, NBC cancelled *The Match Game/Hollywood Squares Hour*. The network was eager to clear the space on its daytime line-up to make room for a lavish, high-budget soap opera, *Santa Barbara*. The network had promised such big returns after the disastrous game show's run that seventeen NBC affiliates who had dropped the 3-4 p.m. hour picked it back up to air the soap opera. 155 NBC stations had aired *The Match Game/Hollywood Squares Hour*, and 172 would air *Santa Barbara*.

The Match Game/Hollywood Squares Hour aired for the last time on July 27, 1984. At final tally, the game had averaged a 4.2 rating and a 14 share in the Neilsen ratings. *Santa Barbara*, which took over the following Monday, averaged a 4.4 rating and a 14 share in the Neilsen ratings, and lasted eight and a half years.

Chapter Eighteen
How Good He Had It

Although *The Match Game/Hollywood Squares Hour* had flopped during the 1983-84 season, another game show had caught fire. *Wheel of Fortune* had been airing on NBC since 1975 to generally so-so ratings, but the nighttime syndicated version that creator Merv Griffin introduced in the fall of 1983 took off virtually overnight, and the show became a national craze. By 1984, networks and syndicators were frantically hunting for the next big game show, and producers were drumming up new shows as fast as they could. And hey, a game show needs a host.

Gene was hired to host two pilots in late 1984. The first, with the humorously vague title *It*, was a word game that involved filling in blanks. Familiar territory, right? The contestants were shown a series of "frames," two words with a blank between them. The blank could be filled in with a single word that would create a pair of two-word phrases. For example,

The Matchless Gene Rayburn

(Fred Wostbrock Collection)

if the contestants saw the phrase "Betty (_____) Christmas," the correct answer would be "White."

Gene's mood on the *It* pilot was transparent. He wasn't very happy on the day it was taped, and he couldn't hide it. At the start of the game, Gene showed the contestants the frame "Baked (_____) Salad." The contestants were stumped. Gene showed them another frame with the same correct answer, "Mashed (_____) Chips." When the contestants were still stumped, Gene blurted out "Oh, this is a wonderful bunch, isn't it?"

Later in the game, the contestants were stumped by "Cultured (_____) Bailey," Gene told them, "I had this one twenty minutes ago!"

Adding to Gene's exasperation was a high-tech set that hadn't quite been debugged. The set was on a series of levels, and contestants were gradually eliminated as the show went along. To start, there were four contestants onstage. Every time one of them advanced to the next round, they would walk up a staircase to the next level, and the podium where they had been standing and ringing in disappeared into the floor. Gene, who didn't have a host's podium, would move closer to the remaining players every time a podium sunk down and became a part of the floor. The problem was that the ring-in button wasn't deactivated when it sank into the floor, so when Gene took a step forward or backward, it triggered the sound of the buzzer, visibly irritating him. Later in the game, a podium malfunctioned and Gene stomped on it to finally get it into the floor. And in the bonus round, played against a sixty-second clock, Gene yelled "Hurry up!" at a game board that revealed the words too slowly, possibly costing the player money.

One could argue that Gene dodged a bullet when *It* didn't get picked up for a regular series. *It* was a Bernstein-Hovis Production. The company, co-founded by former *Hogan's Heroes* cast member Larry Hovis and producer Gary Bernstein, ultimately had a very rocky existence. Although *It* didn't sell in 1984, they did launch a game show for Paramount Television called *Anything for Money*, in which contestants tried to predict the outcome of hidden camera pranks. Bernstein-Hovis Productions was subsequently sued by another game show packager, Ralph Andrews, claiming that he owned the rights to the format. Andrews ultimately won a settlement in 1990. Bernstein-Hovis later produced the original version of *Lingo*, which launched in 1987 and, following its cancellation after one season, was sued by numerous contestants, as well as host Michael Reagan, for non-payment.

Gene hosted another pilot, *Unpredictable Pairs* for The Wohl Company and J. Scott Gilden Productions. And although it was a new company and it was decades after Gene arrived on television, the nature of the game had a decidedly old-school flavor. Gene played host to a team of celebrity panelists—Rhonda Bates, Lyle Alzado, and Beverly Garland—who faced a team of three contestants. For example, one game pitted the panel against fitness guru Jack LaLanne and two men who each claimed to be his son. Only one really was. The panel cross-examined each of the possible sons, and then the panelists and members of the studio audience all voted on whom they believed was telling the truth. The three contestants shared $1,000 for every wrong vote by a panelist, and the total money doubled if the majority of the audience was incorrect, too. It's unlikely that the show ever had a chance of making it to air. Mark Goodson was fiercely protective of his own properties, and in fact, during the 1980s, Goodson had sued Chuck Barris to prevent production from starting on *Bamboozle*, another game show format that bore more than a passing resemblance to *To Tell the Truth*.

Gene returns to TV for *Break the Bank* in 1985. (Author's Collection)

How Good He Had It

Gene also got hired to host a pilot for an upstart production company, Kline & Friends. Founded by long-time game show director Richard S. Kline, Kline & Friends was a company consisting of many former staff members from Jack Barry & Dan Enright Productions. Jack Barry had died suddenly in early May of 1984 and a tremendous amount of infighting erupted in the weeks following his death. Kline left the company, immediately managed to assemble his own production outfit, and by the fall, he was shooting a pilot, titled *Break the Bank*.

Break the Bank seemed to get off to a promising start. The show would be distributed by Blair Entertainment, the company that was syndicating *Divorce Court* and *SCTV* with tremendous results. WCBS, the New York station that signed up for the show, dropped *Let's Make a Deal* to carry the new game, even though *Let's Make a Deal* had seen its ratings go up in the preceding several weeks before the deal was signed.

Gene touted the impending premiere of *Break the Bank* when he appeared as a guest on Regis Philbin's *Lifestyles*. In an unusual interview conducted with interviewer and interviewee both pedaling exercycles, Gene told Regis about his new series. There was something about the tone of his touting that was just slightly off.

He told Philbin, "I'm doing another very exciting [game show] now called *Break the Bank*. Many of them are kind of static but this one is very dynamic. It's got a lot of running around and… When they put it together, Richard Kline, a very creative guy, stole a little bit from *Beat the Clock*, *The Price is Right*, *Let's Make a Deal*, put 'em all together, and it works great!"

There was trouble brewing from the get-go, but Gene had a contract and he was going to be there to host *Break the Bank* whether he liked it or not. And he really, really, really did not like it.

The game pitted two couples against each other. Gene would read a series of trivia questions, each worth an amount of time, ranging from five seconds up to one hundred seconds. The correct answer to every question was a clue to the identity of a famous person, place, or thing—for example, when the correct answers to a series of six questions were "Booth," "Blue," "Davis," "North," "Lincoln," and "Lee," the solution to the puzzle would be "Civil War." The first couple to solve two puzzles took all the time they had accumulated into the Prize Vault.

In the Prize Vault was a series of stunts that the players had to complete in order to earn a Bank Card. As an example, here were the stunts found in the Prize Vault for the first episode of the series:

> Football legend Bubba Smith, who walked onstage wearing a tutu, demonstrated a series of ballet steps and moves. The contestants had to mimic his moves exactly to earn a Bank Card.
>
> Comedienne Louise DuArt performed a series of impressions; the contestant had to identify each celebrity that she was impersonating.
>
> Gene escorted the contestant to a giant stuffed donkey with a basket of money bags in front of it. Each money bag had the name of a foreign currency on it. Gene read a series of names of countries, and the contestant had to hang the corresponding money bags on the donkey.
>
> A contestant had to recite a tongue twister written on a cue card three times.
>
> A contestant climbed into a six-car Ferris wheel. Gene read a series of true-false questions, and the Ferris wheel moved one space for every correct answer given by the contestant. The contestant had to complete one lap on the wheel.

There were forty Bank Cards available in the vault, and one was selected at random after a stunt was successfully completed. After time had expired, the contestants took the bank cards they had earned and inserted them into a slot on the front of the vault. A small marquee on the front of the Vault would light up with either WRONG CODE or BREAK BANK when a card was inserted. If the contestants had chosen the one card in the bank that lit up BREAK BANK, they won a jackpot that started at $20,000 and grew every day until won.

How Good He Had It

**The sprawling set of the bonus round on *Break the Bank*.
(Fred Wostbrock Collection)**

On paper, this is looking like the perfect show for Gene so far, especially that wacky, hijinks-laden bonus round in the Bank Vault. Think of all the potential for fun. The physical comedy if Gene were to try to mimic Bubba's ballet moves, or the reaction if Gene made a wisecrack about the tutu and Bubba reacted by giving Gene an imposing look. Gene could have talked to Louise DuArt and pretended he was actually carrying on a conversation with whoever she was impersonating. He could have tried pretending to ride that giant donkey, or reciting the tongue twister, or climbing into the Ferris wheel himself.

But… none of that happened. By Gene's own account, Richard Kline told him not to play the game for laughs. He wanted it played for suspense. No matter how ludicrous the stunt, the props, or the occasional costumes, none of it could be mined for laughs. And to make sure that Gene didn't play it for laughs, one of the rules of the game was that the clock continued running even as Gene explained the rules for each stunt. He couldn't be funny without potentially costing the contestants money. So he had to rattle as fast as he could while still being coherent.

Seeing the show in execution, it's hard not to ask questions. How can you do such a blatantly silly bonus round without specifically doing it for laughs? And more importantly, if you don't want your game show to be played for laughs, why, of all available masters of ceremonies, did you hire Gene Rayburn?

Fred Wostbrock says, "Gene was there because he had a name that these local station managers would recognize, and they'd buy the show based on that name. Didn't matter if the show was the right fit, didn't matter that Gene had a different sensibility or that he could do different things with the format. He was only there because of his name."

Gene's relationship with his new bosses went south almost immediately. So did the ratings for *Break the Bank*.

> *They blamed me for not making it work.*

Gene was never one to hide his feelings from the audience, whether it was his disdain for a changing time slot or his frustration with a gloomy panelist. Gene couldn't hide his unhappiness with *Break the Bank*. He looked bored and annoyed on the show as the weeks went by. *Break the Bank* had a thirty-nine week commitment to the stations that had signed up for the show, but after the thirteenth week, Gene was fired.

Wostbrock reflects, "The big problem that Gene Rayburn had in the 1980s was this: He didn't know how good he had it. Forty years into his career, this was seriously the first time when Gene was being treated the way that most other performers would be treated, and he wasn't accustomed to that.

"Look at his career. First he's at WNEW, and his boss there is yelling at him to do things her way, but his show is dynamite so she can yell all she wants, but he knows he's not getting fired. So Gene essentially went on the air every morning and did whatever he felt like doing. Then he goes to do *Tonight* with Steve Allen, and there's almost never a rehearsal, and Steve Allen was a big believer in spontaneity, so it was the perfect vehicle for Gene. He does *Dough Re Mi*, and when that show starts to bomb, Jack Barry gives him some control over the show and Gene rebuilds the show to suit his own strengths and gets three years out of it that way. *The Match Game* comes along and Gene ignores Mark Goodson and gets laughs, and then Goodson goes ahead and lets it become a comedy show and that makes it an even better show for him. Gene basically got to do whatever he wanted for forty years. And then in the eighties, he works for these producers with very clear visions of what they wanted their shows to be and they're giving him instructions for how to do it, and when he deviated even slightly, he had to hear about it. He wasn't used to it, and he certainly didn't like it."

Gene during the *Break the Bank* bonus round; Gene's account was that he would be scolded by his bosses for getting laughs from this segment when it was supposed to be played seriously. (Fred Wostbrock Collection)

Gene was replaced by infomercial host Joe Farago. Gene was under contract to host the full season, so to avoid legal troubles, he and Kline & Friends had to agree on a settlement. Part of Gene's settlement, a stipulation that he requested, was that his episodes would never be rerun. During the summer months, only Joe Farago's episodes were rebroadcast. When the show was canceled after a single season, Kline & Friends sold a package of *Break the Bank* reruns to cable channel CBN, and they included only Joe Farago's episodes.

Gene was eager to move on from the experience and get started with a new job. His final episode of *Break the Bank* aired on December 20, 1985, just two days before his birthday, and even though he was fired, being relieved from a job that made him so unhappy was a nice early present for him. But Gene's real birthday present that year wound up being a rude awakening: a well-meaning gesture that had unintentional consequences. And for the rest of his life, Gene would always remember that his career came to a screeching end well before he was ready for it, just because somebody wished him a happy birthday.

Chapter Nineteen
Left Out

Robert Sherman remembers, "What made Gene a great talent was how many mindsets he had for broadcasting. He had been a disc jockey, so he could be the center of attention for four hours and keep it going. He was the Howard Stern of his day. He had been Steve Allen's sidekick, so he could be a straight man. He had been a game show host and was good at interacting with average people and making them interesting for the home viewers. He had been an actor. He sang and danced on Broadway. He brought so much to the table."

But nobody wanted it. At least not after Gene walked away from *Break the Bank*. And for the rest of his life, Gene blamed *Entertainment Tonight* for that.

Entertainment Tonight, which premiered in 1981, had a long-standing regular feature in which each episode concluded with a list of

(Fred Wostbrock Collection)

celebrities celebrating birthdays that day. On December 20, 1985, the same day that Gene's last day of *Break the Bank* aired, *Entertainment Tonight* noted that among the celebrities celebrating birthdays during the upcoming weekend was Gene Rayburn, who was turning sixty-eight years old on Sunday. The secret that Gene had been closely guarding for years was out.

Although Gene never exactly worked as much as he wanted, the phone had at least been steadily ringing for some time now. A regional theater making Gene an offer if he'd spend a few months in their city doing a show, or a game show packager getting ready to tape a pilot, maybe a reporter or a disc jockey was seeking an interview.

> *The day that* Entertainment Tonight *said 'Happy birthday' to me, the phone stopped ringing.*

Few people are as lucky as a man who, at age sixty-eight, doesn't want to retire, loves his work, and is truly great at it. Fewer still are as unlucky as a sixty-eight-year-old man who can still get the job done, but can't get hired.

Lynne remembers, "It was a blow to my dad's ego, especially because for much of his life, he looked younger than he actually was. When I was in my early twenties, my father and I would go out to dinner sometimes and the waiters would call me 'Mrs. Rayburn' because he looked so much younger for his age and I looked older for mine. We looked so close in age. Being told that he looked too old hurt him a lot. It still makes me crazy that my father was deemed too old. Bob Barker got to host *The Price is Right* into his eighties, and to see that and see Alex Trebek in his seventies hosting *Jeopardy!*, and Regis Philbin hosting *Who Wants to be a Millionaire?* in his seventies, and I look back at my dad being told he was too old when he was still in his sixties. Are you kidding me? What's the deal there?

"The problem, I think, was this: Television, when it was mostly based in New York, had sprung from the radio business and was dominated by a lot of people who had some experience in radio. When television migrated to Los Angeles, it was now dominated by people from the movie industry. People in the film industry always think of any sort of performance in terms of film, which means a lot of close-ups on a giant screen, and you want beautiful, glamorous, younger people filling that screen. But television is mostly medium shots on a twenty-four-inch screen. It's okay to have the occasional wrinkled face, I think."

It got worse. His outside business venture, the skating rink, had gone out of business, and Gene was on the hook for the debts. His resources dried up quickly, with no new income on the way. Gene was faced with a tragic irony in the process: As a former chapter president and national board member for AFTRA, Gene helped negotiate the fees that television performers collected for reruns of their programs. The tapes of nearly all of his television work before 1973 had been erased, the result of short-sighted decision-making by employees at every major network, and the majority of his surviving work was game shows, a genre which, at that time, was not commonly rerun. Gene had no income to help him offset the debts. Things turned bad very quickly for Gene.

Randy West remembers, "I had dinner with Gene once and his attitude about his money troubles was interesting because he didn't blame anybody else, he took responsibility for it, but at the same time, you could understand how somebody in the same position would blame others.

"Gene said to me, 'You know, I did something stupid a long time ago and didn't realize what I had done. I hired a manager/accountant guy to handle my affairs and handle my money, and it was the same guy who handled Mark Goodson's finances. I figured it would keep everything in the family, so to speak, and I'd have a favored nations relationship with Mark when it came time to negotiate contracts. It took me decades to realize what a conflict of interest I created by having one guy represent both sides of the table, and it was stupid of me not to recognize that the advocacy would be for the greater of the two clients. Looking back, I cost myself a lot of money.'"

It looked like there might be a light at the end of the tunnel. In early 1987, trade ads first appeared for a new version of *Match Game*, a joint venture of Mark Goodson Productions and Coca-Cola (which dabbled in film & television production during the 1980s). Curiously, some ads included a photo of Gene splashed across them, while some ads made no mention of a host whatsoever. The initial press release from The Television Program Source (the syndication firm that would distribute the show) even stated that "a host for the new show is to be named."

Robert Sherman remembers, "We absolutely wanted Gene involved as I recall. And we were very ambitious about the new version and thought for sure we would make it to air. We were confident enough that Mark Goodson commissioned several set designers to come up with some renderings of new sets. I remember the sets were drastic departures from what we had been using in the 1970s version, and I recall thinking that all the designs they came up with were beautiful, but Mark Goodson didn't like any of them."

Whether Gene would be there or not, plans for *Match Game '87* didn't come to fruition. The game show marketplace was crowded that year with *Wheel of Fortune, Jeopardy!, The New Dating Game, The New Newlywed Game, The New Hollywood Squares, Love Connection, The $100,000 Pyramid, Lingo, The Home Shopping Game, High Rollers*, and *Win, Lose or Draw* gobbling up valuable real estate. There was just no room for Gene and *Match Game*.

Two legendary hosts, Gene Rayburn and Tom Kennedy, backstage at *The Late Show* in 1988. (Fred Wostbrock Collection)

In 1988, Gene arrived at the Fox studios in Los Angeles for a gig. He was appearing as a guest on *The Late Show*. *The Late Show* was one of the first shows introduced on Fox when it launched in 1986 and had been a problem-plagued endeavor from the word "go." Joan Rivers walked away from her lucrative gig guest-hosting *The Tonight Show* each week to host *The Late Show*, making an enemy for life of former boss Johnny Carson. After a tumultuous early going—as Fox executives tried to build a roster of affiliates, many stations agreed to become Fox affiliates on the condition that they didn't have to air *The Late Show*—Rivers was fired. She was briefly replaced by Arsenio Hall, who hosted for thirteen weeks but departed to co-star in *Coming to America*. After auditioning a series of potential hosts, including Howard Stern and Frank Zappa, the network settled on comic Ross Shafer, previously the host of USA Network's cable game show *Love Me, Love Me Not*.

For a special episode, Shafer welcomed Gene, along with Jim Lange, Gary Owens, Tom Kennedy, Dennis James, and Fred Wostbrock to reminisce about classic TV game shows. There was no pretense about the hosts discussing upcoming projects or plans for the future. The discussion stayed squarely in the past. Gene was present not to be promoted, but to be remembered.

Fred Wostbrock explains, "The root of all that was that I had just co-authored a book, *The Encyclopedia of TV Game Shows*, with Steve Ryan and David Schwartz, and they thought that a panel featuring the author and a bunch of game show hosts would be a great segment. Gene actually helped me put that book together. When we were assembling material for it, he invited me to his home and showed me all sorts of photos, because he had saved everything from his career. And he told me stories and just enjoyed reminiscing. It made him happy that anybody wanted to preserve any kind of record of the work that he did.

"What I remember about that night at *The Late Show* was that before the show, all of the hosts convened, and there was quite a bit of respect between the hosts. Everybody thinks of the legendary game show hosts as being of the same generation, but they weren't. Tom Kennedy and Jim Lange were years younger than Gene Rayburn and Dennis James, and I remember Tom and Jim just revered those guys. But Gene and Dennis stood face-to-face at one point, and an argument erupted. It got so heated and so loud that you couldn't really understand what they were saying, but apparently, when they were doing *The Name's the Same* together, they didn't like each other, there was some sort of falling out, and there had always been bad blood there. And these guys were right in each other's faces hollering at each other, and it was almost funny to watch because this was thirty-five years or so of bad blood just coming to the surface out of nowhere. It was just so peculiar. But we got them settled down and we got them onstage. And once they were onstage, they were buddy-buddy. They had that in common, they were both very professional. But then, as the cameras are rolling, Dennis James sneaks in a potshot at Gene. But they left it at that and it didn't get ugly on the air. But offstage it was just so peculiar… although it was fascinating to watch those guys arguing."

But it looked like there was another chance right around the corner. In 1989, Mark Goodson was giving *Match Game* another shot, intending to launch a new version for first-run syndication in the 1990-1991 season. A new set was built, a panel was booked, and tapings were scheduled for a total of five pilots. And at the helm as host would be… Bert Convy. Gene was the first host. He was the only host up to this point. And now he was being told that he wasn't right for the job he had held for a combined seventeen years. Even harder for Gene was learning that he was being replaced by a man who, though they got along fine personally, Gene didn't think much of as a performer.

> *Bert Convy… it's hard for me to be objective about him. But his style was not my style. I remember once, I hosted his show—* Tattletales—*with him as a player. And I found out later that after I had guest-hosted* Tattletales, *the producer was saying to him, "Why don't you try doing this differently? This is the way Rayburn would do it…" And it had to do with the way he moved his body around when he was hosting. And Bert told the producer "I can't do that; I would never turn my back on camera." He wasn't loose. He was a tight guy. He did fourteen shows on Broadway though, so he had talent, I have to give him that.*

Dick DeBartolo remembers, "I honestly believe being rejected for that version of the show took a couple of years off of Gene's life. He was just crushed when he got passed over."

Robert Sherman says, "The company was going into a strange period. *Super Password* got cancelled in March of that year, and after *Super Password* went off the air, Mark Goodson became much more removed from day-to-day operations of the company. But he signed Convy to host this new *Match Game*, and because of my history with the show and because I had produced *Super Password* with Bert Convy hosting, I got picked to produce the *Match Game* pilots. I can't say I was enthusiastic. Again, I was arguing that time had passed the show by and we shouldn't be trying to revive it, but I went along with it. And we wound up doing a fantastic pilot week. The stars were funny, Bert was a very good host, and the contestants played well and gave good answers through the whole thing. It turned me around, opinion-wise."

Gene hosts one more game, AMC's *The Movie Masters*, in 1989. (Fred Wostbrock Collection)

Gene got some consolation, being signed by the American Movie Classics (AMC) cable channel to host a new game. It was low-budget, low-hype, and low-prestige, but it was work, and that was all that mattered to Gene.

The game, called *The Movie Masters*, pitted a regular panel of three players against each other. Film critic Clive Barnes was joined on the panel by two familiar faces to Gene and to game show fans, Peggy Cass and Kitty Carlisle. The channel was geared toward the nostalgic fans of vintage films, and in keeping with that theme, *The Movie Masters* was presented as a vintage game show. The set was a very basic arrangement of desks and curtains, with a manually-operated game board at center stage. The theme music was a vintage arrangement by a string quartet. The show even opened in the same fashion as the classic *What's My Line?*; the panelists introduced each other, and the last panelist in line would introduce Gene.

Gene showed them a grid of nine categories and read trivia questions from those categories. When a correct answer was given, the category was removed from the board, removing a portion of a still from a classic movie. The first panelist to correctly identify that movie won prizes for a randomly-selected home viewer: a VCR plus one videocassette for every correct answer given in the round.

Despite content that celebrated the channel's core programming and a cast of revered stars in their fields, *The Movie Masters* was never intended to be anything more than filler programming for AMC. It didn't even have a regular time slot on the channel; it only aired when AMC had a hole that needed filled during a broadcast day. It wasn't a blockbuster hit; it didn't make Gene a household name. But it was a job, and one that Gene loved. And he got to work with people that he cared about.

> *Peggy Cass knows a little bit about any subject in the world that you can mention, and she's ready to tell you. She speaks up. She's not a shy person. She too was a gifted actress. She was the original Miss Gooch on Broadway in* Auntie Mame. *She was excellent in that.*
>
> *Kitty Carlisle—"Aren't we grand?" She's a sweet, wonderful person. She put on airs a little bit, I thought, but she can be forgiven for that, because she's an attractive person and a great conversationalist.*

The Movie Masters premiered quietly, drifted through six months of episodes quietly, and then disappeared quietly in early 1990. Whether Gene wanted it or not, a period was placed on his television career. There were no more gigs to come as an emcee or an actor.

Chapter Twenty
Game Over

In the 1940s, radio fans heard the name Gene Rayburn and said "I listen to that guy!" In the 1950s, TV fans said "I know that guy!" In the 1960s, they said "I watch that guy!" In the 1970s, they said "I love that guy."

In the 1990s, some of them said "I remember that guy."

The drop in visibility for Gene was almost alarming. The current crop of TV game shows in 1990 was hosted by Pat Sajak, Alex Trebek, Bob Barker, Marc Summers, and a few other names. Reruns of game shows were proliferating on cable, with The Family Channel and USA Network building wildly popular daytime schedules consisting of older games, but somehow, the number-one daytime series of the 1970s wasn't on any of the line-ups. Not only had Gene vanished from the airwaves, he had instantly been forgotten about by so many. When he ran into roadblocks with trying to collect his pension from AFTRA (the union

(Fred Wostbrock Collection)

whose pension plan he had helped create), part of the fight involved having to prove to AFTRA that he really was who he claimed to be. Among other things, the people in charge of issuing the pension checks wanted Gene to provide more proof of identity because they thought that "Jean Rayburn" was a woman!

Orson Bean adds, "Gene told me once that most of his money was gone. He invested in his roller rink and that didn't take off, so Gene tried to recoup his losses by turning his money over to an investor who would build a portfolio for him. Well, it ended up being a Bernie Madoff-style scheme. Gene lost whatever he had left."

With no new income on the way and the pension he was entitled to being held hostage by an incompetent bureaucracy, Gene could be forgiven for the somewhat cynical reaction he had when word got out that Bert Convy's health had taken a turn for the worse.

Dick DeBartolo says, "Bert Convy was diagnosed with a brain tumor a few months after the *Match Game* pilot was taped. The syndicator passed, but ABC was interested and we managed to sell it to ABC. And once word got out that Bert had a brain tumor, as callous as this might come across, I think Gene more or less parked himself next to the telephone for a few weeks and waited for someone to call him. And I can understand that. It's show business. The series had been sold, they needed somebody to host it, so why not the guy who had done the job for twenty years and wanted to keep doing it?"

Fred Wostbrock explains what happened next. "I had just become Gene's agent. I started working at a talent agency the previous year. Gene wasn't working much and he hadn't had an agent of his own in years, so I just went to him and said 'Can I be your agent?' He said 'Sure.' We shook hands. And almost immediately, I get a call from ABC. The folks working in daytime wanted to know Gene's availability in the near future and said they were considering him for *Match Game*. They were very serious for about a week. And Gene was so excited, and so was I. I had just become his agent, I was a big fan of his when I was a kid, and here it looks like I was about to get him a network show. And then after a week passed, the bad news got handed to us that ABC was looking at other people and they weren't interested in Gene. We were both so disappointed by that."

Mark Goodson and ABC briefly considered Bob Eubanks, best known for *The Newlywed Game*. Eubanks even came to Goodson's office to host several run-throughs. But ultimately the job went to Ross Shafer, the talk show host who had spoken to Gene during that infamous night at *The Late Show* on Fox.

Fred Wostbrock says, "If the job had gone to Bob Eubanks, I honestly think Gene could have lived with that. Bob was of a different generation, he wasn't one of Gene's peers, but Gene liked Bob as a performer and respected him, and Gene would have been fine with seeing Bob there. Seeing the job go to Ross Shafer really bothered Gene. It's nothing that Ross could have helped, it was nothing personal against him, but the problem was Ross Shafer wasn't a major name, he had previously been the host of one game show on cable that hadn't had a very long run, so he wasn't a known guy, so giving *Match Game* to somebody like that made Gene feel like he wasn't appreciated. He put so much of himself and his own talents into hosting the show, and giving it to a relative unknown was like saying 'Well, really, anybody can do this job.'"

When Gene learned that he had lost out on the job for a second time, he actually attempted to handle it in graceful fashion. He called Mark Goodson Productions and ABC, offering to pass the torch for the premiere broadcast. He just wanted to make a quick appearance, offer his support for the new series, say a few nice words about Ross Shafer, hand off the microphone, and leave. Request denied.

Randy West remembers, "Gene and I had dinner once and he talked about that so much. He said 'All I wanted to do was hand over the microphone. I wasn't going to try to take over the segment, I wasn't going to try to make the new guy look bad, I just wanted to hand over the microphone and sort of mark the end of my time being the host of that show. They wouldn't let me do it.'"

The new *Match Game* did have a few links to the past. Charles Nelson Reilly signed on to be a regular panelist, sitting right in his old seat on the upper tier. Brett Somers was not a regular but did make occasional appearances. Betty White, Jo Anne Worley, and Marcia Wallace (whose career in 1990 had received an unexpected boost thanks to her role as Mrs. Krabappel on *The Simpsons*) dropped by sometimes, too.

But with all the old faces dropping in, this new *Match Game* really was a new *Match Game*. There were new faces on the panel every week, like comedian Brad Garrett (later of *Everybody Loves Raymond*), ventriloquist Ronn Lucas, and ABC sitcom stars like Bill Kirchenbauer (*Just the Ten of Us*) and Khrystyne Haje (*Head of the Class*).

But the game itself was the most drastic change of all. Robert Sherman explains, "Even though I had produced the pilot week in 1989, when ABC picked up the series, Mark Goodson appointed his son Jonathan to produce the show. Jonathan was like his father in the sense that he wanted the emphasis to be on the game, and he reinvented the show to have more of a game to it."

Jonathan Goodson's innovation was a new wrinkle called Match-Up. After Round 1, each contestant selected a celebrity panelist to partner up with for a thirty second round. On a hidden monitor, the contestant was shown a series of simple blank phrases ("Bar _____") and a pair of choices (BELL or TENDER). The contestant would use a stylus to select one, and the celebrity would try to match. After Round 2, the game would be decided with a second Match-Up round, played for forty-five seconds. Jonathan Goodson also mandated that each episode had to end with the Super Match round; games wouldn't straddle in this version. This meant that a single episode had to contain four traditional *Match Game* questions, four Match-Ups and a Super Match. That was a lot of content for a game that people watched for laughs.

Sherman says, "The game sacrificed entertainment in exchange for game. Editing wasn't going to be enough, we just had to keep the game moving, and as a result, a lot of laughs were sacrificed."

Charles Nelson Reilly stuck it out, but Brett Somers later remembered Reilly privately lamenting, "It's really not the same."

The show was also hampered by its time slot. ABC placed it at noon eastern on the schedule, an awful time slot because by 1990, the majority of network affiliates were airing local newscasts at noon. *Match Game* was floundering. In need of a boost, the show reached out to Gene, asking if he would appear on the show as a guest panelist for one week. Gene, insulted by the request, said no.

Randy West explains, "To deny Gene the job of host and then ask if he'd be on the panel, you're implying that you don't want him, but you need him. And Gene recognized why he was being asked. The show had to boost the ratings and saw Gene as the key. And the show had more to gain from that than Gene. To come in for scale, give this show a boost, and know the whole time that they want you there to help them, but they don't want you to stay… I personally think Gene just looked at the show and the company at that point and thought to himself, 'Screw you.'"

Gene was so hurt by the snub that he couldn't even bring himself to say the title of the show for a time. When a reporter talked to him in

1991, Gene casually mentioned that he had been passed over for "a show at ABC last year" without saying anything more specific.

Gene stayed home and did all he could to avoid becoming stir crazy, devoting himself to a garden and to cooking recreationally. He also helped Helen sort through the personal effects of Adele Astaire, aka "Delly," their friend who had invited them to the castle in Ireland for so many visits, had died in 1981, and left them a wealth of personal material, including diaries. Helen was hoping to turn it into a biography and get it published, but her first draft was an intimidating 1,600-page tome. She was trying to parse it down while continuing to sort through everything.

Gene steps out to Bucks County Playhouse one more time to star in *La Cage Aux Folles*. **(Fred Wostbrock Collection)**

Game Over

Match Game was canceled by ABC after only thirty-nine weeks. It was nearly picked up by CBS, but the network changed its mind. In a bit of retribution for Gene, at the same time that *Match Game* was fizzling and flopping without him, his phone suddenly began ringing again. In 1990, he abruptly popped up on *Saturday Night Live*. Guest host Susan Lucci was performing in a skit where her *All My Children* character, Erica Kane, appeared as a contestant on a game show and had a whirlwind romance with the host (played by Phil Hartman) as the game progressed. By the end of the game, Erica and the master of ceremonies were getting married, with announcer Don Pardo playing the minister for the ceremony. When Pardo asked if anyone objected to the ceremony, in walked Gene Rayburn, revealing that he was secretly married to Erica.

Gene, all dressed up with one more place to go; another performance of *La Cage Aux Folles*. (Fred Wostbrock Collection)

And then the phone suddenly rang once more with a job offer. A familiar home for Gene, the Bucks County Playhouse, wanted him to come back for another performance.

Gene was cast in the lead role of *La Cage Aux Folles*, the Harvey Fierstein musical adaptation of a French film about a gay cabaret owner and his drag queen lover. Gene played the role of Georges the cabaret owner, the role played by Robin Williams when an Americanized version of the story, *The Birdcage*, appeared in movie theaters in 1996.

Seventy-two-year-old Gene was still physically and mentally strong, but the passage of time was creating one unavoidable problem. His voice was starting to give out a little bit. On some episodes of *The Movie Masters*, his voice was noticeably gravelly and soft, nothing like the brassy bellow he had in the prime of his career. And now even nature was starting to prevent him from doing further work in musical theater. He just didn't have the pipes for it.

Gene told a reporter at the time, "It's a difficult play to do. I've never done it before, but I love it... Singing is not my forte. I've been having a hard time because it's a long time since I've done a musical. I'm working on it. I will continue to work on it. And I'm having a good time."

Lynne remembers, "My father was a heavy smoker earlier in his life. It had even been a trademark for him when he was doing *Tonight* with Steve Allen. My father had this really distinctive cigarette holder that he used, and it was a familiar thing that he always had with him on the show. He quit smoking in the 1960s, but he smoked just long enough to age his throat prematurely. He had to work a lot harder hitting certain notes when he sang."

In 1991, he got another bit of retribution following his snub from *Match Game*. The daytime talk show *Geraldo* was doing a retrospective about the history of TV game shows, featuring guests Fred Wostbrock, Monty Hall, Wink Martindale, and Gene. No mention was made at all of the recent version of *Match Game* on ABC. The discussion revolved entirely around Gene and the show's glory days on CBS.

But before long, things were unfortunately right back to normal. *Geraldo* was done taping. *La Cage Aux Folles* ended its run, and Gene went right back home and watched his money dwindle.

Peter Marshall remembers Gene in those retirement years. "Gene wasn't the happiest guy in the world. He never made a lot of money. I made a lot of money, and it drove him crazy because he knew I didn't give a shit, you know? I'd do a gig, get my paycheck, and then he'd hear that I was on my way to New York for a little while for something else. My manager for most of my career was Tom Shields, who was the best negotiator in the business. He's the guy that got Johnny Carson *The Tonight Show*. Gene didn't make very much money, and he lost a fortune on that skating rink, and after that venture failed, he became very bitter."

Fred Wostbrock counters, "I don't agree with that word because it's such an extreme word. I have a vision in my head of 'bitter' and Gene in his later years doesn't fit with that vision. He was frustrated, but anything about him that came off to others as bitter, I just saw as a guy who only wanted to work. That's all."

Gene, Geraldo Rivera, Monty Hall, and Wink Martindale in 1991. The front row audience member with the bushy moustache is *Match Game* writer Dick DeBartolo. (Fred Wostbrock Collection)

(Fred Wostbrock Collection)

Chapter Twenty-One
Don't Forget

"Game shows died in 1991," remembered Fred Wostbrock.

The previous year, a massive wave of new games premiered: Revivals of *Tic-Tac-Dough, Supermarket Sweep, The Joker's Wild, To Tell the Truth, Let's Make a Deal,* and yes, *Match Game* all premiered, as did new formats like *Quiz Kids Challenge, Trump Card, The Challengers, Monopoly,* and *Rodeo Drive*. Of those eleven new arrivals, *Supermarket Sweep* was the only one that made it to a second season. The shows had all failed for a variety of reasons, but TV executives made a rather sweeping assessment that TV viewers just didn't want to watch game shows anymore, and the genre never recovered.

Wostbrock says, "I had just taken on all of these clients who I admired and who I wanted to help, and then immediately, game shows collapsed and I couldn't find work for any of them. Luckily, I didn't get blamed for that, those guys could all see what was happening in the business, but what horrible timing. It wasn't just Gene. Nobody could find work in the early 1990s."

Maybe the television appearances weren't working out, but Gene could find plenty of work away from the cameras, on the convention circuit. Gene became available as a host-for-hire. Businesses or private clubs that were preparing for national or regional conventions would plan a variety of events for attendees, and frequently staged live game shows as part of the events. For the right fee, Gene would attend the conventions and host *Match Game*, with conventioneers acting as contestants and panelists.

Wostbrock says, "It wasn't quite what Gene wanted to do. He still wanted to act, and after *The Simpsons* took off in 1990, Gene became very enthusiastic about cartoons. He wanted to do voice work for cartoons. And those opportunities didn't come, but the convention gigs were very fruitful for him. Everybody remembered the name Gene Rayburn, the conventions would contact me because my name had gotten out there as a representative of TV game show hosts, and whenever they called me, as soon as I said I represented Gene Rayburn, they'd say 'Gene Rayburn! That's who we want! We want Gene Rayburn!' So it wasn't exactly what Gene wanted to do, but he liked to work and he wanted to work as much as he could, and the conventions gave him some steady income and he felt productive."

There was one other guy helping Gene stay productive and employed in the early 1990s: Howard Stern.

Howard Stern had amassed legions of fans and legions of enemies alike with his controversial shock radio program beginning in the early 1980s. But at heart, he genuinely revered the great broadcasters and performers who had dominated the airwaves when he was a child. Soupy Sales recalled in his memoirs that the first time he met Stern, the shock jock showed up clutching an old Soupy Sales record and asking for an autograph. Stern also held Gene Rayburn in high regard.

He invited Gene to be a guest several times, to share old stories from his broadcasting days or even to play *Match Game* with members of Stern's on-air crew. He even appeared on Stern's controversial local TV series on WOR in New York, sitting on the panel of "Homeless

Howiewood Squares" (in which the contestants were actual homeless people).

> *He came to me during a break in the show and he said "You know, when I was a kid growing up, I watched The Match Game every day and I loved it." And it was very flattering. Unfortunately, shock radio is not really my thing. Shock television is not really my style. So I do not wholeheartedly approve of what he does. My generation... we wouldn't think of saying or doing the things he does. But who am I to say if something is right or wrong?*

Gene, with more free time than he would have liked, tried to make the best of it by traveling with Helen. Here, they pay a visit to Rock Island, Illinois. (Fred Wostbrock Collection)

Gene understood Howard Stern. It was a different type of radio than he had done on WNEW or on NBC, to be sure, but yet, in a strange sort of way, it was the same. It was spontaneous like Gene. It was personality-driven like Gene. Gene didn't connect to Howard Stern's brand of radio, but he saw some of himself in Howard and witnessed firsthand how deeply the shock jock appreciated Gene's brand, too.

The appearances on *The Late Show* and *Geraldo* had sparked Fred's imagination and he lucked into a way to find Gene and the other clients some work. He began offering his clients to daytime talk shows as a package. The hosts would bring along clips of their favorite moments from the shows they hosted; they could also bring along some questions and play short-form versions of their games with members of the audience, and swap stories about their careers. Gene was one of several hosts who popped up time and again for these shows, hosted by Phil Donahue, Maury Povich, Marilu Henner, Vicki Lawrence, and Rolanda Watts, among others.

Wostbrock remembers, "The staffs of these talk shows loved doing game show-themed episodes for a couple of reasons. First of all, it took no effort for them. I represented all of the hosts, which meant they only had to make one phone call to finalize everything. I had all the photos, the hosts brought their own videos, which meant the show's staff didn't have to do any research. The only actual work that the show's staff had to do was getting legal clearance from the production companies to air the clips that the hosts were bringing along, and that was nothing. And they always got great ratings because the hosts did have name value and the audience did remember them, so most of these shows did the game show day for their sweeps period. So these episodes got the best ratings of their entire year and it required less effort than a typical episode. How do you say no to that?

"And there was another reason these talk shows liked to do these kinds of shows. In the television business, there are people who sort of fall into their line of work by accident, but by and large, the people who work in the television business do it because they love it, and they loved it from a very young age. And on most of these shows, what happened was all of the hosts would arrive backstage, and a bunch of staff members would be there waiting, and they'd have old magazine covers, or ads that they had clipped out of old *TV Guide*s, or 8x10 glossies, or other memorabilia, and the staffs of these shows would ask Gene and the other guys for autographs."

In 1994, Gene and the rest of the game show legends got some good news. A new satellite TV channel was launching. Sony was launching Game Show Network, a nostalgic romp through forty-five years of TV game show history, as well as a line-up of original programming. In preparations for the channel's launch, Sony secured the full rights to the videotape libraries of Mark Goodson, Bob Stewart, Chuck Barris, and Jack Barry & Dan Enright. Among the videotaped gems from years gone by: 2,213 game show episodes hosted by Gene Rayburn, and 369 episodes featuring Gene as a panelist.

Because game shows had seldom aired in reruns, and because the reruns had never approached the high profile or high profits that sitcom and drama reruns had enjoyed, royalties weren't really a consideration for many producers. Most hosts hadn't had anything in their contracts entitling them to royalties, nor had the panelists and other guests who appeared on the shows. But since Sony had high hopes that the stars from the past would help them promote the channel with public appearances, the company paid millions of dollars in one-time-only deals to begin the channel. Orson Bean's account of the deal was that Game Show Network figured out how many episodes in their library featured him as a guest, and made a single payment that amounted to twenty-five dollars per episode.

Gene got a particularly sweet deal from the channel, a six-figure payment at the launch and residual payments thereafter. Those residual payments ended up being quite fruitful for Gene. From the inception of Game Show Network, *Match Game* was the most popular rerun package on the channel.

Wostbrock muses, "All of the game show hosts were surprised by the success of Game Show Network, and by the idea that reruns of all of their old work had an audience. But *Match Game* endures. These episodes from the 1970s attract an audience, a new audience, even. Young audiences. The show was hilarious, but what keeps it going is that the humor is timeless. Yeah, there are references to political figures or movies very often, but so much of the humor was personality-driven. So much of the humor came from conversations, from how people reacted to everything, from Gene, and there was wordplay. It was a lot of timeless humor. And that helps the show survive."

Gene, in exchange for the residuals, would record promos for the channel and give several interviews. The launch of Game Show Network brought to the end a terrible burden for Gene. Having lost so much of his money to bad investments and a business venture gone sour, and seeing the money dry up at a time when he couldn't find any work, Gene had amassed a sizable amount of debt in a matter of years. The bulk of Gene's initial six-figure payday from the channel went toward paying off all the debts. Gene celebrated the end of the burden by using the money that was left to treat himself to a Cadillac. And with all the problems regarding the union membership status of "Jean Rayburn" finally straightened out, Gene was collecting pension checks from SAG (the screen actors' union), Equity (the theater actors' union), and AFTRA (the radio and television performers' union), as well as Social Security. Gene wasn't rich, but at least he and Helen could be comfortable.

Gene, in 1994, with the Gene of thirty years earlier, selling off some career mementos at a garage sale. (Fred Wostbrock Collection)

And that comfort was important because radio and television were continuing on without him. A pilot for a revival of *Match Game*, titled *MG2*, was taped in September 1996, with former *Dallas* cast member Charlene Tilton acting as host. The pilot wasn't picked up. Two seasons later, a new *Match Game* went into production, hosted by Michael Burger and featuring an entirely new group of panelists. The show ended after one season.

Meanwhile, Gene got to do the occasional interview to keep his name out there, but his acting career was essentially over. He certainly wasn't hosting anything, and voice work wasn't coming up anymore. He was retired, whether he wanted to be or not.

And sadly, for Gene, he wouldn't have anyone to share that retirement with anymore. In October 1996, after fifty-six years of marriage, Helen died.

Lynne remembers, "My father called me and told me that Helen had collapsed and she was taken to Lenox Hill Hospital for surgery. And he told me this after they had already taken her in, so I didn't get a chance to talk to her. My mother was in bad shape, three clogged arteries and a lifelong smoker. She stroked out on the table.

"My father never knew how to deal with things that were traumatic and serious. I've seen movies about people dying and there are the scenes where the family and friends get together, reminisce, share stories, watch the old home movies... And when I see movie scenes like that, I don't see my family. After my mother died, Joan Sullivan came with us to see her laid out in the hospital, and afterward, Joan, my father, and I went out for cocktails. And it was quiet and nobody cried. That's just the way we were."

Lynne may not have seen any signs of grief from Gene, but one witness did: *Today* weatherman Al Roker. In 1999, he published the following story on his blog with this account of a chance encounter with Gene shortly after Helen's death.

> **There's no happy ending to this story. It is a little slice of life in New York, but one that left an impression on both my wife, Deborah and myself. It's a true story, and it happened [on a] Sunday night.**

It was about 7:30 Sunday night. We had just dropped my daughter Courtney back up in Westchester with her mom. Listening to the Yankee pre-game show on the radio, we were in a good mood, talking, chatting. It had been an exciting weekend, what with the storm and all.

We had parked the car in the garage around the corner from where we live and were walking down the street, just steps away from our front door, when a man passed us. Deborah said, "That's the game show guy." Me, I was in a fog just thinking about the Yankees and dreading what the Braves were going to do to them (how did I know?). I turned around, and at the same time, so did the guy.

Lo and behold... it was Gene Rayburn from the *Match Game*, the classic game show from the '60s & '70s. His face lit up, and he called out, "Al... Al Roker... how are you? Gene Rayburn." He stuck out his hand, and I shook it. He looked pretty good, that trademark smile that had the secrets of thousands of game show questions, answers and ad-libs behind it.

I asked him how he was, and suddenly, his face darkened. "Not so good," he replied. Naturally, I asked what was wrong, thinking health, or professional problems. He started to cry. Deborah and I looked at each other. "My wife just died."

We each professed sympathy and condolences. He told us it had just happened last week. "I can't talk anymore, but thank you for your concern. It was nice meeting you." He turned, sobbing and walked away.

We were both stunned. It was something we both are still thinking about today. The loss of one for the other, how suddenly in your later years you're alone, left to deal with grief, loneliness and pain.

The loneliness proved to be more than Gene could handle. Over the years, friend after friend after friend had migrated to the west coast and stayed there, while Gene stayed firmly planted in the east. But faced with a big empty apartment and nobody to share it with, Gene decided it was time to go west, not for his career, but for his morale.

Lynne says "I think my dad just needed to escape from his past. It was the same thing that happened in his childhood. Even though my parents didn't have a truly conventional bond, they still cared about each other, so again, it was my dad getting hurt by somebody he was close to. And I think he just wanted to get away from anything that reminded him of that."

Gene moved to Los Angeles, living with his old friend and producer Ira Skutch while he hunted for a nice apartment to settle down in. He moved into a two-bedroom apartment in Sherman Oaks, which was comfortable for him. Once he got settled in, he was extremely social, visiting friends from his years on *Match Game*, acquaintances like fellow game show host Jack Narz and actor Orson Bean, and his old buddy Fred Wostbrock.

Wostbrock remembers, "We had dinner every Friday night while Gene lived here. Gene picked the place, I always paid—I wouldn't allow Gene to pay… and I just sat there and listened to Gene tell stories. I wish I had brought along a tape recorder looking back, because he told so many stories."

Gene got a chance to tell some stories to a larger audience, thanks to a Game Show Network executive named Ryan Tridenick.

Wostbrock explains, "As I recall, there had been a massive project at ESPN during the 1990s, where that channel had rounded up a bunch of retired athletes and conducted lengthy interviews with them, just to get their memories on tape. And Ryan said he wanted to round up as many game show hosts as possible and do the same thing. He just wanted each host to spend a few hours recounting their lives and careers with a camera rolling the whole time. And the people that Ryan had to answer to at Game Show Network rejected the idea, but they allowed Ryan to interview one guy, and that was Gene. *Match Game* was the channel's highest-rated rerun package, so they allowed Gene to be recorded, with me acting as the interviewer and steering it along."

The date was July 10, 1997. The place was a small studio in Culver City, CA. A small staff was on hand that day; no more than a make-up artist, an audio man, a camera operator, and an interviewer, taking his spot out of view of the camera. The set was low frills; just a chair, a small table big enough for a glass of water and not much else. To a casual observer, nothing about this looked particularly important.

A lavalier microphone—the type that clips onto clothing—was attached to his jacket. As the crew made their preparations, Gene told a story about his friend Charles. The story amused him enough to laugh at himself as he told it, but then he glanced around the room and realized everyone was tending to business and nobody seemed to hear the story. In an instant, the smile disappeared, and a new layer was revealed. Gene looked sad, experiencing the bittersweet effect of living a long life. He now inhabited a world that he helped create, but not one that he was meant to see.

But a few moments later, the make-up was applied, the microphone was working, the lights were beaming, and the camera was rolling, and suddenly, one more change overcame Gene. Pull an average person off the street, give them a microphone, stick them under a bright light, and put a camera in front of their face, and fear-driven silence is all you might get.

But the make-up lady's approach caused the old man to whip his head around and warn her, "Don't touch me unless you love me!"

"I love you," the make-up lady told him.

"Okay, then," Gene replied with a laugh.

As the make-up lady ran a comb through his hair, Gene glanced at a nearby monitor and mumbled "You're doing a great job. I look twenty-nine again."

Gene suddenly sat straight up. The smile returned along with the twinkle in his eye. His gravelly voice became sharp and clear. The lights, camera, and the microphone made it happen. Gene was alive. Not just in the pulse-and-heartbeat sense. He was surrounded by everything that made him look forward to the next heartbeat. A studio or a stage, however tiny, was to him as oxygen was to any other human.

With everything and everyone in place and ready to go, the interviewer began. "Hello, Gene-o!"

Gene talked about his years as an NBC page, his theater career, *Monitor*, *Tonight*, and of course, *Match Game*. And Fred wrapped up the interview by asking Gene if he had anything he wanted his fans to know.

> *"I would just want them to know that I had as much fun doing it as they had watching it. It was a great trip and I loved every minute."*

(Fred Wostbrock Collection)

Chapter Twenty-Two
The End,
and the Continuation

Gene's time in Los Angeles was brief. After living in the city for nine months, he became aware of a problem. He wasn't as sharp as he had been. He began walking into rooms and forgetting why he was in there. He struggled to find words as he spoke. He was experiencing mood swings. Finally, one day, he called Fred Wostbrock and told him the bad news.

"I have to move back east," Gene explained. "I think I have dementia."

Lynne says, "My father had a housekeeper tending to his apartment in Los Angeles. One day the housekeeper called me and said that she was concerned because Dad wasn't taking care of himself. He was on a few medications and he wasn't taking any of them, and I realized that he was starting to go downhill."

Gene returned to Massachusetts and moved into an assisted living apartment near Lynne. Although suffering from dementia, he was in an early stage and still considered himself viable for work, if any happened to come up. Shortly after returning to the east coast, Gene was back on an airplane, returning to Los Angeles for a gig, shooting promos for a new cable series.

FX had picked up a new game show, an oddball entry titled *Bobcat's Big Ass Show*. Hosted by comic Bobcat Goldthwait, contestants on each show revealed embarrassing secrets about themselves, performed stunts, and begged the audience, who voted with their applause to determine which contestant would play a bonus round for a chance at a vacation.

Gene had been brought in at the request of former Game Show Network director of programming Bob Boden, who by this point was FX's vice president of development and production. He had an idea for a series of promos for *Bobcat's Big Ass Show* that would involve legendary game show hosts of the past, like Bob Eubanks, Peter Marshall, and Gene Rayburn, all clients of Fred Wostbrock. Wostbrock was in the studio during the filming of the promos.

He remembers, "Gene had been given a script. They were going to shoot six different promos with each host, so Gene's script was a series of short bursts of dialogue. And we begin filming, and Gene could not deliver his lines. And we stopped and went over what he needed to say again. And Gene nodded, we started filming again, and Gene didn't come close to the scripted line. Gene's capacity for memorizing a script was gone, and it was at a point where he couldn't even be fed the lines. We tried doing 'Gene, say this…' and giving it to him word for word, but by the time the director said 'Action!' it was already gone.

"And my friend Bob Boden was in there, and he looks at me and says 'What are we going to do?' And in show business, 'What are we going to do?' is the polite way of saying 'This is a disaster.' And I stepped forward and I said to the director and Gene, 'Okay, forget this, forget the script, forget cue cards or a teleprompter, we don't need to do that. Just tell me this. What is the essence of what Gene needs to say?'

"The director turns to Gene and just gives him one or two talking points, and we begin filming, and Gene, just off the top of his head, ad-libs for thirty seconds about this new game show and covers the talking points. Did it perfectly, did it in one take. Director says 'Okay, second promo, we need you to mention this and this…' Filming starts, and again, in one take, Gene knocks out the talking points, tells the audience to watch this new show, and manages to make it last for thirty seconds. We got all six promos filmed that way. Even with his mind fading away, Gene, to the very end, had that capacity for ad-libbing and for thinking on his feet. It was actually beautiful to watch him shoot those promos."

That's a wrap… Peter Marshall, agent Fred Wostbrock, Bob Eubanks, and Gene after shooting the promos for *Bobcat's Big-Ass Show*. It was Gene's last professional gig. (Fred Wostbrock Collection)

Gene's dementia advanced. Fred Wostbrock continued to keep tabs on Gene. He had been a friend long before he had been an agent, and Fred was happy to maintain that relationship. Gene still enjoyed sharing the memories he had, and he could still tell stories about the good old days. Fred arranged one final interview for Gene, when A&E's popular series *Biography* devoted an episode to the life of Mark Goodson.

Wostbrock explains, "I would never put somebody in Gene's condition in front of a camera for a project, but A&E wanted to ask him questions about working on Mark Goodson's game shows, which meant the questions were going to be about the 1950s, 1960s, 1970s. And Gene, in his condition, couldn't remember what he did fifteen minutes ago. He couldn't tell you what he had for breakfast that morning. But if you asked him about a TV show that he did in the 1950s, he could talk and talk and talk about it. So I felt comfortable booking Gene for the interview. We brought Gene to a hotel, Gene was wearing a nice suit, and the interviewer asked him questions and it was a great interview. All of the questions were about the past, so Gene was comfortable and he was coherent. That was the last time that I saw him alive."

On October 26, 1999, Gene was invited to a banquet in Manhattan by the National Academy of Television Arts & Sciences. Gene had never won any major awards during his career, but on this night, he was being honored with a lifetime achievement award.

Lynne was there that night. "We had to squeeze him into his tuxedo. He hadn't worn it in years, and he had developed some cardiac issues that affected the shape of his body. But he made it there, and his awareness of his surroundings sort of popped in and out. There were points during the evening where he knew exactly where he was, he knew he was at a banquet being held by the Academy of Television Arts & Sciences. And there were other times when he didn't seem to know that.

"It came time for him to go onstage and accept his award, and he walked up there, looked at the audience, and just began sobbing convulsively. I mean, hard, heavy, crying. In my entire life, I never saw him cry like that. I thought he was about to collapse. And the host walked onstage and put his arms around my dad's elbow and shoulder, and he said, 'Everything is fine, Gene.' And I can't remember if my father finally managed to say anything, but he nodded his head, the audience applauded, and he came to his seat in time for us to have dessert."

Fred Wostbrock remembers, "A few weeks later, I got a call from Lynne saying 'My dad isn't doing well.' And I said 'What do you mean?'

The End, and the Continuation

And Lynne said 'I mean I think we're about to lose him.' And I got right to work assembling photos and preparing the obituary."

On November 29, 1999, Gene Rayburn died. Many game show fans learned the news that night when Game Show Network preceded a rerun of *Match Game PM* with a graphic announcing that Gene was gone and provided a brief list of some of his career highlights. His death made national news. Network newscasts, *The New York Times*, and several major magazines all featured tributes.

Wostbrock says, "He really got one hell of a sendoff, and I think it would have made him happy to know that."

Lynne says, "My father was a pioneer in television and a pioneer in radio. He was a terrific actor, he was well-liked. He was uninvolved but he was kind, and he had a good sense of humor. I remember him being very private, but he was fun to be with during the good times."

Lynne was an avid gardener just like her dad. In accordance with Gene's final wishes, he was cremated, and his ashes were mixed with the soil when she started working on her spring garden. He once said that he considered the idea of helping to grow a plant in that way "the ultimate life cycle."

The following year, for the first time, Game Show Network aired excerpts from the 1997 interview that Fred Wostbrock conducted as part of a *Match Game* marathon. At the time, the interview attracted the largest audience in the channel's history. And well into the 2000s and beyond, *Match Game* continued to be a fixture on Game Show Network.

Meanwhile, the *Match Game* reruns on Game Show Network continued. A *Match Game* home game was released to the general public, with Gene's picture on the box. A *Match Game* DVD set came out, too. *Match Game* slot machines were scattered throughout Las Vegas, with Gene's smiling face adorning each one. Faux-Genes appeared in *Match Game* parodies on *Saturday Night Live* and *Family Guy*. Comedy clubs did *Match Game* nights, with regular performers as panelists and audience members as contestants. Even shows targeting younger audiences, like Nickelodeon's *iCarly* and Logo's *RuPaul's Drag Race*, whipped up *Match Game* spoofs. And far more often than not, the designated host in these spoofs always had a long, thin microphone. Technology offered better options, but everybody seemed to agree that wouldn't really be *Match*

Game without that microphone. In general, the viewing audience loved *Match Game*, but was content to remember it as it was. And that was Gene's legacy.

Many performers in show business are content to find a role that they do well, whether it's breathing life into a character, or singing a song that becomes their signature. Gene's legacy was about absorbing a job, to the point that it seemingly couldn't be done without him. Gene Rayburn never set out to become a game show host; he did it because he couldn't say no to the paying gig. And he found a show that suited his talents more perfectly than anything else that he ever could have done. The reneged promise from years earlier pledging that he could someday host *The Gene Rayburn Show* didn't matter. *Match Game* was exactly what *The Gene Rayburn Show* would have been anyway; jokes, bantering, characters, physical humor, a loose structure. Gene Rayburn wouldn't be remembered for the job that he wanted, but he would always be remembered for the job that he did better than anybody.

Appendix A
Gene Rayburn's Resume

TELEVISION HOST

Where Are You From? (Unsold pilot for NBC; possibly aired October 1, 1953)

Bright Ideas (WNBT-TV, New York, November 16, 1953-February 26, 1954)

The Sky's the Limit (WNBT-TV New York, November 1, 1954-December 27, 1955)

Make the Connection (NBC Primetime, August 4-September 29, 1955)

Choose Up Sides (NBC Saturday mornings, January 7-March 31, 1956)

Dough Re Mi (NBC daytime, February 24, 1958-December 30, 1960)

Head of the Class (Unsold pilot for NBC, 1960)

The 1962 Miss Universe Pageant (CBS-TV, July 14, 1962)

The Match Game (NBC-TV, December 31, 1962-September 26, 1969)

The Matchless Gene Rayburn

(Fred Wostbrock Collection)

The 1963 Miss Universe Pageant (CBS-TV, July 20, 1963)
Helluva Town (WNEW-TV, July 27, 1969-c. 1970)
It's Predictable (Unsold pilot; recorded June 13, 1970)
The Amateur's Guide to Love (CBS-TV, March 27-June 23, 1972)
Celebrity Match Mates (Unsold pilot for CBS-TV, 1972)
Match Game '73, aka *Match Game '74*, etc. (July 2, 1973-April 20, 1979)
Match Game PM (Syndication, once a week, September 1975-September 1981)
Drum Corps International (Public television special, August 19, 1977)

Match Game (Syndication, daily, September 1979-September 1982; only reruns aired during the 1982-83 season and the 1985-86 season)
It Happened Right Here (1982)
Saturday Morning Live (1982-83)
Party Line (Unsold pilot, taped 1983)
The Match Game Hollywood Squares Hour (1983-84)
It (Unsold pilot, taped 1984)
Unpredictable Pairs (Unsold pilot, taped 1984)
Break the Bank (1985)
The Movie Masters (1989)

TELEVISION GUEST-HOST
Tonight! Starring Steve Allen (c. 1955)
Today (NBC, 1954 and 1962)
To Tell the Truth (CBS, October 7, 1963)
The Tonight Show Starring Johnny Carson (NBC, September 1967)
Tattletales (CBS, 1974 and 1975)
The Mike Douglas Show (November 1974)

TELEVISION ANNOUNCER
The Knickerbocker Beer Show, aka *The Steve Allen Show* (WNBT-TV, New York, 1953-September 24, 1954)
Tonight! Starring Steve Allen (NBC late night, September 27, 1954-January 25, 1957)
The Steve Allen Show (NBC primetime, June 24, 1956-June 7, 1959)

TELEVISION GAME SHOW PANELIST/GUEST
The Name's the Same (ABC, 1953-54; at least fifty-five episodes)
What's My Line? (CBS, 1956-67: three episodes as panelist; one episode as Mystery Guest)
To Tell the Truth (CBS, 1956-68: fourteen episodes in primetime; at least 120 episodes in daytime)
Call My Bluff (NBC, 1965: thirty episodes)
Snap Judgment (NBC, 1967-68: forty episodes)
The Hollywood Squares (NBC, 1968-80: twenty-five episodes)

The Matchless Gene Rayburn

(Fred Wostbrock Collection)

What's My Line? (Syndication, 1968-75: At least 160 episodes as panelist, plus one episode as Mystery Guest)
He Said, She Said (Syndication, 1969-70: pilot plus at least twenty episodes)
Beat the Clock (Syndication, 1969-74: At least ten episodes)
To Tell the Truth (Syndication, 1969-78: At least 260 episodes)
All About Faces (Syndication, 1971: seven episodes)
Password (ABC, 1971-74; five episodes)
Password All-Stars (ABC, 1974-75; ten episodes)
I've Got a Secret (Syndication, 1972-73: five episodes)
The $10,000 Pyramid (CBS, 1973: five episodes)
Tattletales (CBS, 1974-78: at least forty-five episodes)
Showoffs (ABC, 1975: ten episodes)
Card Sharks (NBC, 1980: five episodes)
Password Plus (NBC, 1980-82: twenty-six episodes)
Tattletales (CBS, 1982-84: at least five episodes)
Just Men! (NBC, 1983: five episodes)

TELEVISION ACTING
Kukla, Fran, and Ollie (NBC, 1949)

Robert Montgomery Presents "The Man Who Vanished" (February 9, 1956)
Kraft Television Theatre "Heroes Walk on Sand" (December 11, 1957)
The Love Boat "Love Me, Love My Dog/Poor Little Rich Girl/The Decision" (1979)
Here's Boomer "Boomer and Miss 21st Century" (1980)
Aloha Paradise "Best of Friends/Success/Nine Karats" (1981)
The Love Boat "Not So Fast, Gopher/Haven't We Met Before?/Foreign Exchange" (1981)
The Love Boat "April in Boston/Saving Grace/Breaks of Life" (1982)
Fantasy Island "Forget Me Not/The Quiz Masters" (1982)
One Life to Live (1982)
Riptide "Games People Play" (1985)

TV COMMERCIALS
Eno Sparkling Antacid
Greyhound Bus Company
Black & Decker
Pontiac
Cheer
Atari

OTHER TELEVISION GUEST APPEARANCES
Kukla, Fran, and Ollie (NBC, 1949)
The Steve Lawrence-Eydie Gorme Show (NBC, August 24, 1958)
Insight "Prince of Apple Towns" (1970)
Dinah! (1974)
The Jim Nabors Show (1978)
The 35th Primetime Emmy Awards (NBC special, September 25, 1983)
TV's Funniest Game Show Moments (ABC special, May 10, 1984)
TV's Funniest Game Show Moments #2 (ABC special, January 15, 1985)
Regis Philbin's Lifestyles (Syndication, 1985)
NBC 60th Anniversary Celebration (1986)
This is Your Life (NBC, 1987)
The Late Show (Fox, 1988)
Sally Jesse Raphael (Syndicated, November 22, 1989)

Saturday Night Live (NBC, 1990)
The Howard Stern Show (Syndicated, 1992; three episodes)
Marilu (Syndicated, 1994)
Vicki! (Syndicated, 1994)
Donahue (Syndicated, 1995)
The Maury Povich Show (Syndicated, 1996)
Game TV (Game Show Network, 1997; two episodes)
Game Show a Go-Go (VH-1 special, 1997)
Biography (A&E, 2000 – Appearance taped prior to death)

FILM
It Happened to Jane (1959)

RADIO
WNGY-AM, Newburgh, NY (1940-41)
WITH-AM, Baltimore, MD (1941)
WFIL-AM, Philadelphia, NY (1942)
Scream and Dream with Jack & Gene (WNEW, 1946)
Anything Goes with Rayburn & Finch (WNEW, 1946-52)
Let Yourself Go (WNEW, 1948-52)
Rayburn & Finch (ABC Network, 1950 and CBS Network, 1951)
WNBC-AM (November 17, 1952-1953)
Monitor (NBC, 1961-73)

THEATRE
The Seven Year Itch (Sea Cliff, Long Island, NY, 1956)
The Love of Four Colonels (Bucks County Playhouse, 1957)
Will Success Spoil Rock Hunter? (Bucks County Playhouse, 1957)
Our Hearts Were Young and Gay (Bucks County Playhouse, c. 1958)
Who was That Lady I Saw You With? (Bucks County Playhouse, 1959)
Come Blow Your Horn (Bucks County Playhouse, 1960; Broadway
    (substitute), c.1960; National touring company, c.1961)
Bye Bye Birdie (1961, Broadway)
Under the Yum-Yum Tree (Bucks County Playhouse, 1962)
Gypsy (Tenthouse Theater, 1965)
The Impossible Years (Bucks County Playhouse, 1966)

Gene Rayburn's Resume

(Fred Wostbrock Collection)

Rattle of a Simple Man (Playhouse on the Mall, 1966)
Prisoner of Second Avenue (Location and dates unknown)
Lovers Leap (Alhambra Theatre, 1980)
Tribute (Country Dinner Playhouse, 1981)

I Ought To Be in Pictures (Cherry County Playhouse and Elitch Theater Company, 1981)
A Christmas Carol (Charles Playhouse, 1981)

OTHER PERFORMANCES
-1962 Aqua Carnival (New York Coliseum, 1962)

THEATRE, WRITING
Sight Unseen (Vassar, 1941)

Appendix B
Match Game Guests

(Author's Collection)

Research spanning 1962-69 courtesy of NBC.
Research spanning 1973-82 courtesy of Brian Connoy.
Research spanning 1983-84 courtesy of Brendan MacLaughlin.

NBC 1962-63

Dec. 5	Unaired pilot: Peter Lind Hayes & Peggy Cass
Dec. 31, Jan. 2-4	Arlene Francis & Skitch Henderson
Jan. 7-11	Abe Burrows & Sally Ann Howes
Jan. 14-18	Peggy Cass & Peter Lind Hayes
Jan. 21-25	Sam Levenson & Carol Lawrence
Jan. 28-Feb. 1	Darren McGavin & Betty White
Feb. 4-8	Dorothy Collins & Barry Nelson
Feb. 11-15	Ann Sothern & Milt Kamen
Feb. 18-22	Audrey Meadows & Orson Bean
Feb. 25-Mar. 1	Gisele MacKenzie & Milt Kamen
Mar. 4-8	Peggy Cass & Bennett Cerf
Mar. 11-15	Florence Henderson & Paul Ford
Mar. 18-22	Mary Healy & Robert Q. Lewis
Mar. 25-29	Rise Stevens & Henry Morgan
Apr. 1-5	Peggy Cass & Douglas Fairbanks, Jr.
Apr. 8-12	Carol Lawrence & Chester Morris
Apr. 15-19	Florence Henderson & Tom Poston
Apr. 22-26	Jane Wyatt & Henry Morgan
Apr. 29-May 3	Kitty Carlisle & Milt Kamen
May 6-10	Gisele MacKenzie & Mickey Rooney Also appearing during the week: Bob Hope
May 13-17	Art James & Abbe Lane
May 20-24	Sam Levenson & Barbara Cook
May 27-31	Faye Emerson & Jack E. Leonard
Jun. 3-7	Kitty Carlisle & Vaughn Meader (Monday's episode interrupted for coverage of Pope's death)

Jun. 10-14	Joan Fontaine & Rod Serling (Tuesday's episode interrupted for coverage of Alabama crisis)
Jun. 17-21	Faye Emerson & Milt Kamen
Jun. 24-28	Henry Morgan & Florence Henderson
Jul. 1-5	Diana Lynne & Tom Poston
Jul. 8-12	Skitch Henderson & Peggy Cass
Jul. 15-19	Jack E. Leonard & Joan Caulfield
Jul. 22-26	Florence Henderson & Morey Amsterdam
Jul. 29-Aug. 2	Gisele MacKenzie & Chester Morris
Aug. 5-9	Betty White & Sam Levenson
Aug. 12-16	Joan Fontaine & Alan Young
Aug. 19-23	Faye Emerson & Henry Morgan (Friday's program interrupted for coverage of the March on Washington)
Aug. 26-30	Barbara Cook & Milt Kamen
Sep. 2-6	Betty White & Rod Serling
Sep. 9-13	Bess Myerson & Jim Backus
Sep. 16-20	Dorothy Collins & Abe Burrows
Sep. 23-27	Carol Lawrence & Vaughn Meader Also appearing during the week: Richard Egan
Sep. 30-Oct. 4	Jane Withers & Jack Ging
Oct. 7-11	Jinx Falkenberg & Tom Poston
Oct. 14-18	Dick Clark & Fran Allison
Oct. 21-25	Joey Bishop & Arlene Francis
Oct. 28-Nov. 1	Jim Backus & Carol Lawrence (Friday's episode interrupted for bulletin regarding the South Vietnam coup)
Nov. 4-8	Nipsey Russell & Peggy Cass
Nov. 11-15	Van Johnson & Audrey Meadows

Nov. 18-22	Betty White & Shelley Berman (Friday's episode never aired, due to coverage of John F. Kennedy's assassination)
Nov. 25-29	Pat Carroll & Henry Morgan (Monday's episode never aired, due to Kennedy's funeral; Tuesday's episode opened with an announcement that this week's episodes were all taped before Kennedy's death)
Dec. 2-6	Dorothy Kilgallen & Tom Poston
Dec. 9-13	Kitty Carlisle & Chester Morris
Dec. 16-20	Mitch Miller & Audrey Meadows
Dec. 23-27	Peggy Cass & Paul Anka
Dec. 30-31	Milt Kamen & Shari Lewis

NBC, 1964

Jan. 2-3	Milt Kamen & Shari Lewis (continued)
Jan. 6-10	Shirl Conway & Abe Burrows
Jan. 13-17	Arlene Francis & Rod Serling
Jan. 20-24	Special week: Henry Morgan, Bennett Cerf, & Robert Q. Lewis vs. Joan Fontaine, Betty White, & Peggy Cass (all prize money awarded to Boy Scouts and Girl Scouts)
Jan. 27-31	Don Ameche & Jane Withers
Feb. 3-7	Kitty Carlisle & Howard Keel
Feb. 10-14	Joan Bennett & Orson Bean
Feb. 17-21	Betty White & Don Murray
Feb. 24-28	Dorothy Kilgallen & Jack E. Leonard
Mar. 2-6	Carmel Quinn & Morey Amsterdam
Mar. 9-13	Florence Henderson & Henry Morgan (Tuesday's episode interrupted for bulletin announcing that Queen Elizabeth gave birth)
Mar. 16-20	Pat Suzuki & Don Murray
Mar. 23-27	Don Defore & Paula Prentice

Mar. 30-Apr. 3	Arlene Francis & John Payne
Apr. 6-10	Peggy Cass & Howard Keel
Apr. 13-17	Phyllis Diller & Robert Merrill
Apr. 20-24	Phyllis Newman & Robert Q. Lewis
Apr. 27-May 1	Betty White & Pernell Roberts
May 4-8	Douglas Fairbanks, Jr. & Florence Henderson
May 11-15	Tom Poston & Sally Ann Howes
May 18-22	Allan Sherman & Ann Sothern
May 25-29	Rod Serling & Carmel Quinn
Jun. 1-5	Milt Kamen & Dr. Joyce Brothers
Jun. 8-12	Paul Anka & Gretchen Wyler
Jun. 15-19	Betty White & Pat O'Brien
Jun. 22-26	Peggy Cass & Sal Mineo
Jun. 29-Jul. 3	Betty Furness & Allan Sherman
Jul. 6-7, 9-10	Orson Bean & Jayne Mansfield (Pre-empted on the 8th for Republican Convention)
Jul. 14-17	Art James & Florence Henderson (Pre-empted on the 13th for Republican Convention)
Jul. 20-24	Abe Burrows & Carol Lawrence
Jul. 27-31	Jayne Mansfield & Orson Bean
Aug. 3-7	Pat O'Brien & Betty White (Episodes on the 5th and 7th did not air due to United Nations special reports)
Aug. 10-14	Shari Lewis & Mort Sahl
Aug. 17-21	Wally Cox & Selma Diamond

Aug. 24-28	Dale Robertson & Phyllis Diller (Aug. 25th interrupted for news bulletin regarding Gulf Oil; Aug. 26th interrupted for coverage of President Johnson's arrival in Atlantic City for the Democratic Convention)
Aug. 31-Sep. 4	Robert Q. Lewis & Ann Sheridan
Sep. 7-11	Dorothy Kilgallen & Rod Serling
Sep. 14-18	Betty White & Jack E. Leonard
Sep. 21-25	Henry Morgan & Jayne Mansfield Also appearing during the week: Bill Dana and Robert Vaughn
Sep. 28-Oct. 2	Tom Poston & Dr. Joyce Brothers
Oct. 5-9	June Allyson & Abe Burrows Also appearing during the week: Debbie Watson (October 7 and 8 pre-empted for the World Series)
Oct. 12-16	Jayne Wyman & Sidney Chaplin
Oct. 19-23	Roddy McDowell & Peggy Cass
Oct. 26-30	Raymond Massey & Kitty Carlisle
Nov. 2-6	Florence Henderson & Henry Morgan
Nov. 9-13	Gisele MacKenzie & Milt Kamen
Nov. 16-20	Joe Garagiola & Jane Withers
Nov. 23-25, 27	Tom Poston & Dr. Joyce Brothers (Pre-empted on the 26th for NCAA football) (Friday's episode was a special Soldiers vs. WACS game)
Nov. 30-Dec. 4	Selma Diamond & Mel Torme (Dec. 1 pre-empted for Bobby Baker Hearings)
Dec. 7-11	Carmel Quinn & Pat O'Brien
Dec. 14-18	Betty White & Orson Bean (children played on Wednesday's episode)
Dec. 21-25	Y.A. Tittle & Peggy Cass
Dec. 28-31	Don Ameche & Shari Lewis

Match Game Guests

NBC, 1965

Jan. 4-8	Jayne Mansfield & Joe Garagiola
Jan. 11-15	Audrey & Jayne Meadows
Jan. 18-19, 21-22	Florence Henderson & Bill Cosby (Pre-empted on the 20th for Inauguration Day)
Jan. 25-29	Jane Withers & Marty Ingels
Feb. 1-5	Joan Fontaine & Bobby Darin
Feb. 8-12	Sidney Chaplin & Betty White
Feb. 15-19	Lauren Bacall & Abe Burrows
Feb. 22-26	Gisele MacKenzie & Bill Cosby
Mar. 1-5	Jayne Meadows & Bill Leyden
Mar. 8-12	Peggy Cass & Chester Morris (children played on Wednesday)
Mar. 15-19	Orson Bean & Anita Louise
Mar. 22-26	Florence Henderson & Wally Cox (Pre-empted on the 23rd for coverage of the Gemini 3 flight; pre-empted on the 25th by coverage of the March on Montgomery)
Mar. 29-Apr. 2	Selma Diamond & Art James Also appearing during the week: Monty Hall
Apr. 5-9	Jayne Mansfield & Milt Kamen (first week in color)
Apr. 12-16	Bess Myerson & Henry Morgan
Apr. 19-23	Betty White & Gale Gordon
Apr. 26-30	Marty Allen & Steve Rossi (27th pre-empted for Presidential news conference) Also appearing during the week: The Motley Group of the College of New Rochelle
May 3-7	Rita Moreno & Roger Smith
May 10-14	Orson Bean & Dorothy Lamour
May 17-21	Lauren Bacall & Henry Morgan

May 24-28	Peggy Cass & Sal Mineo Also appearing during the week: Bob Barker
May 31-Jun. 4	Whitey Ford & Joe Garagiola (Pre-empted on the 3rd for Gemini 4 coverage)
Jun. 7-11	Vivian Vance & Sydney Chaplin
Jun. 14-18	June Lockhart & Les Crane
Jun. 22-25	Jan Murray & Carol Lawrence (Pre-empted on the 21st due to Presidential news conference)
Jun. 28-Jul. 2	Robert & Alan Alda
Jul. 5-9	Gisele MacKenzie & Bobby Vinton
Jul. 12, 14-16	Audrey Meadows & Pat O'Brien (13th pre-empted for MLB All-Star Game)
Jul. 19-23	Jayne Meadows & Alan Young
Jul. 26-30	Rita Moreno & Cliff Robertson
Aug. 2-6	Henry Morgan & Betty White
Aug. 9-13	Art James & Bill Leyden (on Tuesday, Art James guest-hosted and Gene played)
Aug. 16-20	NO DATA
Aug. 23-27	Elliott Reid & Anna Maris Alberghetti
Aug. 30-Sep. 3	Phyllis Newman & Rod Serling
Sep. 6-10	Whitey Ford & Joe Garagiola (Friday's episode was an all-celebrity game, with Ford & Garagiola joined by Mickey Mantle, Joe Peppetone, Roger Maris, and Tom Tresh)
Sep. 13-17	Phyllis Diller & Wally Cox
Sep. 20-24	Jayne Meadows & Sydney Chaplin
Sep. 27-Oct. 1	Jane Withers & Darryl Hickman

Match Game Guests

Oct. 5, 8	Ethel Merman & Abe Burrows (Pre-empted on the 4th because of Pope Paul's visit to the United States; pre-empted on the 6th & 7th for the World Series)
Oct. 12, 15	Debra Bryant & Sam Levenson (All contestants on the 15th were former Miss Americas) (Pre-empted on the 11th, 13th, and 14th for the World Series)
Oct. 18-22	Gloria Swanson & Chester Morris
Oct. 25-29	Edgar & Candice Bergen
Nov. 1-5	Rita Moreno & Henry Morgan
Nov. 8-12	Vivian Vance & Roddy MacDowell
Nov. 15-19	Whitey Ford & Joe Garagiola
Nov. 22-24, 26	Milt Kamen & Carol Lawrence (Pre-empted on Thursday for NCAA football)
Nov. 29-Dec. 3	Dr. Joyce Brothers & Henry Morgan Also appearing during the week: Juliet Prowse
Dec. 6-10	Betty White & Ray Bolger
Dec. 13-17	Florence Henderson & Edd Byrnes
Dec. 20-24	Joan Rivers & Bill Cullen
Dec. 27-31	Henry Morgan & Rita Moreno

NBC, 1966

Jan. 3-7	Don Adams & Barbara Feldon
Jan. 10-14	Hugh O'Brian & Debbie Bryant
Jan. 17-21	Florence Henderson & Art James
Jan. 24-28	Joe Garagiola & Maury Wills
Jan. 31-Feb. 1, Feb. 3	Rita Moreno & Abe Burrows (Pre-empted on the 2nd for a report on Vietnam)
Feb. 7, 9	Selma Diamond & Rod Serling (Pre-empted on the 6th, 8th, and 10th for Senate hearings on Vietnam)
Feb. 14-16	Ed McMahon & Skitch Henderson (17th & 18th pre-empted for Senate hearings)

Feb. 21-25	Joe Garagiola & Y.A. Tittle
Feb. 28-Mar. 4	Gisele MacKenzie & Milt Kamen
Mar. 7, 9, 11	Bennett Cerf & Jayne Mansfield (pre-empted on the 8th and 10th for Senate hearings on Red China)
Mar. 14-18	Phyllis Newman & Robert Q. Lewis
Mar. 21-25	Nancy Sinatra & Darryl Hickman
Mar. 28-30, Apr. 1	Betty White & Lloyd Bridges (Pre-empted on the 31st by President Johnson's speech about inflation)
Apr. 4-8	Florence Henderson & Ray Bolger
Apr. 11-15	Lee Remick & Abe Burrows
Apr. 18-22	Skitch Henderson & Ed McMahon
Apr. 25-29	Bess Myerson & Henry Morgan
May 2-6	Vivian Vance & John Forsythe
May 9-13	Jacqueline Susann & Sam Levenson
May 16-20	Julia Meade & Roger Smith
May 23-27	Mitch Miller & Carol Lawrence
May 30-Jun. 3	Whitey Ford & Mickey Mantle (31st was a special all-star game, featuring Joe Garagiola, Jerry Coleman, Red Barber, and Phil Rizzuto; 2nd and 3rd were all-star games featuring Tom Tresh, Joe Pepitone, Roger Maris, & Mel Stottlemyre)
Jun. 7-10	Gisele MacKenzie & Paul Anka (pre-empted on the 6th for Gemini coverage)
Jun. 13-17	June Lockhart & Cliff Robertson
Jun. 20-24	Julia Meade & Joe Garagiola
Jun. 27-Jul. 1	Betty White & John Forsythe
Jul. 4-8	Robert Goulet & Carol Lawrence
Jul. 11, 13-15	Debra Bryant & Bert Parks (pre-empted on the 12th for the MLB All-Star Game)

Match Game Guests

Jul. 19, 22	Selma Diamond & Ed McMahon (pre-empted on the 18th for Gemini 10 coverage; pre-empted on the 20th for Presidential news conference; pre-empted on the 21st for coverage of Gemini 10)
Jul. 25-29	Florence Henderson & Durwood Kirby
Aug. 1-5	Rita Moreno & Skitch Henderson
Aug. 8-12	Leslie Uggams & Mitch Miller
Aug. 15-19	Phyllis Newman & Mark Goodson (18th interrupted for coverage of the Lunar Orbiter)
Aug. 22-26	Barbara Feldon & Abe Burrows (all contestants on the 24th were members of the US Navy Blue Angels)
Aug. 29-Sep. 2	Dr. Joyce Brothers & Sam Levenson
Sep. 5-9	Debbie Bryant & Bert Parks
Sep. 12-16	Dina Merrill & Cliff Robertson
Sep. 19-23	Phyllis Newman & Rod Serling. Also appearing during this week: Robert Loggia
Sep. 26-30	Anita Gillette & Les Crane
Oct. 3-4, 7	Carol Lawrence & Soupy Sales (5th and 6th pre-empted for the World Series)
Oct. 10-14	Gisele MacKenzie & Joe Garagiola
Oct. 17-21	Jane Anne Jayroe & Darryl Hickman[1]
Oct. 24-28	Dina Merrill & Mitch Miller
Oct. 31-Nov. 4	1000th Episode Celebration, with Mark Goodson & Phyllis Newman; all contestants during the week were personal friends of Goodson & Newman[2]
Nov. 7-10	Rita Moreno & Henry Morgan. Also appearing during the week: Sandy Baron. (Pre-empted on the 11th for the flight of Gemini 12)

Nov. 14-15, 17-18	Joan Rivers & Ed McMahon (Pre-empted on the 16th for a report on Vietnam from President Johnson)
Nov. 21-23, 25	Sharon K. Ritchie & Soupy Sales (Pre-empted on the 24th for AFL Football)
Nov. 28-Dec. 2	Betty White & Alan King
Dec. 5-9	Dick Clark, Mitch Miller, & Leslie Uggams[3]
Dec. 12-16	Vivian Vance & Henry Morgan
Dec. 19-23	Dr. Joyce Brothers & Robert Q. Lewis
Dec. 26-30	Roger Smith & Betty White

NBC, 1967

Jan. 2-6	NO DATA
Jan. 9-13	Phyllis Newman & Alan Alda
Jan. 16-20	Rita Moreno & George Segal
Jan. 23-27	Fannie Flagg & Noel Harrison
Jan. 30-Feb. 3	Joe Garagiola & Whitey Ford
Feb. 6-8, 10	Audrey Meadows & David Susskind (Pre-empted on the 9th for Secretary of State Dean Rusk's press conference)
Feb. 13-17	Connie Stevens & Robert Culp
Feb. 20-24	Steve Allen & Jayne Meadows
Feb. 27-Mar. 3	Marilyn Van Derbur & Ray Bolger
Mar. 6-10	Henry Morgan & Jane Withers
Mar. 13-17	Betty White & Robert Q. Lewis
Mar. 20-24	Soupy Sales & Fannie Flagg
Mar. 27-31	Phyllis Newman & Ed McMahon
Apr. 3-7	Liza Minelli & Hugh O'Brian
Apr. 10-14	Henry Morgan & Betty White
Apr. 17-21	Bert Parks & Dr. Joyce Brothers
Apr. 24-28	Dom DeLuise & Michelle Lee

May 1-5	Fannie Flagg & Ed McMahon
May 8-12	Mickey Mantle & Whitey Ford
May 15-19	Bill Cullen & Phyllis Newman
May 22-23, 25-26	Victor Borge & Leonid Hambro (pre-empted on the 24th for coverage of the Middle East crisis)
May 29-Jun. 2	Joan Rivers & Joe Garagiola
Jun. 5-9	Claire Bloom & Roger Moore
Jun. 12-16	Ed McMahon & Hugh Downs
Jun. 19-23	Phyllis Newman & Alan King
Jun. 26-30	Joe Pepitone & Mickey Mantle
Jul. 3-7	June Lockhart & Henry Morgan
Jul. 10-14	Lauren Bacall & Abe Burrows
Jul. 17-21	Abby Dalton & Mitch Miller
Jul. 24-28	Betty White & Sandy Baron
Jul. 31-Aug. 4	Sandy Koufax & Y.A. Tittle
Aug. 7-11	Fannie Flagg & Durwood Kirby
Aug. 14-18	Dr. Joyce Brothers & Hal Holbrook
Aug. 21-25	Whitey Ford & Joe Garagiola
Aug. 28-Sep. 1	Phyllis Newman & Alan Alda
Sep. 4-8	Bess Myerson & Bert Parks
Sep. 11-15	Rita Moreno & Cliff Robertson
Sep. 18-22	Michele Lee & James Farentino
Sep. 25-29	Betty White & Sheldon Leonard
Oct. 2-6	Tom Kennedy & Ed McMahon
Oct. 9-13	Lesley Gore & Soupy Sales
Oct. 16-20	Audrey Meadows & Hugh Downs
Oct. 23-27	Carolyn Jones & Henry Morgan
Oct. 30-Nov. 3	Carl Yastrzemski & Joe Garagiola
Nov. 6-10	Vivian Vance & Ed McMahon

Nov. 13-17	Joan Rivers & George Kirby
Nov. 20-24	Florence Henderson & Hugh Downs
Nov. 27-Dec. 1	Betty White & Allen Ludden
Dec. 4-8	Jane Withers & Alan King
Dec. 11-15	Carol Lawrence & Shelley Berman
Dec. 18-22	Bess Myerson & Bill Cullen
Dec. 25-29	Phyllis Diller & Mitch Miller

NBC, 1968

Jan. 2-5	Dina Merrill & Cliff Robertson
Jan. 8-12	Michele Lee & Soupy Sales
Jan. 15-19	Lauren Bacall & Ed McMahon
Jan. 22-26	Liza Minelli & Dustin Hoffman
Jan. 29-Feb. 2	Mickey Mantle & Joe Garagiola
Feb. 5-9	Phyllis Newman & Cliff Robertson
Feb. 12-16	Fannie Flagg & Bill Cullen
Feb. 19-23	Rita Moreno & Eli Wallach
Feb. 26-Mar. 1	Dr. Joyce Brothers & Soupy Sales
Mar. 4-8	Jane Powell & Mitch Miller
Mar. 11-15	Phyllis Newman & Morey Amsterdam
Mar. 18-22	Steve Allen & Jayne Meadows
Mar. 25-29	Bess Myerson & George Hamilton
Apr. 1-5	Lauren Bacall & Peter Lawford
Apr. 8-12	Betty White & George Hamilton
Apr. 15-19	Dorothy Loudon & John Forsythe
Apr. 22-26	Don Meredith & Bart Starr
Apr. 29-May 3	Jessica Walter & Gordon MacRae
May 6-10	Sheila MacRae & Soupy Sales
May 13-17	Judy Carne & John Forsythe
May 20-24	Diana Sands & David Canary

Match Game Guests

May 27-31	Eydie Gorme & Alan King
Jun. 3-7	Fannie Flagg & Joel Grey
Jun. 10-14	Bess Myerson & Nipsey Russell
Jun. 17-21	Joanne Carson & Ed McMahon
Jun. 24-28	Joan Rivers & Noel Harrison
Jul. 1-5	Mickey Mantle & Joe Garagiola
Jul. 8-12	Dina Merrill & Soupy Sales
Jul. 15-19	Meredith MacRae & Peter Lawford (first week with new set)
Jul. 22-26	Barbara McNair & George Hamilton
Jul. 29-Aug. 2	Carol Lawrence & George Hamilton
Aug. 5-9	Judy Carne & Arte Johnson
Aug. 12-16	JoAnne Worley & Henry Morgan
Aug. 19-23	Meredith MacRae & Bennett Cerf
Aug. 26-30	Joanne Carson & Cliff Robertson
Sep. 2-6	Bess Myerson & Bert Parks
Sep. 9-13	JoAnne Worley & Flip Wilson
Sep. 16-20	Michele Lee & Gene Rayburn; guest host Ed McMahon
Sep. 23-27	Connie Hines & Soupy Sales
Sep. 30-Oct. 4	Meredith MacRae & James Brown
Oct. 7-11	Sheila MacRae & Joe Garagiola
Oct. 14-18	Jill Haworth & Orson Bean
Oct. 21-25	All Star Week: Tina Cole, Bridget Hanley & Kathy Garver vs. Don Grady, Bobby Sherman, & James Darren
Oct. 28-Nov. 1	Peggy Cass & Soupy Sales
Nov. 4-8	Joanne Carson & Ed McMahon
Nov. 11-15	Phyllis Newman & Richard Crenna
Nov. 18-22	Lauren Bacall & Patrick O'Neal
Nov. 25-29	Denny McLain & Joe Garagiola

Dec. 2-6	Sheila MacRae & Orson Bean
Dec. 9-13	Robert & Alan Alda
Dec. 16-20	Peggy Cass & Peter Lawford
Dec. 23-27	Bess Myerson & Gordon MacRae
Dec. 30-31	Diana Sands & Bert Convy

NBC, 1969

Jan. 2-3	Diana Sands & Bert Convy (continued)
Jan. 6-10	Joanne Carson & Hugh O'Brian
Jan. 13-17	Fannie Flagg & Soupy Sales
Jan. 20-24	Ethel Merman & Nipsey Russell
Jan. 27-31	Shirley Jones & Jack Cassidy
Feb. 3-7	Meredith & Gordon MacRae
Feb. 10-14	Rita Moreno & Henny Youngman
Feb. 17-21	Bill Cullen & Hugh Downs
Feb. 24-28	Sue Lyon & Carl Betz
Mar. 3-7	Dina Merrill & William Shatner
Mar. 10-14	Patricia Harty & Orson Bean
Mar. 17-21	Sheila MacRae & Jack Cassidy
Mar. 24-28	Lauren Bacall & Vidal Sassoon
Mar. 31-Apr. 4	Carol Lawrence & Soupy Sales
Apr. 7-11	Connie Hines & Garry Moore
Apr. 14-18	Dionne Warwick & Henry Morgan
Apr. 21-25	Meredith MacRae & Keir Dullea
Apr. 28-May 2	Don Meredith & Joe Garagiola
May 5-9	Ali MacGraw & Bob Crane
May 12-16	Edie Adams & Gordon MacRae
May 19-23	Rita Moreno & James Brown
May 26-30	Shani Wallis & Orson Bean
Jun. 2-6	Sue Lyon & Soupy Sales
Jun. 9-13	Connie Stevens & Garry Moore

Match Game Guests

Jun. 16-20	Peggy Cass & Tony Randall
Jun. 23-27	Lauren Bacall & David Frost
Jun. 30-Jul. 4	Sue Lyon & Robert Morse
Jul. 7-11	Joanne Carson & Bennett Cerf
Jul. 14-18	Peter Marshall & Ed McMahon
Jul. 21-25	Brenda Vaccaro & Burt Reynolds
Jul. 28-Aug. 1	Joe Garagiola & Rosey Grier
Aug. 4-8	Fannie Flagg & Soupy Sales
Aug. 11-15	Dr. Joyce Brothers & Bob Crane
Aug. 18-22	E.J. Peaker & William Shatner
Aug. 25-29	Helen O'Connell & Nipsey Russell
Sep. 1-5	Chelsea Brown & Robert Morse
Sep. 8-12	Brenda Vaccaro & Tom Kennedy
Sep. 15-19	Burt Reynolds & Don Meredith
Sep. 22-26	Betty White & Brian Keith

Match Game '73, CBS

Approximate airdates[4]	Panel
Jul. 2-6	Michael Landon, Vicki Lawrence, Jack Klugman, Jo Ann Pflug, Richard Dawson, Anita Gillette
Jul. 9-13	Bob Barker, Arlene Francis, Richard Dawson, Michael Learned, Richard Thomas, Della Reese
Jul. 16-20	Bert Convy, Jaye P. Morgan, Charles Nelson Reilly, Brett Somers, Richard Dawson, Betty White

Jul. 23-27	Dick Gautier, Barbara Stuart, Jack Carter, Jo Ann Pflug, Richard Dawson, Shelley Winters
Jul. 30-Aug. 3	Bert Convy, Loretta Swit, Charles Nelson Reilly, Mary Ann Mobley, Richard Dawson, Kaye Ballard
Aug. 6-10	Bert Convy, Brett Somers, Morey Amsterdam, Carolyn Jones, Richard Dawson, Betty White
Aug. 27-31	Bert Convy, Brett Somers, Jack Carter, Lucie Arnaz, Richard Dawson, Nanette Fabray
Sep. 3-7	Charles Nelson Reilly, Brett Somers, Morey Amsterdam, Loretta Swit, Richard Dawson, Ruta Lee
Sep. 10-14	Stu Gilliam, Brett Somers, Jack Klugman, Stephanie Edwards, Richard Dawson, Betty White
Sep. 17-21	Bobby Van, Elaine Joyce, Charles Nelson Reilly, Brett Somers, Richard Dawson, Nanette Fabray
Sep. 24-28	McLean Stevenson, Loretta Swit, Stu Gilliam, Brett Somers, Richard Dawson, Ann Elder
Oct. 1-5	Robert Culp, Brett Somers, Jack Klugman, Jo Ann Pflug, Richard Dawson, Pat Carroll
Oct. 8-12	Nipsey Russell, Loretta Swit, Charles Nelson Reilly, Brett Somers, Richard Dawson, Betty White

Match Game Guests

Oct. 15-19	Bert Convy, Brett Somers, Nipsey Russell, Mary Ann Mobley, Richard Dawson, Ann Elder
Oct. 22-26	Pat Harrington, Brett Somers, Charles Nelson Reilly, Jo Ann Pflug, Richard Dawson, Betty White
29-Nov. 2	Bert Convy, Brett Somers, Jack Carter, Fannie Flagg, Richard Dawson, Ann Elder
Nov. 5-9	Jim Backus, Brett Somers, Nipsey Russell, Patti Deutsch, Richard Dawson, Betty White
Nov. 12-16	Bill Cullen, Brett Somers, Jack Klugman, Mama Cass Elliot, Richard Dawson, Loretta Swit
Nov. 19-21, 26-27	Robert Vaughn, Brett Somers, McLean Stevenson, Nancy Dussault, Richard Dawson, Betty White
Nov. 28-30, Dec. 3-4	Robert Q. Lewis, Brett Somers, Morey Amsterdam, Joyce Bulifant, Richard Dawson, Ann Elder
Dec. 5-7, 10-11	Bill Daily, Brett Somers, Jack Carter, Judy Carne, Richard Dawson, Fannie Flagg
Dec. 12-14, 17-18	Nipsey Russell, Brett Somers, Charles Nelson Reilly, Beverly Garland, Richard Dawson, Betty White
Dec. 19-21, 24-25	Jack Cassidy, Brett Somers, Charles Nelson Reilly, June Lockhart, Richard Dawson, Loretta Swit

The Matchless Gene Rayburn

Dec. 26-28, 31	Bert Convy, Brett Somers, Charles Nelson Reilly, Lee Meriwether, Richard Dawson, Gail Fisher

(Fred Wostbrock Collection)

Match Game '74, CBS

Jan. 2	Bert Convy, Brett Somers, Charles Nelson Reilly, Lee Meriwether, Richard Dawson, Gail Fisher (continued week)
Jan. 3-4, 7-9	Larry Hovis, Brett Somers, Charles Nelson Reilly, Patti Deutsch, Richard Dawson, Madlyn Rhue
Jan. 10-11, 14-16	Greg Morris, Brett Somers, Morey Amsterdam, Juliet Mills, Richard Dawson, Fannie Flagg
Jan. 17-18, 21-23	Joe Flynne, Brett Somers, Charles Nelson Reilly, Linda Kaye Henning, Richard Dawson, Betty White
Jan. 24-25, 28-30	William Shatner, Anne Meara, Nipsey Russell, Brett Somers, Richard Dawson, Ann Elder
Jan. 31-Feb. 1, 4-6	Orson Bean, Brett Somers, Charles Nelson Reilly, Meredith MacRae, Richard Dawson, Marcia Wallace
Feb. 7-8, 18-20	Larry Hovis, Brett Somers, Rip Taylor, Jo Ann Pflug, Richard Dawson, Peggy Cass
Feb. 21-22, 25-27	Larry Blyden, Brett Somers, Charles Nelson Reilly, Elaine Joyce, Richard Dawson, Kaye Stevens
Feb. 28-Mar. 1, 4-6	Steve Allen, Brett Somers, Charles Nelson Reilly, Fannie Flagg, Richard Dawson, Kaye Ballard
Mar. 7-8, 11-13	Orson Bean, Brett Somers, Charles Nelson Reilly, Mary Ann Mobley, Richard Dawson, Betty White
Mar. 14-15, 18-20	Bert Convy, Brett Somers, Dick Gautier, Elaine Joyce, Richard Dawson, Ann Elder
Mar. 21-22, 25-27	Pat Harrington, Brett Somers, Nipsey Russell, Fannie Flagg, Richard Dawson, Jo Anne Worley

Mar. 28-29, Apr. 1-3	Bill Cullen, Brett Somers, Charles Nelson Reilly, Patti Deutsch, Richard Dawson, Betty White
Apr. 4-5, 8-9	Allen Ludden, Brett Somers, Charles Nelson Reilly, Joyce Bulifant, Richard Dawson, Fannie Flagg
Apr. 11-12, 15-18	Orson Bean, Brett Somers, Charles Nelson Reilly, Chelsea Brown, Richard Dawson, Jo Anne Worley
Apr. 19, 22-25	Rosey Grier, Brett Somers, Charles Nelson Reilly, Loretta Swit, Richard Dawson, Kaye Stevens
Apr. 26, 29-May 2	Ron Masak, Brett Somers, Charles Nelson Reilly, Jo Ann Pflug, Richard Dawson, Fannie Flagg
May 3, 6-9	Bobby Van, Brett Somers, Charles Nelson Reilly, Elaine Joyce, Richard Dawson, Betty White
May 10, 13-16	Jack Carter, Brett Somers, Charles Nelson Reilly, Trish Stewart, Richard Dawson, Kaye Stevens
May 17, 20-23	Greg Morris, Brett Somers, Charles Nelson Reilly, Anne Meara, Richard Dawson, Ann Elder
May 24, 27-30	Orson Bean, Brett Somers, Charles Nelson Reilly, Abby Dalton, Richard Dawson, Fannie Flagg
May 31, Jun 3-6	Nipsey Russell, Brett Somers, Charles Nelson Reilly, Jackie Joseph, Richard Dawson, Jo Anne Worley
Jun. 7, 10-13	Bert Convy, Brett Somers, Charles Nelson Reilly, Louisa Moritz, Richard Dawson, Kaye Stevens
Jun. 14, 17-20	Jack Narz, Brett Somers, Charles Nelson Reilly, Elaine Joyce, Richard Dawson, Fannie Flagg

Match Game Guests

Jun. 21, 24-27	Jimmie Walker, Brett Somers, Charles Nelson Reilly, Joyce Bulifant, Richard Dawson, Loretta Swit
Jun. 28, Jul 1-4	Don Adams, Brett Somers, Charles Nelson Reilly, Mitzi McCall, Richard Dawson, Elaine Joyce
Jul. 5, 8-11	Morey Amsterdam, Brett Somers, George Kirby, Jo Ann Pflug, Richard Dawson, Betty White
Jul. 12, 15-18	Scoey Mitchlll, Brett Somers, Charles Nelson Reilly, Patti Deutsch, Richard Dawson, Marcia Wallace
Jul. 19, 22-25	McLean Stevenson, Brett Somers, Charles Nelson Reilly, Joanie Sommers, Richard Dawson, Ann Elder
Jul. 26, 29-Aug 1	Anson Williams, Brett Somers, Charles Nelson Reilly, Fannie Flagg, Richard Dawson, Kaye Stevens
Aug. 2, 5-8	Alejandro Rey, Brett Somers, Charles Nelson Reilly, Juliet Mills, Richard Dawson, Jo Anne Worley
Aug. 9, 12-15	Orson Bean, Brett Somers, Charles Nelson Reilly, Dr. Joyce Brothers, Richard Dawson, Betty White
Aug. 16, 19-22	Donald Ross, Brett Somers, Charles Nelson Reilly, Patti Deutsch, Richard Dawson, Fannie Flagg
Aug. 23, 26-29	Charlie Brill, Brett Somers, Charles Nelson Reilly, Joyce Bulifant, Richard Dawson, Marcia Wallace
Aug. 30, Sep 2-5	Scoey Mitchlll, Brett Somers, Charles Nelson, Elaine Joyce, Richard Dawson, Fannie Flagg
(Five episodes; exact dates unverified)	Richard Long, Brett Somers, Charles Nelson Reilly, Jo Ann Pflug, Richard Dawson, Kaye Stevens

Sep. 17-20, 23	Nipsey Russell, Brett Somers, Charles Nelson Reilly, Anita Gillette, Richard Dawson, Jo Anne Worley
Sep. 24-27, 30	Robert Morse, Brett Somers, Charles Nelson Reilly, Adrienne Barbeau, Richard Dawson, Fannie Flagg
Oct. 1-4, 7	Orson Bean, Brett Somers, Charles Nelson Reilly, Penny Marshall, Richard Dawson, Betty White
Oct. 8-11, 14	Gary Burghoff, Brett Somers, Charles Nelson Reilly, Ann Elder, Richard Dawson, Patti Deutsch
Oct. 15-18, 21	Richard Deacon, Brett Somers, Nipsey Russell, Gunilla Hutton, Richard Dawson, Mitzi McCall
Oct. 22-25, 28	Jimmie Walker, Brett Somers, Charles Nelson Reilly, Lynda Day George, Richard Dawson, Kaye Stevens
Oct. 29- Nov. 1, 4	Arte Johnson, Brett Somers, Charles Nelson Reilly, Michele Lee, Richard Dawson, Betty White[5]
Nov. 5-8, 11	Michael Evans, Brett Somers, Gary Burghoff, Joyce Bulifant, Richard Dawson, Fannie Flagg
Nov. 12-15, 18	Charlie Brill, Brett Somers, Richard Deacon, Jo Ann Pflug, Richard Dawson, Patti Deutsch
Nov. 19-22, 25-26	Allen Ludden, Brett Somers, Gary Burghoff, Elaine Joyce, Richard Dawson, Fannie Flagg
Nov. 27, 29, Dec. 2-4	Gene Wood, Brett Somers, Gary Burghoff, Amanda Blake, Richard Dawson, Joyce Bulifant
Dec. 5-6, 9-11	Jack Carter, Brett Somers, Orson Bean, Louisa Moritz, Richard Dawson, Betty White

Match Game Guests

Dec. 12-13, 16-18	Bobby Van, Brett Somers, Gary Burghoff, Adrienne Barbeau, Richard Dawson, Fannie Flagg
Dec. 19-20, 23-24, 26	Avery Schreiber, Brett Somers, Gary Burghoff, Phyllis Newman, Richard Dawson, Patti Deutsch
Dec. 27, 30-31	James Darren, Brett Somers, Nipsey Russell, Juliet Mills, Richard Dawson, Betty White

Match Game '75, CBS

Jan. 2-3	James Darren, Brett Somers, Nipsey Russell, Juliet Mills, Richard Dawson, Betty White (continued week)
Jan. 6-10	Robert Vaughn, Brett Somers, Gary Burghoff, Patty Duke Astin, Richard Dawson, Mitzi McCall
Jan. 13-17	Greg Morris, Brett Somers, Gary Burghoff, Joyce Bulifant, Richard Dawson, Fannie Flagg
Jan. 20-24	Bert Convy, Brett Somers, Gary Burghoff, Mary Ann Mobley, Richard Dawson, Betty White
Jan. 27-31	Dwayne Hickman, Brett Somers, Gary Burghoff, Carol Lawrence, Richard Dawson, Marcia Wallace
Feb. 3-7	Avery Schreiber, Brett Somers, Gary Burghoff, Trish Stewart, Richard Dawson, Patti Deutsch
Feb. 10-14	Clifton Davis, Brett Somers, Gary Burghoff, Jo Ann Pflug, Richard Dawson, Fannie Flagg
Feb. 17-21	Shecky Greene, Brett Somers, Gary Burghoff, Elaine Joyce, Richard Dawson, Betty White

Feb. 24-28	Bob Barker, Brett Somers, Gary Burghoff, Rona Barrett, Richard Dawson, Fannie Flagg
Mar. 3-7	Jimmie Walker, Brett Somers, Gary Burghoff, Lee Meriwether, Richard Dawson, Joyce Bulifant
Mar. 10-14	Leslie Nielsen, Brett Somers, Gary Burghoff, Patti Deutsch, Richard Dawson, Marcia Wallace[6]
Mar. 17-21	Tom Bosley, Brett Somers, Gary Burghoff, Meredith MacRae, Richard Dawson, Fannie Flagg
Mar. 24-27, 31	Charlie Brill, Brett Somers, Gary Burghoff, Sarah Kennedy, Richard Dawson, Betty White
Apr. 1-4, 7-8	Nipsey Russell, Brett Somers, Gary Burghoff, Elaine Joyce, Richard Dawson, Fannie Flagg
Apr. 9-11, 14-15	Dick Martin, Brett Somers, Gary Burghoff, Mary Ann Mobley, Richard Dawson, Patti Deutsch
Apr. 16-18, 21-22	Orson Bean, Brett Somers, Gary Burghoff, Lynda Day George, Richard Dawson, Betty White
Apr. 23-25, 28-29	Ron Masak, Brett Somers, Gary Burghoff, Patty Duke Astin, Richard Dawson, Joyce Bulifant
Apr. 30-May 2, 5-6	Avery Schreiber, Brett Somers, Gary Burghoff, Arlene Francis, Richard Dawson, Betty White
May 7-9, 12-13	Buck Owens, Brett Somers, Gary Burghoff, Gloria DeHaven, Richard Dawson, Patti Deutsch
May 14-16, 19-20	John Forsythe, Brett Somers, Gary Burghoff, Elaine Joyce, Richard Dawson, Fannie Flagg

May 21-23, 26-27	Scoey Mitchlll, Brett Somers, Gary Burghoff, Karen Morrow, Richard Dawson, Fannie Flagg
May 29-30, Jun. 2-4	Gary Burghoff, Brett Somers, Charles Nelson Reilly, Madlyn Rhue, Richard Dawson, Betty White
Jun. 5-6, 9-11	Jack Albertson, Brett Somers, Charles Nelson Reilly, Lynne Redgrave, Richard Dawson, Patti Deutsch
Jun. 12-13, 16-18	Nipsey Russell, Brett Somers, Charles Nelson Reilly, Lee Meredith, Richard Dawson, Joyce Bulifant
Jun. 19-20, 23-25	Johnny Brown, Brett Somers, Charles Nelson Reilly, Trish Stewart, Richard Dawson, Marcia Wallace
Jun. 26-27, 30-Jul. 2	Bobby Van, Brett Somers, Charles Nelson Reilly, Sarah Kennedy, Richard Dawson, Ann Elder
Jul. 3-4, 7-9	Bill Daily, Brett Somers, Charles Nelson Reilly, Ethel Merman, Richard Dawson, Fannie Flagg
Match Game PM episode 1	Clifton Davis, Brett Somers, Charles Nelson Reilly, Elaine Joyce, Richard Dawson, Joyce Bulifant
Match Game PM episode 2	Clifton Davis, Brett Somers, Charles Nelson Reilly, Lee Meriwether, Richard Dawson, Betty White

Match Game PM episode 3	William Shatner, Brett Somers, Charles Nelson Reilly, Lee Meriwether, Richard Dawson, Joyce Bulifant
Match Game PM episode 4	Bill Macy, Brett Somers, Charles Nelson Reilly, Elaine Joyce, Richard Dawson, Betty White
Match Game PM episode 5	Orson Bean, Brett Somers, Charles Nelson Reilly, Lynda Day George, Richard Dawson, Patti Deutsch
Match Game PM episode 6	Orson Bean, Brett Somers, Charles Nelson Reilly, Sarah Kennedy, Richard Dawson, Marcia Wallace
Match Game PM episode 7	Avery Schreiber, Brett Somers, Charles Nelson Reilly, Joan Collins, Richard Dawson, Patti Deutsch
Match Game PM episode 8	Avery Schreiber, Brett Somers, Charles Nelson Reilly, Sarah Kennedy, Richard Dawson, Marcia Wallace
Match Game PM episode 9	Sheldon Leonard, Brett Somers, Charles Nelson Reilly, Dr. Joyce brothers, Richard Dawson, Fannie Flagg

Match Game PM episode 10	Gary Burghoff, Brett Somers, Charles Nelson Reilly, Madlyn Rhue, Richard Dawson, Betty White
Match Game PM episode 11	Bill Daily, Brett Somers, Charles Nelson Reilly, Kate Jackson, Richard Dawson, Betty White
Match Game PM episode 12	Gary Burghoff, Brett Somers, Charles Nelson Reilly, Adrienne Barbeau, Richard Dawson, Fannie Flagg
Jul. 10-11, 14-16	Jack Cassidy, Brett Somers, Charles Nelson Reilly, Conny Van Dyke, Richard Dawson, Betty White
Jul. 17-18, 21-23	Bert Convy, Brett Somers, Charles Nelson Reilly, Jo Ann Pflug, Richard Dawson, Joyce Bulifant
Jul. 24-25, 28-Aug 1	Avery Schreiber, Brett Somers, Charles Nelson Reilly, Kate Jackson, Richard Dawson, Fannie Flagg
Aug. 4-8	Allen Ludden, Brett Somers, Charles Nelson Reilly, Dolly Martin, Richard Dawson, Betty White
Aug. 11-15	Gary Burghoff, Brett Somers, Charles Nelson Reilly, Brenda Dickson, Richard Dawson, Patti Deutsch
Aug. 18-22	Orson Bean, Brett Somers, Charles Nelson Reilly, Pat Finley, Richard Dawson, Joyce Bulifant

Aug. 25-29	Bill Macy, Brett Somers, Charles Nelson Reilly, Elaine Joyce, Richard Dawson, Betty White
Sep. 1-5	Scoey Mitchlll, Brett Somers, Charles Nelson Reilly, Joan Collins, Richard Dawson, Patti Deutsch
Sep. 8-12	Robert Urich, Brett Somers, Gary Burghoff, Jamie Lynne Bauer, Richard Dawson, Fannie Flagg
Sep. 15-19	Avery Schreiber, Brett Somers, Charles Nelson Reilly, Lana Wood, Richard Dawson, Joyce Bulifant
Sep. 22-24, 26, 29	Bobby Van, Brett Somers, Charles Nelson Reilly, Sarah Kennedy, Richard Dawson, Betty White
Sep. 30-Oct. 3, 6	Bill Daily, Brett Somers, Charles Nelson Reilly, Dr. Joyce Brothers, Richard Dawson, Patti Deutsch
Oct. 7-10, 13	Bob Barker, Brett Somers, Charles Nelson Reilly, Arlene Francis, Richard Dawson, Fannie Flagg**
Oct. 14-17, 20	Sheldon Leonard, Brett Somers, Charles Nelson Reilly, Louisa Moritz, Richard Dawson, Fannie Flagg**
Oct. 21-24, 27	Alex Karras, Brett Somers, Charles Nelson Reilly, Barbara McNair, Richard Dawson, Joyce Bulifant
Oct. 28-31, Nov. 3	Scoey Mitchlll, Brett Somers, Charles Nelson Reilly, Patty Duke Astin, Richard Dawson, Patti Deutsch**

Match Game Guests

Nov. 4-7, 10	Orson Bean, Brett Somers, Charles Nelson Reilly, Mary Ann Mobley, Richard Dawson, Patti Deutsch**
Nov. 11-14, 17	Dick Gautier, Brett Somers, Charles Nelson Reilly, Melinda O. Fee, Richard Dawson, Betty White**
Nov. 18-21, 24	William Shatner, Brett Somers, Charles Nelson Reilly, Julie Harris, Richard Dawson, Fannie Flagg**
Nov. 25-26, 28, Dec. 1-2	Joe Silver, Brett Somers, Charles Nelson Reilly, Esther Rolle, Richard Dawson, Fannie Flagg**
Dec. 3-5, 8-9	Clifton Davis, Brett Somers, Charles Nelson Reilly, Rona Barrett, Richard Dawson, Betty White**
Dec. 10, 12, 15-17	Edward Asner, Brett Somers, Charles Nelson Reilly, Julie London, Richard Dawson, Fannie Flagg**
Dec. 18-19, 22-24	Gary Burghoff, Brett Somers, Charles Nelson Reilly, Pat Crowley, Richard Dawson, Joyce Bulifant**
Dec. 29-31	Dick Martin, Brett Somers, Charles Nelson Reilly, Jody Donovan, Richard Dawson, Fannie Flagg**

** - denotes a week when the panel taped a sixth episode for *Match Game PM*.

Match Game '76, CBS

CBS	Panel
Jan. 2, 5	Dick Martin, Brett Somers, Charles Nelson Reilly, Jody Donovan, Richard Dawson, Fannie Flagg (continued week)
Jan. 6-9, 12	Marvin Hamlisch, Brett Somers, Charles Nelson Reilly, Isabel Sanford, Richard Dawson, Betty White**
Jan. 13-16, 19	Jimmie Walker, Brett Somers, Charles Nelson Reilly, Elaine Joyce, Richard Dawson, Marcia Wallace**
Jan. 20-23, 26	Bill Daily, Brett Somers, Charles Nelson Reilly, Lee Meriwether, Richard Dawson, Fannie Flagg**
Jan. 27, 29-30, Feb 2-3	Scoey Mitchlll, Brett Somers, Charles Nelson Reilly, Bonnie Franklin, Richard Dawson, Patti Deutsch**
Feb. 4-6, 9-10	Edward Asner, Brett Somers, Gary Burghoff, Marcia Rodd, Richard Dawson, Betty White**
Feb. 11-13, 16-17	Gary Burghoff, Brett Somers, Jimmie Walker/Charles Nelson Reilly, Susan Howard, Richard Dawson, Fannie Flagg**[7]
Feb. 12-20, 23-24	Joey Bishop, Brett Somers, Charles Nelson Reilly, Arlene Francis, Richard Dawson, Joyce Bulifant**
Feb. 25-27, Mar. 1-2	Jimmie Walker, Brett Somers, Charles Nelson Reilly, Kate Jackson, Richard Dawson, Patti Deutsch**

Mar. 3-5, 8-9	Avery Schreiber, Brett Somers, Charles Nelson Reilly, Jo Ann Pflug, Richard Dawson, Fannie Flagg**
Mar. 10-12, 15-16	George Kennedy, Brett Somers, Charles Nelson Reilly, Lee Meriwether, Richard Dawson, Betty White**
Mar. 17-19, 22-23	Clifton Davis, Brett Somers, Charles Nelson Reilly, Patty Duke Astin, Richard Dawson, Joyce Bulifant**
Mar. 24-26, 29-30	Bill Anderson, Brett Somers, Charles Nelson Reilly, Bonnie Franklin, Richard Dawson, Fannie Flagg**
Mar. 31-Apr. 2, 5-6	Scoey Mitchlll, Brett Somers, Charles Nelson Reilly, Susan Howard, Richard Dawson, Fannie Flagg**
Apr. 7-9, 12-13	Orson Bean, Brett Somers, Charles Nelson Reilly, Pat Delany, Richard Dawson, Betty White**
Apr. 14-16, 19-20	Bill Cullen, Brett Somers, Charles Nelson Reilly, Janice Pennington, Richard Dawson, Fannie Flagg**
Apr. 21-23, 26-27	Joey Bishop, Brett Somers, Charles Nelson Reilly, Janice Lynde, Richard Dawson, Patti Deutsch**
Apr. 28-30, May 3-4	Donald H. Ross, Brett Somers, Charles Nelson Reilly, Isabel Sanford, Richard Dawson, Betty White
May 5-7, 10, 12	Ron Palillo, Brett Somers, Charles Nelson Reilly, Jo Anne Worley, Richard Dawson, Fannie Flagg

May 13-14, 17-19	Tom Poston, Brett Somers, Charles Nelson Reilly, Barbara Sharma, Richard Dawson, Patti Deutsch
May 20-21, 24-26	Greg Morris, Brett Somers, Charles Nelson Reilly, Anitra Ford, Richard Dawson, Betty White
May 27-28, Jun. 1-2	Jimmie Walker, Brett Somers, Charles Nelson Reilly, Elaine Joyce, Richard Dawson, Fannie Flagg
Jun. 4, 7-10	Avery Schreiber, Brett Somers, Charles Nelson Reilly, Ethel Merman, Richard Dawson, Joyce Bulifant
Jun. 11, 14-17	Dick Gautier, Brett Somers, Charles Nelson Reilly, Mary Ann Mobley, Richard Dawson, Betty White
Jun. 18, 21-24	Dick Martin, Brett Somers, Charles Nelson Reilly, Juliet Prowse, Richard Dawson, Fannie Flagg
Jun. 25, 28-Jul. 1	George Kennedy, Brett Somers, Charles Nelson Reilly, Donna Mills, Richard Dawson, Patti Deutsch
Jul. 2, 5-9	Joey Bishop, Brett Somers, Charles Nelson Reilly, Mary Wickes, Richard Dawson, Joyce Bulifant
Jul. 12-16	Bill Daily, Brett Somers, Charles Nelson Reilly, Bennye Getteys, Richard Dawson, Fannie Flagg
Jul. 19-23	Gary Burghoff, Brett Somers, Charles Nelson Reilly, Sarah Kennedy, Richard Dawson, Fannie Flagg

Date	Guests
Jul. 26-30	Pat Morita, Brett Somers, Charles Nelson Reilly, Lee Meriwether, Richard Dawson, Patti Deutsch**
Aug. 2-6, 9-10	Robert Hegyes, Brett Somers, Charles Nelson Reilly, Ethel Merman, Richard Dawson, Fannie Flagg**
Aug. 11-13, 16-17	Soupy Sales, Brett Somers, Charles Nelson Reilly, Madlyn Rhue, Richard Dawson, Betty White**
Aug. 18-20, 23-24	Ron Palillo, Brett Somers, Charles Nelson Reilly, Joyce Bulifant, Richard Dawson, Mary Wickes**
Aug. 25-27, 30-31	Bert Convy, Brett Somers, Charles Nelson Reilly, Patty Duke Astin, Richard Dawson, Fannie Flagg**
Sep. 1-3, 6-7	Joey Bishop, Brett Somers, Charles Nelson Reilly, Lynne Deerfield, Richard Dawson, Betty White**
Sep. 8-10, 13-14	Edward Asner, Brett Somers, Charles Nelson Reilly, Trish Stewart, Richard Dawson, Patti Deutsch**
Sep. 15-17, 20-21	Dick Gautier, Brett Somers, Charles Nelson Reilly, Della Reese, Richard Dawson, Fannie Flagg**
Sep. 22-24, 27-28	Scoey Mitchlll, Brett Somers, Charles Nelson Reilly, Debralee Scott, Richard Dawson, Joyce Bulifant**
Sep. 29-Oct. 1, 4-5	Gary Burghoff, Brett Somers, Charles Nelson Reilly, Mary Wickes, Richard Dawson, Betty White**

Oct. 6-8, 11-12	Greg Morris, Brett Somers, Charles Nelson Reilly, Elaine Joyce, Richard Dawson, Fannie Flagg**
Oct. 13-15, 18-19	Bill Daily, Brett Somers, Charles Nelson Reilly, Lee Meriwether, Richard Dawson, Betty White**
Oct. 20-22, 25-26	Dick Martin, Brett Somers, Charles Nelson Reilly, Didi Conn, Richard Dawson, Patti Deutsch**
Oct. 27-29, Nov. 1-2	Avery Schreiber, Brett Somers, Charles Nelson Reilly, Nancy Kulp, Richard Dawson, Joyce Bulifant**
Nov. 3-5, 8-9	Jimmie Walker, Brett Somers, Charles Nelson Reilly, Roz Kelly, Richard Dawson, Betty White**
Nov. 10-12, 15-16	Nipsey Russell, Brett Somers, Charles Nelson Reilly, Dr. Joyce Brothers, Richard Dawson, Patti Deutsch**
Nov. 17-19, 22-23	Bill Anderson, Brett Somers, Charles Nelson Reilly, Debralee Scott, Richard Dawson, Fannie Flagg**
Match Game PM episode 57	Gary Burghoff, Brett Somers, Charles Nelson Reilly, Lee Meriwether, Richard Dawson, Fannie Flagg
Nov. 24, 26, 29-30	Don Sutton, Brett Somers, Charles Nelson Reilly, Mary Wickes, Richard Dawson, Fannie Flagg**
Dec. 1-3, 6-7	George Kennedy, Brett Somers, Charles Nelson Reilly, Loretta Swit, Richard Dawson, Betty White**

Match Game Guests

Dec. 9-10, 13-15	Bob Barker, Brett Somers, Charles Nelson Reilly, Patty Duke Astin, Richard Dawson, Fannie Flagg**
Dec. 16-17, 20-22	Gary Burghoff, Brett Somers, Charles Nelson Reilly, Susan Sullivan, Richard Dawson, Joyce Bulifant**
Dec. 23-24, 27-29	Orson Bean, Brett Somers, Charles Nelson Reilly, Mary Wickes, Richard Dawson, Betty White**
Dec. 30-31	Joey Bishop, Brett Somers, Charles Nelson Reilly, Elizabeth Allen, Richard Dawson, Fannie Flagg**

Match Game '77, CBS

Jan. 3-5	Joey Bishop, Brett Somers, Charles Nelson Reilly, Elizabeth Allen, Richard Dawson, Fannie Flagg (continued)**
Jan. 6-7, 10-12	Edward Asner, Brett Somers, Charles Nelson Reilly, Mary Ann Mobley, Richard Dawson, Patti Deutsch**
Jan. 13-14, 17-19	Mel Tillis, Brett Somers, Charles Nelson Reilly, Bonnie Franklin, Richard Dawson, Fannie Flagg**
Jan. 21, 24-27	Avery Schreiber, Brett Somers, Charles Nelson Reilly, Della Reese, Richard Dawson, Betty White**
Jan. 28, 31-Feb. 3	Nipsey Russell, Brett Somers, Charles Nelson Reilly, Rosemary Forsyth, Richard Dawson, Joyce Bulifant**

Feb. 4, 7-10	Dick Martin, Brett Somers, Charles Nelson Reilly, Sarah Kennedy, Richard Dawson, Fannie Flagg**
Feb. 11, 14-17	Bill Daily, Brett Somers, Charles Nelson Reilly, Elaine Joyce, Richard Dawson, Betty White**
Feb. 18, 21-24	Ron Palillo, Brett Somers, Charles Nelson Reilly, Patty Duke Astin, Richard Dawson, Patti Deutsch**
Feb. 25, 28-Mar. 3	Dick Gautier, Brett Somers, Charles Nelson Reilly, Jo Ann Pflug, Richard Dawson, Fannie Flagg**
Mar. 4, 7-10	Peter Isacksen, Brett Somers, Charles Nelson Reilly, Mary Wickes, Richard Dawson, Fannie Flagg**
Mar. 11, 14-17	Orson Bean, Brett Somers, Charles Nelson Reilly, Lynda Day George, Richard Dawson, Joyce Bulifant**
Mar. 18, 21-24	Bill Anderson, Brett Somers, Charles Nelson Reilly, Eva Gabor, Richard Dawson, Betty White**
Mar. 25, 28-31	Scoey Mitchlll, Brett Somers, Charles Nelson Reilly, Susan Sullivan, Richard Dawson, Betty White**
Apr. 1, 4-7	Leslie Nielsen, Brett Somers, Charles Nelson Reilly, Barbara Rhoades, Richard Dawson, Joyce Bulifant**
Apr. 8, 11-14	Dick Martin, Brett Somers, Charles Nelson Reilly, Debralee Scott, Richard Dawson, Betty White**

Match Game Guests

Apr. 15, 18-21	Abe Burrows, Brett Somers, Charles Nelson Reilly, Rosemary Forsyth, Richard Dawson, Betty White**
Apr. 22, 25-28	Nipsey Russell, Brett Somers, Charles Nelson Reilly, Arlene Francis, Richard Dawson, Patti Deutsch
Apr. 29, May 2-5	Don Sutton, Brett Somers, Charles Nelson Reilly, Ethel Merman, Richard Dawson, Fannie Flagg
May 6, 9-12	Tom Hallick, Brett Somers, Dick Martin, Mary Wickes, Richard Dawson, Betty White
May 13, 16-19	Ron Palillo, Brett Somers, Nipsey Russell, Tudi Wiggins, Richard Dawson, Betty White
May 20, 23-25, 27	Dick Smothers, Brett Somers, Charles Nelson Reilly, Meg Bennett, Richard Dawson, Fannie Flagg
May 30-Jun. 3	Scoey Mitchlll, Brett Somers, Charles Nelson Reilly, Elaine Joyce, Richard Dawson, Fannie Flagg
Jun. 6-10	Arte Johnson, Brett Somers, Charles Nelson Reilly, Barbara Rhoades, Richard Dawson, Patti Deutsch
Jun. 13-17	Avery Schreiber, Brett Somers, Charles Nelson Reilly, Jo Ann Haris, Richard Dawson, Fannie Flagg
Jun. 20-24	Orson Bean, Brett Somers, Charles Nelson Reilly, Lee Meriwether, Richard Dawson, Fannie Flagg

Jun. 27-Jul. 1	Bill Daily, Brett Somers, Charles Nelson Reilly, Trish Stewart, Richard Dawson, Mary Wickes
Jul. 4-8	Edward Asner, Brett Somers, Charles Nelson Reilly, Debralee Scott, Richard Dawson, Patti Deutsch
Jul. 11-15	Dick Martin, Brett Somers, Charles Nelson Reilly, Patty Duke Astin, Richard Dawson, Fannie Flagg**
Jul. 18-22	Greg Morris, Brett Somers, Charles Nelson Reilly, Roz Kelly, Richard Dawson, Joyce Bulifant**
Jul. 25-29	Anson Williams, Brett Somers, Charles Nelson Reilly, Mary Ann Mobley, Richard Dawson, Fannie Flagg**
Aug. 1-5	Gary Burghoff, Brett Somers, Charles Nelson Reilly, Eva Gabor, Richard Dawson, Joyce Bulifant**
Aug. 8-12	Adam Arkin, Brett Somers, Charles Nelson Reilly, Elaine Joyce, Richard Dawson, Fannie Flagg**
Aug. 15-19	Nipsey Russell, Brett Somers, Charles Nelson Reilly, Suzanne Somers, Richard Dawson, Patti Deutsch**
Aug. 22-26	Hans Conried, Brett Somers, Charles Nelson Reilly, Sarah Kennedy, Richard Dawson, Betty White**
Aug. 29-Sep. 2	Dick Martin, Brett Somers, Charles Nelson Reilly, Conny Van Dyke, Richard Dawson, Fannie Flagg**

Dates	Guests
Sep. 6-9	Dick Smothers, Brett Somers, Charles Nelson Reilly, Minnie Pearl, Richard Dawson, Fannie Flagg**
Sep. 12-16, 19	Gary Crosby, Brett Somers, Charles Nelson Reilly, Mary Wickes, Richard Dawson, Joyce Bulifant**
Sep. 20-23	George Kennedy, Brett Somers, Charles Nelson Reilly, Lee Meriwether, Richard Dawson, Betty White**
Sep. 26-30	Bill Cullen, Brett Somers, Charles Nelson Reilly, Debralee Scott, Richard Dawson, Fannie Flagg**
Oct. 3-7	Avery Schreiber, Brett Somers, Charles Nelson Reilly, Barbara Rhoades, Richard Dawson, Marcia Wallace**
Oct. 10-14	Dick Martin, Brett Somers, Charles Nelson Reilly, Elaine Joyce, Richard Dawson, Patti Deutsch**
Oct. 17-21	Gary Burghoff, Brett Somers, Charles Nelson Reilly, Meg Bennett, Richard Dawson, Fannie Flagg**
Oct. 24-28	Nipsey Russell, Brett Somers, Charles Nelson Reilly, Patty Duke Astin, Richard Dawson, Betty White**
Oct. 31-Nov. 4	Bob Barker, Brett Somers, Charles Nelson Reilly, Eva Gabor, Richard Dawson, Joyce Bulifant**
Nov. 7-11	Nipsey Russell, Brett Somers, Charles Nelson Reilly, Sarah Purcell, Richard Dawson, Betty White** (First week of shows in the 11:00 am time slot)

Nov. 14-18	Dick Martin, Brett Somers, Charles Nelson Reilly, Polly Holliday, Richard Dawson, Fannie Flagg**
Nov. 21-23, 28-29	Orson Bean, Brett Somers, Charles Nelson Reilly, Connie Stevens, Richard Dawson, Fannie Flagg**
Nov. 30- Dec. 2, 5-6	David Landsberg, Brett Somers, Charles Nelson Reilly, Lee Meriwether, Richard Dawson, Marcia Wallace**
Dec. 7-9, 12-13	David Doyle, Brett Somers, Charles Nelson Reilly, Juliet Prowse, Richard Dawson, Patti Deutsch**
Dec. 14-16, 19-20	Tom Poston, Brett Somers, Charles Nelson Reilly, Mary Ann Mobley, Richard Dawson, Betty White** (Fourth episode is the first day in the 4:00 pm time slot)
Dec. 21-23, 26-27	Ron Palillo, Brett Somers, Charles Nelson Reilly, Elaine Joyce, Richard Dawson, Fannie Flagg**
Dec. 28-30	Richard Deacon, Fannie Flagg, Charles Nelson Reilly, Mary Wickes, Richard Dawson, Joyce Bulifant**

Match Game '78, CBS

Jan. 3-4	Richard Deacon, Fannie Flagg, Charles Nelson Reilly, Mary Wickes, Richard Dawson, Joyce Bulifant (continued)**
Jan. 5-6, 9-11	Gary Burghoff, Brett Somers, Charles Nelson Reilly, Jo Ann Pflug, Richard Dawson, Fannie Flagg**

Match Game Guests

Jan. 12-13, 16-19	Dick Martin, Brett Somers, Charles Nelson Reilly, Helaine Lembeck, Richard Dawson, Betty White**
Jan. 20, 23-26	Joe Garagiola, Brett Somers, Charles Nelson Reilly, Debralee Scott, Richard Dawson, Betty White**
Jan. 27, 31-Feb. 2	David Doyle, Brett Somers, Charles Nelson Reilly, Didi Conn, Richard Dawson, Fannie Flagg**
(Five	Bill Anderson, Brett Somers, Charles Nelson Reilly, Dr. Joyce Brothers, Richard Dawson, Marcia Wallace**
Feb. 15-17, 20-22	Avery Schreiber, Brett Somers, Charles Nelson Reilly, Barbara Rhoades, Richard Dawson, Betty White**
Feb. 23-24, 27-Mar. 1	Nipsey Russell, Brett Somers, Charles Nelson Reilly, Susan Sullivan, Richard Dawson, Marcia Wallace**
Mar. 2-3, 6-8	George Kennedy, Brett Somers, Charles Nelson Reilly, Patty Duke Astin, Richard Dawson, Patti Deutsch**
Mar. 10, 13-16	Dick Martin, Brett Somers, Charles Nelson Reilly, Elaine Joyce, Richard Dawson, Fannie Flagg**
Mar. 17, 20-23	Gary Crosby, Brett Somers, Charles Nelson Reilly, Mary Wickes, Richard Dawson, Fannie Flagg**
Mar. 24, 27-31	David Doyle, Brett Somers, Charles Nelson Reilly, Eva Gabor, Richard Dawson, Betty White**

Apr. 3-5	Nipsey Russell, Brett Somers, Charles Nelson Reilly, Ethel Merman, Richard Dawson, Fannie Flagg**
(Five	Tom Dreesen, Brett Somers, Charles Nelson Reilly, Debralee Scott, Richard Dawson, Joyce Bulifant**
Apr. 18-21, 24	Bernie Kopell, Brett Somers, Charles Nelson Reilly, Lee Meriwether, Richard Dawson, Betty White**
Apr. 25-28	Bill Daily, Brett Somers, Charles Nelson Reilly, Sarah Purcell, Richard Dawson, Betty White
May 1-5	Dick Martin, Brett Somers, Charles Nelson Reilly, Arlene Francis, Richard Dawson, Patti Deutsch
May 8-10, 12, 15	Don Sutton, Brett Somers, Charles Nelson Reilly, Patty Duke Astin, Richard Dawson, Betty White
May 16-19, 22	Bill Anderson, Brett Somers, Charles Nelson Reilly, Didi Carr, Richard Dawson, Marcia Wallace
May 23-26, 29	Nipsey Russell, Brett Somers, Charles Nelson Reilly, Denise DuBarry, Richard Dawson, Mary Wickes
May 30-Jun. 2, 5	David Doyle, Brett Somers, Charles Nelson Reilly, Elaine Joyce, Richard Dawson, Betty White
Jun. 6-7, 9, 12-13	Gary Burghoff, Brett Somers, Charles Nelson Reilly, Hope Lange, Richard Dawson, Patti Deutsch

Jun. 14-16, 19-20	Richard Paul, Brett Somers, Charles Nelson Reilly, Barbara Rhoades, Richard Dawson, Fannie Flagg
Jun. 21-23, 26-27	Dick Martin, Brett Somers, Charles Nelson Reilly, Vicki Lawrence, Richard Dawson, Betty White
Jun. 28-30, Jul. 3-4	Scoey Mitchlll, Brett Somers, Charles Nelson Reilly, Sharon Farrell, Richard Dawson, Mary Wickes (First week with the Star Wheel)
Jul. 5-7, 10-11	McLean Stevenson, Brett Somers, Charles Nelson Reilly, Didi Carr, Richard Dawson, Betty White
Jul. 12-14, 17-18	Henry Morgan, Brett Somers, Charles Nelson Reilly, Debralee Scott, Richard Dawson, Joyce Bulifant
Jul. 19-21, 24-26	Nipsey Russell, Brett Somers, Charles Nelson Reilly, Susan Richardson, Richard Dawson, Fannie Flagg (First week with the new set)
Jul. 27-28, 31-Aug. 2	Bill Daily, Brett Somers, Charles Nelson Reilly, Bonnie Franklin, Richard Dawson, Marcia Wallace**
Aug. 3-4, 7-9	Avery Schreiber, Brett Somers, Charles Nelson Reilly, Elaine Joyce, Richard Dawson, Fannie Flagg**
Aug. 10-11, 14-16	Richard Paul, Brett Somers, Charles Nelson Reilly, Jo Ann Harris, Richard Dawson, Betty White**

Aug. 17-18, 21-23	Dick Martin, Brett Somers, Charles Nelson Reilly, Lorrie Mahaffey, Richard Dawson, Joyce Bulifant** (Richard Dawson's final week)
Aug. 24-25, 28-30	Richard Deacon, Brett Somers, Charles Nelson Reilly, Patty Duke Astin, Bob Barker, Fannie Flagg**
Aug. 31-Sep. 1, 5-7	Robert Mandan, Brett Somers, Charles Nelson Reilly, Lee Meriwether, Richard Paul, Betty White**
Sep. 8, 11-14	Gary Burghoff, Brett Somers, Charles Nelson Reilly, Loni Anderson, McLean Stevenson, Marcia Wallace**
Sep. 15, 18-22	Tab Hunter, Brett Somers, Charles Nelson Reilly, Marilu Henner, Dick Martin, Fannie Flagg**
Sep. 25-29	David Doyle, Brett Somers, Charles Nelson Reilly, Debralee Scott, Nipsey Russell, Betty White**
Oct. 2-6	Ed Asner, Brett Somers, Charles Nelson Reilly, Valerie Bertinelli, Nipsey Russell, Patty Duke Astin**
Oct. 9-13, 16	Greg Morris, Brett Somers, Charles Nelson Reilly, Barbara Rhoades, Bill Daily, Fannie Flagg**
Oct. 17-20, 23-24	Bill Anderson, Brett Somers, Charles Nelson Reilly, Donna Pescow, Jack Klugman, Betty White**

Match Game Guests

Oct. 25-27, 30-31	Robert Walden, Brett Somers, Charles Nelson Reilly, Loretta Swit, Richard Paul, Mary Wickes**
Nov. 1-3, 6-7	David Doyle, Brett Somers, Charles Nelson Reilly, Elaine Joyce, Raymond Burr, Joyce Bulifant**
Nov. 8-10, 13-14	Nipsey Russell, Brett Somers, Charles Nelson Reilly, Judy Landers, Gary Burghoff, Betty White**
Nov. 15-17, 20-21	Robert Pine, Brett Somers, Charles Nelson Reilly, Loni Anderson, Bob Barker, Patti Deutsch**
Nov. 22, 24, 27-29	Bart Braverman, Brett Somers, Charles Nelson Reilly, Erica Hope, Arte Johnson, Fannie Flagg**
Nov. 30-Dec. 1, 11-13	Jon Bauman, Brett Somers, Charles Nelson Reilly, Nancy Lane, Don Sutton, Betty White**
Dec. 14-15, 18-20	Guich Koock, Brett Somers, Charles Nelson Reilly, Mabel King, Ken Olfson, Marcia Wallace**
Dec. 21-22, 26-29	Joe Santos, Brett Somers, Charles Nelson Reilly, Carol Jones, Dick Martin, Fannie Flagg**
Jan. 2	**David Doyle, Brett Somers, Charles Nelson Reilly, Connie Stevens, Jack Jones, Betty White****

Match Game '79, CBS

Jan. 3-5, 8	David Doyle, Brett Somers, Charles Nelson Reilly, Connie Stevens, Jack Jones, Betty White (continued)
Jan. 9-12, 15	Robert Walden, Brett Somers, Charles Nelson Reilly, Audrey Landers, Bert Convy, Patty Duke Astin**
Jan. 16-19, 22	Nipsey Russell, Brett Somers, Charles Nelson Reilly, Dolly Martin, Dick Martin, Patti Deutsch**
Jan. 23-26, 29	Robert Pine, Brett Somers, Charles Nelson Reilly, Susan Richardson, Richard Deacon, Fannie Flagg**
Jan. 30-31, Feb. 2, 5-6	Jon Bauman as "Bowzer," Brett Somers, Charles Nelson Reilly, Brianne Leary, Bob Barker, Joyce Bulifant**
Feb. 7-9, 12-14	Avery Schreiber, Brett Somers, Charles Nelson Reilly, Elaine Joyce, Gary Burghoff, Fannie Flagg**
Feb. 15-16, 19-21	Joe Santos, Brett Somers, Charles Nelson Reilly, Lorrie Mahaffey, Bill Daily, Marcia Wallace**
Feb. 22-23, 26-28	Bart Braverman, Brett Somers, Charles Nelson Reilly, Barbara Rhoades, Dick Martin, Fannie Flagg**
Mar. 2, 5-7	Guich Koock, Brett Somers, Charles Nelson Reilly, Debralee Scott, Paul Williams, Betty White**

Match Game Guests

Mar. 8-9, 12-14	Daryl Anderson, Brett Somers, Charles Nelson Reilly, Donna Pescow, Richard Paul, Patti Deutsch**
Mar. 15-16, 19-23	David Doyle, Brett Somers, Charles Nelson Reilly, Loretta Swit, Scoey Mitchlll, Fannie Flagg**
Mar. 26-30	Foster Brooks, Brett Somers, Charles Nelson Reilly, Lorna Patterson, Dick Martin, Betty White**
Apr. 2-4, 6, 9	Nipsey Russell, Brett Somers, Charles Nelson Reilly, Loni Anderson, Jack Jones, Joyce Bulifant**
Apr. 10-13	Kukla & Ollie, Brett Somers, Charles Nelson Reilly, Eva Gabor, Arte Johnson, Fannie Flagg** (five episodes were taped but only four aired on CBS)
Apr. 16-17	Don Galloway, Brett Somers, Charles Nelson Reilly, Lee Meriwether, Bill Daily, Patti Deutsch** (five episodes were taped but only two aired on CBS)
Apr. 18-20	Fred Grandy, Brett Somers, Charles Nelson Reilly, Connie Stevens, Bill Cullen, Marcia Wallace**(five episodes were taped but only three aired on CBS)
n/a	Orson Bean, Brett Somers, Dick Martin, Brianne Leary, Bill Daily, Fannie Flagg** (none aired on CBS)

n/a	Bart Braverman, Brett Somers, Gary Burghoff, Elaine Joyce, Bill Daily, Marcia Wallace** (none aired on CBS)
Match Game PM episode 156	Joe Santos, Brett Somers, Charles Nelson Reilly, Elaine Joyce, Dick Martin, Marcia Wallace
Match Game PM episode 157	Conrad Janis, Brett Somers, Charles Nelson Reilly, Dolly Martin, Dick Martin, Marcia Wallace
Match Game PM episode 158	Robert Walden, Brett Somers, Charles Nelson Reilly, Brianne Leary, Bart Braverman, Betty White
Match Game PM episode 159	Jon Bauman as "Bowzer," Brett Somers, Charles Nelson Reilly, Lorrie Mahaffey, Gary Crosby, Betty White
Match Game PM episode 160	Don Galloway, Brett Somers, Charles Nelson Reilly, Mary Ann Mobley, Richard Paul, Joyce Bulifant
Match Game PM Episode 161	Fred Grandy, Brett Somers, Charles Nelson Reilly, Susan Richardson, Richard Paul, Joyce Bulifant
Match Game PM episode 161	Fred Grandy, Brett Somers, Charles Nelson Reilly, Mary Ann Mobley, Richard Paul, Joyce Bulifant

Match Game PM episode 162	Ted Lange, Brett Somers, Charles Nelson Reilly, Lorna Patterson, Foster Brooks, Marcia Wallace
Match Game PM episode 163	Foster Brooks, Brett Somers, Charles Nelson Reilly, Sarah Purcell, Robert Pine, Patti Deutsch

Syndication, 1979-80

Because of the nature of syndication at the time, exact airdates varied from city to city. Tape dates are provided where known.

June 30, 1979	Bart Braverman, Brett , Charles Nelson Reilly, Eva Gabor, Bill Daily, Fannie Flagg**
July 1, 1979	David Doyle, Brett Somers, Charles Nelson Reilly, Debralee Scott, Dick Martin, Patty Duke Astin**
	George Kennedy, Brett Somers, Charles Nelson Reilly, Judy Landers, Richard Paul, Joyce Bulifant**
July 21, 1979	Robert Pine, Brett Somers, Charles Nelson Reilly, Jamie Lee Curtis, Dick Martin, Betty White**
	Jack Carter, Brett Somers, Charles Nelson Reilly, Barbara Rhoades, Bill Daily, Abigail Van Buren**
	Robert Walden, Brett Somers, Charles Nelson Reilly, Elaine Joyce, Bill Daily, Joyce Bulifant**

	Nipsey Russell, Brett Somers, Charles Nelson Reilly, Loretta Swit, Dick Martin, Nancy Lane**
	Alfie Wise, Brett Somers, Charles Nelson Reilly, Patty Duke Astin, Jack Jones, Debralee Scott**
	Joe Santos, Brett Somers, Charles Nelson Reilly, Donna Pescow, Bill Daily, Patty Duke Astin**
	Richard Deacon, Brett Somers, Charles Nelson Reilly, Charlene Tilton, Bob Barker, Betty White**
August 26, 1979	Foster Brooks, Brett Somers, Charles Nelson Reilly, Sarah Purcell, Scoey Mitchlll, Fannie Flagg**
	Bart Braverman, Brett Somers, Charles Nelson Reilly, Rita Moreno, Bill Daily, Patti Deutsch**
	David Doyle, Brett Somers, Charles Nelson Reilly, Randi Oakes, Bill Daily, Marcia Wallace**
	Ronny Graham, Brett Somers, Charles Nelson Reilly, Susan Richardson, Arte Johnson, Fannie Flagg**
	Steve Kanaly, Brett Somers, Charles Nelson Reilly, Jamie Lee Curtis, Richard Paul, Fannie Flagg**

Match Game Guests

	Bill Cullen, Brett Somers, Charles Nelson Reilly, Lee Meriwether, Bill Daily, Betty White**
	Jim Staahl, Brett Somers, Charles Nelson Reilly, Anita Gillette, Bart Braverman, Debralee Scott**
	David Doyle, Brett Somers, Charles Nelson Reilly, Phyllis Diller, Fred Travalena, Joyce Bulifant
	Jon Bauman as "Bowzer," Brett Somers, Charles Nelson Reilly, Charlene Tiliton, Bill Daily, Patty Duke Astin**
	Jimmie Walker, Brett Somers, Charles Nelson Reilly, Dolly Martin, Dick Martin, Betty White**
	Wesley Eure, Brett Somers, Charles Nelson Reilly, Debralee Scott, Bob Barker, Marcia Wallace**
	Bill Anderson, Brett Somers, Charles Nelson Reilly, Barbara Rhoades, Bart Braverman, Joyce Bulifant**
	Clifton Davis, Brett Somers, Charles Nelson Reilly, Gail Farrell, Paul Williams, Betty White
	Freeman King, Brett Somers, Charles Nelson Reilly, Betty Kennedy, Bill Daily, Joyce Bulifant**

	Fred Grandy, Brett Somers, Charles Nelson Reilly, Eva Gabor, Gary Burghoff, Marcia Wallace**
	Alfie Wise, Brett Somers, Charles Nelson Reilly, Patty Duke Astin, Bill Daily, Betty White**
	Steve Kanaly, Brett Somers, Charles Nelson Reilly, Elaine Joyce, Richard Paul, Patty Duke Astin**
January 12, 1980	Jon Bauman as "Bowzer," Brett Somers, Charles Nelson Reilly, Gina Hecht, Bill Daily, Fannie Flagg**
January 13, 1980	Robert Pine, Brett Somers, Charles Nelson Reilly, Stephanie Edwards, Bill Daily, Fannie Flagg**
January 26, 1980	Gary Collins, Brett Somers, Dick Martin, Debralee Scott, Bill Daily, Betty White**
January 27, 1980	Robert Walden, Brett Somers, Bart Braverman, Connie Stevens, Bill Daily, Marcia Wallace**
	Fred Grandy, Brett Somers, David Doyle, Dawn Jeffory, Bill Daily, Rita Moreno**
February 23, 1980	Joe Santos, Brett Somers, Fred Grandy, Eva Gabor, Bill Daily, Betty White**
	Peter Marshall, Brett Somers, Dick Martin, Bonnie Franklin, Bill Daily, Marcia Wallace**

Match Game Guests

	Jim Staahl, Brett Somers, Bart Braverman, Holly Hallstrom, Bill Daily, Debralee Scott

Syndication, 1980-81
All panels during this season taped a sixth episode for *Match Game PM*.

	Gary Burghoff, Brett Somers, Charles Nelson Reilly, Holly Halstrom, Dick Martin, Joyce Bulifant
May 11, 1980	George Kennedy, Brett Somers, Charles Nelson Reilly, Elaine Joyce, Dick Martin, Betty White
	Jimmie Walker, Brett Somers, Charles Nelson Reilly, Connie Stevens, Bart Braverman, Debralee Scott
	David Doyle, Brett Somers, Charles Nelson Reilly, Betty Kennedy, Robert Donner, Marcia Wallace
	Gary Collins, Brett Somers, Charles Nelson Reilly, Susan Richardson, Richard Paul, Joyce Bulifant
	Alan Oppenheimer, Brett Somers, Charles Nelson Reilly, Laurie Walters, Dick Martin, Betty White
	Fred Grandy, Brett Somers, Charles Nelson Reilly, Phyllis Diller, Bill Daily, Debralee Scott
	Robert Walden, Brett Somers, Charles Nelson Reilly, Judy Landers, Bill Daily, Marcia Wallace
June 29, 1980	David Doyle, Brett Somers, Charles Nelson Reilly, Rita Moreno, Gary Crosby, Joyce Bulifant
	Bart Braverman, Brett Somers, Charles Nelson Reilly, Eva Gabor, Dick Martin, Betty White

	Richard Kiel, Brett Somers, Charles Nelson Reilly, Mary Ann Mobley, Paul Williams, Marcia Wallace
	Scoey Mitchlll, Brett Somers, Charles Nelson Reilly, Dolly Martin, Bill Daily, Debralee Scott
	Peter Marshall, Brett Somers, Dick Martin, Elaine Joyce, Bill Cullen, Betty White
	Richard Deacon, Brett Somers, Fred Grandy, Louise Sorel, Bill Daily, Joyce Bulifant
	Jimmie Walker, Brett Somers, Charles Nelson Reilly, Jonelle Allen, Allen Ludden, Betty White
	Charles Siebert, Brett Somers, Charles Nelson Reilly, Phyllis Davis, Robert Donner, Marcia Wallace
	Bart Braverman, Brett Somers, Charles Nelson Reilly, Jamie Lee Curtis, Richard Paul, Fannie Flagg
	Fred Travelena, Brett Somers, Charles Nelson Reilly, Betty Kennedy, Robert Donner, Fannie Flagg
	Jon Bauman as "Bowzer," Brett Somers, Charles Nelson Reilly, Eva Gabor, Arte Johnson, Joyce Bulifant
	Don Galloway, Brett Somers, Charles Nelson Reilly, Holly Halstrom, Bart Braverman, Fannie Flagg
	George Kennedy, Brett Somers, Charles Nelson Reilly, Elaine Joyce, Dick Martin, Betty White
	David Doyle, Brett Somers, Charles Nelson Reilly, Susan Howard, Gary Burghoff, Marcia Wallace

	Fred Grandy, Brett Somers, Charles Nelson Reilly, Dolly Martin, Bart Braverman, Mary Wickes
	Robert Donner, Brett Somers, Charles Nelson Reilly, Marjorie Wallace, Bill Daily, Marcia Wallace
	Richard Paul, Brett Somers, Charles Nelson Reilly, Jo Ann Pflug, Bill Daily, Joyce Bulifant
October 31, 1980	Bill Anderson, Brett Somers, Charles Nelson Reilly, Jonelle Allen, McLean Stevenson, Debralee Scott
	Fred Travalena, Brett Somers, Charles Nelson Reilly, Elaine Joyce, Dick Martin, Debralee Scott
November 16, 1980	Don Sutton, Brett Somers, Charles Nelson Reilly, Phyllis Davis, Bart Braverman, Marcia Wallace
	Ted Lange, Brett Somers, Charles Nelson Reilly, Susan Richardson, Robert Donner, Joyce Bulifant
	Jimmie Walker, Brett Somers, Charles Nelson Reilly, Dolly Martin, Bill Daily, Debralee Scott
	Bart Braverman, Brett Somers, Charles Nelson Reilly, Diana Soviero, Bill Daily, Betty White
	Fred Grandy, Brett Somers, Charles Nelson Reilly, Marjorie Wallace, Gary Crosby, Fannie Flagg
December 26, 1980	George Kennedy, Betty Kennedy, Charles Nelson Reilly, Phyllis Diller, McLean Stevenson, Fannie Flagg
December 27, 1980	Brian Patrick Clarke, Jack Klugman, Charles Nelson Reilly, Elaine Joyce, Robert Donner, Marcia Wallace

| December 28, 1980 | Bart Braverman, Betty White, Charles Nelson Reilly, Joyce Bulifant, Bill Daily, Marcia Wallace |

Syndication, 1981-82

	Richard Paul, Brett Somers, Dick Martin, Holly Halstrom, McLean Stevenson, Elaine Joyce
	Fred Travalena, Brett Somers, Fred Grandy, Mary Ann Mobley, McLean Stevenson, Joyce Bulifant
	Bart Braverman, Brett Somers, Richard Deacon, Connie Stevens, McLean Stevenson, Debralee Scott
	Joe Santos, Brett Somers, Dick Martin, Eva Gabor, McLean Stevenson, Elaine Joyce
	David Doyle, Brett Somers, Charles Nelson Reilly, Edie McClurg, Paul Williams, Joyce Bulifant
	Jimmie Walker, Brett Somers, Charles Nelson Reilly, Lilibet Stern, Bill Cullen, Elaine Joyce
	Robert Donner, Patty Duke Astin, Charles Nelson Reilly, Betty Kennedy, McLean Stevenson, Joyce Bulifant
	Bill Anderson, Brett Somers, Charles Nelson Reilly, Jonelle Allen, Bill Daily, Patty Duke Astin
	George Kennedy, Brett Somers, Charles Nelson Reilly, Barbara Rhoades, Bill Daily, Betty White
	Bernie Kopell, Brett Somers, Charles Nelson Reilly, Marjorie Wallace, Scoey Mitchlll, Edie McClurg
	Fred Travalena, Brett Somers, Charles Nelson Reilly, Lee Meriwether, McLean Stevenson, Fannie Flagg

Match Game Guests

	Robert Pine, Brett Somers, Charles Nelson Reilly, Dolly Martin, McLean Stevenson, Fannie Flagg
	Tom Kennedy, Brett Somers, Charles Nelson Reilly, Gail Farrell, McLean Stevenson, Joyce Bulifant
	Robert Donner, Brett Somers, Charles Nelson Reilly, Lilibet Stern, McLean Stevenson, Edie McClurg
	David Doyle, Brett Somers, Charles Nelson Reilly, Holly Halstrom, McLean Stevenson, Betty White
	Bart Braverman, Brett Somers, Charles Nelson Reilly, Eva Gabor, McLean Stevenson, Marcia Wallace
	Bill Daily, Brett Somers, Charles Nelson Reilly, Dolly Martin, McLean Stevenson, Elaine Joyce
	Conrad Janis, Brett Somers, Paul Williams, Edie McClurg, McLean Stevenson, Debralee Scott
	Richard Paul, Brett Somers, Dick Martin, Sharon Farrell, McLean Stevenson, Betty White
	David Doyle, Brett Somers, Bill Daily, Sydney Goldsmith, McLean Stevenson, Joyce Bulifant
	Robert Donner, Brett Somers, Charles Nelson Reilly, Melody Thomas, McLean Stevenson, Marcia Wallace
	Ted Lange, Brett Somers, Charles Nelson Reilly, Audrey Landers, McLean Stevenson, Edie McClurg
	Bill Daily, Brett Somers, Charles Nelson Reilly, Dolly Martin, McLean Stevenson, Betty White

	George Gobel, Brett Somers, Charles Nelson Reilly, Stephanie Edwards, McLean Stevenson, Elaine Joyce
	Fred Grandy, Brett Somers, Charles Nelson Reilly, Leslie Easterbrook, McLean Stevenson, Fannie Flagg
	Willie Tyler & Lester, Brett Somers, Charles Nelson Reilly, Lynne Redgrave, McLean Stevenson, Marcia Wallace
	Bill Cullen, Brett Somers, Charles Nelson Reilly, Sharon Farrell, McLean Stevenson, Edie McClurg
	Skip Stephenson, Brett Somers, Charles Nelson Reilly, Irlene Mandrell, McLean Stevenson, Fannie Flagg
	Marty Cohen, Brett Somers, Charles Nelson Reilly, Debralee Scott, McLean Stevenson, Edie McClurg
	Scoey Mitchlll, Brett Somers, Charles Nelson Reilly, Elaine Joyce, McLean Stevenson, Betty White
	Fred Travalena, Brett Somers, Charles Nelson Reilly, Monique Van Vooren, McLean Stevenson, Joyce Bulifant
	Bill Anderson, Brett Somers, Charles Nelson Reilly, Irlene Mandrell, McLean Stevenson, Fannie Flagg
	Bill Daily, Brett Somers, Charles Nelson Reilly, Jenilee Harrison, McLean Stevenson, Edie McClurg
	Bart Braverman, Brett Somers, Charles Nelson Reilly, Abby Dalton, McLean Stevenson, Marcia Wallace
January 15, 1982	Skip Stephenson, Brett Somers, Charles Nelson Reilly, Melinda O. Fee, McLean Stevenson, Betty White

Match Game Guests

(Fred Wostbrock Collection)

NBC, 1983-84: *The Match Game/Hollywood Squares Hour*

October	Tom Villard, Barbi Benton, Bill Daily, Jimmie Walker, Phil Proctor, Twyla Littleton, Skip Stephenson, Alison Arngrim
November 7-11	Arsenio Hall, Eddie Mekka, Bonnie Urseth, Charles Nelson Reilly, Shannon Tweed, Nedra Volz, Fred Travalena, Ed Begley, Jr.
November 14-18	James Widdoes, Brian Mitchell, Paul Provenza, Lydia Cornell, Marty Cohen, Richard Kline, Gloria Loring, Edie McClurg
November 21-25	Rebecca Holden, Jimmy Brogan, Tim Reid, Matt McCoy, Tom Poston, Lois Bromfield, Alison Arngrim, Leonard Frey
November 28-December 2	Markie Post, Jim Staahl, Blake Clark, Audrey Landers, Fred Travalena, Shawn Stevens, Nedra Volz, Arsenio Hall
December 5-9	Jay Leno, Karen Witter, Charlie Siebert, Martha Smith, McLean Stevenson, Michael Winslow, Edie McClurg, Fred Grandy
December 12-16	Alfie Wise, Vicki McCarty, Stan Freberg, Kim Miyori, Marcia Wallace, Bill Rafferty, Willie Tyler & Lester, Bruce Baum
December 19-23	Marty Cohen, Victoria Hallman, Jimmie Walker, Judy Landers, Tom Poston, Leonard Frey, Nedra Volz, Jm J. Bullock
December 26-30	"Salute to *Leave It to Beaver*": Rich Correll, Frank Bank, Jeri Weil, Barbara Billingsley, Jerry Mathers, Ken Osmond, Richard Deacon, Gallagher

Match Game Guests

January 2-6	David Ruprecht, Christie Claridge, Nathan Cook, Arsenio Hall, Dick Martin, Alison Arngrim, Dorothy Lyman, Vic Dunlop
January 9-13	Jenilee Harrison, Sybil Danning, Phil Proctor, Anson Williams, Pat McCormick, Mark Russell, Mary Page Keller, Leonard Frey
January 16-20	Linda Dano, Brian Mitchell, Jay Leno, Ellen Bry, Richard Kline, Lyle Waggoner, Phyllis Diller, Bill Cullen
January 23-27	David Oliver, Leah Ayres, Nedra Volz, Matt McCoy, Teri Copley, Tom Villard, Bonnie Urseth, Gary Burghoff
January 30-February 3	Stephen Schnetzer, Gloria Loring, Nipsey Russell, Marty Cohen, Tom Poston, Alan Thicke, Constance McCashin, Fern Fitzgerald
February 6-10	Tim Reid, Sally Julian, Bruce Baum, Larry Manetti, Charles Nelson Reilly, Marcia Wallace, Helen Reddy, Pat Sajak
February 13-17	Tom Wiggin, Elaine Joyce, Jimmie Walker, Leonard Frey, George Gobel, Richard Kline, Nancy Stafford, Bill Daily
February 20-24	Nedra Volz, Richard J. Porter, Gordon Jump, Ken Kercheval, Fannie Flagg, Robert Donner, Debra Sue Maffett, Nathan Cook
February 27-March 2	"Salute to *Too Close for Comfort*" with Arsenio Hall, Elyse Knight, Bart Braverman, Nancy Dussault, Ted Knight, Lydia Cornell, Deborah Van Valkenburgh, Jm J. Bullock
March 5-9	Martha Smith, Christopher Rich, Bob Eubanks, Nancy Frangione, Charles Nelson Reilly, James Sloyan, Erin Moran, Fred Travalena

March 12-16	Anson Williams, Jesse Welles, Tim Thomerson, Kim Morgan Greene, Phyllis Diller, Pat Paulsen, Thom Bray, Paula Kelly
March 19-23	Tom Villard, Anna Stuart, Carlo Imperato, Lois Hamilton, Leonard Frey, Fannie Flagg, James B. Sikking, Nedra Volz
March 26-30	Kim Miyori, Eric Laneuville, Norman Lloyd, Howie Mandel, Nancy Stafford, Terence Knox, Ellen Bry, Ed Begley, Jr.
April 2-6	Judy Landers, Stephen Schnetzer, Roxie Roker, Brian Mitchell, Steve Allen, Jayne Meadows, Gloria Loring, Bruce Baum
April 9-13	Jayne Kennedy, Michael Lembeck, Sorrell Brooke, Rod Arrants, Marcia Wallace, Bill Rafferty, Fern Fitzgerald, Marty Cohen
April 16-20	Tim Reid, Bill Anderson, Edie McClurg, Debra Sue Maffett, Fred Travalena, Joe Santos, Linda Dano, Soupy Sales
April 23-27	Leonard Frey, Chuck Wagner, Lydia Cornell, Rene Enriquez, Phyllis Diller, Richard Kline, Abby Dalton, Charles Nelson Reilly
April 30-May 4	McLean Stevenson, Richard Moll, Nathan Cook, Martha Smith, Charles Nelson Reilly, Bonnie Urseth, Larry Linville, Nedra Volz
May 7-11	Wayne Northrop, Deidre Hall, John de Lancie, Leann Hunley, Christopher Rich, Nancy Frangione, David Forsyth, Marcia McCabe
May 14-18	"Salute to the '50s": David Nelson, Angela Cartwright, Edd Byrnes, Bob Denver, Jay Leno, Fabian, Elinor Donahue, Troy Donahue

Match Game Guests

May 21-25	Carlo Imperato, Kim Hood, Jayne Kennedy, Tom Poston, Nancy Lane, Thom Bray, Jimmie Walker, Ed Begley, Jr.
May 28-June 1	Mindy Cohn, Lynda Goodfriend, Eddie Mekka, Erin Moran, Nedra Volz, David L. Lander, Lauri Hendler, Michael Winslow
June 4-8	Bruce Baum, Kari Michaelsen, Marilyn Michaels, William Christopher, Fannie Flagg, Teresa Ganzel, Robert Donner
June 11-15	Marty Cohen, Anna Stuart, Brian Mitchell, Fern Fitzgerald, George Gobel, Rene Enriquez, Randi Oakes, Richard Moll
June 18-22	Richard Kline, Petronia Paley, Charlie Siebert, Roger E. Mosley, Marcia Wallace, Ken Kercheval, Lois Hamilton, Pat Sajak
June 25-29	Paula Kelly, Arlene Francis, Chuck Woolery, Jamie Farr, McLean Stevenson, Heidi Bohay, Linda Dano, Arsenio Hall
July 2-6	Lydia Cornell, Christina Pickles, Anson Williams, Carlo Imperato, Phyllis Diller, Nathan Cook, Abby Dalton, Charles Nelson Reilly
July 9-13	Tom Villard, Jayne Kennedy, Terence Knox, Tom Poston, Fred Travalena, Kate McGeehan, Mindy Cohn, Nedra Volz
July 16-20	Didi Conn, Alex Cord, Michael Lembeck, Audrey Landers, Marty Cohen, Judy Landers, Anne-Marie Martin, Jimmie Walker
July 23-27	Leonard Frey, Barry Gordon, Roxie Roker, Roger E. Mosley, Phyllis Diller, Fannie Flagg, Constance McCashin, Charles Nelson Reilly

Footnotes

[1] One source states that Sal Mineo played during this week, but NBC's program file lists Darryl Hickman. It's possible that Mineo was originally scheduled but replaced.

[2] Another source lists a completely different week of special all-celebrity episodes.
- Monday: Carol Lawrence, Betty White, & Peggy Cass vs. Joe Garagiola, Cliff Robertson, & Ed McMahon.
- Tuesday: Hugh Downs, Bob Clayton, & Paolo Diva vs. Luke Kalpin, Tommy Norden, & Brian Kelly.
- Wednesday: Don Adams, Barbara Feldon, & Ed Platt vs. Larry Hagman, Barbara Eden, & Bill Daily.
- Thursday: MacDonald Carey, Peter Hansen, & Frances Reid vs. Susan Trustman, Shepperd Strudwick, & Audra Lindley.
- Friday: Andrew Prine, Brenda Scott, & Barry Sullivan vs. Michael Landon, Dan Blocker, & Lorne Greene.

[3] Dick Clark appeared on the first two shows of the week, Mitch Miller appeared on the other three.

[4] Because of CBS coverage of the Watergate hearings, the show was subject to frequent pre-emptions in 1973 and 1974. As such, airdates from Summer 1973 through Summer 1974 varied from city to city.

[5] Charles Nelson Reilly missed the third episode of this taping session and was replaced by Mark Goodson.

[6] Gary Burghoff missed the first episode of this taping and was replaced by announcer Johnny Olson.

[7] Jimmie Walker was a panelist on the first two episodes of the week, with Charles Nelson Reilly returning on the third episode.

Bibliography

"Adoption Group Plans a Benefit." *The New York Times*. 13 Apr. 1958.

"Adoption Service to Hold Benefit in Westchester." *The New York Times*. 26 Oct. 1958.

"AFRA Vote; New York Local Elects." *Broadcasting Magazine*. 20 Dec. 1948.

Anderson, Dave. "Koufax Playing Watch My Lines.' *The New York Times*. 2 Jul. 1967.

"Ask Them Yourself." Ocala Star-Banner. 10 Jul. 1984.

"Audience Fills Avery Hall to See 'Sight Unseen.'" *Vassar Miscellany News*. 19 Apr. 1941.

Baber, David. *Television Game Show Hosts: Biographies of 32 Stars*. McFarlane and Co. Jefferson, NC. 2008.

Bauer, Nancy. "Rayburn and Exhuberance—That's a Match." *The Boston Globe*. 22 Sep. 1982.

http://www.bcptheater.org/about-us/history/

Bean, Orson. Personal interview. 11 Mar. 2014.
Behind the Blank. 2006. Game Show Network. Television.
Benson, Ray. "Rayburn the Instantaneous Editor." *The Columbia Record.* 1 Apr. 1972.
http://www.biography.com/people/brett-somers-246042
"Brett Somers, Match Game Wit, Dies at 83." *The New York Times.* 18 Sep. 2007.
Calta, Louis. "Theater: 1962 Aqua Carnival Opens." *The New York Times.* 29 Jun. 1962.
"CBS to Televise Bouts by Kinescope." *The New York Times.* 8 Jun. 1951.
Coleman, Emily. "From Red Barn to Package and Tent." *The New York Times.* 19 Jul. 1964.
Crosby, John. "Wishbones and Kinkajous." *The Portsmouth Times.* 23 Feb. 1955.
Dahlin, Robert. "Down Memory Lane with Gene Rayburn." *The Litchfield County Times.* 29 Oct. 1993.
Danzig, Fred. "Treasure Hunt TV Quiz Adroitly Kills Viewers' Time." *Oxnard Press-Courier.* 24 Jul. 1958.
Davidson, Donald W. "Rayburn Commutes from Cape to LA." *Boston Herald American.* 22 Nov. 1981.
"Dee Finch, Disk Jockey with WNEW 26 Years." *The New York Times.* 31 Mar. 1983.
"Dough Re Mi Offers Treats for Visitors." *The Southern Missourian.* Cape Girardeau, MO. 8 Jul. 1960.
Dresser, Norman. "ABC Calls It 'Sugar Time' But Critic Has Sour View." *Toledo Blade.* 15 Aug. 1977.
DuBrow, Rick. "TV Squeezes Mileage from First Family." *Sarasota Journal.* 3 Jan. 1963.
Eckstein, Warren. Personal interview. 15 Nov. 2013.
"Election Results." *Broadcasting Magazine.* 9 Dec. 1946.
http://emceesteve.tripod.com/column_10_10_99.htm
"ERA Supporters Rally in Chicago." *St. Joseph Gazette.* 24 Aug. 1981.
"February Sweeps: CBS Wins Totals, NBC Demographics." *Broadcasting Magazine.* 4 Mar. 1985.
Fowler, Glenn. "Ray Goulding, 68, Genial Satirist as Part of Bob and Ray, Is Dead." *The New York Times.* 26 Mar. 1990.

Freeman, Don. "Rayburn… Matched Up for His New Show." *The San Diego Union.* 30 Jun. 1973.

Gautier, Dick. Personal interview. 28 Mar. 2014.

Gaver, Jack. "ABC Again Tries a Network-Wide Disc Jockey." *St. Petersburg Times.* 26 Apr. 1950.

"Gene Rayburn in Play." *The New York Times.* 9 Feb. 1956.

Gould, Jack. "TV: Cliche-Ridden Play." *The New York Times.* 12 Dec. 1957.

Grace, Arthur. "Dough Re Mi Not Bad Show." *The Miami News.* 11 Jul. 1958.

Grace, Art. "He Didn't Quit Quiz—He Was Canned." *The Miami News.* 13 Sep. 1958.

Greenberg, Ron. Personal interview. 25 Jan. 2014.

Hart, Dennis. *Monitor (Take Two): The Revised, Expanded Inside Story of Network Radio's Greatest Program.* iUniverse. Lincoln, NE. 2003.

"Heating Up: Network Fight for Leadership in Daytime TV." *Broadcasting* Magazine. 3 Jun. 1974.

Heffernan, Virginia. "Filling in the Blanks on a Staple of Daytime." *The New York Times.* 25 Nov. 2006.

Hoerburger, Rob. "A Perfect Match." *The New York Times.* 30 Dec. 2007.

Holmberg, Ted. "Gene Rayburn's Girl Watching." *Providence Sunday Journal.* 14 Jul. 1963.

Hoogesteger, John. "Always a Pioneer, Gene Rayburn Did What Came Naturally." *Traverse City Record-Eagle.* 30 Jun. 1981.

"How Well the Games Play On Television." *Broadcasting Magazine.* 9 Sep. 1974.

"In Review." *Broadcasting Magazine.* 11 Oct. 1954.

"In the Suites." *Broadcasting Magazine.* 7 Jan. 1985.

Jory, Tom. "Bauman's Alter-Ego a Loud Success." *The Prescott Courier.* 17 Oct. 1980.

Kelly, Kevin. "Humbug for Christmas Carol." *The Boston Globe.* 12 Dec. 1981.

Kern, Janet. "Rayburn Career Work, Not Luck." *The Milwaukee Sentinel.* 26 May 1958.

Lester, John. "Rayburn and Finch are Funny, Even at 6 A.M." *The Newark Star-Ledger.* 30 Mar. 1950.

Lowry, Cynthia. "Fannie Flagg Just Luckily in Right Place." *Pittsburgh Post-Gazette.* 3 Jan. 1972.

Lowry, Cynthia. "Match Game Cooked Up by Old Formula." *Evening Independent.* St. Petersburg, FL. 2 Jan. 1963.

Marshall, Peter. 15 Jan. 2014.

Martin, Douglas. "Gene Klavan, Radio Show Host, Dies at 79." *The New York Times.* 9 Apr. 2004.

Martin, Douglas. "Teresa Brewer, Cheerful Chart-Topper on the Hit Parade, is Dead at 76." *The New York Times.* 18 Oct. 2007.

McMahon, James. "Gene Rayburn." *Meriden Journal.* 25 Jun. 1960.

http://mentalfloss.com/article/18082/4-famous-tv-co-workers-who-struggled-get-along

Monroe, Bob. "Union Insists Big Studios Stop Television Reruns of Shows in Event of Strike." *Gettysburg Times.* 18 Nov. 1966.

Mosby, Wade H. "As I See It." *The Milwaukee Journal.* 15 Jul. 1973.

http://www.mrpopculture.com/files/html/oct15-1953/

"New TPS Game Show." *Television/Radio Age.* 10 Nov. 1986.

"Promotion." *Broadcasting Magazine.* 7 Mar. 1949.

"Radio and Television: Rayburn and Finch, Disk Jockey Team, to Take Over Bob Crosby ABC Spot." *The New York Times.* 10 Feb. 1950.

"Radio-TV Notes." *The New York Times.* 11 Nov. 1952.

"Radio-TV Notes." *The New York Times.* 13 Nov. 1953.

Rahn, Pete. "Miss Universe Show on TV." *St. Louis Globe-Democrat.* 20 Jul. 1963.

"Rayburn Creates Scholarship." *Broadcasting Magazine.* 20 Jul. 1953.

"Rayburn, Finch Split." *Broadcasting Magazine.* 30 Jun. 1952.

"Rayburn's 'Helluva Town' Opens Sunday on Channel 5." *The New York Times.* 24 Jun. 1969.

Rayburn, Lynne. Personal interviews. 5 May 2014 and 8 May 2014.

http://roker.com/journal_archive_display.cfm?journal_id=5106

Ryan, Steve. *Classic Concentration: The Game, The Show, The Puzzles.* Sterling Publishing. New York.

Sabatino, Carl. "No Match for Gene's Games." *The New York Post.* 18 Nov. 1980.

Schwartz, David, and Steve Ryan and Fred Wostbrock. *The Encyclopedia of TV Game Shows.* New York Zoetrope. 1987.

"Scrooge Likely Role for Dickens." *The Press-Courier.* Oxnard, CA. 13 Dec. 1981.

Shain, Percy. "Rayburn's a Cape-to-Coast Commuter." *Boston Evening Globe.* 6 Jul. 1973.

Shanley, J.P. "TV: Solid Vanishing Act; Gene Rayburn Proves Versaility in Drama." *The New York Times.* 15 Feb. 1956.

Sherman, Robert. Personal interview. 22 Nov. 2013.

Skutch, Ira. *I Remember Television.* Scarecrow Press. Metuchen, NJ. 1989.

"Steve Allen Visit Set for Monday." *The Milwaukee Journal.* 28 Jul. 1957.

Sullivan, Dan. "The Games Day People Play." *The New York Times.* 17 Dec. 1967.

"Tartikoff: I See Us Getting Out of Third Place." 18 Jun. 1984.

"To Play First Straight Role." *The New York Times.* 22 Aug. 1957.

"Veteran Game Show Host Also At Home On Stage." *The Morning Call.* New Hope, PA. 22 Aug. 1991.

Werts, Diane. "Rayburn Doesn't Play Games" in 'Tribute.'" *Dallas Morning News.* 1981.

Werts, Diane. "Rayburn Stops Playing Games for Make-Believe of Theater." *Dallas Morning News.* 1981.

West, Randy. *Johnny Olson: A Voice in Time.* BearManor Media. Albany, GA. 2006.

West, Randy. Personal interview. 17 Dec. 2013.

White, Laura. "Cape Charm Lures TV Star." *Boston Herald.* 1 Feb. 1972.

Wilson, Earl. "Fortune Hangs On One Word." *The Miami News.* 1 Mar. 1957.

Wister, Emery. "New Game Show Joins Daily Battle." *The Charlotte News.* 29 Mar. 1972.

Witbeck, Charles. "Patti Keeps Laugh-In Chuckling." *The Miami News.* 21 Nov. 1972.

"WNBC's 'Ain't We Devils' Promotional Bally to Herald Rayburn Shift." *Variety.* 12 Nov. 1952.

"The Worm Turns, And Listeners to the Giving, Not Station or Sponsor." *Broadcasting Magazine.* 5 Apr. 1948.

Wostbrock, Fred. Personal interview. 23 Mar. 2014.

Zolotow, Sam. "'Blow Your Horn' to Star Rayburn." *The New York Times.* 3 Sep. 1962.

Endnotes

1 One source states that Sal Mineo played during this week, but NBC's program file lists Darryl Hickman. It's possible that Mineo was originally scheduled but replaced.

2 Another source lists a completely different week of special all-celebrity episodes.
   Monday: Carol Lawrence, Betty White, & Peggy Cass vs. Joe Garagiola, Cliff Robertson, & Ed McMahon.
   Tuesday: Hugh Downs, Bob Clayton, & Paolo Diva vs. Luke Kalpin, Tommy Norden, & Brian Kelly.

  Wednesday: Don Adams, Barbara Feldon, & Ed Platt vs. Larry Hagman, Barbara Eden, & Bill Daily.
  Thursday: MacDonald Carey, Peter Hansen, & Frances Reid vs. Susan Trustman, Shepperd Strudwick, & Audra Lindley.
  Friday: Andrew Prine, Brenda Scott, & Barry Sullivan vs. Michael Landon, Dan Blocker, & Lorne Greene.

3 Dick Clark appeared on the first two shows of the week, Mitch Miller appeared on the other three.

4 Because of CBS coverage of the Watergate hearings, the show was subject to frequent pre-emptions in 1973 and 1974. As such, airdates from Summer 1973 through Summer 1974 varied from city to city.

5 Charles Nelson Reilly missed the third episode of this taping session and was replaced by Mark Goodson.

6 Gary Burghoff missed the first episode of this taping and was replaced by announcer Johnny Olson.

7 Jimmie Walker was a panelist on the first two episodes of the week, with Charles Nelson Reilly returning on the third episode.

Index

Numbers in **bold** indicate photographs

Abernathy, Ken **156**
Adams, Don 449, 463, 506, 514
Adams, Edie 456
Alberghetti, Anna Marie 448
Albertson, Jack 467
Alda, Alan 186, **187**, 448, 452, 453, 456
Alda, Robert 448, 456
All About Faces 195, 436
Allen, Elizabeth 477
Allen, Jonelle 496, 497, 498
Allen, Marty 447
Allen, Steve 61, 63, 64-79, **67**, 81, 90, 92, 93, 96, 97, **98**, 103, 115, 133, 174, 200, 228, 343, 392, 395, 412, 435, 452, 454, 461, 504
Allison, Fran 46, 443
Allyson, June 446
Aloha Paradise 437
Alzado, Lyle 388

Amateur's Guide to Love, The **197**, 198-203, **199**, 213, 434
Ameche, Don 157, 444, 446
Ames, Art 178, 367, 442, 445, 447, 448, 449
Ames, Ed 136
Amsterdam, Morey 64, 443, 444, 454, 458, 459, 461, 463
Anderson, Bill 473, 476, 478, 483, 484, 486, 493, 497, 498, 500, 504
Anderson, Daryl 489
Anderson, Loni 486, 487, 489
Andrews, Ralph 387
Anka, Paul 444, 445, 450
Anything for Money 387
Anything Goes with Rayburn & Finch 31-43, **32**, **35**, **42**, 51, 52, 438
"April in Boston/Saving Grace/Breaks of Life" 437
Aqua Carnival 138-140, 440
Arkin, Adam 480
Arnaz, Lucie 458
Arngrim, Alison **380**, 502, 503
Arrants, Rod 504
Artists and Models Ball, The 161, **162**
Asner, Ed 252, 339, 364, 471, 472, 475, 477, 480, 486
Astaire, Adele 410
Astaire, Fred 285-286, **287**
Ayres, Leah 503

Baber, David 140, 201
Bacall, Lauren 157, 159-160, 447, 453, 454, 455, 456, 457
Backus, Jim 443, 459
Ballard, Kaye 458, 461
Bamboozle 388
Bank, Frank 502
Barbeau, Adrienne 464, 465, 469
Barber, Red 450
Barker, Bob 159, 203, 261, 288, 318, 397, 405, 448, 457, 466, 470, 477, 481, 486, 487, 488, 492, 493
Barnes, Clive **402**, 403
Baron, Sandy 451, 453
Barrett, Rona 163, 466, 471
Barris, Chuck 294, 308, 340, 388, 419
Barry, Jack 92, 94, 103, 104, 105-106, 108, 111, 112, 113, 114-115, 121, 146, 203, 215, 345, 389, 392, 419
Bates, Rhonda 388
Bauer, Jamie Lynne 470
Bauman, Jon **375**, 376, 377, **378**, 379, 381-382, **383**, 487, 488, 490, 493, 494, 496
Baum, Bruce 502, 503, 504, 505

Bean, Orson 61, 70, 112-113, 160-163, 189, 218-220, **223**, 226, 265-266, **267**, 270, 272-273, 280, 298, 406-407, 419, 423, 442, 444, 445, 446, 447, 455, 456, 461, 462, 463, 464, 466, 468, 469, 471, 473, 477, 478, 479, 482, 489, **501**
Beat the Clock 84, 143, 146, 292, 389, 436
Begley, Jr., Ed 502, 504, 505
Bennett, Joan 444
Bennett, Meg 479, 481
Benton, Barbi **380**, 502
Bergen, Candice 449
Bergen, Edgar 449
Berman, Shelley 444, 454
Bernstein, Gary 387-388
Bertinelli, Valerie 486
"Best of Friends/Success/Nine Karats" 437
Betz, Carl 456
Beverly, Steve 151, 178, 215
Billingsley, Barbara 502
Biography 430, 438
Bishop, Joey 443, 472, 473, 474, 475, 477
Blake, Amanda 464
Blocker, Dan 506, 514
Bloom, Claire 453
Blyden, Larry 179, 193, 461
Bob & Ray 41-42, 53, 61, 133
Bobcat's Big Ass Show 428-429, **429**
Boden, Bob 428
Bohay, Heidi 505
Bolger, Ray 449, 450, 452
Bono, Sonny 270-271, 264
"Boomer and Miss 21st Century" 437
Borge, Victor 453
Bosley, Tom 466
Bowman, Joyce **208**
Bowzer see Bauman, Jon
Bracken, Eddie 90
Branigan, Hugh 112, 118
Brattar, Bill 188
Braverman, Bart **326**, **327**, 487, 488, 490, 491, 492, 493, 494, 495, 496, 497, 498, 499, 500, 503
Bray, Thom 504, 505
Break the Bank **388**, 389-393, **391**, **393**, 395, 396, 435
Breslow, Marc 233, 259
Brewer, Teresa 36-37
Bridges, Lloyd 157, 450
Brill, Charlie 463, 464, 466
Broadway Open House 63-64, 65

Brogan, Jimmy 502
Bromfield, Lois 502
Brooke, Sorrell 504
Brooks, Foster 489, 491, 492
Brothers, Dr. Joyce 445, 446, 449, 451, 452, 453, 454, 457, 463, 468, 470, 476, 483
Brown, Chelsea 457, 462
Brown, James 157, 455, 456
Brown, Johnny 467
Bruner, Wally 184, 185, **187**
Bryant, Debra 449, 450, 451
Bry, Ellen 503, 504
Bulifant, Joyce 246-247, **247**, 302, **313**, **320**, 459, 462, 463, 464, 465, 466, 467, 468, 469, 470, 471, 472, 473, 474, 475, 476, 477, 478, 480, 481, 482, 484, 485, 486, 487, 488, 489, 490, 491, 493, 495, 496, 497, 498, 499, 500
Bullock, Jm J. 502, 503
Burger, Michael 421
Burghoff, Gary 222, 226, **264**, 272-273, 302, 464, 465, 466, 467, 469, 470, 471, 472, 474, 475, 476, 477, 480, 481, 482, 484, 486, 487, 488, 490, 494, 495, 496, 503, 506, 514
Burrows, Abe 61, 442, 443, 444, 445, 446, 447, 449, 450, 451, 453, 479
Burr, Raymond **320**, 487
Bye Bye Birdie xi, 121-129, **124**, **125**, 138, 163, 172, 265, 438
Byrnes, Edd 449, 504

Call My Bluff 435
Canary, David 454
Card Sharks 339, 436
Carey, Macdonald 506, 514
Carlisle, Kitty 61, 189, 190, 191, **402**, 403, 442, 444, 446
Carne, Judy 454, 455, 459
Carroll, Pat 444, 458
Carson, Joanne 455, 456, 457
Carson, Johnny 72, 136, 141, 167, 173-174, 226, 301, 400, 413, 435
Carter, Jack 458, 459, 462, 464, 491
Cartwright, Angela 504
Cassidy, Jack 456, 459, 469
Cass, Peggy 61, 101, 163, 172, 189, 190, **402**, 403, 442, 443, 444, 445, 446, 447, 448, 455, 456, 457, 461, 506, 513
Caulfield, Joan 443
Celebrity Match Mates **208**, 209, 255-256, 434
Cerf, Bennett 61, 172, 184, 442, 444, 450, 455, 457
Chancellor, John **141**
Chaplin, Sidney 446, 447
Cher 270-271, 330, 364
Chester, Jerry 204, 328
Choose Up Sides **89**, 90-92, **91**, 286, 433

Christmas Carol, A 347, **347**, 348, 440
Christopher, William 505
Claridge, Christie 503
Clark, Blake 502
Clark, Dick 443, 452, 506, 514
Clarke, Brian Patrick 497
Clayton, Bob 506, 513
Clementson, Chris 272, 335
Coe, Fred 83
Cohen, Marty 500, 502, 503, 504, 505
Cohn, Mindy 505
Cole, Kay 123, 126, 127, 128, 264-265
Coleman, Jerry 450
Cole, Tina 455
Collins, Dorothy 442, 443
Collins, Gary 363, 494, 495
Collins, Joan 252, **253**, **302**, **310**, 468, 470
Collyer, Bud 188, 202
Come Blow Your Horn 121, 140, 438
Concentration 103, 112, 181, 292
Conn, Didi 476, 483, 505
Conried, Hans 480
Convy, Bert **210**, 211, 256-257, 266, 401-402, 407, 456, 457, 458, 459, 460, 461, 462, 465, 469, 475, 488
Conway, Shirl 444
Cook, Barbara 442, 443
Cook, Nathan 503, 504, 505
Copley, Teri 503
Cord, Alex 505
Cornell, Lydia 502, 503, 504, 505
Correll, Rich 502
Cosby, Bill 157, **237**, 247, 447
Cox, Wally 445, 447, 448
Crane, Bob 456, 457
Crane, Les 448, 451
Crenna, Richard 455
Crockett, Keane 11
Cronkite, Walter 235, 265
Crosby, Bing 45
Crosby, Bob 40, 51
Crosby, Gary 481, 483, 490, 495, 497
Crosby, Miles 34
Crowley, Pat 471
Cullen, Bill 56, 61, 161, 168, 179, 185, 189, 190, 193, 228, 263, 271, 288, 304, 366, 449, 453, 454, 456, 459, 462, 473, 481, 489, 493, 496, 498, 500, 503
Culp, Robert 452, 458
Curtis, Jamie Lee 491, 492, 496

Daily, Bill 302, **326**, **327**, **378**, **380**, 382, 459, 467, 469, 470, 472, 474, 476, 478, 480, 484, 485, 486, 488, 489, 490, 491, 492, 493, 494, 495, 496, 497, 498, 499, 500, 502, 503, 506, 514
Dalton, Abby 382, 453, 462, 500, 504, 505
Daly, John Charles 184, 304
Dana, Bill 93, 446
Danning, Sybil 503
Dano, Linda 503, 504, 505
Darin, Bobby 447
Darren, James 455, 465
Dating Game, The 202
Davidson, Donald 263, 266
Davis, Audrey **156**
Davis, Clifton 465, 467, 471, 473, 493
Davis, Phyllis 496, 497
Dawson, Richard 204, **210**, 211, **214**, 218, **219**, 220, 231, 232, **242**, 244, **246**, **247**, 248, **250**, **251**, 252, **253**, 256, 257, 259, **264**, **267**, **276**, 280, 281, 282, **283**, 284, **285**, 288-289, 292-294, 295, 301-303, **302**, 310-316, **310**, **313**, **315**, 317-319, 341-342, 348, **349**, 350, 366, 382, 457, 458, 459, 460, 461, 462, 463, 464, 465, 466, 467, 468, 469, 470, 471, 472, 473, 474, 475, 476, 477, 478, 479, 480, 481, 482, 483, 484, 485, 486
DeBartolo, Dick 105, 146-147, 152-153, 154-155, 157, 158-159, 163-164, 167, 168, 172-173, 179, 185, 186-188, 190-192, 209-211, 224, 226, 234-235, 239, 240, 241-242, 263, 276, 302, 308, 311, 316, 330, 384, 402, 407, **413**
Deacon, Richard 464, 482, 486, 488, 492, 496, 498, 502
Deerfield, Lynne 475
Defore, Don 444
DeHaven, Gloria 90, 466
De Lancie, John 504
Delany, Pat 473
DeLuise, Dom 452
Denver, Bob 504
Deutsch, Patti **187**, 244-245, **246**, **253**, 256, **267**, **302**, 302, 459, 461, 462, 463, 464, 465, 466, 467, 468, 469, 470, 471, 472, 473, 474, 475, 476, 477, 478, 479, 480, 481, 482, 483, 484, 487, 488, 489, 491, 492
Diamond, Selma 445, 446, 447, 449, 451
Dickson, Brenda 469
Diller, Phyllis 445, 446, 448, 454, 493, 495, 497, 503, 504, 505
Dinah! 437
Diva, Paolo 506, 513
Dobkowitz, Roger 295-297
Donahue 351, 438
Donahue, Elinor 504
Donahue, Phil 418, 438
Donahue, Troy 504
Donner, Robert 495, 496, 497, 498, 499, 503, 505
Donovan, Jody 256, 471, 472

Dors, Diana 280
Dotto 110-111, 114, 115
Dough Re Mi 103-115, **104**, **105**, **109**, **111**, **113**, **114**, 118-120, **119**, 140, 146, 345, 392, 433
Downs, Hugh 103, 133, 453, 454, 456, 506, 513
Doyle, David **320**, **330**, **335**, 482, 483, 484, 486, 487, 488, 489, 491, 492, 493, 494, 495, 496, 498, 499
"Do You Remember Radio?" 40-41
Drake, Bud 135
Dreesen, Tom 484
DuArt, Louise 390, 391
DuBarry, Denise 484
Duke, Patty 302, **330**, **335**, 465, 466, 470, 473, 475, 477, 478, 480, 481, 483, 484, 486, 488, 491, 492, 493, 494, 498
Dullea, Keir 456
Dunlop, Vic 503
Dussault, Nancy 459, 503

Easterbrook, Leslie 500
Eckstein, Warren 356-364, **357**
Eden, Barbara 506, 514
Edwards, Geoff 292, 367
Edwards, Stephanie 458, 494, 500
Egan, Richard 443
Elder, Ann 458, 459, 461, 462, 463, 464, 467
Elliott, Bob 41-42
Elliott, Chris 42
Elliot, Mama Cass 459
Ellis, Michael 101-102
Ellis, Peggy Ann 44, 52
Emerson, Faye 60, 61, 442, 443
Enright, Dan 92, 103, 104, 105-106, 108, 111, 112, 113, 115, 121, 146, 345, 389, 419
Enriquez, Rene 504, 505
Entertainment Tonight 395-397
Eubanks, Bob 274, 366, 407-408, 428, **429**, 503
Eure, Wesley 493
Evans, Michael 464
Eye Guess 179, 193

Fabe, Maxine 240
Fabian 504
Fabray, Nanette 458
Face is Familiar, The 193
Fadiman, Clifton 61, 133
Fairbanks, Jr., Douglas 442, 445
Falkenberg, Jinx 443

Family Feud xii, 291-294, 301, 302, 312, 318, 326, 341-342, 366
Fantasy Island 353, 437
Farago, Joe 393
Farentino, James 453
Farrell, Gail 493, 499
Farrell, Sharon 485, 499, 500
Farr, Jamie 505
Fates, Gil 186, **187**, 187
Fee, Melinda O. 471, 500
Feldman, Elliott 239
Feldon, Barbara 449, 451, 506, 514
Felsher, Howard 140, 342
Fenton, Mildred 45
Finch, Betty 46, 56-57
Finch, Durwood "Dee" 31-32, **32**, **33**, 34, 35, **35**, 36, 37, **39**, 41, 42-43, **42**, 44, 46, 51-52, **52**, 53, 56-57, 63, 79, 133, 438
Finley, Pat 469
Fisher, Eddie 265
Fisher, Gail 244, 460, 461
Fitzgerald, Fern 503, 504, 505
Flagg, Fannie 168, 248-249, 252, **293**, 302, 303, 325, **326**, **327**, **349**, 382, 452, 453, 454, 455, 456, 457, 459, 461, 462, 463, 464, 465, 466, 467, 468, 469, 470, 471, 472, 473, 474, 475, 476, 477, 478, 479, 480, 481, 482, 483, 484, 485, 486, 487, 488, 489, 491, 492, 494, 496, 497, 498, 499, 500, 503, 504, 505
Fleming, Art 367, 372
Flynn, Joe 461
Fontaine, Joan 443, 444, 447
Ford, Anitra 474
Ford, Paul 442
Ford, Whitey 448, 449, 450, 452, 453
"Forget Me Not/The Quiz Masters" 353, 437
Forsyth, David 504
Forsythe, John 450, 454, 466,
Forsyth, Rosemary 477, 479
Francis, Arlene 61, 66, 148, 149, 184, **184**, **187**, **210**, 211, 442, 443, 444, 445, 457, 466, 470, 472, 479, 484, 505
Frangione, Nancy 503, 504
Franklin, Bonnie 472, 473, 477, 485, 494
Freberg, Stan 502
Freeman, Stan 56
Frey, Leonard **380**, 502, 503, 504, 505
Frost, David 157, 457
Furness, Betty 445

Gabor, Eva **326**, **327**, 478, 480, 481, 483, 489, 491, 494, 495, 496, 498, 499
Gaines, William M. 190-191

Gallagher 502
Gallagher, Mike 356
Galloway, Don 489, 490, 496
Gambit 203, 275
Game Show a Go-Go 438
"Games People Play" 437
Game TV 438
Ganzel, Teresa 505
Garagiola, Joe 209, 446, 447, 448, 449, 450, 451, 452, 453, 454, 455, 456, 457, 483, 506, 513
Garland, Beverly 388, 459
Garnes, Gene 136
Garroway, Dave 12, 46, **47**, 48-49, 60, 63, 133
Garver, Kathy 455
Gautier, Dick 128, 129, 163, 171-172, **208**, 266, 279-280, 346, 458, 461, 471, 474, 475, 478
Gelman, Michael 364
Gene Rayburn's Bright Ideas 60, 433
George, Lynda Day **267**, 464, 466, 468, 478
Geraldo 412, **413**, 418
Getteys, Bennye 474
Gillette, Anita **214**, 451, 457, 464, 493
Gilliam, Stu 458
Ging, Jack 443
Gobel, George 382, 500, 503, 505
God's Favorite 226
Goldsmith, Sydney 499
Goldstein, Lenore **156**
Goldthwait, Bobcat 428-429, **429**
Gong Show, The 294, 340
Goodfriend, Lynda 505
Goodson, Jonathan 210, 408-409
Goodson, Mark 60, 61, 62, 63, 84, 87, 88, 90, 112, 140, 141, 142, 143, 145, 146, 147, 150, 151, 155, 157, 161, 163-166, 172, 179, 183, 184, 188, 189, 191, 192, 193, 198, 204, 205, 209, 210-211, 212, 214, 217, 218, 219-220, 223, 228-229, 236, 238, 239, 244, 253, 255, 256, 259, 270, 272, 275, 276, 286-288, 291, 292, 296, 298, 299, 301, 304, 305, 310, 312, 321, 325, 326, 328, 329, 330, 334-336, 341-342, 367, 368, 373, 375, 376, 377, 378-379, 380-381, 383-384, 388, 392, 398-399, 401, 402, 407, 408-409, 419, 430, 451, 506, 514
Gordon, Barry 505
Gordon, Gale 447
Gore, Lesley 453
Gorme, Eydie 70, 437, 455
Goulet, Robert 450
Grady, Don 455
Graham, Ronny 492

Grandy, Fred 489, 490, 494, 495, 496, 497, 498, 500, 502
Grant, Bud 200, 203
Greenberg, Ron 70, 103-105, **105**, 107, 108-109, 110, 113, 118, **119**, 120
Greene, Kim Morgan 504
Greene, Lorne 506, 514
Greene, Shecky 465
Greeting to a New Day 55
Grey, Joel 455
Grier, Rosey 457, 462
Griffin, Joseph 111-112, 114-115
Griffin, Merv 101, 141, 142, 146, 249, 385
Grundy, Reg 367
Gypsy 169, **170**, 438

Hagman, Larry 506, , 514
Hall, Arsenio 400, 502, 503, 505
Hall, Deidre 504
Hallick, Tom 479
Hallman, Victoria 502
Hall, Monty 114, 133, 159, 274, 275, 367, 412, **413**, 447
Halstrom, Holly 495, 496, 498, 499
Hambro, Leonid 453
Hamilton, George 454, 455
Hamilton, Lois 504, 505
Hamlisch, Marvin 472
Hammett, David 376, 381
Hanley, Bridget 455
Hansen, Peter 506, 514
Harlem Globetrotters, The 72
Harrington, Jr., Pat 93, 459, 461
Harris, Jo Ann 479, 485
Harris, Julie 127, 471
Harrison, Jenilee 500, 503
Harrison, Noel 452, 455
Hart, Dennis 135, 136
Harty, Patricia 456
Harwood, Joe 279
Haworth, Jill 455
Hayes, Peter Lind 442
Head of the Class 121, 433
Healy, Mary 442
Heatter, Merrill 196, 198, 211, 266, 267, 268, 270, 275, 371-372, 379
Hecht, Gina 494
Hecht, Joel 295
Heffernan, Virginia 265
Hegyes, Robert 475
Helluva Town 182-183, 434

Henderson, Florence 247, 442, 443, 444, 445, 446, 447, 449, 450, 451, 454
Henderson, Skitch 76, 77, 148, 442, 443, 449, 450, 451
Hendler, Lauri 505
Henley, Kay 244
Henner, Marilu 418, 486
Henning, Linda Kaye 461
Here's Boomer 437
"Heroes Walk on Sand" 103, 437
He Said, She Said 209, 436
Hickman, Darryl 448, 450, 451, 506, 513
Hickman, Dwayne **239**, **242**, **258**, **264**, 465
Hines, Connie 455, 456
Hoffman, Dustin 157, 454
Holbrook, Hal 453
Holden, Rebecca 502
Holliday, Polly 482
Hollywood Squares, The 198, 211, 266, 267, 268-270, 275, 280, 344, 371-372, 374, 375, **375**, 378, 379, 381, 382, 384, 435
Hollywood's Talking 215
Holmberg, Ted 140
Hood, Kim 505
Hope, Bob 159, 442
Hope, Erica 487
"Hop Scotch Polka" 37-40, **39**
Hot Streak see *Party Line*
Houston, Jean 135
Hovis, Larry 387-388, 461
Howard Stern Show, The 416-417, 418, 438
Howard, Susan 472, 473, 496
Howes, Sally Ann 442, 445
Hunley, Leann 504
Hunter, Tab 486
Huste, Annemarie 356, 365
Hutton, Gunilla 464

Imperato, Carlo 504, 505
Impossible Years, The 169, **171**, 438
Ingels, Marty 447
Insight 437
I Ought to Be in Pictures 345, 440
I Remember Television 141-142
Isacksen, Peter 478
It 385, **386**, 387, 435
It Had to be You 209
It Happened Right Here 355, 435
It Happened to Jane 118, 438

It's Predictable 434
I've Got a Secret 61, 88, 101, 161, 189, 204-205, 218, 223, 253, 436

Jackson, Kate 469, 472
James, Art 178, 367, 442, 445, 447, 448, 449
James, Dennis 61, 267, 400-401
Janaver, Diane 254
Janis, Conrad 490, 499
Jayroe, Jane Anne 451
Jeffory, Dawn 494
Jeopardy! xii, 181, 351, 372, 397, 399
Jim Nabors Show, The 437
Johnson, Arte 455, 464, 479, 487, 489, 492, 496
Johnson, Van 443
Joker's Wild, The 203, 415
Jones, Carol 487
Jones, Carolyn 453, 458
Jones, Jack 487, 488, 489, 492
Jones, Shirley 456
Joseph, Jackie 462
Joyce, Elaine 248, 252, 256, **320**, 458, 461, 462, 463, 464, 465, 466, 467, 468, 470, 472, 474, 476, 478, 479, 480, 481, 482, 483, 484, 485, 487, 488, 490, 491, 494, 495, 496, 497, 498, 499, 500, 503
Judis, Bernice 27, 31, 32, 34, 35, 36, 37, 40, 44
Julian, Sally 503
Jump, Gordon 503
Just Men! 365-366, 436

Kaempfert, Bert 148
Kalehoff, Edd 377
Kalpin, Luke 506, 513
Kamen, Milt 162, 442, 443, 444, 445, 446, 447, 449, 450
Kanaly, Steve 492, 494
Karras, Alex 470
Katz, Ruth 356
Keaton, Buster 90
Keel, Howard 444, 445
Keith, Brian 457
Keller, Mary Page 503
Kelly, Brian 506, 513
Kelly, Paula 504, 505
Kelly, Roz **313**, 476, 480
Kennedy, Betty 493, 495, 496, 497, 498
Kennedy, George 473, 474, 476, 481, 483, 491, 495, 496, 497, 498
Kennedy, Jayne 504, 505
Kennedy, John F. 444
Kennedy, Sarah 466, 467, 468, 470, 474, 478, 480

INDEX

Kennedy, Tom 179, 274, 366, **399**, 400, 453, 457, 499
Kercheval, Ken 503, 505
Kiel, Richard 496
Kilgallen, Dorothy 61, 163, 184, 444, 446
King, Alan 452, 453, 454, 455
King, Freeman 493
King, Mabel 487
Kirby, Durwood 451, 453
Kirby, George 454, 463
Klavan, Gene 56, 90
Kline, Richard **380**, 502, 503, 504, 505
Kline, Richard S. 389, 391, 393
Klugman, Jack **208**, **210**, 211, **214**, 221-222, 457, 458, 459, 486, 497
Knickerbocker Beer Show, The see *Steve Allen Show, The*
Knight, Elyse 503
Knight, Ted 503
Knotts, Don 70, 93
Knox, Terence 504, 505
Koock, Guich 487, 488
Kopell, Bernie 484, 498
Kopelman, Jean 152, **156**
Koufax, Sandy 157-158, **158**, 453
Kovacs, Ernie 93, 96, 118
Kraft Television Playhouse 103, 437
Kukla, Fran and Ollie 46, 47, 436, 437
Kulp, Nancy 476

La Cage Aux Folles 344, **410**, **411**, 412
LaLanne, Jack 388
Lamour, Dorothy 157, 447
Lander, David L. 505
Landers, Audrey 488, 499, 502, 505
Landers, Judy 487, 491, 495, 502, 504, 505
Landon, Michael **214**, 217, 457, 506, 514
Landsberg, David 482
Lane, Abbe 442
Lane, Nancy 487, 492, 505
Laneuville, Eric 504
Lange, Hope **85**, 85, **86**, 87, **88**, 484
Lange, Jim 202, 366, 367, 400
Lange, Ted 491, 497, 499
Late Show, The **399**, 400-401, 407, 418, 437
Lawford, Peter 157, **199**, 454, 455, 456
Lawrence, Carol **239**, **242**, **258**, **264**, 442, 443, 445, 448, 449, 450, 451, 454, 455, 456, 465, 506, 513
Lawrence, Mark 83
Lawrence, Steve 70, 437

Lawrence, Vicki **214**, 418, 457, 485
Layne, Jerry **156**
Learned, Michael 457
Leary, Brianne 488, 489, 490
Lee, Michelle 452
Lee, Ruta 458
Lembeck, Helaine 483
Lembeck, Michael 504, 505
Lemmon, Jack 118, 342, 343
Leno, Jay 502, 503, 504
Leonard, Jack E. 442, 443, 444, 446
Leonard, Sheldon 453, 468, 470
Lescoulie, Jack 29-31, **30**, 96, 133
Lesko, Karen 232-233
Lester, Jerry 64
Let's Make a Deal 159, 275, 389, 415
Letterman, David 266, 356
Let Yourself Go 44, 438
Levenson, Sam 442, 443, 449, 450, 451
Lewis, Jerry 108, **109**
Lewis, Robert Q. 60-61, 62, 142, 312, 442, 444, 445, 446, 450, 452, 459
Lewis, Shari 444, 445, 446
Leyden, Bill 193, 447, 448
Liebmann, Norm 108
Lindley, Audra 506, 514
Lingo 388, 399
Linville, Larry 504
Littleton, Twyla 502
Lloyd, Norman 504
Lockhart, June 448, 450, 453, 459
Loggia, Robert 451
Lombardo, Guy 40, 63
London, Julie 471
Long, Richard 463
Loring, Gloria 502, 503, 504
Loudon, Dorothy 454
Louise, Anita 447
Love Boat, The 323-325, 353, 437
Love of Four Colonels, The 101-102, 438
Lovers Leap 338, 439
Lucci, Susan 411
Ludden, Allen 101, 144-145, 223, 250, 251, **251**, 256, **285**, 285, 454, 462, 464, 469, 496
Lyman, Dorothy 503
Lynde, Janice 473
Lynde, Paul 127, 257, 270

INDEX

Lynn, Diana 443
Lyon, Sue 456, 457

MacGraw, Ali 456
MacKenzie, Gisele 442, 443, 446, 447, 448, 450, 450, 451
MacRae, Gordon 454, 456
MacRae, Meredith **184**, 455, 456, 461, 466
MacRae, Sheila 454, 455, 456
Macy, Bill 468, 470
Maffett, Debra Sue 503, 504
Mahaffey, Lorrie 486, 488, 490
Make the Connection 87-90, 286, 433
Malone, Michael 279
Mandan, Robert 486
Mandel, Howie 504
Mandrell, Irlene 500
Manetti, Larry 503
Mansfield, Jayne 160-161, **160**, **162**, 445, 446, 447, 450
Mantle, Mickey 157, 448, 450, 453, 454, 455
"Man Who Vanished, The" 102-103, 348, 437
March, Hal 121, 140
Marilu 418, 439
Maris, Roger 448, 450
Marshall, Penny 464
Marshall, Peter 82-83, 120, 127, 129, 136, 267, 268-270, 292, 304-305, 310, 312, 344-345, 366, 367, 372, 378, 381, 412-413, 428, **429**, 457, 494, 496
Martin, Anne-Marie 505
Martindale, Wink 203, 412, **413**
Martin, Dean 108
Martin, Dick 301, **330**, **335**, 466, 471, 472, 474, 476, 478, 479, 480, 481, 482, 483, 484, 485, 486, 487, 488, 489, 490, 491, 492, 493, 494, 495, 496, 497, 498, 499, 503
Martin, Dolly Read **285**, **349**, 469, 488, 490, 493, 496, 497, 499
Martin, Mary 117
Masak, Ron 462, 466
Massey, Raymond 446
Match Game, The xi, xii, 143, 145-168, **147**, **149**, **153**, **156**, **158**, **160**, **165**, 169, 172, 174, 175-179, **177**, **180**, 182, 183, 185, 186, 192, 198, 200, 203, 209-230, **210**, **211**, **213**, **214**, **216**, **219**, **221**, **223**, **225**, 231-259, **232**, **239**, **242**, **243**, **246**, **247**, **250**, **251** 253, **258**, **260**, 261-289, **262**, **264**, **267**, **269**, **271**, **273**, **274**, **276**, **279**, **283**, **285**, **290**, 291, 292, 293, **293**, 294-305, **297**, **298**, **300**, **302**, **305**, **306**, 307-321, **310**, **313**, **315**, **317**, **320**, 325-336, **326**, **327**, **330**, **332**, **333**, **335**, 338, 340, **341**, 341, 346, 347, 348-352, **349**, 353, 355, 356, 365, 366, 367-368, 369-384, **370**, **373**, **375**, **378**, **380**, **383**, 385, 392, 398, 399, 401, 402, 407-410, 411, 412, 415, 416, 417, 419-420, 421, 422, 423, 424, 431-432, 433, 434, 435, 441-505, **441**, **460**, **501**

Match Game/Hollywood Squares Hour, The 369-384, **370**, **373**, **375**, **378**, **380**, **383**, 385, 435, **501**, 502-505
Match Game PM see *Match Game, The*
Match Game '74 see *Match Game, The*
Match Game '73 see *Match Game, The*
Mathers, Jerry 502
Matthau, Walter 135, 161
Maury Povich Show, The 418, 438
McCabe, Marcia 504
McCall, Mitzi 463, 464, 465
McCarty, Vicki 502
McCashin, Constance 503, 505
McClurg, Edie 498, 499, 500, 502, 504
McCormick, Pat 503
McCoy, Matt 502, 503
McDowall, Roddy 157, 446
McGavin, Darren 442
McGeehan, Kate 505
McKay, Jim 87-88
McLain, Denny 455
McMahon, Ed 178, 209, 449, 450, 451, 452, 453, 454, 455, 457, 506, 513
McNair, Barbara 455, 470
Meade, Julia 101, 450
Meader, Vaughn 442, 443
Meadows, Audrey 70, 442, 443, 444, 447, 448, 452, 453
Meadows, Jayne 61, 70, 447, 448, 452, 454, 504
Meara, Anne 461, 462
Mekka, Eddie 502, 505
Meredith, Don 158, 454, 456, 457
Meredith, Lee 467
Meriwether, Lee 460, 461, 466, 467, 468, 472, 473, 475, 476, 479, 481, 482, 484, 486, 489, 493, 498
Merman, Ethel 157, 159, 325, 449, 456, 467, 474, 475, 479, 484
Merrill, Dina 451, 454, 455, 456
Merrill, Robert 445
MG2 421
Michaelsen, Kari 505
Michaels, Marilyn 505
Miller, Mitch 444, 450, 451, 452, 453, 454, 506, 514
Mills, Donna 474
Mills, Juliet 461, 463, 465
Minelli, Liza 452, 454
Mineo, Sal 157, 445, 448, 506, 513
Miss Universe pageant 138, **139**, 433, 434
Mitchell, Brian 502, 503, 504, 505
Mitchell, Scoey 463, 467, 470, 472, 473, 475, 478, 479, 486, 489, 492, 496, 498, 500

Miyori, Kim 502, 504
Mobley, Mary Ann 458, 459, 461, 465, 466, 471, 474, 477, 480, 482, 490, 496, 498
Moll, Richard 504, 505
Monitor 132-138, **134**, 192, 198, **202**, 203, 207, 213, 424, 438
Moore, Garry 60, 66, 118, 167, 185, 189, 190-191, 192, 202, 228, 288, 456
Moore, Roger 157, 453
Moran, Erin 503, 505
Moreno, Rita 447, 448, 449, 451, 452, 453, 454, 456, 492, 494, 495
Morgan, Henry 61, 101, 442, 443, 444, 446, 447, 448, 449, 450, 451, 452, 453, 455, 456, 485
Morgan, Jaye P. 457
Morita, Pat 475
Moritz, Louisa 231-232, 462, 464, 470
Morris, Chester 442, 443, 444, 447, 449
Morris, Greg **313**, 461, 462, 465, 474, 476, 480, 486
Morris, Marsha 239
Morrow, Karen 467
Morse, Robert 457, 464
Mosley, Roger E. 505
Movie Masters, The **402**, 402-404, 412, 435
Murray, Don 444
Murray, Jan 448
"Music! Music! Music!" 36, 37
Myerson, Bess 443, 447, 450, 453, 454, 455, 456
My Fair Lady 116

Name's the Same, The 60-62, 142, 218, 401, 435
Narz, Jack 114, 274, 292, 423, 462
NBC 60th Anniversary Celebration 437
Neary, Patrick 239
Nelson, Barry 442
Nelson, David 504
Neustein, Joe 239
Newhart, Bob 108, 249
Newlywed Game, The 256, 407
Newman, Phyllis 445, 448, 450, 451, 452, 453, 454, 455, 465
New Price is Right, The 203, 205
Nicolette, David 331, 339
Nielsen, Leslie 252, 466, 478
Noah, Robert 104-105, 146-147, 150, **197**, 198, 201-202, 266-267, 268, 367
Norden, Tommy 506, 513
Northrop, Wayne 504
"Not So Fast, Gopher/Haven't We Met Before?/Foreign Exchange" 437
Nye, Louis 70, 93

Oakes, Randi 492, 505
O'Brian, Hugh 449, 452, 456
O'Brien, Pat 445, 446, 448
O'Connell, Helen 457
Ogiens, Mike 308-309
Olfson, Ken 487
Oliver, David 503
Olson, Johnny 148, 150, 152, 168, 177, **210**, 245, 254-255, 259, **269**, 272, **273**, 293, 310, 311, 506, 514
O'Neal, Patrick 455
One Life to Live 353, 354-355, 437
Oppenheimer, Alan 495
Osmond, Ken 502
Our Hearts Were Young and Gay 438
Owens, Buck 466
Owens, Gary 400

Paar, Jack 60, 96, 97
Paley, Petronia 505
Palillo, Ron 473, 475, 478, 479, 482
Pantomime Quiz 162
Pardo, Don 90, 411
Parks, Bert 367, 450, 451, 452, 453, 455
Party Line **366**, 367, 435
Password 87, 120, 143-145, 146, 148, 149, 151, 154, 163, 200, 244, 250, 350, 436
Password All-Stars 436
Password Plus 365, 436
Patterson, Lorna 489, 491
Paul, Richard 485, 486, 487, 489, 490, 491, 492, 494, 495, 496, 497, 498, 499
Paulsen, Pat 504
Payne, John 445
Peaker, E.J. 457
Pearl, Minnie 481
Pennington, Janice 205, 473
Pepitone, Joe 448, 450, 453
Perry, Jim 366
Personality 179, 193
Pescow, Donna 486, 489, 492
Pflug, JoAnn **210**, 211, **214**, **293**, 457, 458, 459, 461, 462, 463, 464, 465, 469, 473, 478, 482, 497
Philbin, Regis 70, 389, 397, 437
Pichon, Rae **156**, 157, 158
Pickles, Christina 505
Pine, Robert **349**, 487, 488, 491, 494, 499
Platt, Ed 506, 514
Play Your Hunch 140-142, 146, 286
Porter, Richard J. 503

INDEX

Post, Markie 502
Poston, Tom 61, 93, **378**, **380**, 442, 443, 444, 445, 446, 474, 482, 502, 503, 505
Povich, Maury 438, 438
Powell, Jane 454
Prentice, Paula 444
Presley, Elvis 121, 128
Price is Right, The xii, 87, 143, 168, 205, 255, 261, 304, 318, 351, 389, 397
Price, Vincent 270
"Prince of Apple Towns" 437
Prine, Andrew 506, 514
Prisoner of Second Avenue 338, 343, 439
Proctor, Phil 502, 503
Provenza, Paul 502
Prowse, Juliet 449, 474, 482
Purcell, Sarah 481, 484, 491, 492

Quigley, Bob 196, 198, 211, 266, 270, 275, 371-372, 379
Quinn, Carmel 444, 445, 446

Rafferty, Bill 502, 504
Randall, Tony 457
Rapp, Joel 356
Rattle of a Simple Man **439**, 439
Rayburn, Helen 16, **17**, 18, 19, 24-25, 26, 27, 56, 73, **74**, 116, **116**, **117**, 117, 136, 152, 168, 169, 174, 191, 194, 195, 196, 209, **234**, 235, 256, 256-257, 284, 285-286, 298, 329, 336-338, **338**, 348, 349, 410, **417**, 420, 421-422, 423
Rayburn, Lynne 19-20, **20**, 24, 25, 26, 27, 48-49, 50-51, 56, 57, 61, 66, 72-73, 82, 83-84, 93-94, 116, **117**, 117-118, 129, 164-167, 169, 171, 174, 181, 193, **194**, 195-196, 238, 244, 305, 308, 333, 337-338, 339-340, 348, 349, 381-382, 397, 412, 421, 423, 427-428, 430-431
Reagan, Michael 388
Reagan, Ronald 60
Reddy, Helen 503
Redgrave, Lynn 467, 500
Reese, Della 457, 475, 477
Regis Philbin's Lifestyles 389, 437
Reid, Elliott 448
Reid, Frances 506, 514
Reid, Tim 502, 503, 504
Reilly, Charles Nelson 126-127, **199**, 204-205, **221**, **223**, 223-227, **225**, 241, 242, **243**, 244, **246**, **247**, 249, **250**, **251**, 252, 257, **267**, 268, **276**, 281, 282, **283**, **285**, **293**, 295, 301, **302**, 303, **310**, **313**, 316, 320, **320**, **326**, **327**, **330**, **335**, **341**, **349**, 350, 362, 382, 408, 409, 457, 458, 459, 460, 461, 462, 463, 464, 467, 468, 469, 470, 471, 472, 473, 474, 475, 476, 477, 478, 479, 480, 481, 482, 483, 484, 485, 486, 487, 488, 489, 490, 491, 492, 493, 494, 495, 496, 497, 498, 499, 500, 502, 503, 504, 505, 506, 514

Remick, Lee 450
Rey, Alejandro **208**, 463
Reynolds, Burt 158, 233, 457
Rhoades, Barbara 478, 479, 481, 483, 485, 486, 488, 491, 493, 498
Rhue, Madlyn 461, 467, 469, 475
Richardson, Susan 485, 488, 490, 492, 495, 497
Rich, Christopher 503, 504
Riptide 437
Ritchie, Sharon K. 452
Rivers, Joan 400, 449, 452, 453, 454, 455
Rizzuto, Phil 450
Robert Montgomery Presents 102-103, 348, 437
Robertson, Cliff 157, 448, 450, 451, 453, 454, 455, 506, 513
Robertson, Dale 446
Roberts, Pernell 445
Robins, Cynthia 336
Rodd, Marcia 472
Roker, Al 421-422
Roker, Roxie 504, 505
Rolle, Esther 471
Rooney, Mickey 442
Ross, Donald 256, 463, 473
Rossi, Steve 447
Rowan & Martin's Laugh-In 204, 245
Rubaloff, Noel 381
Ruprecht, David 503
Russell, Mark 503
Russell, Nipsey 302, 366, 443, 455, 456, 457, 458, 459, 461, 462, 464, 465, 466, 467, 476, 477, 479, 480, 481, 483, 484, 485, 486, 487, 488, 489, 492, 503

Sahlin, Don **47**, 48
Sahl, Mort 445
Sajak, Pat 405, 503, 505
Sale of the Century 179, 367
Sales, Soupy 184, **184**, 416, 451, 452, 453, 454, 455, 456, 457, 475, 504
Sally Jesse Raphael 437
Sands, Diana 454, 456
Sanford, Isabel 472, 473
Santos, Joe 487, 488, 490, 492, 494, 498, 504
Sarnoff, David 15, 133
Sarnoff, Robert 133
Sassoon, Vidal 157, 456
Saturday Morning Live 355-365, **357**, **360**, 367-368, 376, 435
Saturday Night Live 42, 90, 270, 321, 356, 411, 431, 438
Schnetzer, Stephen 503, 504
Schreiber, Avery 282, **283**, **293**, 302, **310**, 465, 466, 468, 469, 470, 473, 474, 476, 477, 479, 481, 483, 485, 488

Scott, Brenda 506, 514
Scott, Debralee 302, **330**, **335**, 475, 476, 478, 480, 481, 483, 484, 485, 486, 488, 491, 492, 493, 494, 495, 496, 497, 498, 499, 500
Scream & Dream with Jack & Gene **30**, 31, 438
Segal, George 452
Serling, Rod 157, 443, 444, 445, 446, 448, 449, 451
Seven Year Itch, The 90, 99, 221, 438
Shafer, Ross 400-401, 407-408
Sharma, Barbara 474
Shatner, William 456, 457, 461, 468, 471
Sheldon, Gail 185
Sheridan, Ann 446
Sherman, Allan 88, 445
Sherman, Bobby 455
Sherman, Robert 205, 212, 214, 215, 216-217, 220, 227, 228-230, 236, 238, 239, 240-241, 243, 244, 253-255, 270-272, 278-279, 287-288, 293, 294, 299, 301, 302-303, 311, 312, 319, 320-321, 328-329, 334, 336, 350, 351, 369, 371, 374, 375, 376-377, 379-381, 382-383, 395, 398-399, 402, 408-409
Shogun 350
Showoffs 436
Siebert, Charles 496, 502, 505
Sight Unseen 18-19, 440
Sigman, Carl 37
Sikking, James B. 504
Silver, Joe 471
Simon, Neil 121, 207, 338, 343, 345
Simpsons, The 408, 416
Sinatra, Frank 60, **137**
Sinatra, Nancy 450
$64,000 Question, The 111, 115, 121
Skutch, Ira 141-142, 146, 151, 154, 155, 204, 211, 215, 217, 221-222, 226-227, 229, 231, 238-239, 240, 244, 264, 299, 312, 314, 316, 318, 342, 351, 375, 423
Skyscraper 127, 344
Sky's the Limit, The 84-87, **85**, **86**, **88**, 90, 188, 192, 193, 433
Sloyan, James 503
Smith, Bubba 390
Smith, Martha 502, 503, 504
Smith, Roger 447, 450, 452
Snap Judgment 435, **436**
Somers, Brett **208**, 220-225, **221**, **223**, **225**, 235, **239**, **242**, 244, **246**, **247**, 248-249, **250**, 251, **251**, 252, 257, **258**, 259, **264**, 264, 266, **267**, 268, **276**, 281-282, **283**, **285**, **293**, 295, 301, **302**, 303, **310**, 313, 316, 320, **320**, **326**, **327**, **330**, **341**, **335**, **349**, 408, 409, 457, 458, 459, 460, 461, 462, 463, 464, 465, 466, 467, 468, 469, 470, 471, 472, 473, 474, 475, 476, 477, 478, 479, 480, 481, 482, 483, 484, 485, 486, 487, 488, 489, 490, 491, 492, 493, 494, 495, 496, 497, 498, 499, 500

Somers, Suzanne 252, 480
Sorel, Louise 496
Sothern, Ann 442, 445
Soviero, Diana 497
Split Second 275
Staahl, Jim 493, 495, 502
Stafford, Nancy 503, 504
Starr, Bart 454
Stephenson, Skip 500, 502
Stern, Howard 395, 400, 416-417, 418, 438
Stern, Lilibet **380**, 498, 499
Steve Allen Show, The 93, 96, 115, 435, 435
Steve Lawrence-Eydie Gorme Show, The 437
Stevens, Connie 452, 456, 482, 487, 488, 489, 494, 495, 498
Stevens, Kaye 231, 461, 462, 463, 464
Stevenson, McLean 259, 318, 348-351, **349**, 458, 459, 463, 485, 486, 497, 498, 499, 500, 502, 504, 505
Stevens, Rise 442
Stevens, Shawn 502
Stewart, Bob 44, 87, **88**, 144, 188, 192-194, 304, 328, 419
Stewart, Trish 462, 465, 467, 475, 480
Stiller, Jerry 109
Stottlemyre, Mel 450
Strouse, Charles 127-128
Strudwick, Shepperd 506, 514
Stuart, Anna 504, 505
Stuart, Barbara **208**, 266, 458
Sullivan, Barry 506, 514
Sullivan, Ed 92-93, 231
Sullivan, Joan 83, 421
Sullivan, Susan 477, 478, 483
Summers, Marc 405
Super Password xii, 402
Susann, Jacqueline 450
Susskind, David 452
Sutton, Don 476, 479, 484, 487, 497
Suzuki, Pat 444
Swanson, Gloria 157, 449
"Swingin' Safari, A" 148, 178
Swit, Loretta 458, 459, 462, 463, 476, 487, 489, 492

Tattletales 256-257, 266, 309, 350, 365, 401, 435, 436
Tauber, Jake 239
Taubman, Paul 106
Taylor, Rip 461
$10,000 Pyramid, The 192, 328, 436
That's My Line! 210

Thicke, Alan 503
This is Your Life 437
Thomas, Melody 499
Thomas, Richard 457
Thomerson, Tim 504
Three on a Match 193
Ticknor, Helen *see* Rayburn, Helen
Tic Tac Dough xii, 92, 103, 105, 112, 115, 140, 415
Tillis, Mel 477
Tillstrom, Burr 46, **47**, 48
Tilton, Charlene 421, 492
Tinker, Grant 372
Tittle, Y.A. 446, 450, 453
Today 12, 63, 66, 75, 96, **141**, 173, 363, 364, 421, 435
Todman, Bill 60, 61, 62, 63, 84, 87, 88, 90, 112, 140, 141, 142, 143, 145, 146, 147, 155, 161, 163, 172, 183, 184, 188, 189, 192, 193, 198, 204, 205, 209, 210, 211, 212, 214, 218, 223, 238, 239, 244, 253, 255, 256, 259, 272, 275, 276, 286, 288, 291, 292, 301, 304, 321, 325, 328, 329, 330, 341-342, 367
Tonight: America After Dark 96
Tonight Show, The xi, 66, 68, 92, **95**, 97, 136, 141, 161, 174, 200, 226, 301, 400, 413, 435
Tonight! Starring Steve Allen 66-79, **67**, **71**, **73**, **78**, 81, 92, 93, 96, 97, 200, 392, 412, 435
Torme, Mel 157, 446
Toscanini, Arturo 13-15, 16, 148
To Tell the Truth 61, 87, 101, 112, 140, 154, 185, 188, 190-192, 193, 202-203, 218, 219-220, 235, 253, 388, 415, 435, 436
Travalena, Fred **378**, **380**, 493, 497, 498, 500, 502, 503, 504, 505
Trebek, Alex 367, 397, 405
Tresh, Tom 448, 450
Tribute 342-343, 345-346, 439
Tridenick, Ryan 423
Trustman, Susan 506, 514
Truth or Consequences 159
Tuttle, Roger 108
TV's Funniest Game Show Moments 437
TV's Funniest Game Show Moments #2 437
Tweed, Shannon 502
Twenty One 92, 94, 103, 105, 111, 112, 114, 115
$20,000 Pyramid, The 329
242nd Street: The Low-Rent District 172

Uggams, Leslie 366, 451, 452
Urich, Robert 470
Under the Yum-Yum Tree 438
Unpredictable Pairs 388, 435

Urseth, Bonnie 502, 503, 504
Ustinov, Peter 101-102

Vaccaro, Brenda 457
Valentine, Karen **199**
Van, Bobby 256, 458, 462, 465, 467, 470
Van Buren, Abigail 491
Vance, Vivian 448, 449, 450, 452, 453
Van Derbur, Marilyn 452
Van Doren, Charles 92, 112
Van Dyke, Conny 469, 480
Van Dyke, Dick 108, 121, 123, 126, 127, 128, 129, 248
Van Valkenburgh, Deborah 503
Van Vooren, Monique 500
Vaughn, Robert 159, 446, 459, 465
Vicki! 418, 438
Video Village 120, 200
Villard, Tom 502, 503, 504, 505
Vinton, Bobby 448
Volz, Nedra 502, 503, 504, 505

Waggoner, Lyle 503
Wagner, Chuck 504
Walden, Robert 226, 332, 487, 488, 490, 491, 494, 495
Walker, Jimmie 463, 464, 466, 472, 474, 475, 493, 495, 496, 497, 498, 502, 503, 505, 506, 514
Wallace, Marcia 249-250, **250**, **264**, 302, 408, 461, 463, 465, 466, 467, 468, 472, 481, 482, 483, 484, 485, 486, 487, 488, 489, 490, 491, 492, 493, 494, 495, 496, 497, 498, 499, 500, 502, 503, 504, 505
Wallace, Marjorie 497, 498
Wallach, Eli 454
Wallis, Shani 456
Walter, Jessica 454
Walters, Laurie 495
Warwick, Dionne 157, 456
Watson, Debbie 446
Watts, Rolanda 418
Wayne, Frank 143, 145
Weaver, Charley 376, 378
Weaver, Pat 63, 66, 75, 96, 132, 133
Weil, Jeri 502
Welles, Jesse 504
Werts, Diane 343, 346
West, Mae 158-159
West, Randy 150, 183, 198, 200, 238-239, 286-287, 312, 398, 408, 409

INDEX

What's My Line? 61, 65, 88, 184-188, **184**, **187**, 189, 202, 218, 235, 253, 304, 403, 435, 436
Wheel of Fortune 351, 385, 399
Where Are You From? 59-60, 433
Whitaker, Jack 193
White, Betty 90, 172, **210**, 211, 222-223, 250-251, **251**, 252, 256, **285**, 285, 303, 333, **333**, 365-366, 387, 408, 442, 443, 444, 445, 446, 447, 448, 449, 450, 452, 453, 454, 457, 458, 459, 461, 462, 463, 464, 465, 466, 467, 468, 469, 470, 471, 472, 473, 474, 475, 476, 477, 478, 479, 480, 481, 482, 483, 484, 485, 486, 487, 488, 489, 490, 491, 492, 493, 494, 495, 496, 497, 498, 499, 500, 506, 513
White, Stanford 196
Whitlock, Billy 37, 40
Who Was That Lady I Saw You With? 438
Wickes, Mary 474, 475, 476, 477, 478, 479, 480, 481, 482, 483, 484, 485, 487, 497
Widdoes, James 502
Wiggins, Tudi 479
Wiggin, Tom 503
Williams, Andy 70
Williams, Anson 463, 480, 503, 504, 505
Williams, Paul 265, 488, 493, 496, 498, 499
Williams, Robin 412
Willie Tyler & Lester 500, 502
Wills, Maury 449
Will Success Spoil Rock Hunter? 102, **102**, 161, 438
Wilson, Flip 157, 455
Winslow, Michael 502, 505
Winters, Shelley 458
Wise, Alfie 492, 494, 502
Withers, Jane 443, 444, 446, 447, 448, 452, 454
Witter, Karen 502
Wood, Gene 376, 381, 464, 470
Wood, Lana 470
Woolery, Chuck 505
Worley, JoAnne 408, 455, 461, 462, 463, 464, 473
Wostbrock, Fred ix, xii, xiii, 185, 274, 288, 336, 392-393, 400-401, 407-408, 412, 413, 415-416, 418-420, 423, 427, 428, 429-431
Wyatt, Jane 442
Wyler, Gretchen 445
Wyman, Jane 446

Yastrzemski, Carl 453
You Don't Say! 179, 244
Young, Alan 443, 448

Youngman, Henny 456
You're Putting Me On 193

Zimbalist, Jr., Efrem 12
Zirato, Jr., Bruno 191

www.ingramcontent.com/pod-product-compliance
Lightning Source LLC
Chambersburg PA
CBHW060219230426
43664CB00011B/1482